GAINING MOMENTUM
Managing the Diffusion of Innovations

Series on Technology Management*

Series Editor: J. Tidd (Univ. of Sussex, UK)   ISSN 0219-9823

---

*For the complete list of titles in this series, please write to the Publisher.

SERIES ON TECHNOLOGY MANAGEMENT – VOL. 15

GAINING MOMENTUM

Managing the Diffusion of Innovations

editor

Joe Tidd

SPRU, University of Sussex, UK

Imperial College Press

ICP

Published by

Imperial College Press
57 Shelton Street
Covent Garden
London WC2H 9HE

Distributed by

World Scientific Publishing Co. Pte. Ltd.
5 Toh Tuck Link, Singapore 596224
USA office: 27 Warren Street, Suite 401-402, Hackensack, NJ 07601
UK office: 57 Shelton Street, Covent Garden, London WC2H 9HE

British Library Cataloguing-in-Publication Data
A catalogue record for this book is available from the British Library.

Series on Technology Management — Vol. 15
GAINING MOMENTUM
Managing the Diffusion of Innovations
Copyright © 2010 by Imperial College Press

For photocopying of material in this volume, please pay a copying fee through the Copyright Clearance Center, Inc., 222 Rosewood Drive, Danvers, MA 01923, USA. In this case permission to photocopy is not required from the publisher.

ISBN-13 978-1-84816-354-6
ISBN-10 1-84816-354-1

Typeset by Stallion Press
Email: enquiries@stallionpress.com

Printed by FuIsland Offset Printing (S) Pte Ltd. Singapore

Preface

Diffusion, or the widespread adoption, of innovations is critical, but underresearched and ill-understood. It is the means by which innovations — technological, commercial and organizational — are translated into social and economic benefits. Existing treatments of this important, but neglected, topic tend to adopt a single discipline to try to explain the phenomenon, typically economics, sociology or marketing. However, the diffusion of innovations is inherently multi-disciplinary, and this book adopts a managerial, process approach to understanding and promoting the adoption of innovations, based upon the latest research and practice.

The title *Gaining Momentum* was chosen to reflect an important omission in most treatments of diffusion. The term "momentum" is often used simply to indicate some critical mass of adoption or threshold level, or a successful marketing or communication campaign. Most studies are concerned only with the rate of adoption or the final proportion of a population that adopts an innovation. However, diffusion, like momentum, should be treated as a vector in that it has both magnitude and *direction*. The direction of the diffusion of innovations needs more attention: how and why different types of innovations are adopted (or not). This is critical for innovations which have profound social and economic implications, such as those affecting development, health and the environment.

Most innovation research, management and policy focus on the *generation* of innovations, especially new product development. However, a better understanding of why and how innovations are *adopted* (or not) can help us to develop more realistic management and business plans and public policies. There is a wide chasm between the development and successful adoption of an innovation, and around half of all innovations never reach the intended markets. Conventional marketing approaches are fine for many products and services, but not for innovations. Marketing texts often refer to "early adopters" and "majority adopters", and even go so far as to apply numerical estimates of these, but these simple categories are based on the very early studies of the state-sponsored diffusion of hybrid-seed varieties in farming communities, and are far from universally applicable. To better plan for innovations, we need a deeper understanding of what factors promote and constrain adoption, and how these influence the rate and level of diffusion within different markets and populations.

There are many barriers to the widespread adoption of innovations, including:

- Economic — personal costs versus social benefits, access to information, insufficient incentives;
- Behavioral — priorities, motivations, rationality, inertia, propensity for change or risk;
- Organizational — goals, routines, power and influence, culture and stakeholders; and
- Structural — infrastructure, sunk costs, governance.

The literature on diffusion is vast and highly fragmented. However, a number of different approaches to diffusion research can be identified, each focusing on particular aspects of diffusion and adopting different methodologies. The main contributions have been from economics, marketing, sociology and anthropology. Economists have developed a number of econometric models of the diffusion of new products and processes in an effort to explain past behavior and to predict future trends. Prediction is a common theme of the marketing literature. Marketing studies have adopted a wide range of different research instruments to examine buyer behavior, but most recent research has focused on social and psychological factors. Developmental economics and rural sociology have both examined the adoption of agricultural innovations, using statistical analysis of secondary data and collection of primary data from surveys. Much of the anthropological research has been based on case studies of the diffusion of new ideas in tribes, villages or communities. Most recently, there has been a growing number of multi-disciplinary studies which have examined the diffusion of educational, medical and other policy innovations.

This book is organized in three parts. The first part examines the generic factors which influence the diffusion of innovations, from concept through development, trials and commercialization. Chapter 1 presents a review of the major models of diffusion and highlights some key issues in the management of diffusion. In Chapter 2, J. Roland Ortt identifies the critical role of "pre-diffusion" phases in the subsequent success or failure of diffusion. Federico Frattini in Chapter 3 identifies the pre-development factors which contribute to market and network acceptance. In Chapter 4, Susan Hart and Nikolaos Tzokas review how launch strategies affect market adoption; and in Chapter 5, John Christiansen *et al.* argue that, in many cases, it is necessary to co-develop a new product and the associated brand. Qing Wang reviews the evidence on how consumers respond to innovations in Chapter 6. The influence of market and technical standards on the adoption of innovations is examined by Davide Chiaroni and Vittorio Chiesa in Chapter 7. In Part II, we look at the sector-specific dynamics of diffusion. Chapter 8 reviews the experience of pharmaceutical innovation in health care systems; Chapter 9, mobile telecommunications; and Chapter 10, environmental products and services. Each of these three cases demonstrates the importance of generic factors such as network effects and regulatory context, but also exhibits strong contingency influences due to the unique national and sectoral systems of innovation. Finally, in Part III we apply our understanding of diffusion to help predict and forecast future patterns of adoption. Chapter 11 reviews methods of forecasting, and Chapter 12 surveys the evidence and support for different models of forecasting diffusion.

We hope that this book will encourage others to re-examine research, policy and management practice on the diffusion of innovations in order to help translate innovations into social and economic benefits.

Joe Tidd
SPRU, University of Sussex, UK
April 2009

Contents

List of Contributors

Rifat A. Atun
Imperial College Business School, UK

Nuri Basoglu
Boğaziçi University, Turkey

Birgitte C. Blomberg
L'Oréal, Denmark

Davide Chiaroni
Politecnico di Milano, Italy

Vittorio Chiesa
Politecnico di Milano, Italy

John K. Christiansen
Copenhagen Business School, Denmark

Wen-Lin Chu
*Graduate Institute of Technology and Innovation Management,
National Chengchi University, Taiwan*

Tugrul Daim
Portland State University, USA

Federico Frattini
Politecnico di Milano, Italy

Nathasit Gerdsri
Mahidol University, Thailand

Ipek Gurol-Urganci
Imperial College Business School, UK

Susan Hart
University of Strathclyde, UK

Birgitte Hollensen
IBM A/S, Denmark

Towhidul Islam
University of Guelph, Canada

Xielin Liu
Graduate University of the Chinese Academy of Sciences, China

Nigel Meade
Imperial College Business School, UK

J. Roland Ortt
TU Delft, The Netherlands

Desmond Sheridan
Imperial College Business School, UK

Kwok L. Shum
Hong Kong University of Science and Technology, Hong Kong

Joe Tidd
*Science and Technology Policy Research (SPRU),
University of Sussex, UK*

Thien Tran
Portland State University, USA

Nikolaos Tzokas
University of East Anglia, UK

Claus J. Varnes
Copenhagen Business School, Denmark

Qing Wang
Warwick Business School, UK

Chihiro Watanabe
Tokyo Institute of Technology, Japan

Feng-Shang Wu
Graduate Institute of Technology and Innovation Management, National Chengchi University, Taiwan

Part I

Generic Factors Influencing the Diffusion of Innovations

Chapter 1

From Models to the Management of Diffusion

Joe Tidd

1.1 Introduction

A better understanding of why and how innovations are adopted (or not) can help us to develop more realistic business plans and public policies.

Diffusion is the means by which innovations are translated into social and economic benefits. We know that the impact of the *use* of innovations is around four times that of their *generation* (Geroski, 1991, 1994). In particular, the widespread adoption of *process* innovations has the most significant benefit (Griliches, 1984): technological innovations are the source of productivity and quality improvements; organizational innovations are the basis of many social, health and educational gains; and commercial innovations create new services and products (Bessant and Tidd, 2007; Tidd and Bessant, 2009). However, the benefits of innovations can take 10–15 years to be fully effected (Jaffe, 1986), and in practice most innovations fail to be adopted widely, so they have limited social or economic impact. There are many barriers to the widespread adoption of innovations, including:

- Economic — personal costs versus social benefits, access to information, insufficient incentives;

- Behavioral — priorities, motivations, rationality, inertia, propensity for change or risk;
- Organizational — goals, routines, power and influence, culture and stakeholders; and
- Structural — infrastructure, sunk costs, governance.

The title of this book, *Gaining Momentum*, was chosen to reflect an important omission in most treatments of diffusion. The term "momentum" is often used simply to indicate some critical mass of adoption or threshold level, or a successful marketing or communication campaign. Most studies are concerned only with the rate of adoption or the final proportion of a population that adopts an innovation. However, diffusion, like momentum, should be treated as a vector in that it has both magnitude and *direction*. The direction of the diffusion of innovations needs more attention: how and why different types of innovations are adopted (or not). This is critical for innovations which have profound social and economic implications, such as those affecting development, health and the environment.

In this chapter, we review what we know about the diffusion and adoption of innovations, identify some of the shortcomings of research and practice, and finally suggest some ways to better understand and manage this critical part of the innovation process. We begin with a brief review of the research in the field, beginning with the pioneering work of Rogers and other sociological approaches, through treatments in the economics literature and finally the most recent insights from marketing. Next, we identify some of the key themes to emerge from these studies, and also some of the common weaknesses. The chapter concludes with a discussion of two contemporary issues in the understanding and management of the diffusion of innovations: dealing with risk and uncertainty, such as the unintended consequences of adoption or non-adoption, through experimentation and learning; and the central role of networks in the diffusion and evolution of innovations.

1.2 Disciplinary Research on Diffusion

Conventional marketing approaches are adequate for promoting many products and services, but are not sufficient for the majority of innovations. Marketing texts often refer to "early adopters" and "majority adopters", and even go so far as to apply numerical estimates of these, but these simple categories are based on the very early studies of the state-sponsored diffusion of hybrid-seed varieties in farming communities, and are far from universally applicable. To better plan for innovations, we need a deeper understanding of what factors promote and constrain adoption, and how these influence the rate and level of diffusion within different markets and populations.

Rogers' (2003) definition of diffusion is used widely: "the process by which an innovation is communicated through certain channels over time among members of a social system. It is a special type of communication, in that the messages are concerned with new ideas" (p. 5). However, there are no generally accepted definitions of associated terms such as "technology transfer", "adoption", "implementation", or "utilization". Diffusion usually involves the analysis of the spread of a product or idea in a given social system, whereas technology transfer is usually a point-to-point phenomenon. Technology transfer usually implies putting information to use, or more specifically moving ideas from the laboratory to the market. The distinction between adoption, implementation and utilization is less clear. Adoption is generally considered to be the decision to do or acquire something, whereas implementation and utilization imply some action and adaptation.

The literature on diffusion is vast and highly fragmented. However, a number of different approaches to diffusion research can be identified, each focusing on particular aspects of diffusion and adopting different methodologies. The main contributions have been from economics, marketing, sociology and anthropology. Economists have developed a number of econometric models of the diffusion of new products and processes in an effort to explain past behavior.

Prediction is a common theme of the marketing literature. Marketing studies have adopted a wide range of different research instruments to examine buyer behavior, but most recent research has focused on social and psychological factors. Developmental economics and rural sociology have both examined the adoption of agricultural innovations, using statistical analysis of secondary data and collection of primary data from surveys. Much of the anthropological research has been based on case studies of the diffusion of new ideas in tribes, villages or communities. Most recently, there has been a growing number of multi-disciplinary studies which have examined the diffusion of educational, medical and other policy innovations.

The economists' view of the innovation process begins with the assumption that it is simply the cumulative aggregation of individual, rational calculations (Hall, 2005). These individual decisions are influenced by an assessment of the costs and benefits, under conditions of limited information and environmental uncertainty. An underlying assumption is that adoption represents a sunk cost and so any net benefit is perceived to be positive, but that under uncertainty about the future benefits of adopting an innovation, there is an option value in postponing adoption, which will slow diffusion. However, this perspective ignores the effects of social feedback and learning and externalities. The initial benefits of adoption may be small; but with improvement, re-invention and growing externalities, the benefits can increase over time and the costs decrease. These increasing returns from positive feedback are particularly evident with innovation clusters and networks, in which standards and complementary assets are important. This self-sustaining dynamic can result in inferior innovations and standards becoming "locked in" prematurely. Conversely, failure to establish standards and complementary innovations can slow or prevent diffusion.

Everett Rogers originally published his seminal book, *Diffusion of Innovations*, in 1962, and has since revised it every 8–10 years to reflect developments in the field. Over that period, the focus has shifted from the initial interest in rural sociology, in particular the promotion of adoption of innovations in agriculture, through public health and education in developed and developing economies, and most recently more narrow marketing and economic quantitative research on the adoption of specific technologies and products (especially consumer durables, such as mobile telephones, and pharmaceuticals).

Rogers (2003) conceptualizes diffusion as a social process in which actors create and share information through communication. Reflecting its roots in rural sociology and early interest in the adoption of agricultural innovations, the emphasis of this approach is on the roles of opinion leaders and change agents working within social structures and systems. Therefore, a focus on the relative advantage of an innovation is insufficient, as different social systems will have different values and beliefs, which will influence the costs, benefits and compatibility of an innovation, and different social structures will determine the most appropriate channels of communication as well as the type and influence of opinion leaders and change agents. In summary, this model of diffusion has five significant elements: an *innovation*, which is *communicated* through certain *channels* over *time* by members of a *social system* (emphasis in original).

Rogers contrasts this rich sociological perspective to the more narrow instrumental approaches, and warns that the "bias in marketing diffusion studies may lead to highly applied research that, although methodologically sophisticated, deals with trivial diffusion problems" (p. 90). Clearly, the motivations, questions, methods and foci of the research and practice of innovation diffusion are varied. However, we need to distinguish between the disciplines and methods used to understand and influence the diffusion of innovation, from the motivation and focus of such work. For example, sociological methods have been applied to segment markets and sell more products, whereas marketing techniques have been used successfully to promote beneficial social and health changes.

It is true that many more recent economic and marketing studies have typically focused on the diffusion of a specific technology or product, but an innovation may also be an idea, information, belief or practice. This includes the patterns of adoption of a philosophy, religion or doctrine (such as Marxism), or a management practice (such as Six Sigma or lean production), or changes in attitude and behavior (such as changes in lifestyle, exercise and diet). Similarly, the diffusion of many technologies or products also requires the adoption of complementary beliefs or practices, for example training or education. This can demand clusters or networks of interrelated innovations to be adopted to fully benefit. Moreover, the ordering or sequence of related innovations can influence diffusion, and prior innovations can restrict or promote adoption. In this way, an innovation may evolve over the process of diffusion through the adaptation and re-invention by users. Re-invention is more common where the focal innovation has a broad range of potential uses and can be adapted for different applications or contexts, or where local ownership and control are necessary or desirable.

The time dimension is important, and many studies are particularly interested in understanding and influencing the rate of adoption. It can take years for a new drug to be prescribed after license, a decade for a new crop variety, or 50 years for educational or social changes. This leads to a focus on the communication channels and the decision-making criteria and process. Generally, mass marketing media channels are more effective for generating awareness and disseminating information and knowledge, whereas interpersonal channels are more important in the decision-making and action stages. Rogers distinguishes between three types of decision-making relevant to the adoption of an innovation:

(1) *Individual*, in which the individual is the main decision-maker, independent of peers. Decisions may still be influenced by social norms and interpersonal relationships, but the individual makes the ultimate choice. For example, the purchase of a consumer durable such as a mobile telephone.
(2) *Collective*, where choices are made jointly with others in the social system, and there is significant peer pressure or formal requirement to conform. For example, the sorting and recycling of domestic waste.
(3) *Authoritative*, where decisions to adopt are taken by a few individuals within a social system, due to their power, status or expertise. For example, the adoption of enterprise resource planning (ERP) systems by businesses, or hospital management systems by hospitals.

Based upon an idealized diffusion curve, Rogers proposes five ideal types of adopters for the purpose of segmentation: innovators, early adopters, early majority, late majority and laggards. Many models and most marketing texts go further and (wrongly) assume a normal distribution, and assign the resultant proportion of the adopting population: 2.5%, 13.5%, 34%, 34% and 16%, respectively. Innovators are characterized as being technically sophisticated and risk-taking, and as a result are atypical; early adopters, in contrast, are more integrated with and respected by peers, and help to reduce perceived uncertainty for latter adopters. The early majority are well-connected in the social system and include opinion leaders; the late majority are more skeptical, and adoption is more the result of peer pressure and economic necessity. Finally, laggards, despite the label, have the least innovation bias and are the most rational of adopters.

Rogers argues that the innovativeness of potential adopters is a continuous variable, and that the five ideal types are abstractions. However, Moore (1991) takes a different view and makes the case for a significant "chasm" between the early adopters and the majority that must be overcome for mass market, high-technology products. Rogers' five categories are used widely in marketing, but a simpler two-fold distinction between early and late adopters is also common. Generalizations of the contrasting characteristics of early and late adopters are commonplace, but are often crude caricatures rather than empirical taxonomies, and reflect a strong innovation bias. For example, Rogers makes the assertion that early adopters are more educated, literate, intelligent and upwardly socially mobile, as well as less dogmatic and fatalistic, than late adopters. Consider this claim when you next meet someone with the very latest mobile telephone and sports shoes! Clearly, more subtle segmentation is necessary on a case-by-case basis. Cross-country comparisons of diffusion reveal that cultural factors play an important role. For example, high individuality limits the influence of imitation and contagion mechanisms; whereas high power distance, a measure of the hierarchies, promotes diffusion, possibly because innovations may be adopted faster within class strata (Van den Bulte and Stremersch, 2004). Similarly, at the national level, "industriousness" and "need for achievement",

measured by the ratio of Protestants to Catholics in a country (!),
speed up the diffusion of new consumer durables (Tellis *et al.*, 2002).

There is much evidence that opinion leaders are critical to diffusion, especially for changes in behavior or attitude (see Exhibit 1.1).
Therefore, they tend to be a central feature of social and health change
programs, such as sex education. However, they are also evident in
more routine examples of product diffusion, ranging from sports shoes
to hybrid cars. Opinion leaders carry information across boundaries
between groups, much like knowledge bridges. They operate at the
edge of groups, rather than from the top; they are not leaders within
a group, but brokers between groups. In the language of networks,
they have many weak ties rather than a few strong ties. They tend to
have extended personal networks, be accessible and have high levels of
social participation. They are recognized by peers as being both competent and trustworthy. They have access and exposure to mass media.
Whether they are more innovative than peers is less clear. Rogers suggests that in a social system that favors change, opinion leaders tend to
be more innovative; but in a social system with norms which do not
support change, opinion leaders will not necessarily be innovative.
A common mistake made by change agents is to choose opinion leaders
who are too innovative compared to the social system, making the
opinion leaders too atypical to act as a model and promote change.

Exhibit 1.1. Evolution of Hybrid Cars

The car industry is an excellent example of a large, complex sociotechnical system which has evolved over many years, such that the
current system of firms, products, consumers and infrastructure interact to restrict the degree and direction of innovation. Since the 1930s,
the dominant design has been based around a gasoline (petrol)- or
diesel-fueled reciprocating combustion engine/Otto cycle, mass produced in a wide variety of relatively minimally differentiated designs. This
is no industrial conspiracy, but rather the almost inevitable industrial
trajectory, given the historical and economic context. This has resulted

(Continued)

Exhibit 1.1. (*Continued*)

in car companies spending more on marketing than on research and development. However, growing social and political concerns over vehicle emissions and their regulation have forced the industry to reconsider this dominant design, and in some cases develop new capabilities to help create new products and systems. For example, zero/low-emission targets and legislation have encouraged experimentation with alternatives to the combustion engine, whilst retaining the core concept of personal, rather than collective or mass, travel.

For example, the zero-emission law passed in California in 1990 required manufacturers selling more than 35,000 vehicles a year in the state to have 2% of all vehicle sales as zero-emission vehicles by 1998, 5% by 2001 and 10% by 2003. This most affected GM, Ford, Chrysler, Toyota, Honda and Nissan, and potentially BMW and VW, if their sales increased sufficiently over that period. However, the USA automobile industry subsequently appealed, and had the quota reduced to a maximum of 4%. As fuel cells were still very much a longer-term solution, the main focus was on developing electric vehicles. At first sight, this would appear to represent a rather "autonomous" innovation, i.e. the simple substitution of one technology (combustion engine) for another (electric). However, the shift has implications for related systems such as power storage, drivetrain, controls, weight of materials used, and the infrastructure for re-fueling/re-charging and servicing. Therefore, it is much more of a "systemic" innovation than it first seems. Moreover, it challenges the core capabilities and technologies of many of the existing car manufacturers. The American manufacturers struggled to adapt, and early vehicles from GM and Ford were not successful. In contrast, the Japanese were rather more successful in developing the new capabilities and technologies, and new products from Toyota and Honda have been particularly successful.

However, zero-emission legislation was not adopted elsewhere, and more modest emission reduction targets were set. Since then, hybrid petrol-electric cars have been developed to help reduce emissions.

(*Continued*)

Exhibit 1.1. (*Continued*)

These are clearly not long-term solutions to the problem, but do represent valuable technical and social prototypes for future systems such as fuel cells. In 1993, Eiji Toyoda (Toyota's chairman) and his team embarked on project G21: "G" stands for global, and "21" stands for the 21st century. The purpose of the project was to develop a small hybrid car that could be sold at a competitive price in order to respond to the growing needs and eco-awareness of many consumers worldwide. A year later, a concept vehicle was developed called the Prius, taken from the Latin for "before". The goal was to reduce fuel consumption by 50%, and emissions by more than that. To find the right hybrid system for project G21, Toyota considered 80 alternatives before narrowing the list to 4. Development of the Prius required the integration of different technical capabilities, including, for example, a joint venture with Matsushita Battery.

The prototype was revealed at the Tokyo Motor Show in October 1995. It is estimated that the project cost Toyota US$1 billion in R&D. The first commercial version was launched in Japan in December 1997 and, after further improvements such as battery performance and power source management, introduced to the American market in August 2000. The fuel economy is 60 MPG for urban driving, and 50 MPG for motorways — the opposite consumption profile of a conventional vehicle, but roughly twice as fuel-efficient as an equivalent Corolla. From the materials used in production, through driving, maintenance and finally its disposal, the Prius reduces CO_2 emissions by more than a third, and has a recyclability potential of approximately 90%. The Prius was launched in the USA at a price of US$19,995, and sales in the USA were 15,556 in 2001 and 20,119 in 2002. However, industry experts estimate that Toyota was losing some US$16,000 for every Prius it sold because it costs between US$35,000 and US$40,000 to produce. Toyota did make a profit on its second-generation Prius launched in 2003, and on other hybrid cars such as the Lexus range in 2005, because of improved technologies and lower production costs.

(*Continued*)

Exhibit 1.1. (*Continued*)

Hollywood celebrities soon discovered the Prius: Leonardo DiCaprio bought one of the first in 2001, followed by Cameron Diaz, Harrison Ford and Calista Flockhart at the 2003 Academy Awards. British politicians took rather longer to jump on the hybrid bandwagon, with the leader of the opposition, David Cameron, driving a hybrid Lexus in 2006. In 2005, 107,897 cars were sold in the USA, about 60% of global Prius sales, and four times more than the sales in 2000 and twice as many in 2004. Toyota plans to sell a million hybrids by 2010.

In addition to the direct income and indirect prestige the Prius and other hybrid cars have created for Toyota, the company has also licensed some of its 650 patents on hybrid technology to Nissan and Ford, which are expected to launch hybrid vehicles in 2010, and Ford plans to sell 250,000 hybrids by 2010. Mercedes-Benz showed a diesel-electric S-Class at the Frankfurt Auto Show in autumn 2005. Honda has developed its own technology and range of hybrid cars, and is probably the world leader in fuel cell technology for vehicles.

Sources: Pilkington and Dyerson (2004); [Anonymous] (2004); Naim (2005); Taylor (2006); [Anonymous] (2006).

1.3 Models of Diffusion

Research on diffusion attempts to identify what influences the rate and direction of the adoption of an innovation. The diffusion of an innovation is typically described by an S-shaped (logistic) curve. Initially, the rate of adoption is low, and adoption is confined to so-called "innovators". Next to adopt are the "early adopters", then the "early majority" and "late majority", and finally the curve tails off as only the "laggards" remain. Such taxonomies are fine with the benefit of hindsight, but provide little guidance for future patterns of adoption (Geroski, 2000).

Hundreds of marketing studies have attempted to fit the adoption of specific products to the S-curve, ranging from television sets to new drugs. In most cases, mathematical techniques can provide a relatively good fit with historical data, but research has so far failed to identify robust generic models of adoption. In practice, the precise pattern of the adoption of an innovation will depend on the interaction of demand-side and supply-side factors:

- *Demand-side factors* — direct contact with or imitation of prior adopters, adopters with different perceptions of benefits and risks.
- *Supply-side factors* — relative advantage of an innovation, availability of information, barriers to adoption, feedback between developers and users.

The epidemic S-curve model is the earliest model and is still the most commonly used. It assumes a homogeneous population of potential adopters, and assumes that innovations spread via information transmitted by personal contact, observation and the geographical proximity of existing and potential adopters. This model suggests that the emphasis should be on communication, and on the provision of clear technical and economic information. However, the epidemic model has been criticized because it assumes that all potential adopters are similar and have the same needs, which is unrealistic.

The probit model takes a more sophisticated approach to the population of potential adopters. It assumes that potential adopters have different threshold values for costs or benefits, and will only adopt beyond some critical or threshold value. In this case, differences in threshold values are used to explain different rates of adoption. This suggests that the more similar potential adopters are, the faster the diffusion.

However, adopters are assumed to be relatively homogeneous, apart from some difference in progressiveness or threshold values. The probit model does not consider the possibility that the rationality and profitability of adopting a particular innovation might be different for different adopters. For example, local "network externalities", such as the availability of trained skilled users, technical assistance and maintenance, or complementary technical or organizational innovations, are likely to affect the cost of adoption and use, as distinct from the cost of purchase.

Also, it is unrealistic to assume that adopters will have perfect knowledge of the value of an innovation. Therefore, Bayesian models of diffusion introduce lack of information as a constraint to diffusion. Potential adopters are allowed to hold different beliefs regarding the value of an innovation, which they may revise according to the results of trials to test the innovation. Because these trials are private, imitation cannot take place and other potential adopters cannot learn from the trials. This suggests that better-informed potential adopters may not necessarily adopt an innovation earlier than the less well-informed ones, which was an assumption of earlier models (Griffiths and Tenenbaum, 2006).

The most influential marketing model of diffusion was developed by Frank Bass in 1969, and has been applied widely to the adoption of consumer durables. The Bass model assumes that potential adopters are influenced by two processes: individual independent adopters are initially influenced mostly by media; and later, adopters are more influenced by interpersonal communication and channels. The addition of these two adoption processes generates the famous bell-shaped diffusion curve, or cumulatively, the S-curve.

Slightly more realistic assumptions, such as those of the Bass model, include two different groups of potential adopters: innovators, who are not subject to social emulation; and imitators, for whom the diffusion process takes the epidemic form. This produces a skewed S-curve because of the early adoption by innovators, and suggests that different marketing processes are needed for the innovators and subsequent imitators. The Bass model is highly influential in economics and marketing research, and the distinction between the two types of potential adopters is critical in understanding the different mechanisms involved in the two user segments.

The main models of the diffusion of innovations were established by 1970 (Meade and Islam, 2006). These were developed to explain historical data, rather than to predict or manage future diffusion. More recently, attempts have been made to develop models which incorporate the effects of active marketing efforts, and how these influence the market potential and probability of adoption. For example, the generalized Bass model (GBM) introduces a factor representing "current marketing effort" into the hazard function, or probability of adoption. Such models tend to provide better forecasts for the diffusion of consumer durables. The Norton–Bass model (1987) adapts the Bass model for cases where there are successive generations of a product or technology, for example mobile phones. In such cases, a new generation can lead to incremental adoption by new market segments, and in addition may result in substitution or upgrading by adopters of earlier generations. This model has been applied to the diffusion of a wide range of electronic devices, industrial processes and pharmaceuticals (Norton and Bass, 1992).

The "critical mass" or "take-off" is the point after which diffusion becomes self-sustaining. The term is borrowed from physics, where it is used to describe the point at which a nuclear chain reaction occurs. In diffusion, the point is usually less explosive, but can mark a significant increase in adoption and changes in the mechanisms driving adoption. For example, many information and communication technology (ICT) innovations follow this pattern as their value increases with interaction. Research on the diffusion of 25 different ICT innovations found that external influence and imitation were the main drivers of adoption, rather than internal individual factors (Teng *et al.*, 2002). Such innovations become more valuable as the number of users increases, creating so-called "network externalities" and clusters of complementary innovations. The Internet reached this point in the mid-1990s, following developments in HTML and web browsers. Similarly, bandwagons can occur beyond the critical mass, where peer pressure or fashion becomes more important than other mechanisms.

Bandwagons may occur where an innovation is adopted because of pressure caused by the sheer number of those who have already adopted an innovation, rather than because of individual assessments of the benefits of an innovation (see Exhibit 1.2). In general, as soon as the number of adopters has reached a certain threshold, the greater the level of ambiguity of the innovation's benefits, the greater the subsequent number of adopters. This process allows technically inefficient innovations to be widely adopted, or technically efficient innovations to be rejected. Examples include the QWERTY keyboard, originally designed to prevent professional typists from typing too fast and jamming typewriters; and the DOS operating system for personal computers, designed by and for computer enthusiasts.

Exhibit 1.2. Diffusion of Management Fads and Fashions

Over the past 40 years, we have seen many apparent panaceas for the problems of becoming competitive. Organizations are constantly seeking new answers to old problems, and the scale of investment in the new fashions of management thinking has often been considerable. The original evidence for the value of these tools and techniques was strong, with case studies and other reports testifying to their proven value within the context of origin. But there is also extensive evidence to suggest that these changes do not always work, and in many cases lead to considerable dissatisfaction and disillusionment. Examples include:

- total quality management (TQM);
- business process re-engineering (BPR);
- best practice benchmarking;
- networking/clustering;
- knowledge management; and
- disruptive or open innovation.

New management practices diffuse in less than optimal ways. They often begin with a large, public firm developing or adapting some new method, technique or tool (e.g. Six Sigma began at Motorola, lean production began at Toyota). The apparent benefits of such innovations are observed by other firms, and adopted or adapted. However, if imitation was the only mechanism driving adoption, such innovations would be restricted to specific sectors or countries and would diffuse slowly. The equivalent of the role of mass media in the Bass model are the popular business journals and case studies written by business schools. Critical mass requires further codification of ideas and practices, through professional associations and active change agents such as management consultants. Finally, the innovation becomes a full bandwagon. Further pressure is created by peers and stakeholders to adopt the latest "modern" management practices to remain competitive. Many public sector organizations also feel under pressure

(Continued)

Exhibit 1.2. (*Continued*)

to adopt, and have been criticized for "fad-lag", i.e. adopting out-of-date management fashions. The problem with this process is that, however worthy the original innovation may be, it becomes diluted and taken out of the original context and so may offer limited value or indeed be dysfunctional.

What is going on here demonstrates well the principles behind behavioral change in organizations. It is not that the original ideas were flawed or that the initial evidence was wrong. Rather, other organizations assumed that they could simply be copied, without the need to adapt, customize, modify or change them to suit their circumstances. In other words, there was no learning or progress towards making them become routines as part of the underlying culture within the firm.

Sources: Alexander and Korine (2008); Tidd and Bessant (2009).

Bandwagons occur due to a combination of competitive and institutional pressures (Abrahamson and Plosenkopf, 1993). Where competitors adopt an innovation, a firm may also adopt it because of the threat of lost competitiveness, rather than as a result of any rational evaluation of benefits. For example, many firms adopted business process re-engineering (BPR) in the 1980s in response to increased competition, but most failed to achieve significant benefits (Isaksen and Tidd, 2006). The main institutional pressure is the threat of lost legitimacy, for example, being considered by peers or customers as being less progressive or less competent.

The critical difference between bandwagons and other types of diffusion is that the former require only limited information to flow from early to later adopters. Indeed, the more ambiguous the benefits of an innovation, the more significant bandwagons are on rates of adoption. Therefore, the process of diffusion must be managed with as much care as the process of development. In short, better products do not necessarily result in more sales. Not everybody requires a better mousetrap.

Finally, there are more sociological and psychological models of adoption that are based on interaction and feedback between the developers and potential adopters (Williams and Gibson, 1990). These perspectives consider how individual psychological characteristics such as attitude and perception affect adoption. Individual motivations, perceptions, likes and dislikes determine what information is reacted to and how it is processed. Potential adopters will be guided and prejudiced by experience, and will have "cognitive maps" which filter information and guide behavior. Social context will also influence individual behavior. Social structures and meaning systems are locally constructed, and therefore highly context-specific. These can distort the way in which information is interpreted and acted upon. Therefore, the perceived value of an innovation, and thus its subsequent adoption, is not some objective fact, but instead depends on individual psychology and social context. These factors are particularly important in the later stages of diffusion. For example, lifestyle aspirations, such as exercising more and adopting a healthy diet, have created the opportunity for many new products and services.

Initially, the needs of early adopters or innovators dominate, and therefore the characteristics of an innovation are most important. Innovations tend to evolve over time through improvements required by these early users, which may reduce the relative cost to later adopters. However, early adopters are almost by definition atypical; for example, they tend to have superior technical skills. As a result, the preferences of early adopters can have a disproportionate impact on the subsequent development of an innovation, and can result in the establishment of inferior technologies or the abandonment of superior alternatives.

The choice between the different models of diffusion and factors which will most influence adoption will depend on the characteristics of the innovation and the nature of potential adopters. The simple epidemic model appears to provide a good fit to the diffusion of new processes, techniques and procedures; whereas the Bass model appears to best fit the diffusion of consumer products. However, the mathematical structure of the epidemic and Bass models tends to overstate the importance of differences in adopter characteristics while underestimating the effect of macroeconomic and supply-side factors. In general, both these models of diffusion work best where the total potential market is known, that is, for derivatives of existing products and services rather than for totally new innovations.

1.4 Factors Influencing Adoption

Numerous variables have been identified as affecting the diffusion and adoption of innovations, but these can be grouped into three clusters: characteristics of the innovation itself; characteristics of individual or organizational adopters; and characteristics of the environment. Characteristics of an innovation found to influence adoption include relative advantage, compatibility, complexity, trialability and observability. Individual characteristics include age, education, social status and attitude to risk. Environmental and institutional characteristics include economic factors such as the market environment and sociological factors such as communications networks. However, whilst there is a general agreement regarding the relevant variables, there is very little consensus on the relative importance of the different variables, and in some cases disagreements over the direction of relationships.

1.4.1 *Characteristics of an innovation*

Diffusion rates of different innovations are highly variable. In predicting the rate of adoption of an innovation, five factors explain 49–87% of the variance: relative advantage, compatibility, complexity, trialability and observability. However, the contextual or environmental factors are also important, as demonstrated by the fact that the diffusion rates for the same innovation in different contexts also vary significantly.

1.4.1.1 *Relative advantage*

Relative advantage is the degree to which an innovation is perceived as better than the product it supersedes, or competing products. Relative advantage is typically measured in narrow economic terms like cost or financial payback, but non-economic factors such as convenience, satisfaction and social prestige may be equally important. In theory, the greater the perceived advantage, the faster the rate of adoption.

It is useful to distinguish between the primary and secondary attributes of an innovation. Primary attributes, such as size and cost, are invariant and inherent to a specific innovation, irrespective of the adopter. Secondary attributes, such as relative advantage and compatibility, may vary from adopter to adopter, being contingent upon the perceptions and context of adopters. In many cases, a so-called "attribute gap" will exist. An attribute gap is the discrepancy between a potential user's perception of an attribute or characteristic of an item of knowledge and how the potential user would prefer to perceive that attribute. The greater the sum of all attribute gaps, the less likely a user is to adopt the knowledge. This suggests that preliminary testing of an innovation is desirable in order to determine whether significant attribute gaps exist. Not all attribute gaps require changes to the innovation itself — a distinction needs to be made between knowledge content and knowledge format. The idea of pre-testing information for the purposes of enhancing its value and acceptance is not widely practiced.

1.4.1.2 *Compatibility*

Compatibility is the degree to which an innovation is perceived to be consistent with the existing values, experience and needs of potential adopters. There are two distinct aspects of compatibility: existing skills and practices, and values and norms. The extent to which the innovation fits the existing skills, equipment, procedures and performance criteria of the potential adopter is important, and relatively easy to assess. But, compatibility with existing practices may be less important than the fit with existing values and norms (Leonard-Barton and Sinha, 1993). Significant misalignments between an innovation and an adopting organization will require changes in the innovation or organization, or both. In the most successful cases of implementation, mutual adaptation of the innovation and organization occurs

(Leonard-Barton, 1990). However, few studies distinguish between compatibility with values and norms, and compatibility with existing practices.

The extent to which the innovation fits the existing skills, equipment, procedures and performance criteria of the potential adopter is critical. Few innovations initially fit the user environment into which they are introduced. Significant misalignments between the innovation and the adopting organization will require changes in the innovation or organization or, in the most successful cases of implementation, mutual adaptation of both. Initial compatibility with existing practices may be less important, as it may provide limited opportunity for mutual adaptation to occur.

In addition, so-called "network externalities" can affect the adoption process. For example, the cost of adoption and use, as distinct from the cost of purchase, may be influenced by the availability of information about the technology from other users, the availability of trained skilled users, technical assistance and maintenance, and the availability of complementary innovations (both technical and organizational).

1.4.1.3 *Complexity*

Complexity is the degree to which an innovation is perceived as being difficult to understand or use. In general, innovations which are simpler for potential users to understand will be adopted more rapidly than those which require the adopter to develop new skills and knowledge.

However, complexity can also influence the *direction* of diffusion, not just the rate of adoption. Evolutionary models of diffusion focus on the effect of "network externalities", i.e. the interaction of consumption, pecuniary and technical factors which shape the diffusion process. For example, within a region, the cost of adoption and use — as distinct from the cost of purchase — may be influenced by the availability of information about the technology from other users, the availability of trained skilled users, technical assistance and maintenance, and the availability of complementary innovations (both technical and organizational).

1.4.1.4 *Trialability*

Trialability is the degree to which an innovation can be experimented with on a limited basis. An innovation that is trialable represents less uncertainty to potential adopters, and allows learning by doing. Innovations which can be trialed will generally be adopted more quickly than those which cannot. The exception is where the undesirable consequences of an innovation appear to outweigh the desirable characteristics. In general, adopters wish to benefit from the functional effects of an innovation, but avoid any dysfunctional effects. However, where it is difficult or impossible to separate the desirable from the undesirable consequences, trialability may reduce the rate of adoption.

Developers of an innovation may have two different motives for involving potential users in the development process. First is to acquire the knowledge from users needed in the development process so as to ensure usability and add value. Second is to attain user "buy-in", that is, user acceptance of the innovation and commitment to its use. The second motive is independent of the first, because increasing user acceptance does not necessarily improve the quality of the innovation. Rather, involvement may increase users' tolerance of any inadequacies. In the case of point-to-point transfer, both motives are typically present.

However, in the case of diffusion, it is not possible to involve all potential users, and therefore the primary motive is to improve usability rather than attain user buy-in. But even the representation of user needs must be indirect, using surrogates such as specially selected user groups. These groups can be problematic for a number of reasons. Firstly, they may possess atypically high levels of technical knowledge, and therefore may not be representative. Secondly, where the group must represent diverse user needs, such as both experienced and novice users, the group members may not work well together. Finally, when user representatives work closely with developers over a long period of time, they may cease to represent users and instead absorb the developers' viewpoint. Thus, there is no simple relationship between user involvement and user satisfaction. Typically, very low levels of user involvement are associated with user dissatisfaction, but extensive user involvement does not necessarily result in user satisfaction.

1.4.1.5 *Observability*

Observability is the degree to which the results of an innovation are visible to others. The easier it is for others to see the benefits of an innovation, the more likely the innovation will be adopted. The simple epidemic model of diffusion assumes that innovations spread as potential adopters come into contact with existing users of an innovation.

Peers who have already adopted an innovation will have what communication researchers call "safety credibility", because potential adopters seeking their advice will believe that they know what it is really like to implement and utilize the innovation. Therefore, early adopters are well positioned to disseminate "vicarious learning" to their colleagues. "Vicarious learning" is simply learning from the experience of others, rather than direct personal experimental learning. However, the process of vicarious learning is neither inevitable nor efficient because, by definition, it is a decentralized activity. Centralized systems of dissemination tend to be designed and rewarded on the basis of being the source of technical information, rather than for facilitating learning among potential adopters.

Over time, learning and selection processes foster both the evolution of the technologies to be adopted and the characteristics of actual and potential adopters. Thus, an innovation may evolve over time through improvements made by early users, thereby reducing the relative cost to later adopters. In addition, where an innovation requires the development of complementary features, for example a specific infrastructure, late adopters will benefit. This suggests that, instead of a single diffusion curve, a series of diffusion curves will exist for the different environments. However, there is a potential drawback to this model. The short-term preferences of early adopters will have a disproportionate impact on the subsequent development of the innovation, and may result in the establishment of inferior technologies or the abandonment of superior alternatives. In such cases, interventionalist policies may be necessary to postpone the lock-in phenomenon.

From a policy perspective, high visibility is often critical. However, high visibility, at least initially, may be counterproductive. If users' expectations about an innovation are unrealistically high and adoption is immediate, subsequent disappointment is likely. Therefore, in some circumstances, it may make sense to delay dissemination or to slow the rate of adoption. However, in general, researchers and disseminators are reluctant to withhold knowledge.

Demonstrations of innovations are highly effective in promoting adoption. Experimental, private demonstrations or pilots can be used to assess the attributes of an innovation and the relative advantage for different target groups, and to test compatibility. Exemplary, public demonstrations can improve observability, reduce perceived complexity, and promote private trials. However, note the different purpose and nature of experimental and exemplary demonstrations. Resources, urgency and uncertainty should determine the appropriate type of demonstration. Public demonstrations for experimental purposes are ill-advised and are likely to stall diffusion.

In the case of systemic or network innovations, a wider range of factors have to be managed to promote adoption and diffusion. In such cases, a wider set of actors and institutions on the supply side and demand side are relevant, in what has been called an *adoption network* (Chakravorti, 2003, 2004a, 2004b). On the supply side, other organizations may provide the infrastructure, support and complementary products and services that can promote or prevent adoption and diffusion. For example, in 2008 the two-year battle between the new high-definition optical disc formats was decided not by price or any technical superiority, but rather because the Blu-ray consortium managed to recruit more film studios to its format than the competing HD DVD format. As soon as the uncertainty over the future format was resolved, there was a step-change increase in the rate of adoption.

On the demand side, the uncertainty of potential adopters as well as communication with and between them need to be managed. Whilst early adopters may emphasize technical performance and novelty above other factors, the mainstream mass market is more likely to be concerned with factors such as price, quality, convenience and support. This transition from the niche market and needs of early adopters through to the requirements of more mass markets has been referred to as "crossing the chasm" by Moore (1991, 1998). Moore studied the successes and many failures of Silicon Valley and other high-technology products, and argued that the critical success factors for early adopters and mass markets were fundamentally different but most innovations failed to make this transition. Therefore, the successful launch and diffusion of a systemic or network innovation demand not only attention to traditional marketing issues such as the timing and positioning of the product or service (Lee and O'Connor, 2003), but also significant effort to demand-side factors such as communication and interactions *between* potential adopters (Van den Bulte and Lilien, 2001).

The continued improvement in health in the advanced economies over the past 50 years can be attributed in part to the supply of new diagnostic techniques, drugs and procedures, and also to changes on the demand side, such as increases in the levels of education, income and service infrastructure. However, the focus of innovation (and policy) in health care is too often on the development and commer-cialization of new pharmaceuticals, but this is only part of the story. This is a clear case of systemic innovation, in which firm and public R&D are necessary but not sufficient to promote improved health. The adoption network includes regulatory bodies, national health assessment and reference pricing schemes, regional health agencies, public and private insurers, as well as the more obvious hospitals, doc-tors, nurses and patients (Atun *et al.*, 2007). However, too often the management and policy for innovation in health are confined to the regulation of prices and the effects of intellectual property regimes. There is a clear need for new methods of interaction, involvement and engagement in such cases (Flowers and Henwood, 2008).

1.5 Towards a Process for Managing Diffusion

Diffusion research and practice has been criticized for an increasingly limited scope and methodology. For example, economic and marketing studies have focused narrowly on the diffusion of consumer durables such as mobile phones, in contrast to the pioneering work on the adoption of health, educational and agricultural innovations. Rogers (2003) identifies a number of shortcomings in diffusion research and practice:

(1) Diffusion has been seen as a *linear, unidirectional communication* activity in which the active source of research or information attempts to influence the attitudes and/or behaviors of essentially passive receivers. However, in most cases, diffusion is an interactive process of adaptation and adoption.

(2) Diffusion has been viewed as a *one-to-many communication* activity, but point-to-point transfer is also important. Both centralized and decentralized systems exist. Decentralized diffusion is a process of convergence as two or more individuals exchange information in order to move toward each other in the meanings they ascribe to certain events.

(3) Diffusion research has been preoccupied with an *action-centered and issue-centered communication* activity, such as selling products, actions or policies. However, diffusion is also a social process that is affected by social structure, position and interpersonal networks.

(4) Diffusion research has used *adoption as the dependent variable* — the decision to use the innovation, rather than implementation itself. Hence, adoption is seen as a consequence of the innovation. Most studies have used attitudinal change as the dependent variable, rather than change in overt behavior.

(5) Diffusion research has suffered from an implicit *pro-innovation bias*, which assumes that an innovation should be adopted by all members of a social system as rapidly as possible. Therefore, the process of adaptation or rejection of an innovation has been overlooked, and there have been relatively few studies of how to prevent the diffusion of "bad" innovations.

Rogers makes the important point that the diffusion of an innovation may not be economically or socially desirable, or conversely anti-diffusion programs may seek to limit or prevent the adoption of "bad" innovations. However, the research and practice of innovation diffusion has an inherent pro-innovation bias: marketing studies seek to promote the sale and purchase of products, and social programs seek to promote changes in behavior and practice. This "source bias", whereby diffusion researchers and practitioners side with the promoters of an innovation, can result in individual blame for rejection, non-adoption or late adoption of an innovation. Many apparently individual decisions to reject or adopt late are locally rational, or are more the result of systemic conditions than individual choice. For example, surveys of the European Union consistently reveal that around half of the population do not support innovation and change, as broadly defined. Such widespread beliefs cannot simply be labeled as "regressive" by firms and policy-makers. Therefore, we need a better framework for anticipating and managing the consequences of the adoption or rejection of an innovation by a social system:

(1) Desirable versus undesirable consequences, depending on the functional and dysfunctional aspects of an innovation within a specific social system;
(2) Direct versus indirect consequences, due to second-order effects or time delays; and
(3) Anticipated versus unanticipated consequences, due to ignorance, complex interactions or uncertainty.

1.5.1   *Unintended consequences: dealing with risk and uncertainty*

At the group or social level, many factors influence our perception and response to risk. How managers assess and manage risk is also a social and political process. It is influenced by prior experience of risk, perceptions of capability, status and authority, and the confidence and ability to communicate with the relevant people at the appropriate times (Genus and Coles, 2006). In the context of managing innovation, risk is less about personal propensity for risk taking or rational assessments of probability, and more about the interaction of experience, authority and context. In practice, managers deal with risk in different ways in different situations. General strategies include delaying or delegating decisions, or sharing risks and responsibilities. Generally, when managers are performing well and achieving their targets, they have less incentive to take risks. Conversely, when under pressure to perform, managers will often accept higher risks, unless these threaten survival.

Studies confirm that measures of cognitive ability are associated with project performance. In particular, differences in reflection, reasoning, interpretation and sense making influence the quality of problem formulation, evaluation and solution, and therefore ultimately the performance of research and development. A common weakness is the oversimplification of problems characterized by complexity or uncertainty, and the associated simplification of problem framing and evaluation of alternatives (Tenkasi, 2000). This includes adopting a single prior hypothesis, selectively using information that supports this hypothesis, devaluing alternatives, and maintaining the illusion of control and predictability. Similarly, marketing managers are likely to share similar cognitive maps, and tend to make the same assumptions concerning the relative importance of different factors contributing to new product success (such as the degree of customer orientation versus competitor orientation) and the implications of relationship between these factors (such as the degree of interfunctional coordination) (Tyler and Gnyawali, 2002).

At the individual, cognitive level, risk assessment is characterized by overconfidence, loss aversion and cognitive bias (Westland, 2008). Overconfidence in our ability to make accurate assessments is a common failing, and results in unrealistic assumptions and uncritical assessment. Loss aversion is well documented in psychology, and essentially means that we prefer to avoid loss rather than risk gain. Finally, cognitive bias is widespread and has profound implications for the identification and assessment of risk. Cognitive bias results in us seeking and overemphasizing evidence which supports our beliefs, thus reinforcing our bias, but at the same time leads us to avoid and undervalue any information which contradicts our view (Gardner, 2008). Therefore, we need to be aware of and challenge our own biases, and encourage others to debate and critique our data, methods and decisions.

So, the evidence indicates the importance of cognitive processes at the senior management, functional, group and individual levels of an organization. More generally, problems of limited cognition include (Walsh, 1995):

- *Reasoning by analogy*, which oversimplifies complex problems;
- *Adoption of a single, prior hypothesis bias*, even where information and trials suggest this is wrong;
- *Limited problem set*, i.e. the repeated use of a narrow problem-solving strategy;
- *Single outcome calculation*, which focuses on a simple single goal and a course of action to achieve it, denying value trade-offs;
- *Illusion of control and predictability*, based on an overconfidence in the chosen strategy, a partial understanding of the problem and limited appreciation of the uncertainty of the environment; and
- *Devaluation of alternatives*, emphasizing negative aspects of alternatives.

In most organizations, risk has become a negative term — something which should be minimized or avoided — and implies hazard or failure. This view, particularly common in the policy domain, is enshrined in the "precautionary principle" and the many regulatory regimes it has spawned, which, as the title suggests, promotes wherever possible the avoidance of risk taking (Fischoff, 1995; Renn, 1998; Stirling, 1998).

However, this interpretation perverts the nature of risk and opportunity, which are both central to successful innovation, and promotes inaction and the status quo rather than improvement or change. The term "risk" is derived from the Latin for "to dare", but has become associated with hazard or danger. We must consider the risks of success as well as the risks associated with *not* changing (Sunstein, 2005). Berglund (2007) provides a good working definition of risk in the context of innovation, as "the pursuit of perceived opportunities under conditions of uncertainty".

Research on returns to new technology indicates that the diffusion of very novel technology is associated with very high costs and uncertainty, but conversely mature technology provides limited opportunity (Heeley and Jacobson, 2008). This suggests a "Goldilocks" strategy of exploiting median-age technologies (in the relevant patent classes) which have reduced much of the very high cost and uncertainty, but retain significant scope for further development and commercialization. Similarly, a study of organizational innovation and performance confirms the need for this delicate balance between risk and stability. Risk taking is associated with a higher relative novelty of innovation (how different it is to what the organization has done before) and absolute novelty of innovation (how different it is to what *any* organization has done before), and both types of novelty are correlated with financial and customer benefits (Totterdell *et al.*, 2002). However, the same study concludes that:

> [I]ncremental, safe, widespread innovations may be better for internal considerations, but novel, disruptive innovations may be better for market considerations. . . . [A]bsolute novelty benefits customers and quality of life, relative innovation benefits employee relations (but) risk is detrimental to employee relations. [Totterdell *et al.*, 2002, p. 362]

In fact, many of the critical risks that need to be identified and managed are internal to organizations, rather than the more obviously anticipated external risks such as markets, competition and regulation (Keizer *et al.*, 2005). The inherent uncertainty in some projects limits the ability of managers to predict the outcomes and benefits of projects. In such cases, changes to project plans and goals are commonplace, being driven by external factors (such as technological breakthroughs or changes in markets) as well as internal factors (such as changes in organizational goals). Together, the impact of changes to project plans and goals can overwhelm the benefits of formal project planning and management (Dvir and Lechler, 2004).

This is consistent with the real options approach to investing in risky projects, because investments are sequential and managers have some influence on the timing, resourcing and continuation or abandonment of projects at different stages. By investing relatively small amounts in a wide range of projects, a greater range of opportunities can be explored (see Exhibit 1.3). Once uncertainty has been

Exhibit 1.3. The Value of Uncertainty

The real options approach has been used to evaluate R&D at both the project and firm levels. The idea is that investment in (or, more strictly speaking, spending on) R&D creates greater flexibility and a portfolio of options for future innovations, especially where the future is uncertain. Faced with uncertainty, managers can choose to commit additional resources to R&D to create an *option to grow*, or alternatively delay additional R&D to hold an *option to wait*.

This study (see source below) examined the different and combined effects of market and technological uncertainty on the financial valuation of firms' investments in R&D. The authors examined the behavior and performance of 290 firms over 10 years, and found that the relationship between R&D and firm valuation depended on the source and degree of uncertainty. They identified a U-shaped relationship between market uncertainty and R&D capital: increasing market uncertainty initially reduces the value of any unit of investment in R&D until a point of inflection, beyond which it augments the value. The higher the rate of market growth, the lower the point of inflection. Conversely, the relationship between technological uncertainty and R&D capital is an inverted U-shape. This suggests that investors put a limit on the value of technology hedging: at low levels of technological uncertainty, there is limited value in creating options; and at very high levels, the cost of maintaining many alternatives is too high.

Therefore, it is important to identify the main sources of uncertainty, technological or market, in order to make better decisions about the potential value of investments in R&D options.

Source: Oriani and Sobrero (2008).

reduced, only the most promising projects should be allowed to continue. For a given level of investment, this real options approach should increase the value of the project portfolio. However, because decisions and the options they create interact, a decision regarding one project can affect the option value of another project (McGrath and

Nerkar, 2004; Paxon, 2001). Nonetheless, the real options perspective remains a useful way of conceptualizing risk, particularly at the portfolio level. The goal is not to calculate or optimize, but rather to help identify risks and payoffs, key uncertainties, decision points and future opportunities that might be created (Loch and Bode-Greual, 2001). Combined with other methods, such as decision trees, the real options approach can be particularly effective where high volatility demands flexibility, placing a premium on the certainty of information and the timing of decisions.

1.6 Role of Innovation Networks

Different authors adopt different meanings, levels of analysis and attribute networks with different characteristics. For example, academics on the Continent have focused on social, geographical and institutional aspects of networks, and the opportunities and constraints these present for innovation (Camagni, 1991). In contrast, Anglo-Saxon studies have tended to take a systems perspective, and have attempted to identify how best to design, manage and exploit networks for innovation (Nohria and Eccles, 1992).

Whilst there is little consensus on the aims or means, there appears to be some agreement that a network is more than an aggregation of bilateral relationships or dyads, and therefore the configuration, nature and content of a network impose additional constraints and present additional opportunities. A network can be thought of as consisting of a number of positions or nodes — occupied by individuals, firms, business units, universities, governments, customers and other actors — and the links or interactions between these nodes. By the same token, a network perspective is concerned with how these economic actors are influenced by the social context in which they are embedded and how actions can be influenced by the position of actors.

A network can influence the actions of its members in two ways (Gulati, 1998). First is through the flow and sharing of information within the network. Second is through differences in the position of actors in the network, which cause power and control imbalances.

J. Tidd

Therefore, the position an organization occupies in a network is a matter of great strategic importance, and reflects its power and influence in that network. Sources of power include technology, expertise, trust, economic strength and legitimacy (see Table 1.1). Networks are appropriate where the benefits of co-specialization, sharing of joint infrastructure and standards, and other network externalities outweigh the costs of network governance and maintenance. Where there are high transaction costs involved in purchasing technology, a network approach may be more appropriate than a market model; and where uncertainty exists, a network may be superior to full integration or acquisition.

Networks can be tight or loose, depending on the quantity (number), quality (intensity) and type (closeness to core activities) of the interactions or links. Such links are more than individual transactions, and require significant investment in resources over time. Historically, networks have often evolved from long-standing business relationships. Any firm will have a group of partners that it does regular business with — universities, suppliers, distributors, customers and competitors. Over time, mutual knowledge and social bonds develop through repeated dealings, increasing trust and reducing transaction

Table 1.1. Competitive dynamics in network industries.

	Type of network	
	Unconnected, closed	**Connected, open**
System attributes	Incompatible technologies	Compatible technologies across vendors and products
	Custom components and interfaces	Standard components
Firm strategies	Control standards by protecting proprietary knowledge	Shape standards by sharing knowledge with rivals and complementary markets
Source of advantage	Economies of scale, customer lock-in	Economies of scope, multiple segments

Source: Adapted from Garud and Kumaraswamy (1993).

costs. Therefore, a firm is more likely to buy or sell technology from members of its network (Bidault and Fischer, 1994).

Research has examined the opportunities networks might provide for innovation, and the potential to explicitly design or selectively participate in networks for the purpose of innovation, that is, a path-creating rather than path-dependent process (Galaskiewicz, 1996). A study of 53 research networks found two distinct dynamics of formation and growth. The first type of network emerges and develops as a result of environmental interdependence and through common interests — an emergent network. However, the other type of network requires some triggering entity to form and develop — an engineered network (Conway and Steward, 1998). In an engineered network, a nodal firm actively recruits other members to form a network, without the rationale of environmental interdependence or similar interests. Table 1.2 gives an idea of the different ways in which such engineered networks can be configured to help with the innovation process. Innovation networks are more than just ways of assembling and deploying knowledge in a complex world; they can also have what are termed as "emergent properties" — the potential for the whole to be greater than the sum of its parts. Being in an effective innovation network can deliver a wide range of benefits beyond the collective knowledge efficiency mentioned above. These include gaining access to different and complementary knowledge sets, reducing risks by sharing them, accessing new markets and technologies, and pooling complementary skills and assets.

Research suggests that the challenge facing firms in building new networks can be broken down into two separate activities: identifying the relevant new partners, and learning how to work with them. It is a little like the recipe for effective team-working (forming, storming, norming and performing), except that here it is a three-stage process: finding, forming and performing (Birkinshaw *et al.*, 2007). Finding refers essentially to the breadth of search that is conducted. Finding is enabled by the scope and diversity of current operations as well as by the capacity to move beyond the dominant models in the industry,

Table 1.2.   Types of innovation networks.

Network type	Examples
Entrepreneur-based	Bringing different complementary resources together to help take an opportunity forward. Often a combination of formal and informal networks. Depends a lot on the entrepreneur's energy and enthusiasm in getting people interested to join — and stay in — the network.
Internal project teams	Formal and informal networks of knowledge and key skills which can be brought together to help enable some opportunity to be taken forward. Essentially like entrepreneur networks, but on the inside of established organizations. May run into difficulties because of having to cross internal organizational boundaries.
Communities of practice	Networks which can involve players inside and across different organizations — what binds them together is a shared concern with a particular aspect or area of knowledge.
Spatial clusters	Networks which form because of the players being close to each other, for example, in the same geographical region. Silicon Valley is a good example of a cluster which thrives on proximity — knowledge flows amongst and across the members of the network, but is hugely helped by the geographical closeness and the ability of key players to meet and talk.
Sectoral networks	Networks which bring different players together because they share a common sector — and often have the purpose of shared innovation to preserve competitiveness. Often organized by sector or business associations on behalf of their members. Shared concern to adopt and develop innovative good practice across a sector or product market grouping, for example, the SMMT Industry Forum or LOGIC (Leading Oil and Gas Industry Competitiveness), a gas and oil industry forum.

(*Continued*)

Table 1.2. (*Continued*)

Network type	Examples
New product or process development consortium	Sharing knowledge and perspectives to create and market a new product or process concept, for example, the Symbian consortium (Sony, Ericsson, Motorola and others) working towards developing a new operating system for mobile phones and PDAs.
Sectoral forum	Working together across a sector to improve competitiveness through product, process and service innovation.
New technology development consortium	Sharing and learning around newly emerging technologies, for example, the pioneering semiconductor research programs in the US and Japan.
Emerging standards	Exploring and establishing standards around innovative technologies, for example, the Moving Picture Experts Group (MPEG) working on audio and video compression standards.
Supply-chain learning	Developing and sharing innovative good practice and possibly shared product development across a value chain, for example, the SCRIA initiative in aerospace.

Source: Tidd and Bessant (2009).

but is hindered by a combination of geographical, technological and institutional barriers (see Table 1.3). Forming refers to the attitude of prospective partners. How likely is a link-up and what are the advantages or barriers? Finally, performing refers to how to make the network function.

Operating an innovation network depends heavily on the type of network and the purposes it is set up to achieve. Challenges include keeping the network up to date and engaged, building trust and reciprocity, positioning oneself within the network and decoupling from

Table 1.3. Barriers to new network formation.

Primary objective	Type of barrier	Description
Finding prospective partners	Geographical	Discontinuities often emerge in unexpected corners of the world. Geographical and cultural distance makes complex opportunities more difficult to assess, and as a result they typically get discounted.
	Technological	Discontinuous opportunities often emerge at the intersection of two technological domains.
	Institutional	Institutional barriers often arise because of the different objectives or origins of two groups, such as those dividing the public sector from the private sector.
Forming relationships with prospective partners	Ideological	Many potential partners do not share the values and norms of the focal firm, which can blind it from seeing the threats or opportunities that might arise at the interfaces between the two world views.
	Demographic	Barriers to building effective networks can arise from the different values and needs of different demographic groups.
	Ethnic	Ethnic barriers arise from deep-rooted cultural differences between countries or regions of the world.

Source: Based on Birkinshaw *et al.* (2007).

existing networks. For example, there is a big difference between the demands for an innovation network working at the frontier where issues of intellectual property management and risk are critical, and one where there is an established innovation agenda (as might be the case in using supply chains to enhance product and process innovation).

For example, LEGO's decision to develop its next-generation Mindstorms product involved using a network of lead users of the first-generation product. LEGO's experience after the first Mindstorms product had been that the enthusiastic user community was an asset, despite its approaches such as hacking into the old software and sharing this information on the Web. As described by the LEGO senior vice president, Mads Nipper, "We came to understand that this is a great way to make the product more exciting. It's a totally different business paradigm." In other cases, potential partners are easy to find but may be reluctant to engage. This might occur for ideological reasons, or because of institutional or demographic barriers. An illustration of this approach can be seen in the Danish pharmaceutical company, Novo Nordisk. Faced with long-term changes in the business environment towards greater obesity and rising healthcare costs associated with diabetes (its core market), Novo Nordisk realized that it needed to start exploring opportunities for discontinuous innovation in its products and offerings. Its "Diabetes 2020" process involved exploring radical alternative scenarios for chronic disease treatment and the roles which a player like Novo Nordisk could play. As part of the follow-up from this initiative, in 2003 the company helped set up the Oxford Health Alliance, a non-profit collaborative entity that brought together key stakeholders — medical scientists, doctors, patients and government officials — with views and perspectives which were sometimes quite widely disparate. To make it happen, Novo Nordisk made clear that its goal was nothing less than the prevention of or cure for diabetes — a goal which, if it were achieved, would potentially kill off the company's main line of business. As Lars Rebien Sørensen, CEO of Novo Nordisk, explained:

> In moving from intervention to prevention — that's challenging the business model where the pharmaceuticals industry is deriving its revenues! . . . We

Table 1.4. Challenges in managing innovation networks.

Set-up stage	Operating stage	Sustaining (or closure) stage
Issues here are around providing the momentum for bringing the network together and clearly defining its purpose. It may be crisis-triggered, e.g. perception of the urgent need to catch up via adoption of innovation. Equally, it may be driven by a shared perception of opportunity — the potential to enter new markets or exploit new technologies. Key roles here will often be played by third parties, e.g. network brokers, gatekeepers, policy agents and facilitators.	The key issues here are about trying to establish some core operating processes for which there is support and agreement. These need to deal with: • Network boundary management: how the membership of the network is defined and maintained; • Decision making: how (where, when, who) decisions get taken at the network level; • Conflict resolution: how conflicts are resolved effectively; • Information processing: how information flows among members and is managed; • Knowledge management: how knowledge is created, captured, shared and used across the network; • Motivation: how members are motivated to join/remain within the network; • Risk/benefit sharing: how the risks and rewards are allocated across members of the network; and • Coordination: how the operations of the network are integrated and coordinated.	Networks need not last forever — sometimes, they are set up to achieve a highly specific purpose (e.g. development of a new product concept) and once this has been done the network can be disbanded. In other cases, there is a case for sustaining the networking activities for as long as members see benefits. This may require periodic review and "re-targeting" to keep the motivation high. For example, CRINE, a successful development program for the offshore oil and gas industry, was launched in 1992 by key players in the industry such as BP, Shell and major contractors with support from from the UK government, with the target of cost reduction. Using a network model, it delivered extensive innovation in products/services and processes. Having met its original cost-reduction targets, the program moved to a second phase with a focus aimed more at capturing a bigger export share of the global industry through innovation.

Source: Tidd and Bessant (2009).

believe that we can focus on some major global health issue — mainly diabetes — and at the same time create business opportunities for our company. [Tidd and Bessant, 2009, p. 264]

Different types of networks have different issues to resolve, but we can identify some common challenges (Tidd and Bessant, 2009):

(1) How to manage something we do not own or control;
(2) How to see system-level effects, not narrow self-interests;
(3) How to build trust and shared risk-taking without tying the process up in contractual red tape; and
(4) How to minimize unintended consequences and spillovers.

Table 1.4 summarizes some of the key management questions associated with each stage.

1.7 Conclusions

The successful diffusion of innovations is necessary to achieve any widespread economic or social benefit. It demands much more than marketing. Research and experience have created several predictive models of the process(es) of diffusion that apply in different contexts, and we know many of the attributes of an innovation that influence adoption. Many disparate fields such as economics and sociology also provide useful insights, but alone are not sufficient to understand and manage this process. Instead, we need to integrate this knowledge to tackle some of the key common challenges, such as dealing with the inevitable risk of unintended consequences, and building coalitions and maintaining innovation networks to help to mitigate and share the risks and benefits of adoption. This suggests a strategy of experimentation and learning, in contrast to the "precautionary principle". It favors incrementalism, the step-by-step modification of objectives and resources, in light of new evidence, such that key uncertainties — technical, market and social — are revealed and reduced before any irreversible commitments are made.

Most studies are concerned only with the rate of adoption or the final proportion of a population that adopts an innovation. However, diffusion should be treated as a vector in that it has both magnitude and *direction*. The direction of the diffusion of innovations needs more attention: how and why different types of innovations are adopted (or not). This is critical for innovations which have profound social and economic implications, such as those affecting development, health and the environment.

References

[Anonymous]. (2004). Why the future is hybrid. *The Economist*, December 4.

[Anonymous]. (2006). Toyota: the birth of the Prius. *Wall Street Journal*, February 13.

Abrahamson, E. and Plosenkopf, L. (1993). Institutional and competitive bandwagons: using mathematical modeling as a tool to explore innovation diffusion. *Academy of Management Journal*, 18(3), 487–517.

Alexander, M. and Korine, H. (2008). When you shouldn't go global. *Harvard Business Review*, December, 70–77.

Atun, R.A., Gurol-Urganci, I. and Sheridan, D. (2007). Uptake and diffusion of pharmaceutical innovations in health systems. *International Journal of Innovation Management*, 11(2), 299–322.

Berglund, H. (2007). Risk conception and risk management in corporate innovation. *International Journal of Innovation Management*, 11(4), 497–514.

Bessant, J. and Tidd, J. (2007). *Innovation and Entrepreneurship*. Chichester: Wiley.

Bidault, F. and Fischer, W. (1994). Technology transactions: networks over markets. *R&D Management*, 24(4), 373–386.

Birkinshaw, J., Bessant, J. and Delbridge, R. (2007). Finding, forming, and performing: creating networks for discontinuous innovation. *California Management Review*, 49(3), 67–83.

Camagni, R. (1991). *Innovation Networks: Spatial Perspectives*. London: Belhaven Press.

Chakravorti, B. (2003). *The Slow Pace of Fast Change: Bringing Innovation to Market in a Connected World*. Boston: Harvard Business School Press.

Chakravorti, B. (2004a). The new rules for bringing innovations to market. *Harvard Business Review*, 82(3), 58–67.

Chakravorti, B. (2004b). The role of adoption networks in the success of innovations. *Technology in Society*, 26, 469–482.

Conway, S. and Steward, F. (1998). Mapping innovation networks. *International Journal of Innovation Management*, 2(2), 165–196.

Dvir, D. and Lechler, T. (2004). Plans are nothing, changing plans is everything: the impact of changes on project success. *Research Policy*, 33, 1–15.

Fischoff, B. (1995). Risk perception and communication unplugged: twenty years of progress. *Risk Analysis*, 15(2), 137–145.

Flowers, S. and Henwood, F. (2008). Special Issue on User-Centered Innovation. *International Journal of Innovation Management*, 12(3).

Galaskiewicz, J. (1996). The "new" network analysis. In: D. Iacobucci (ed.), *Networks in Marketing*, London: Sage, pp. 19–31.

Gardner, D. (2008). *Risk: The Science and Politics of Fear.* London: Virgin Books.

Garud, R. and Kumaraswamy, A. (1993). Changing competitive dynamics in network industries. *Strategic Management Journal*, 14, 351–369.

Genus, A. and Coles, A.M. (2006). Firm strategies for risk management in innovation. *International Journal of Innovation Management*, 10(2), 113–126.

Geroski, P.A. (1991). Innovation and the sectoral sources of UK productivity growth. *Economic Journal*, 101, 1438–1451.

Geroski, P.A. (1994). *Market Structure, Corporate Performance and Innovative Activity.* Oxford: Oxford University Press.

Geroski, P.A. (2000). Models of technology diffusion. *Research Policy*, 29, 603–625.

Griffiths, T.L. and Tenenbaum, J.B. (2006). Optimal predictions in everyday cognition. *Psychological Science*, 45, 56–63.

Griliches, Z. (1984). Market value, R&D and patents. In: Z. Griliches and A. Pakes (eds.), *Patents, R&D and Productivity*, Chicago: University of Chicago Press, pp. 249–252.

Gulati, R. (1998). Alliances and networks. *Strategic Management Journal*, 19, 293–317.

Hall, B.H. (2005). Innovation and diffusion. In: J. Fagerberg, D.C. Mowery and R.R. Nelson (eds.), *The Oxford Handbook of Innovation*, Oxford: Oxford University Press, pp. 459–484.

Heeley, M.B. and Jacobson, R. (2008). The recency of technological inputs and financial performance. *Strategic Management Journal*, 29, 723–744.

Isaksen, S. and Tidd, J. (2006). *Meeting the Innovation Challenge: Leadership for Transformation and Growth.* Chichester: Wiley.

Jaffe, A.B. (1986). Technological opportunity and spillovers of R&D: evidence from firms' patents, profits and market values. *American Economic Review*, 76, 948–999.

Keizer, J.A., Vos, J.P. and Halman, J.I.M. (2005). Risks in new product development: devising a reference tool. *R&D Management*, 35(3), 297–306.

Lee, Y. and O'Connor, G.C. (2003). New product launch strategy for network effects products. *Journal of the Academy of Marketing Science*, 31(3), 241–255.

Leonard-Barton, D. (1990). Implementing new production technologies: exercises in corporate learning. In: M.A. von Glinow and S.A. Mohmian (eds.), *Managing Complexity in High Technology Organizations*, New York: Oxford University Press, pp. 160–187.

Leonard-Barton, D. and Sinha, D.K. (1993). Developer–user interaction and user satisfaction in internal technology transfer. *Academy of Management Journal*, 36(5), 1125–1139.

Loch, C.H. and Bode-Greual, K. (2001). Evaluating growth options as sources of value for pharmaceutical research projects. *R&D Management*, 31(2), 231–245.

McGrath, R.G. and Nerkar, A. (2004). Real options reasoning and a new look at the R&D investment strategies of pharmaceutical firms. *Strategic Management Journal*, 25, 1–21.

Meade, N. and Islam, T. (2006). Modelling and forecasting the diffusion on innovation: a 25-year review. *International Journal of Forecasting*, 22, 519–545.

Moore, G. (1991). *Crossing the Chasm: Marketing and Selling Technology Products to Mainstream Customers*. New York: HarperBusiness.

Moore, G. (1998). *Inside the Tornado: Marketing Strategies from Silicon Valley's Cutting Edge*. Chichester: Capstone/Wiley.

Naim, G. (2005). Too soon to write off the dinosaurs. *Financial Times*, November 18.

Nohria, N. and Eccles, R. (1992). *Networks and Organizations: Structure, Form and Action*. Boston: Harvard Business School Press.

Norton, J.A. and Bass, F.M. (1987). A diffusion theory model of adoption and substitution for successive generations of high-technology products. *Management Science*, 33, 1069–1086.

Norton, J.A. and Bass, F.M. (1992). Evolution of technological generations: the law of capture. *Sloan Management Review*, 33, 66–77.

Oriani, R. and Sobrero, M. (2008). Uncertainty and the market value of R&D within a real options logic. *Strategic Management Journal*, 29, 343–361.

Paxon, D.A. (2001). Introduction to real R&D options. *R&D Management*, 31(2), 109–113.

Pilkington, A. and Dyerson, R. (2004). Incumbency and the disruptive regulator: the case of the electric vehicles in California. *International Journal of Innovation Management*, 8(4), 339–354.

Renn, O. (1998). Three decades of risk research: accomplishments and new challenges. *Journal of Risk Research*, 1(1), 49–72.

Rogers, E.M. (2003). *Diffusion of Innovations*, 5th ed. New York: Free Press.

Stirling, A. (1998). Risk at a turning point? *Journal of Risk Research*, 1(2), 97–110.

Sunstein, C.R. (2005). *Laws of Fear: Beyond the Precautionary Principle*. Cambridge: Cambridge University Press.

Taylor, A. (2006). Toyota: the birth of the Prius. *Fortune*, February 21.

Tellis, G.J., Stremersch, S. and Yin, E. (2002). The international takeoff of new products: the role of economics, culture and country innovativeness. *Marketing Science*, 22(2), 188–208.

Teng, T.C., Grover, V. and Guttler, W. (2002). Information technology innovations: general diffusion patterns and its relationships to innovation characteristics. *IEEE Transactions on Engineering Management*, 49, 13–27.

Tenkasi, R.V. (2000). The dynamics of cognitive oversimplification processes in R&D environments: an empirical assessment of some consequences. *International Journal of Technology Management*, 20(5/6/7/8), 782–798.

Tidd, J. and Bessant, J. (2009). *Managing Innovation: Integrating Technological, Market and Organizational Change*, 4th ed. Chichester: Wiley.

Totterdell, P., Leach, D., Birdi, K., Clegg, C. and Wall, T. (2002). An investigation of the contents and consequences of major organizational innovations. *International Journal of Innovation Management*, 6(4), 343–368.

Tyler, B.B. and Gnyawali, D.R. (2002). Mapping managers' market orientations regarding new product success. *Journal of Product Innovation Management*, 19, 259–276.

Van den Bulte, C. and Lilien, G.L. (2001). Medical innovation revisited: social contagion versus marketing effort. *The American Journal of Sociology*, 106(5), 1409–1435.

Van den Bulte, C. and Stremersch, S. (2004). Social contagion and income heterogeneity in new product diffusion. *Marketing Science*, 23(4), 530–544.

Walsh, J.P. (1995). Managerial and organizational cognition: notes from a field trip. *Organization Science*, 6(1), 1–41.

Westland, J.C. (2008) *Global Innovation Management: A Strategic Approach*. Basingstoke: Palgrave Macmillan.

Williams, F. and Gibson, D.V. (1990). *Technology Transfer: A Communications Perspective*. London: Sage.

Chapter 2

Understanding the Pre-diffusion Phases

J. Roland Ortt

2.1 Introduction

The development and diffusion of high-tech product categories is a fascinating topic. The managerial relevance and the complicated nature of the topic — how to turn inventions into successful products — have inspired scientists from diverse disciplines to examine technological innovation (for an overview, see Rosenberg, 1982; Gopalakrishnan and Damanpour, 1997; Nieto, 2003). The invention of new technological principles, their application in new product categories, and the subsequent diffusion of products based on these principles often result in an erratic process stretching out for decades. The case of the television illustrates the kind of process that can be expected prior to the emergence of the well-known S-shaped diffusion curve (see Exhibit 2.1).

Many individuals, companies and organizations are usually involved in the process of development and diffusion of high-tech product categories. Some of the pioneering companies that set these processes in motion turn out to be very successful, but it is remarkable that many of them fail before their products manage to reach a mass market (Tellis and Golder, 1996; Olleros, 1986). Tellis and Golder (1996) focus on pioneers of successful new high-tech product categories. They estimate that 47% of these pioneers demise before

Exhibit 2.1. The Pre-diffusion Phases for Television

During the first three decades of the 20th century, essential components to enable television were developed by many different inventors. The first rudimentary television systems were demonstrated almost simultaneously in the late 1920s by different inventors such as Baird in the UK (1926), Tihanyi from Hungary (1926) and Farnsworth in the US (1927). Baird made an electromechanical television system, whereas Farnsworth and Tihanyi created full electronic systems. The first experimental broadcasting trials appeared in 1928 in the US and during 1929–1935 in the UK. From 1935 on, a regular broadcasting service began almost simultaneously in Germany and the UK. In Germany, television was first a kind of semi-public small-scale service provided in dedicated television theaters and later on in military field hospitals. Television sets were commercially sold from 1939 on by RCA in the US. Large-scale diffusion, represented by the S-shaped diffusion curve, would start in the US after the Second World War.

Sources: Encyclopaedia Britannica (2010); http://www.tvhandbook.com/History/History_timeline.htm/; http://www.bvws.org.uk/405alive/history/revisionist_history.html/; http://www.nyu.edu/classes/stephens/History%20of%20Television%20page.htm/; http://www.earlytelevision.org/german_prewar.html/.

their technological innovations reach the mass market. Olleros (1986) refers to this phenomenon as "the burnout of the pioneers".

This chapter will focus on the phases prior to large-scale production and diffusion, referred to as the pre-diffusion phases. In practice, the S-shaped diffusion curve invariably starts several years after the first attempt to introduce versions of a specific product category in the market (Ortt and Schoormans, 2004). The television case illustrates that these pre-diffusion phases can last decades. The empirical data from Tellis and Golder (1996) and Olleros (1986) show the devastating effect of these phases on the pioneers.

In diffusion research, Rogers (2005) noticed an almost complete lack of attention to the pre-diffusion period. By ignoring this period, mainstream diffusion research seems to imply that large-scale diffusion starts directly after the market introduction of a new high-tech product. Indicating that this large-scale diffusion can be represented by an S-shaped diffusion curve also implies that the diffusion process is quite predictable. A systematic study of the pre-diffusion period is likely to provide useful insight and lead to more realistic business plans.

In this chapter, the pre-diffusion phases for high-tech product categories will be explored. The term "new high-tech product category" refers to a new combination of a technological principle and a specific functionality (at the time of invention). In other words, in these categories, the technological principle is new, the functionality is new, or both are new. Examples of new high-tech product categories, at the time of their invention, were digital photography (the digital imaging technology used to make photographs) and video cassette recorders (VCRs) (the technology to store data on a tape with magnetized particles that is used to store and later replay video material).

This chapter will address several issues related to the pre-diffusion phases. In Section 2.2, we will discuss some of the theories and ideas that describe the development and diffusion of high-tech product categories over time. In Section 2.3, the pre-diffusion phases will be defined, while their length for high-tech product categories will be discussed in Section 2.4. The causes and consequences of these phases will be explored in Sections 2.5 and 2.6, respectively. Conclusions and discussions are in Section 2.7.

2.2 Patterns in Technological Innovation and Diffusion

Ever since the effect of the Industrial Revolution was felt in society, i.e. from the 1830s on (Hobsbawn, 1962), scientists from different disciplines have investigated technology innovation and diffusion. For example, in the 1840s Marx was already a careful student of technological progress (for a discussion, see Chapter 2 in Rosenberg, 1982). Marx was ahead of his time in various respects. He described technology as an endogenous variable and a gradual process of improvement, rather than the exogenous flash of an inventor's ingenuity that some contemporary writers later on would make us believe. Subsequently, various schools of economists (for an overview, see Deane, 1978; Ekelund and Hébert, 1983; Landreth and Colander, 1994), sociologists (such as Bijker, 1995), historians of technology (for a short overview, see Chapter 1 in Rosenberg, 1982) and technologists (such as Sahal, 1985) have studied technological innovation and diffusion. The emphasis on the topic is understandable because of its effect on the gross national product (GNP) of countries, on competition in industries as well as on the daily lives of individuals.

Observing the variety of scientific disciplines studying technological innovation and diffusion, it may come as no surprise that many different types of innovation/diffusion-related patterns have been distinguished thus far. Some of them will be mentioned here to illustrate the variety. Rogers (2005) is one of the founding fathers of diffusion research. He distinguishes patterns by describing the subsequent groups of adopters or customers of a product category. In doing so, he focuses on the diffusion rather than the development of products, and on the demand side (the customers) rather than the supply side (including complementary products and services) or the wider market environment. Furthermore, the assumption that innovation occurs prior to diffusion means that diffusion researchers assume that the product essentially remains invariant over the diffusion process. Rogers (2005) also explains why diffusion researchers traditionally focus on the demand side of the market to explain the diffusion pattern and why subsequent innovations in the product during the diffusion process are usually ignored. One of the first well-known cases in which diffusion was studied happened to be hybrid corn in the US. Hybrid corn was an innovation that performed well and remained essentially invariant over the diffusion process. At that time, the institutions supplying and distributing corn were well developed, which meant that the main factors to explain actual diffusion in this particular case were the customers or farmers, i.e. the demand side of the market. Diffusion research has been applied in a broad variety of cases, some of which may not justify the same assumption of invariance or the focus on the demand side of the market. Rogers concludes that this hybrid corn case has set the standard of working for researchers investigating other cases.

By contrast, Utterback *et al.* (Utterback and Abernathy, 1975; Abernathy and Utterback, 1978; Utterback, 1994) focus on a pattern by distinguishing subsequent types of innovations that emerge in a given industry. They explain that, in a new industry, the focus is on (major) product innovations; whereas later on, when a dominant design has appeared, the focus shifts toward process innovations that fundamentally change the production and distribution chain rather than the product in question. A dominant product design is a design that consists of a configuration of components that represents the standard in the market for an extended period of time because it meets the requirements and needs of a wide range of users (Abernathy and Utterback, 1978). Abernathy and Utterback (1978) focus on the supply side of the market and on innovation rather than the diffusion process. The particular pattern that they distinguish might be the result of their focus on technology-oriented industries such as the automotive industry. Tushman and Rosenkopf (1992) elaborate on Utterback's idea when they describe a technology cycle. The first stage of the cycle, which they call variation, starts with a technological discontinuity that emerges either through scientific advance or through a unique combination of existing technologies. In the next stage, referred to as the era of ferment, parallel processes of substitution, competition and ongoing technical change unfold. In the third stage, the selection stage, a dominant design emerges. Finally, an era of incremental change sets in, where the dominant design essentially remains the same. Rogers' representation of the diffusion process is found to be valid for a wide variety of product categories (see Chapter 2 in Rogers, 2005). The same applies to the points of view adopted by Utterback and Tushman, although these are claimed to apply in particular to complicated technological products (Murmann and Frenken, 2006).

This chapter focuses on a specific pattern — the time between invention and large-scale production and diffusion, also referred to as the pre-diffusion phases, for high-tech product categories. Upon closer inspection, many scientists have already described the pre-diffusion period, some of them by describing separate cases, others by comparing multiple cases. Marx, for example, described that new production

technologies have to go through a process of adaptation and improvement before they become economically viable, and as a result of that
start to diffuse on a large scale long after its first application. Similar
results are obtained for other cases. Bloch (1935) described the lag
(an entire millennium) between the invention of the water mill and its
widespread adoption. David (1966) described that although the
reaper had been invented in the early 1830s, it was only in the mid-
1850s that Midwestern farmers adopted the reaper on a large scale.
Some other scientists tried to distinguish patterns by studying the pre-
diffusion period for multiple cases. Mansfield (1968), for example,
claimed that the average time from invention to the start of the commercial development process is about 10–15 years. From the start of
this process up to the market introduction, again, a few more years
elapse. Utterback and Brown (1972) estimated that, on average, this
development process takes an additional 5–8 years. So, according to
these authors, the period from invention to the first market introduction comprises 15–23 years. Agarwal and Bayus (2002) found an
average period of 28 years between invention and commercialization
for 30 breakthrough innovations from diverse industries.[1]

The message from all these authors is clear and can be summarized using the following text: "A review of past forecasts for video
recorders and microwave ovens illustrates the length of time required
for even the most successful innovations to diffuse through a mass
market. . . . Both took more than twenty years to catch fire in a large
market" (Schnaars, 1989, p. 120). What is lacking in these studies is
a systematic comparison of the length of the pre-diffusion period for
many cases and across industries. A systematic investigation of the
causes and consequences of the pre-diffusion period is also lacking.

---

[1] The fact that the estimates in Agarwal and Bayus (2002) differ from the findings of
other authors can be attributed to various reasons such as different types of cases
(later on, this chapter will show that industry has an effect), different types of definitions for the milestones, and statistical variation or dispersion around the average
(both will be discussed later on in the chapter). Given this dispersion, the data from
Agarwal and Bayus (2002) are considered to be in line with the data from Mansfield
(1968) and Utterback and Brown (1972).

These inquiries require a definition of this period, i.e. a definition of milestones between which time intervals can be assessed. We will turn to this topic in the next section.

2.3 Defining the Pattern

The previous section showed that it can take a long period of time before the industrial production and large-scale diffusion begins. A systematic comparison of the length of this period for multiple cases requires a clear definition of the start and end moments. At first sight, the emergence of the idea seems a good candidate for the start of this period and the first sales (adoption) of products seems a good candidate for the end of this period. In Exhibit 2.2, some elements of the helicopter case are described. This case is used to discuss whether the first idea for the product is actually a good choice for the starting point.

The case of the helicopter illustrates a couple of issues that hamper our effort to define the start of the pre-diffusion period. Firstly, the idea for a new high-tech product may be considered a natural starting point. In practice, however, it is almost impossible to assess with certainty whether the documented idea is actually the first. A patented idea is more easily traceable but patent behavior depends on the

Exhibit 2.2. The Invention of the Helicopter

The first idea for the helicopter or "rotary-wing aviation" originated in China in the 4th century BC. The helicopter was a children's toy that was powered manually. Centuries later, around 1500, Da Vinci designed the "Helical Air Screw", which is usually seen as the first attempt to make an effective helicopter. It was an experimental design never put into practice. Subsequently, multiple helicopter-like models powered by strings, gun powder, steam power, and so on were tried until the start of the 20th century, when the first helicopters were built that could be controlled by a person inside the helicopter.

Sources: Carey (1986) and Leishman (2000).

industry and culture involved, so it can hardly be used as a general starting point for different types of cases. Secondly, upon closer inspection, the case of the helicopter illustrates the evolutionary nature of the development process. This evolutionary nature seems to conflict with the idea of assessing milestones. Are there milestones in an evolutionary process? There is definitely a first time that a person inside a helicopter was able to control it while being lifted with the helicopter which was powered by means of an engine (inside the helicopter). This description shows that the more evolutionary a development process is, the more careful a milestone has to be defined (in our case, the first time a helicopter (1) lifted an individual; (2) could be controlled by that same person; and (3) was powered by an engine inside the helicopter).

A similar discussion is possible for the end of the pre-diffusion period. The start of the sales seems a good candidate to represent the start of the diffusion period. Upon closer inspection, however, this choice has a disadvantage. For many cases of new high-tech product categories, there is no clear start of the diffusion. In practice, a product can be introduced, withdrawn from the market, redesigned, aimed at a different customer segment and introduced again. Easingwood and Lunn (1992) argue that because of this iterative process, the diffusion of some communication products cannot be captured in a simple S-shaped curve. In these cases, there is no single smooth diffusion curve but rather an erratic process with multiple small efforts (each of which can be represented by a separate curve). This observation is in line with the fact that the first products of a new high-tech product category are often sold and applied years before the S-shaped diffusion curve starts.

Therefore, assessing the length of the pre-diffusion period, if possible at all, requires a very careful selection and definition of milestones. Three criteria that these milestones should fulfill are:

(1) Generic nature of the milestone — it should exist in (almost) all cases.
(2) Data availability of the milestone — data should be available for (almost) all cases.

(3) Objective timing of the milestone — milestones can be dated objectively.

These three criteria ensure that the milestones can be assessed for different types of cases. Using these criteria, the following milestones have been selected: (1) invention, (2) first market introduction, and (3) start of large-scale production and diffusion. Each of the milestones will be discussed and defined below.

2.3.1 *Milestone 1: invention*

Invention is considered to be the first demonstration of the working principle of a new high-tech product category. Materials are sometimes discovered in nature. Discovery, however, does not mean that the technology is understood and can be reproduced. So, the discovery of aspirin was much earlier than the invention of the process to produce this medicine. Similarly, the material aluminum was discovered in nature long before mankind started to master its process of production. We consider the latter moment as the invention.

> **Definition:** The invention of a new high-tech product category is defined to be the first time that the technical principle of this category is demonstrated and mastered.

The technical principle can be defined in terms of the physical or chemical processes on which the product category is based and in terms of the functionality that is enabled by the product category. The technical principle of the VCR, for example, is that particles on a tape are magnetized (technical principle) to store video data (functionality). The new high-tech product category can be defined in terms of a number of attributes that are considered to represent the core of this category.

An example will illustrate the relevance of distinguishing basic product attributes in addition to the technical principle and the functionality. Mobile telephony can be defined as a new high-tech product category that requires at least two stations with senders and receivers (attributes) to enable communication (functionality) via radio contact (technical principle). Using this definition, the invention of mobile telephony goes back to the work of Marconi and his predecessors in the late 19th century. Mobile telephony can also be defined as the ability to communicate, i.e. to have a conversation (functionality) via radio contact (technical principle) which requires stations with a sender and receiver and a switching station to connect them (attributes). In the latter case, the invention date is the time that the Bell labs devised the first switched mobile telecommunication system in 1947. So, establishing an invention date requires a very careful definition. Or, to put it differently, when definitions are changed, the invention dates may shift by decades.

2.3.2 *Milestone 2: introduction*

The introduction of a technological product is part of an array of subsequent activities. In the course of time, a product is developed, maybe produced on a small scale for testing and pilots, produced for actual use, maybe put in stock, then sold or transferred to the users in some way or another, and finally used in practice or implemented in the daily practice of the users.

> **Definition:**   The introduction date is defined to be the date at which the product is available for sales or can be transferred to users. In some cases, products are not sold, for example, if a government institute develops a new weapon that is used by the military forces.

For some cases, only information about the first pilots or the start of the production is available; whereas for other cases, the first sales or the first application in practice is the only available information. It is important to discuss the change in the introduction date that may result from the specific information available. If that change is small compared to the time scale used (in years) or if it is small compared to the time intervals observed for the phases of the case (multiple years), then the changes do not create a problem. However, if the change is relatively large, then additional information is required to find the actual date of selling or transferring the product to the user. If a large uncertainty in the dates of the milestones may completely shift conclusions about the length of the phases, these phases cannot be assessed.

2.3.3 *Milestone 3: large-scale production and diffusion*

This milestone is important because it separates the pre-diffusion phases from the standard diffusion process represented by the S-shaped diffusion curve. On the other hand, it is also a difficult milestone to define and assess in practice. Do the small-scale attempts to introduce the first products from a high-tech product category represent the start of the diffusion process or do they precede this process? In the latter case, it is important to define a milestone that distinguishes the pre-diffusion phases from the diffusion phase.

Definition: This milestone is defined using three elements:

- A standard product that can be reproduced multiple times (or standard product modules that can be combined in many different ways but are based on the same standard platform);
- A (large-scale) production unit with dedicated production lines (industrial production of a standard product); and
- Diffusion of the product.

The first element in the definition of the milestone is the existence of a standard product (or product modules) that is reproduced multiple times. This element is required to distinguish made-to-order products or experimental batches of products from the standard product. In the automotive industry, for example, cars were first produced as made-to-order products by small workshops. Industrial large-scale production in factories started with the emergence of the Model T Ford. This example also illustrates that, together with the emergence

of the standard product, another type of production facility emerges —
this phenomenon represents the second element in the definition of
the milestone. In some cases, large-scale production units are built for
products that are never sold. The standard product and the dedicated
production unit alone do not suffice to assess the start of the large-
scale diffusion; products should be sold as well (third element). A
dedicated production facility for the point-contact transistor made
out of germanium, for example, was built by Raytheon in the late
1940s, but this particular type of transistor was difficult to manufacture and was not successful. At the time of the opening of the
production facility, a much better type of transistor, the junction or
sandwich transistor, was invented; its large-scale production would
start around 1953.[2]

2.3.4 *Pattern of development and diffusion using the milestones*

Now that the milestones to assess the pre-diffusion phases have been
defined, the time interval of the pre-diffusion period can be assessed.
The pre-diffusion phases are defined to be the time that elapses
between the invention and the industrial production and large-scale
diffusion of a high-tech product category. This time period can be
further subdivided into two subsequent phases: the innovation phase
(from invention to initial market introduction) and the adaptation
phase (from initial market introduction to industrial production and
large-scale diffusion).

A typical representation of the development and diffusion pattern
of high-tech products is shown in Figure 2.1.

2.4 Length of the Pre-diffusion Phases

After defining milestones in the process of development and diffusion
of high-tech product categories, it is possible to compare the length

---

[2] The information on the transistor is from http://www.pbs.org/transistor/album1/
index.html/.

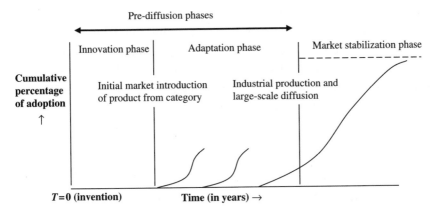

Figure 2.1. The pattern of development and diffusion of high-tech product categories.

of the pre-diffusion phases between cases.[3] I will shortly describe the method of assessing the milestones in practice for individual cases and then proceed with an overview of the results.

2.4.1 *Method*

An extensive case-study approach was used in the sense that each high-tech product category was examined as a separate case. The similarity of the approach in each case study later enabled a comparison of the data for multiple cases between industries. The exact time pattern for each case was assessed after conducting an extensive literature search. After combining various sources to find the relevant data, the data were categorized based on when relevant events took place. This approach is also referred to as a "chronology-of-events approach" (Sahal, 1981). In practice, literal copies of the information from various sources were combined in a table that described what happened before and after a new high-tech product was invented. These tables,

---

[3] This section is based on three conference papers presented at the IAMOT 2007, IAMOT 2008 and IAMOT 2009, respectively (Ortt *et al.*, 2007b; Ortt and Delgoshaie, 2008; Ortt *et al.*, 2009).

which covered between 10 and 20 pages, were then analyzed and discussed by at least two researchers to determine the dates of invention, market introduction, and large-scale production and diffusion, which resulted in an outline of the development and diffusion pattern. In some cases, additional literature was needed to resolve uncertainties or controversies concerning the correct pattern.

2.4.2 Results

The results are based on 50 cases of new high-tech product categories in five different industries.[4] The results will be described in three parts. Firstly, the length of the pre-diffusion phases for the entire set of cases will be discussed. Secondly, different scenarios or types of patterns will be distinguished within the set. Thirdly, the patterns of cases from different industries will be compared. In the Appendix is a table with an overview of the length (in years) of the pre-diffusion phases for all cases. A summary of this information can be found in Table 2.1. Both tables will be used when discussing the results.

2.4.2.1 Length of the pre-diffusion phases for all cases

On closer inspection, the data presented in Table 2.1 reveal some interesting information about the pre-diffusion phases. Firstly, the last column ("Total") shows that, on average, the pre-diffusion phases take about 17 years, which is a remarkably long time, especially given the term patents typically provide inventors with protection (about 20 years). The standard deviation is also relatively large (about 15 years),

---

[4] Standard industry categorizations from the Central Bureau of Statistics were used and condensed into comparable industry definitions on a relatively high level of aggregation: (1) chemicals, metals & materials; (2) pharma & healthcare equipment; (3) telecom, media & Internet; (4) electronic equipment; and (5) aerospace & defense. Individual cases were assigned to these industries by five different researchers. Their categorizations were then compared. When the researchers disagreed, their line of reasoning was discussed. In some cases, the experts reached an agreement after the discussion. When no such agreement could be reached, the cases were removed from the set.

Table 2.1. Duration (in years) of the pre-diffusion phases for 50 cases in five different industries.

Industry → Mean value (std. deviation) →	Chemicals, metals & materials	Pharma & healthcare equipment	Telecom, media & Internet	Electronic equipment	Aerospace & defense	Total
Total duration of pre-diffusion phases (P)[a]	11.4 (7.4)	26.1 (24.2)	15.3 (10.8)	19.2 (10.5)	11.6 (10.6)	16.7 (14.5)
Duration of innovation phase (I)[b]	4.9 (3.2)	21.6 (23.3)	8.9 (10.8)	7.2 (5.4)	7.6 (10.2)	10.0 (13.5)
Duration of adaptation phase (A)[c]	6.5 (5.8)	4.5 (6.2)	6.4 (7.1)	12.0 (11.2)	4.0 (4.3)	6.7 (7.6)

[a]Pre-diffusion phases (P) = Innovation and adaptation phases combined.
[b]Innovation phase (I) = The time period between invention and initial market introduction.
[c]Adaptation phase (A) = The time period between the initial market introduction and the industrial production and large-scale diffusion of products.

indicating a high dispersion around the average value. This implies considerable levels of uncertainty about the length of pre-diffusion phases for companies. The duration of the pre-diffusion phases is significantly different from zero (one-sample t-test: $p = 0.000$).[5] The innovation and adaptation phases are about 10 and 7 years long, respectively. Although the innovation phase seems somewhat longer than the adaptation phase, this difference is insignificant (two-sample t-test: $p = 0.15$). The lengths of the separate phases are all significantly different from zero (one-sample t-tests: all $p = 0.000$).

2.4.2.2 *Different scenarios for the pattern*

The results in the Appendix show that each phase can disappear in specific situations. These ideas are summarized in two propositions: (1) the phases can vary considerably in length, and one or more phases may even disappear; and (2) the entire process can break off in each phase.

These propositions convey a more unpredictable process than the S-shaped pattern. In practice, the actors involved in the commercialization of new high-tech product categories may face different scenarios. After studying the pattern of development and diffusion for 50 cases, three important scenarios are distinguished (see Figure 2.2 and Table 2.2). Scenario 1 is a situation in which a long innovation phase emerges, which means that it takes a long time before a product based on a new technology is introduced in the market. Scenario 2 is a situation in which a product is introduced shortly after the invention yet it requires a long market adaptation phase, which means that it takes a long time before this product diffuses in a mass market. Scenario 3 is a situation in which a new high-tech product, almost directly after the invention, diffuses in a mass market, which means that both the innovation and

---

[5] The value $p = 0.05$ means that there is a chance of 5 in 100 that the relationship (for which the p-value is established) does not hold. Although a critical p-value of 0.05 is often chosen, the value may depend on the research project. Below this value ($p < 0.05$), the relationship is statistically significant; above this value, it is not significant.

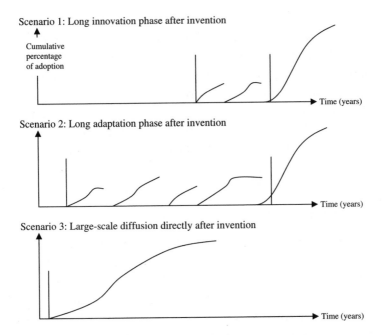

Figure 2.2. Three scenarios after the invention of a breakthrough technology.

Table 2.2. Data for some cases representing the (extreme) scenarios.

Scenario	Cases	Length of innovation phase (years)	Length of adaptation phase (years)	Length of pre-diffusion phases (years)
1	Radar technology	34	1	35
	Aspirin	44	3	47
2	Magnetic recording	5	30	35
	Plasma display	7	29	36
3	Dynamite	1	0	1
	X-ray	1	0	1

market adaptation phases almost completely disappear. Each scenario is illustrated in Table 2.2 using two cases.

Table 2.2 illustrates that these three extreme scenarios are possible in practice. Most of the cases, however, will result in innovation and adaptation phases that are less extreme in duration. It is interesting to notice that two medical high-tech product categories (at the time of their invention), aspirin and X-ray, represent different scenarios. Similarly, two product categories important in warfare, radar technology and dynamite, also represent different scenarios. Magnetic recording and plasma display, however, are both electronic equipment and represent the same scenario. It is interesting to more systematically explore the differences in cases from different industries, using the data from Table 2.1.

2.4.2.3 *Differences in pattern across the five industries*

We now focus on the question of whether the innovation and adaptation phases vary significantly across the five industries. The first row in Table 2.1 reveals that there are two industries with relatively short pre-diffusion phases, "chemicals, metals & materials" (column 1: 11 years) and "aerospace & defense" (column 5: 12 years). By contrast, "pharma & healthcare equipment" is characterized by relatively long pre-diffusion phases (column 2: 26 years). The other two industries are in between these extremes.

The significance of the differences between industries using analysis of (co)variance[6] was also checked, and a summary of the findings is presented here (for a full description, see Ortt *et al.*, 2009). When the effect of the date of invention is taken into account, the pre-diffusion phases do vary in duration significantly among the industries. The differences between the industries can almost completely be attributed to a difference in the duration of the innovation phase, which turns out to be highly significant. On closer inspection, the difference in the duration of the innovation phase can largely be attributed to a very long innovation phase in the case of "pharma & healthcare equipment" (22 years) and a relatively short innovation

---

[6] Analysis of variance investigates the variances of the duration of the pre-diffusion phases *between* industries and *within* industries. If the variance *between* the industries is relatively large compared to the variance *within* the industries, it can be inferred that the industries are homogeneous but different.

phase in the case of "chemicals, metals & materials" (5 years). Although the differences in terms of the adaptation phase are not significant, when individual pairs of industries are compared, it becomes clear that "electronic equipment" has a significantly longer adaptation phase (12 years) than "aerospace & defense" (4 years).

To conclude, the type of industry is related to the length of the pre-diffusion phases.

2.5 Causes of the Pre-diffusion Phases

2.5.1 *Introduction*

As explained in the first sections of this chapter, many scientists from different disciplines have studied patterns of technological innovation and diffusion. Some of them focused in particular on the factors that explain whether a delay can be expected between invention and large-scale diffusion. Bloch (1935), for example, explained the lag of an entire millennium between the invention of the water mill and its widespread adoption primarily in terms of legal and economic conditions. Rosenberg (1972) also pointed at the availability and introduction of other complementary inputs that make an original invention more useful and thereby demarcate the start of large-scale diffusion. David (1966) explained the delay in the diffusion of the reaper in terms of the relative cost of labor and the threshold for farm size, implying that, after farms obtained a particular size and after labor costs increased to a specific level, it became economically viable to use a reaper rather than the old labor-intensive techniques of cutting grain. Finally, Rogers (2005) used the characteristics of farmers to explain the diffusion of new appliances in agriculture.

The overview of scientists who describe specific factors to explain the delay between invention and large-scale diffusion is almost endless. Many factors can be mentioned, depending on the (sub)discipline of the scientists. Depending on the theory that is adopted, different factors and mechanisms are used to explain the delay between invention and large-scale diffusion. Diffusion researchers (see Rogers, 2005), for example, traditionally explain the start and the speed of diffusion in terms of the characteristics of potential adopters and their perception of the innovation, whereas institutional economists (such as North (1994)) tend to focus on legal and institutional characteristics in the market environment when doing so.

One of the ways to make sense of the variety of factors is to categorize them. Instead of a literature review to find the factors, the results of a multi-case study approach have been summarized to find many factors, to categorize them, and to explore the mechanisms by which they have an effect on the delay between invention and large-scale diffusion (Ortt and Delgoshaie, 2008). The advantage of a multi-case study approach is that the interaction between the factors can be observed; whereas in a review of articles, the factors are described separately.

Three categories for these factors will be distinguished: characteristics of (1) the main organizations involved, (2) the technological system, and (3) the wider market environment (around the main organizations). Using this categorization, one can argue that the economic conditions mentioned by Bloch (1935) belong to the wider market environment. The size of the farms (David, 1966) and the characteristics of farmers (Rogers, 2005) can be considered to represent characteristics of the customers (which belong to the main organizations involved).

2.5.2 *Method to assess factors*

The first step was to select a heterogeneous set of cases. Heterogeneity was assessed in terms of the industries involved, the length of the pre-diffusion phases and the time of invention. For each case, the pattern was first assessed (for the approach, see Section 2.4). Once the pattern was clear, the factors and mechanisms that may have influenced the length of the pre-diffusion phases were considered. Again, each case was studied by at least two researchers, each of whom made a list of factors and mechanisms that may have determined the length of the pre-diffusion phases in that specific case. The factors and mechanisms were discussed and a form was completed in which the factors and mechanisms were described, to which a copy was added containing the information that was used to infer this information. Because this procedure was carried out for all cases, the result was 18 forms containing detailed information. The information was then summarized and stored in a single data file to make it possible to analyze all the cases. In all, there were 118 occasions where a factor was identified that affected the length of the pre-diffusion phases.

2.5.3 Results

2.5.3.1 Categorization of these factors

To categorize the types of factors that affect the length of the pre-diffusion phases, a simple model of the market environment of the new high-tech product was adopted. This model describes the relevant environment for a new high-tech product:

(1) The main organization(s) responsible for the development, production, supply and use of the new high-tech product;
(2) The technological system required to use the new high-tech product; and
(3) The market environment, including all the other actors (than the main organizations) and factors involved (e.g. the availability of regulations and standards).

When the factors found in the cases were categorized depending on the question to which part of the environment they belong, they could be divided into three categories (see Table 2.3).

2.5.3.2 Mechanisms by which these factors affect the delay between invention and large-scale diffusion

While investigating the factors, the mechanisms by which these factors influence the delay between invention and large-scale production and diffusion were also explored. Four mechanisms are distinguished.

Table 2.3.   Categories of factors found to affect the pre-diffusion phases.

The main organization(s)	
Fit with mission and other criteria of companies to evaluate the importance of the product for the company	Customer need and other customer-related criteria needed to evaluate the product
Cheapness for producer/supplier (overview of costs/benefits)	Cheapness for customer (overview of costs/benefits)
Resources of main actor (to develop, produce and supply)	Resources of customer (ability to adopt and use)
Expertise (to develop, produce and supply innovation)	Expertise (to use innovation)
Market (supply) strategy	Adoption strategy
Number of suppliers for product and technological system; number and resources of suppliers of alternative products/technological systems	Number of potential customers (market potential)
	Network effects on the customers' or suppliers' side
	Cooperation/competition among different actors

The technological system	The market environment
Relative performance compared to alternative technology	Regulatory environment
Competition with other new/old technologies	Availability of rules and standards
Required and available complementary products	General public attitude
Reliability, certainty and risk of technology	Accidental changes in the macro-environment
Complexity and network requirements of technology	Accidents during development/exploitation
Availability of knowledge components (newness)	
Difficulty in controlling production	
Type of technology (basic, general purpose and/or competence-destroying technology)	
Visibility of benefits	
Unknown applications of technology (newness)	
Ease of translation from invention to innovation	
Compatibility with similar systems in other regions or with previous systems	

The first and simplest type of relationship can be represented via a regression model in which independent factors determine the length of the pre-diffusion phases. An example of this is the required presence of an infrastructure. In the case of telecommunication products and services or in the case of a navigation system like GPS, a complete infrastructure is required that consists of a network and complementary products and services. In some cases (for instance, SMS), an existing infrastructure can be re-used; while in other cases (like GPS and the mobile telephone at the time of their introduction), the infrastructure has to be built from scratch. The latter option usually implies that long pre-diffusion phases are to be expected. The more extensive the new infrastructure that has to be built, the longer the adaptation phase is likely to be.

A second type of relationship cannot be represented via a regression model, because it emerges when a factor serves as a necessary condition for the start or emergence of a new phase in the development and diffusion of a product. If the condition is not met, the emergence of the phase is impossible or highly unlikely. An example of this is the case of Dyneema, an ultra-strong fiber. In this case, because there was no controllable and scalable production method available, large-scale production and diffusion of the fiber were impossible. A controllable and scalable production method is a necessary condition for the emergence of the phase of large-scale production and diffusion.

A third type of relationship emerges when various factors have a combined effect on the dependent variable, the length of the pre-diffusion phases. Although the combination of the factors determines the length of phases, separate effects are hard to identify. Interaction effects between factors may be very complex when several factors are involved. An example of such an interaction involves the factors "fit of new high-tech product with the mission of the main organization responsible for developing, producing and supplying this product" (in short: "fit with mission") and "resources of the main company". Large organizations with many resources are only willing to invest in a product/technology when it fits their mission. Again, Dyneema provides an example. Dyneema was invented in the labs of DSM (a large Dutch chemical company), but because it did not fit the company's mission at the time,

DSM tried to sell the business unit involved. At the time, attempts to sell the business unit were unsuccessful, and almost 10 years later DSM reformulated its mission so as to include chemical specialities like Dyneema. This chain of events delayed the large-scale production and diffusion of the fiber, increasing the length of the pre-diffusion phases.

Finally, a fourth type of relationship emerges when the effect of the factors involved is highly contextual and time-dependent. The effect of a factor can, for example, depend to a large extent on the type of industry in which an organization operates. Military high-tech innovations, like radar and nuclear bombs, would never have been developed and used so quickly in the absence of war. In the telecommunication industry, to name another example, the existence of a compatible infrastructure is extremely important when new telecommunication products or services are introduced in the market.

The implication of these results is that the pre-diffusion phases are somewhat erratic. Although in all we identified many factors, we noticed that only a limited number of factors are important in individual cases. On average, we found fewer than seven factors to be decisive in each of the cases. We identified factors that serve as a precondition for the end of the pre-diffusion period, for instance, the ability to develop scalable production for new materials. We also found complex interactions among multiple factors that, for example, cause network effects or complicated patterns of substitution. We also found that the effect of factors on the pre-diffusion phases is context-dependent. Moreover, the importance of the factors may depend to a large extent on the industry involved. It is therefore believed that erratic patterns emerging during the pre-diffusion phases, in particular the adaptation phase, are the result of the complex interaction among many factors with an opposite effect.

2.6 Consequences of the Pre-diffusion Phases

From the perspective of a company trying to commercialize a new high-tech product (category), the pre-diffusion period has profound consequences. In the previous sections, several characteristics of the pre-diffusion period were described that have an important effect. Firstly, the average length of the pre-diffusion phases is large (about

17 years) (Section 2.4). Secondly, the dispersion around the average is considerable (about 15 years) (Section 2.4). Thirdly, there is a large number of factors that can determine the length of the pre-diffusion phases in individual cases, and these factors interact in complex ways (Section 2.5). The effect of these three characteristics on companies will be explored below.

2.6.1 *Consequence of the average length of the pre-diffusion phases*

The duration of the pre-diffusion phases has considerable implications for companies trying to commercialize their new high-tech products. In general, one may assume that the pre-diffusion phases represent an investment rather than a source of income for the organizations involved. Profits are usually generated during the phases of industrial production and large-scale diffusion. If that is the case, high-tech product categories require a tremendous investment over a long period of time.

2.6.2 *Consequence of the dispersion in the length of the pre-diffusion phases*

There is a relatively large dispersion around the average length of the pre-diffusion phases (about 15 years). In other words, the average duration of the pre-diffusion phases may be long, but in individual cases it can be very short or more than twice the average of 17 years. In general, the type of industry is shown to explain some of this variation; but at the time of the invention of a new high-tech product category, the overall uncertainty about the type of pattern that will unfold remains huge.

2.6.3 *Consequence of the lack of good market research tools in the pre-diffusion phases*

The trial-and-error process in the pre-diffusion period that results from the complex interactions between the factors makes it very difficult to use standard market research methods. Most methods assume that segments of potential customers are identified, and that individual customers invited in consumer research projects are able to understand the product and its use and are able to estimate the consequences of using the product on their daily lives. Furthermore, those types of predictions also assume that the product, once introduced in the market, will remain essentially the same, as will the market circumstances (such as the types of competitors); otherwise, the market research predictions no longer hold. These assumptions are rarely met in the pre-diffusion period, and therefore adapted or completely different methods are required to explore the market (Ortt *et al.*, 2007a).

So, at the time a new high-tech product is invented, there is a large uncertainty about the type of pre-diffusion period that will emerge. The general pattern that can be expected was described earlier (Figure 2.1); but it was also mentioned that for individual cases different scenarios might appear (Figure 2.2), each of which may require another production and market introduction strategy. The wrong strategy is found to entail large losses (Ortt *et al.*, 2007b).

In short, for the pioneers the stakes are high (in terms of the investment over years to turn the invention into a successful new high-tech product category), the return is uncertain (because the length of the period is uncertain, as is the ultimate return on the investment), and one of the instruments (market research) to reduce that risk does not function exactly in the situation that we need it most. It is not so remarkable that many companies involved in the commercialization of new high-tech product categories lose out before their products are applied on a large scale (Olleros, 1986; Pech, 2003). Projects dedicated to these high-tech products are risky, expensive, and usually take several years to produce results (Leifer *et al.*, 2000). Technical, market and organizational uncertainties associated with these projects are much higher than with projects aimed at incremental improvement (Burgelman and Sayles, 1986).

2.7 Conclusions and Discussion

This chapter started with the observation that the diffusion of new high-tech products rarely follows the well-known S-shaped diffusion pattern. In practice, after the first introduction a long period tends to elapse before the diffusion really starts. There appears to be a scientific gap in the mainstream diffusion literature regarding the pre-diffusion period. Managerially, it is also relevant to explore this period because many of the pioneers that invent new high-tech products no longer exist by the time their findings are successfully diffused in a mass market.

The pre-diffusion phases are defined using three milestones: (1) the invention, (2) the (first) introduction, and (3) the start of large-scale production and diffusion. Two phases are distinguished in the pre-diffusion period: the innovation phase (from invention to introduction) and the adaptation phase (from introduction to large-scale production and diffusion).

Using data from a multiple-case study, covering 50 cases from five different industries, we could explore the pre-diffusion phases in more detail. On average, the pre-diffusion phases last about 17 years, the innovation and adaptation phases each covering about half of this period. The actual length of the pre-diffusion period for an individual case may diverge considerably from this average, as can be inferred from a large standard deviation (about 15 years). In practice, after the invention of a new high-tech product category, different scenarios can emerge, only one of which resembles the original S-shaped diffusion curve directly after the invention. Yet that is exactly what mainstream diffusion researchers made us expect. If the data set presented in this chapter is a representative sample (the heterogeneity of the sample implies that it is quite random), then the findings imply that only a small percentage of these cases follow the S-shaped diffusion pattern. To be more precise: if we assume that cases with a pre-diffusion period of 3 years or less resemble the S-shaped diffusion curve, then our data reveal that only 6 out of 50 cases fulfill that requirement.

The causes of the pre-diffusion phases have also been explored. Our findings indicate that many factors can play a role and these factors can be categorized into three groups, covering characteristics of (1) the main organizations, (2) the technological system, and (3) the wider market environment. The type of industry is shown to explain some of the variation in the length of the pre-diffusion period. This makes sense because industries often refer to specific types or clusters of companies and customers, specific types of technologies and products, and a specific broader market environment. The mechanisms by which the factors affect the duration of the pre-diffusion period have been examined, and these mechanisms include complex interactions among many factors that explain the erratic nature of the pre-diffusion period. For each case, different subsets of factors turn out to be determinant. In addition, the consequences of the length of the pre-diffusion period and the uncertainty about this length for those companies that try to commercialize a new high-tech product have been discussed.

2.7.1 _Discussion_

This chapter showed that the pre-diffusion period is visible for many cases before the well-known S-shaped diffusion pattern. The sample of 50 heterogeneous cases implied that the emergence of this pre-diffusion period can be generalized to the population of new high-tech product categories. The particular way in which this pre-diffusion period was represented, by defining three milestones and distinguishing two phases between them, is based on a number of assumptions.

Firstly, the approach assumes that the milestones — invention, introduction, and the start of large-scale production and diffusion — can be distinguished quite accurately in time. Or to put it differently, the uncertainty in the estimates of the milestones should be relatively small (typically a year) compared to the length of the phases between these milestones (typically a decade). In some cases, such as the development and diffusion of fiber-reinforced concrete, the steps of improvement are very small while the application in practice proceeds. It is impossible in these types of cases to validly assess the timing for the pre-diffusion phases; the idea of the pre-diffusion period, however, still holds.

Secondly, we assume that the pre-diffusion phases are a kind of exogenous factor for those companies that try to commercialize a new high-tech product. From this perspective, these companies are advised to assess the stage of the pattern and to adapt their strategies accordingly. However, some companies are able to shape the pattern in a form that suits their goals. Philips, for example, deliberately postponed the market introduction of the DVD in order to be able to form an alliance of companies that supported the same DVD format before it was introduced in the market. Thus, the innovation phase was deliberately lengthened and the adaptation phase was shortened. As a result, the company was able to directly start large-scale production and introduce the DVD at a relatively low cost. Standardization battles (Suarez, 2004) show that this strategy is not without risk.

Thirdly, the type of research that was conducted — a chronology of events for historical cases to assess the entire pattern of development and diffusion — almost inevitably created a pro-innovation bias. By selecting cases that went through the entire pattern, we also selected cases of successful new high-tech product categories. It is, of course, possible that a specific product category never reaches the stabilization phase. Likewise, some inventions are never introduced in the market, or some new high-tech products that are introduced in the market are never produced on a large scale. The uncertainty for the cases that were investigated is reflected in the large dispersion around the average length of each pre-diffusion phase. The real uncertainty is even bigger because of the risk that the pattern may break off.

Finally, further research is definitely required to quantitatively assess the interaction between factors in the pre-diffusion period and their combined effect on the length of the pre-diffusion phases. Further research is also required to advise companies on how they can explore the market and adapt their strategy while they are in the pre-diffusion period. This chapter sets the scene by describing the pre-diffusion period and indicating the relevance of taking it into account when making new business plans.

Appendix

Table A2.1.　Duration (in years) of the pre-diffusion phases for all cases.

Name	Innovation phase (I)	Adaptation phase (A)	I and A
Chemicals, metals & materials			
1 Memory metal	7	4	11
2 Kevlar	6	2	8
3 Nylon	3	3	6
4 Bakelite	0	4	4
5 Dyneema	11	15	26
6 Cellophane	4	0	4
7 Polyurethane	1	15	16
8 Rayon	7	14	21
9 Buna S	4	4	8
10 Lycra	6	4	10
Mean	**4.90**	**6.50**	**11.40**
Std. deviation	**3.213**	**5.778**	**7.382**
Pharma & healthcare equipment			
1 Aspirin	44	3	47
2 Antibiotics	14	1	15
3 Viagra	2	1	3
4 CT scanner	5	2	7
5 MRI	7	3	10
6 X-ray	1	0	1
7 Heart-lung machine	54	10	64
8 Pacemaker	10	20	30
9 SSRI (Prozac)	15	5	20
10 Paracetamol	64	0	64
Mean	**21.60**	**4.50**	**26.10**
Std. deviation	**23.291**	**6.205**	**24.205**
Telecom, media & Internet			
1 Bluetooth	6	0	6
2 Fiber optic communications	9	8	17
3 Mobile telephone	15	1	16
4 Internet	0	15	15
5 Telegraphy	7	21	28

(Continued)

Table A2.1. (*Continued*)

Name	Innovation phase (I)	Adaptation phase (A)	I and A
6 Wi-Fi	2	9	11
7 Satellite phone	36	0	36
8 Telephone	1	2	3
9 UMTS	1	1	2
10 Television technology	12	7	19
Mean	**8.90**	**6.40**	**15.30**
Std. deviation	**10.775**	**7.121**	**10.750**
Electronic equipment			
1 Digital camera	3	21	24
2 Optical disc	16	4	20
3 Magnetic recording	5	30	35
4 Plasma display	7	29	36
5 VCR	5	1	6
6 Photocopier	11	11	22
7 Polaroid	15	3	18
8 Microwave oven	2	8	10
9 Air conditioning	0	13	13
10 Electronic microscope	8	0	8
Mean	**7.20**	**12.00**	**19.20**
Std. deviation	**5.371**	**11.165**	**10.475**
Aerospace & defense			
1 Helicopter	16	4	20
2 Aircraft	5	6	11
3 Dynamite	1	0	1
4 Nuclear bomb	4	2	6
5 Sonar	1	2	3
6 Radar technology	34	1	35
7 IFF	3	3	6
8 GPS	6	15	21
9 Jet engine	4	2	6
10 Torpedo	2	5	7
Mean	**7.60**	**4.00**	**11.60**
Std. deviation	**10.233**	**4.269**	**10.585**
(Total 50) Mean	**10.0**	**6.7**	**16.7**
Std. deviation	**13.5**	**7.6**	**14.5**

References

Abernathy, W.J. and Utterback, J.M. (1978). Patterns of industrial innovation. *Technology Review* (June/July), 41–47.

Agarwal, R. and Bayus, L. (2002). The market evolution and sales takeoff of product innovations. *Management Science*, 48(8), 1024–1041.

Bijker, W.E. (1995). *Of Bicycles, Bakelites, and Bulbs: Toward a Theory of Sociotechnical Change.* Cambridge, MA: MIT Press.

Bloch, M. (1935). Avènement et conquêtes du moulin à eau. *Annales d'Histoire Economique et Social*, 7, 538–563.

Burgelman, R.A. and Sayles, L.R. (1986). *Structure and Managerial Skills.* London: Collier-Macmillan.

Carey, K. (1986). *The Helicopter.* Blue Ridge Summit, PA: Tab Books.

David, P. (1966). The mechanization of reaping in the Ante-Bellum Midwest. In: H. Rosovsky (ed.), *Industrialization in Two Systems: Essays in Honor of Alexander Gerschenkron*, New York: Wiley, pp. 3–39.

Deane, P. (1978). *The Evolution of Economic Ideas.* Cambridge: Cambridge University Press.

Easingwood, C.J. and Lunn, S.O. (1992). Diffusion paths in a high-tech environment: clusters and commonalities. *R&D Management*, 1, 69–80.

Ekelund, R.B. and Hébert, R.F. (1983). *A History of Economic Theory and Method.* New York: McGraw-Hill.

Gopalakrishnan, S. and Damanpour, F. (1997). A review of innovation research in economics, sociology and technology management. *Omega*, 25(1), 5–28.

Hobsbawn, E.J. (1962). *The Age of Revolution.* London: Weidenfeld & Nicolson.

Landreth, H. and Colander, D.C. (1994). *History of Economic Thought.* Boston: Houghton Mifflin.

Leifer, R., McDermott, C.M., Colarelli-O'Connor, G., Peters, L.S., Rice, M.P. and Veryzer, R.W. (2000). *Radical Innovation: How Mature Companies Can Outsmart Upstarts.* Cambridge, MA: Harvard Business School Press.

Leishman, J.G. (2000). *Principles of Helicopter Aerodynamics.* Cambridge: Cambridge University Press.

Mansfield, E. (1968). *Industrial Research and Technological Innovation: An Econometric Analysis.* London: Longmans, Green & Co.

Murmann, J.P. and Frenken, K. (2006). Toward a systematic framework for research on dominant designs, technological innovations, and industrial change. *Research Policy*, 35(7), 925–952.

Nieto, M. (2003). From R&D management to knowledge management: an overview of studies of innovation management. *Technological Forecasting and Social Change*, 70(2), 135–161.

North, D.C. (1994). Economic performance through time. *American Economic Review*, 84(3), 359–368.

Olleros, F. (1986). Emerging industries and the burnout of pioneers. *Journal of Product Innovation Management*, 3(1), 5–18.

Ortt, J.R. and Delgoshaie, N. (2008). Why does it take so long before the diffusion of new high-tech products takes off? In: *Proceedings of IAMOT (International Association for Management of Technology) Conference, 6–10 April 2008, Dubai.*

Ortt, J.R., Langley, D.J. and Pals, N. (2007a). Exploring the market for breakthrough technologies. *Technological Forecasting and Social Change*, 74, 1788–1804.

Ortt, J.R. and Schoormans, J.P.L. (2004). The pattern of development and diffusion of breakthrough communication technologies. *European Journal of Innovation Management*, 7(4), 292–302.

Ortt, J.R., Shah, C.M. and Zegveld, M.A. (2007b). Strategies to commercialise breakthrough technologies. In: *Proceedings of IAMOT (International Association for Management of Technology) Conference, 13–17 May 2007, Miami.*

Ortt, J.R., Tabatabaie, S., Alva, G., Balini, G. and Setiawan, Y. (2009). From invention to large-scale diffusion in five high-tech industries. In: *Proceedings of IAMOT (International Association for Management of Technology) Conference, 5–9 April 2009, Orlando.*

Pech, R.J. (2003). Memetics and innovation: profit through balanced meme management. *European Journal of Innovation Management*, 6(2), 111–117.

Rogers, E.M. (2005). *Diffusion of Innovations.* New York: The Free Press.

Rosenberg, N. (1972). Factors affecting the diffusion of technology. *Explorations in Economic History*, 10, 3–33.

Rosenberg, N. (1982). *Inside the Black Box: Technology and Economics.* Cambridge: Cambridge University Press.

Sahal, D. (1981). *Patterns of Technological Innovation.* Reading, MA: Addison-Wesley.

Sahal, D. (1985). Technological guideposts and innovation avenues. *Research Policy*, 14(2), 61–82.

Schnaars, S.P. (1989). *Megamistakes: Forecasting and the Myth of Rapid Technological Change.* New York: The Free Press.

Suarez, F.F. (2004). Battles for technological dominance: an integrative framework. *Research Policy*, 33, 271–286.

Tellis, G.J. and Golder, P.N. (1996). First to market, first to fail? Real causes of enduring market leadership. *Sloan Management Review* (Winter), 65–75.

Tushman, M.L. and Rosenkopf, L. (1992). Organizational determinants of technological change. Towards a sociology of technological evolution. *Research in Organizational Behavior*, 14, 311–347.

Utterback, J.M. (1994). *Mastering the Dynamics of Innovation.* Boston: Harvard Business School Press.

Utterback, J.M. and Abernathy, W.J. (1975). A dynamic model of process and product innovation. *Omega*, 3(6), 639–656.

Utterback, J.M. and Brown, J.W. (1972). Monitoring for technological opportunities. *Business Horizons*, 15(October), 5–15.

Websites Visited

Encyclopaedia Britannica. (2010). Television. In: *Encyclopaedia Britannica Online Academic Edition*, available at http://www.search.eb.com/eb/article-235378/.
http://www.bvws.org.uk/405alive/history/revisionist_ history.html/.
http://www.earlytelevision.org/german_prewar.html/.
http://www.nyu.edu/classes/stephens/History%20of%20Television%20page.htm/.
http://www.pbs.org/transistor/album1/index.html/.
http://www.tvhandbook.com/History/History_timeline.htm/.

Chapter 3

Achieving Adoption Network and Early Adopters Acceptance for Technological Innovations

Federico Frattini

3.1 Introduction

It has been extensively documented in management literature that an incredibly large share of firms' investments in technological innovation do not generate substantial financial returns (Bianchi, 2004; Elton *et al.*, 2002; Rivette and Kline, 2000). Three main reasons underlying this phenomenon can be identified. Firstly, technological innovation creates knowledge and technological assets that often remain largely unexploited. As noted by Lichtenthaler (2005), various studies show that 70–90% of corporate technology assets often never get used in core products or lines of business. This technology underutilization problem has been recently mitigated by the diffusion of external technology commercialization and open innovation approaches (Lichtenthaler, 2008). Secondly, the likelihood that an innovation project reaches completion and that the new product is introduced into the market is strikingly low. It has been estimated that the probability of new product commercialization is about 40% in many industries (Gourville, 2006), and in some cases (e.g. pharmaceutics) the mortality of innovation projects is much higher. Finally, a large share of the innovations that ultimately reach the market do not experience a satisfactory diffusion and their sales are discontinued. Empirical studies have shown that, on average, 40–50% of fully commercialized new products turn out to be commercial failures (Cierpicki et al., 2000).

This chapter focuses on this last aspect to investigate what lies behind the poor customer acceptance that innovations often experience once their technical development is complete and they are introduced into the market. When managers and consultants are asked to comment on the surprisingly high failure rates for fully commercialized new products, they generally conclude that these new products were destined to fail. But, as noted by Gourville (2006), this is too simple an explanation: if these innovations had such a poor technical and functional content, why wasn't this apparent before firms invested large amounts of financial resources in executing their market launch? The truth is that the market acceptance and diffusion of a new product needs to be appropriately managed, and accordingly conceived as a critical phase of the innovation process (Schilling, 2005) — yet managers often underestimate its importance (Calantone and Montoya-Weiss, 1993), somehow blinded by the so-called "technology seduction" phenomenon (Meldrum, 1995).

Furthermore, literature has not yet reached a complete understanding of how to gain momentum for a new product that has a given functional content and is launched within a given competitive and product strategy. Much has been written about the factors that are able to discriminate between success and failure in the technological innovation process (for a review, see Van der Panne et al., 2003). Most of the variables this body of literature takes into account concern the technical or functional characteristics of the product (e.g. its capability to incorporate users' needs, relative advantage and innovativeness) or the decisions taken during the earlier stages of the process (e.g. organization of pre-development activities, cross-functional teamwork, interaction between marketing and R&D). What remains largely overlooked is the impact that the approaches used to introduce a given innovation into the market might have on its diffusion and market acceptance. Diffusion of innovation research has instead developed a number of interpretative models (e.g. epidemic or disequilibrium, probit or rank, sociological models) that are useful to describe the diffusion patterns of new products (Geroski, 2000; Van den Bulte and Stremersch, 2004). However, a strong limitation of this body of research is that it has largely failed to consider the role played by supply-side variables (i.e. endogenous variables controlled by the firm commercializing the innovation) in explaining new products' market acceptance (Frambach *et al.*, 1998).

The purpose of this chapter is to understand on which levers and how managers should act with the aim to successfully administer the market acceptance of an innovation that has a given set of technical and functional characteristics, and that is launched within the framework of a given competitive and product strategy. The chapter focuses in particular on innovations introduced into high-tech markets, because poor or too slow market acceptance can be very detrimental for the firm's competitive advantage in these industries (Nevens *et al.*, 1990). Because of their volatility and fast-moving nature (Wolf, 2006; Bayus, 1994), the window of opportunity during which new products must be introduced and established in high-tech markets has significantly reduced over the last years. Moreover, the demand-side increasing returns that often characterize high-tech markets make a rapid and large-scale acceptance of a new product a critical determinant of competitive advantage (McDade *et al.*, 2002). Furthermore, the chapter focuses specifically on consumer product innovations, and purposefully neglects service and process ones as well as new products introduced in industrial markets. It is left to future research to broaden the external validity of the research to also include these forms of innovations.

The chapter is structured as follows. Section 3.2 develops an interpretative, theoretical framework that helps unravel the research problem addressed in the chapter and serves as a basis for the subsequent empirical analysis. Section 3.3 illustrates the methodology of the empirical investigation, whereas Section 3.4 discusses the results of this analysis. Finally, Section 3.5 concludes and describes some avenues for future research.

3.2 Theoretical Framework

It is possible to identify two main factors that are influenced by the decisions managers take during the commercialization of a high-tech innovation, and that have a crucial impact over the customer acceptance it experiences once launched into the market. They are labeled in this chapter as "adoption network acceptance" and "early adopters acceptance", and are discussed in more detail hereinafter.

3.2.1 Adoption network acceptance

In the last years, an increasing number of high-tech markets have assumed the characteristics of networks as a result of improved communications technologies, the diffusion of the Internet, and the increasing incidence of unbundling, industrial specialization and de-verticalization phenomena (Chakravorti, 2003; Borrus and Zysman, 1997; Yoffie, 1997; Davies, 2004). As a consequence, the decisions concerning the large-scale adoption of an innovation are dispersed among a large number of interconnected players today, whose behavior can significantly affect the level of market acceptance that the innovation experiences. Compare a firm that launched a new technology in the market of traditional photography with one that enters the digital photography industry with a new image format. When introducing its innovation, the first company had to secure the support of film producers to ensure that the proprietary technology experienced large-scale acceptance. In the case of digital photography, the diffusion of the new image format has an impact on a wider set of players, whose support becomes key in determining large-scale acceptance: printer and PC manufacturers, companies that produce software for editing and organizing pictures, broadband communication firms, and manufacturers of cellular phones and handsets. It is the interconnected nature of many high-tech markets that explains, according to Chakravorti (2003), the "slow pace" with which very promising innovations have diffused into the market (e.g. information technology in the healthcare business).

The set of interconnected players who, with their behavior and strategic decisions, can significantly affect the market acceptance of a high-tech innovation is called the "adoption network" (Chakravorti, 2004). This network fundamentally includes, besides the end users of the new product, (1) companies that develop and provide products and services complementary to the innovation; (2) firms involved in distributing the innovation and information about it; and (3) industrial associations, institutions and governmental agencies that might affect the regulatory framework within which the adoption of the innovation occurs. If a high-tech innovation lacks support from some of the critical members of the adoption network, its customer acceptance will be significantly reduced.

Obviously, depending on the characteristics of the high-tech innovation being commercialized, the adoption network will include different players that can affect its customer acceptance to varying extents. Systemic innovations are those new products that necessitate significant readjustments of the other components of the system they are part of to be successfully commercialized, whereas autonomous (or stand-alone) innovations can be introduced without modifying the rest of the system (Teece, 1984). The main components that need to be altered to successfully commercialize a high-tech systemic innovation are: physical devices or pieces of equipment (e.g. a new hydrogen car calls for an infrastructure of dedicated filling stations); complementary software (e.g. a new DVD format requires the development of a library of compatible recorded movies); and services (e.g. a new music format calls for the distribution of a wide selection of pre-recorded albums, which might be in competition for shelf space with other, established formats). These components are largely unchanged when an autonomous innovation (e.g. a faster microprocessor or a larger memory) is commercialized. This indicates that many different players in the adoption network have to be persuaded to give support to a systemic innovation, as opposed to an autonomous innovation, and their behavior needs to be affected to a greater extent.

Therefore, it becomes a priority for a company commercializing a systemic innovation to administer its market introduction so as to influence the behavior of the critical players in the adoption network in order to secure their support for the new product. Differently put, achieving the support of the adoption network is particularly critical to ensure large-scale acceptance of a systemic innovation.

3.2.2 Early adopters acceptance

Psychology and economics research has demonstrated that individuals often deviate from rational economic behavior (Kahneman *et al.*, 1990; Kahneman and Tversky, 1979). This helps explain why people tend to resist innovations even when they offer substantial benefits that outweigh the economic switching costs they entail (e.g. learning and obsolescence costs) as well as the benefits offered by alternative products. This is due to the fact that innovations determine, albeit to a varying extent, changes in customers' behavior and consumption patterns. These changes are costly, due to the endowment and status quo biases perceived by potential customers, whereby they value products that they already possess more than those they do not have yet and tend to stick with what they have even if a better alternative is available (Gourville, 2006). As explained by sociological theories of innovation diffusion (Turnbull and Meenaghan, 1980; Burt, 1987; Deroïan, 2002), adoption decisions are also surrounded by a thick curtain of uncertainty: purchasers are often unsure of how a new product will perform for them, although specifications are available and the cost of the purchase is exactly known. Therefore, they try to address this uncertainty by asking previous adopters how they have fared with the use of the new product. These early adopters are more exposed to external communication channels (e.g. mass media) and have a higher reputation in comparison with the average population, and consequently exercise a strong opinion leadership on subsequent adopters (Czepiel, 1975; Rogers, 2003). The attitude they develop toward the innovation and their satisfaction with it are therefore decisive in affecting subsequent purchasers' adoption decisions and in overcoming their resistance. If early adopters are not satisfied with the new product, they will discourage subsequent adopters from purchasing it (Wind and Mahajan, 1987; Leonard-Barton, 1985; Richins, 1984).

These dynamics are particularly critical in high-tech consumer markets, which are strongly characterized by imitation, observation and bandwagon phenomena (Rohlfs, 2001).

Obviously, not all innovations lead to the same level of resistance and uncertainty in potential adopters. The greater the changes in customers' behavior and consumption patterns required by the innovation, the higher the level of resistance and uncertainty (Gourville, 2006; Hoeffler, 2003). Marketing research has developed the concept of "really-new" product to denote an innovation whose consumption utility is hard to estimate by customers before purchase (Alexander *et al.*, 2008). This concept is similar to the notion of radical innovation introduced by the Product Development and Management Association (PDMA) and often employed in innovation management research, according to which a radical innovation is "a new product, generally containing new technologies, that significantly changes behavior and consumption patterns"[1] in the target market. On the contrary, an incremental innovation is a new product that enhances a currently delivered benefit, without requiring a change in consumption or behavior.

Therefore, it is a main concern for a firm commercializing a radical innovation to manage its market introduction so as to stimulate a positive post-purchase attitude among early adopters, who play a fundamental role in overcoming prospective customers' resistance to change and uncertainty. Differently put, stimulating a positive post-purchase attitude in early adopters is particularly critical to ensure large-scale acceptance of a radical innovation. Figure 3.1 summarizes the arguments developed so far in this section of the chapter.

An important managerial question is, however, left unanswered: which levers can a manager act upon to achieve adoption network acceptance and early adopters acceptance for a high-tech innovation, having a given functional content and a set of technical specifications, that is introduced within the scope of a given competitive and product strategy? Literature on launch strategy and tactics (Hultink *et al.*, 1997, 1998; Hultink and Robben, 1999; Hultink *et al.*, 2000) and

---

[1] See the PDMA glossary available at http://pdma.org/library/glossary.html/.

88   *F. Frattini*

TYPE OF INNOVATION   CRITICAL SUCCESS FACTOR   DESIRED PERFORMANCE

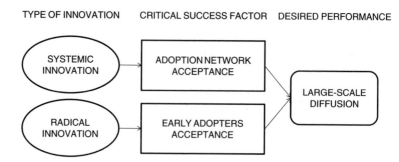

Figure 3.1.   Schematic representation of the theoretical framework.

high-tech marketing (Davies and Brush, 1997; Beard and Easingwood, 1996; Easingwood and Harrington, 2002) helps identify the decisions a manager is required to take when introducing into the market a high-tech new product. For the purpose of this chapter, the variables listed in Table 3.1 are focused on.

The empirical analysis described in the remainder of the chapter has been undertaken with the aim to understand how and why the decisions a manager takes along the variables reported in Table 3.1 can affect adoption network acceptance and early adopters acceptance of high-tech innovations.

3.3 Research Methodology

The methodology employed in the empirical research is historical analysis, which entails the systematic collection and analysis of data published on publicly available sources (periodicals, books, reports, etc.). The commercialization processes of 11 technological innovations, launched in high-technology markets in the past 30 years, have been investigated using this approach. Historical analysis was selected as a research method because it has a number of advantages over surveys and case studies carried out using direct, personal interviews (Gottschalk, 1969). In particular, it is effective in overcoming post-hoc rationalizations and in allowing researchers to identify the real causes of managerial drawbacks. This explains why it has been largely used in business and marketing research (Nevett, 1991; Golder and Tellis, 1993).

Table 3.1. Critical decisions in the market introduction of a high-tech new product.

Variable	Description
Timing	— When will the innovation first be launched into the market? — Will the firm announce the innovation to the press long before its market launch? — Will the firm partner with external organizations long before the official market launch?
Targeting and positioning	— Which market segments will the innovation be addressed to? — What will be the position of the innovation in the eyes of potential adopters in each of the targeted market segments? — Will the firm target different segments as long as the commercialization process progresses?
Interfirm relationships	— Which external organizations will the firm partner with during the commercialization of the innovation? — Which forms of relationships will be most appropriate (e.g. licensing agreements, strategic or long-term partnerships) to organize such relationships?
Product	— Which bundle of additional add-ons, services and functionalities surrounding the core innovation will be included in the basic configuration of the new product?
Distribution	— Which type of distribution strategy (e.g. push or pull) will be needed to streamline the market penetration of the innovation? — Which types of distribution channels will be chosen to deliver the innovation to market (e.g. retail or specialized distributors)? — Which critical functions (e.g. customer education) will these distributors be required to perform?
Advertising and promotion	— What message will be communicated during the pre-announcement and post-launch advertising campaign? — Which types of communication channels will be employed for these advertising and promotion initiatives (e.g. mass or specialized channels)?
Pricing	— Which pricing strategy (e.g. skimming or penetration) will be used for the market introduction of the new product? — Which pricing strategy will be adopted for complementary goods and additional services?

As far as the sampling of the 11 innovations is concerned, I decided to use a "polar-type" sampling design. Accordingly, I built a sample comprising some new products that had experienced a very poor customer acceptance after launch, together with a number of innovations that, on the contrary, were very successful from this point of view. This was done with the aim to unravel more straightforwardly the impact of managers' commercialization decisions on adoption network and early adopters acceptance, as suggested by Eisenhardt and Graebner (2007). Moreover, I decided to focus my attention only on systemic and radical innovations. This choice was suggested by the fact that, as explained in the last section, these types of new products are particularly susceptible to the effects of adoption network and early adopters acceptance. Therefore, they give the opportunity to study the phenomenon we are interested in under paradigmatic and particularly insightful circumstances (Siggelkow, 2007). More in detail, I interviewed a panel of seven experts in information and communication technology (ICT) and consumer electronics (consultants, professors and managers in ICT firms), who were asked to identify two successful and two unsuccessful high-tech consumer innovations that were launched in the last 30 years. They were also asked to classify them as either radical or incremental and systemic or autonomous, according to the definitions adopted in this research. The experts were in agreement in classifying the 11 innovations reported in Table 3.2 as being either systemic or radical.[2]

Table 3.3 provides some preliminary information about the 11 innovations. In particular, it reports data about the expected and actual sales of the new products, hence corroborating the experts' opinions about the degree of customer acceptance that they received once launched in the market.[3]

---

[2] Apple Newton and Sony Betamax were identified by all the experts as being both radical and systemic. Moreover, they suggested that I should focus on the commercialization of the MiniDisc in Europe and the USA and the commercialization of the BlackBerry in the USA.

[3] The comparison of expected and actual sales of a new product is a widely employed method to evaluate its degree of customer acceptance (e.g. Cooper and Kleinschmidt, 1987; Kleinschmidt and Cooper, 1991).

Table 3.2.   The innovations included in the sample.

	Radical innovations	Systemic innovations
Unsuccessful innovations	Apple Newton IBM PC Junior Sony Betamax	3DO Interactive Multiplayer Sony MiniDisc Apple Newton Sony Betamax
Successful innovations	TomTom GO Sony Walkman RIM BlackBerry	PalmPilot Nintendo NES Apple iPod

The main source used to collect data on the 11 innovations was periodicals. I gathered and analyzed more than 200 articles for each new product, for a total of more than 2,000 articles. The most helpful periodicals in this research were *Advertising Age, Billboard, Brandweek, Financial Times, The Wall Street Journal* and *The New York Times*. I used professional journal databases (i.e. LexisNexis Professional™ and InfoTrac™) to search through these periodicals, and thematic content analysis procedures (see, e.g., Weber, 1990) to classify and easily access the information they contained. As a first step, these data were used to analyze the extent to which the critical members of the innovations' adoption network provided support to the new products, and the attitude their early adopters developed after purchase. Table 3.4 summarizes the results of this analysis, suggesting that support from the adoption network is critical for systemic innovations to achieve a satisfactory customer acceptance, whereas the post-purchase attitude of early adopters has a significant influence over the diffusion of radical innovations. Unsuccessful radical innovations roused a very negative post-purchase attitude in their early adopters, whereas unsuccessful systemic innovations received very limited support from some critical members of their adoption network.[4] Successful innovations, on the other hand, did not encounter these

---

[4] Apple Newton was the only unsuccessful systemic innovation that did not lack support from the critical members of its adoption network. Similarly, Sony Betamax was the only unsuccessful radical innovation that did not stimulate a negative post-purchase attitude in early adopters.

Table 3.3. Preliminary information about the 11 innovations included in the sample.

Innovation	Brief description	Target market	Sales target	Actual sales
Unsuccessful Innovations				
Apple Newton	Apple Newton, the forerunner of the modern personal digital assistant (PDA), was launched in 1993. It had an advanced handwriting recognition software and an operating system based on an object-oriented programming language.	— Mass consumer market, with a focus on young men and adults who often travel and are used to working with a PC	— After 1 year: 50,000–100,000 — In 5 years: tens of millions	— After 1 year: 80,000–100,000 — In 5 years: 350,000 (withdrawal due to poor sales in February 1998)
Sony Betamax	Sony Betamax was the first home videocassette tape recording format launched in 1975. It was derived from the earlier U-matic technology by Sony, and was beaten in the market by the VHS technology by JVC.	— All the people who have a TV set — Families with heterogeneous TV preferences	— After 1 year: 50,000 — In 5 years: 1.5 million	— After 1 year: 30,000 — In 5 years: 800,000

(Continued)

Table 3.3. (*Continued*)

Innovation	Brief description	Target market	Sales target	Actual sales
IBM PC Junior	IBM PCjr was introduced by IBM in 1984. It was the first home computer developed by IBM, and it featured the same microprocessor used in the traditional PC and a wireless keyboard.	— Families with children — Elementary and secondary schools/universities	— After 1 year: 1 million	— After 1 year: 26,000 (withdrawal due to poor sales in mid-1985)
3DO Interactive Multiplayer	The Interactive Multiplayer was released in 1993 by 3DO, a start-up firm founded by Trip Hawkins, who had already created Electronic Arts some years earlier. The Interactive Multiplayer was a multimedia gaming, entertainment and learning platform that used a CD-ROM as support.	— All family members, from young children to teenagers to adults	— After 1 year: 500,000 — In 5 years: 50 million	— After 1 year: 250,000 (200,000 in Japan) — In 3–4 years: 1.38 million (withdrawal due to poor sales in early 1996)

(*Continued*)

Table 3.3. (*Continued*)

Innovation	Brief description	Target market	Sales target	Actual sales
Sony MiniDisc	MiniDisc was a new magneto-optical disc format launched by Sony in 1992 to replace the analog cassette. It could be recorded on repeatedly and was able to store data in different formats (sound, image and text).	— Young people fond of music — Men and women between 22 and 32 years old	— After 1 year: 500,000 (worldwide) — In 5 years: 25–30 million (worldwide)	— After 1 year: 50,000 in US; 100,000 in Europe — In 5 years: 550,000 in US; 1.2 million in Europe
Successful Innovations TomTom GO	The GO was the first portable all-in-one GPS car navigation system launched by TomTom in 2004. It had a very simple configuration and cost three times less than the integrated satellite navigators then available on the market.	— Mass consumer market, and in particular men between 22 and 40 years old who frequently travel for work	— After 1 year: 800,000 — In 3 years: 2 million	— After 1 year: 1.5 million — In 3 years: 3 million

(*Continued*)

Table 3.3. (*Continued*)

Innovation	Brief description	Target market	Sales target	Actual sales
Sony Walkman	Walkman was the first portable music cassette player launched by Sony in 1979 that featured stereo sound reproduction quality.	— Young people from 12 to 25 years old — Adults fond of sport and outdoor living, and commuters	— After 2 years: 1.5 million — After 5 years: 7 million	— After 2 years: 2 million — After 5 years: 10 million
RIM BlackBerry	The BlackBerry was the first palm-held device, launched by RIM in 1999, that allowed the user to receive e-mails in real time using a revolutionary "push" technological approach.	— Managers who need to read e-mail messages everywhere and in real time — Professionals who travel a lot for work	— After 2 years: 150,000 — In 4 years: 500,000	— After 2 years: 220,000 — In 4 years: 1 million
PalmPilot	The Pilot was launched in 1996 as a substitute for paper daybooks. It was a palm-held device with a simplified handwriting recognition functionality, and allowed instant connectivity with PC and Macintosh.	— Mass consumer market, and in particular adults who travel frequently and are accustomed to using a PC	— After 1 year: 200,000 — In 5 years: 2 million	— After 1 year: 1 million — In 5 years: 7 million

(*Continued*)

Table 3.3. (*Continued*)

Innovation	Brief description	Target market	Sales target	Actual sales
Nintendo NES	NES was the first 8-bit home video game system introduced by Nintendo in 1983. It had improved graphic performance and was less expensive than previous-generation consoles. It came with a broad collection of game titles.	— Children and teenagers, mainly male, between 6 and 16 years old	— After 1 year: 2 million — After 5 years: 5 million	— After 1 year: 3.6 million — After 5 years: 27 million
Apple iPod	iPod was a digital music player launched by Apple in 2001. It was based on hard disk technology and it supported several different music formats (e.g. MP3, WAV, ACC). It had an essential but sophisticated design, and was complemented by the iTunes software allowing the purchasing of music from the Web.	— Young people between 12 and 25 years old — People who already possess an Internet flat connection and download music from the Web	— After 1 year: 100,000 — In 4 years: 4 million	— After 1 year: 140,000 — In 4 years: 28 million

Table 3.4. Analysis of adoption network acceptance and early adopters acceptance for the 11 innovations in the sample.

Innovation	Early adopters	Early adopters acceptance	Key players of the adoption network	Adoption network acceptance
Apple Newton	— Businessmen and executives who need a device that allows them to work while traveling — Museums (as an interactive wireless guide) — Companies (for sales force automation applications)	Very negative: — Some key functions were not perfectly working at launch (in particular, the handwriting recognition system). — The inability to communicate with PC and Mac in the basic configuration was perceived as a strong limitation by early adopters.	— Software companies that develop applications for the Newton OS operating system — Complementary product manufacturers	Very positive: — After the launch of the new product, a wide library of software applications and complementary add-ons was available in the market to improve the value of the innovation for potential adopters. This result was achieved by Apple through the establishment of a number of agreements with the providers of hardware devices based on the Newton technology as well as software applications (e.g. Motorola, Rolm, Cirrus Logic, Siemens, State of the Art, Dendrite, Intuit, RR Donnelley).

(Continued)

Table 3.4. (*Continued*)

Innovation	Early adopters	Early adopters acceptance	Key players of the adoption network	Adoption network acceptance
Sony Betamax	— Professional recording studios — Universities and institutions working with many workstations	Very positive: — The quality of the music and video reproduction technology was extremely high and allowed Betamax to be successfully employed for professional reasons.	— Motion picture production companies that supply films and titles in the Betamax format — Distributors (video rentals, electronic outlets, supermarkets) — Competitors that might decide to give their preference to a different format	Very negative: — Film producers strongly resisted the new format (Disney and Universal Studios even sued Sony for copyright issues). Sony was not able to win their support (it attempted to recover from this situation by setting up a joint venture with Paramount Home Video). — Video rentals decided to give support to the competing technology — VHS — promoted by JVC. — Competitors found it difficult to manufacture products based on the Betamax technology, since it was closely protected (Sony accepted to out-license it to Zenith only one year after the launch of the product).

(*Continued*)

Table 3.4. (*Continued*)

Innovation	Early adopters	Early adopters acceptance	Key players of the adoption network	Adoption network acceptance
IBM PC Junior	— Managers or professionals using a traditional IBM PC at the office and willing to also work at home — Elementary and secondary schools/ universities for educational and learning purposes	Very negative: — It was perceived as a downscaled version of the PC with strong limitations in terms of processing capabilities (memory, disc drive, expansion slots). — The keyboard was especially criticized because it was uncomfortable to use for long periods.	— Software companies that develop video games as well as professional and educational software — Firms that develop and manufacture compatible equipment and add-ons	Very positive: — The recognition of the IBM brand and the early success of the PC were critical for convincing software developers and distributors to ensure full support to the new product.

(*Continued*)

Table 3.4. (*Continued*)

Innovation	Early adopters	Early adopters acceptance	Key players of the adoption network	Adoption network acceptance
3DO Interactive Multiplayer	— Middle-aged consumers (mainly male) who are driven to own the latest and most-performing home gaming system	Very positive: — The graphic capabilities of the machine were particularly appreciated and aligned with the compelling reason to purchase among the early adopters. — It was perceived as a technologically advanced platform, which allowed a big step toward realism in interactive technology.	— Manufacturers that produce the console under their own brands — Software developers and publishers supplying video games and other applications for the console	Very negative: — The Interactive Multiplayer suffered from a lack of games and applications that were capable of exploiting its graphic capabilities, even though 3DO had sold a number of licenses for software development before the market launch (only 60 applications were available by June 1994, despite over 200 titles being officially under development). — 3DO suffered from a shortage of multi-brand production from manufacturers that had accepted to produce the console on the basis of a manufacturing license (e.g. Goldstar, Sanyo, Panasonic).

(*Continued*)

Table 3.4. (*Continued*)

Innovation	Early adopters	Early adopters acceptance	Key players of the adoption network	Adoption network acceptance
Sony MiniDisc	— Middle-aged men and women who travel a lot for work — Young people who are "gadget addicts"	Very positive: — The MiniDisc was perceived as a revolutionary technology because it allowed the recording of data multiple times, while maintaining a high sound reproduction quality. — The portability of the machine was particularly important for satisfying the compelling reason to buy among early adopters.	— Record labels that supply pre-recorded music in MD format — Retailers of pre-recorded music that ensure the availability of a wide range of titles on the new recording format	Very negative: — Only Sony Music and EMI Music decided to produce and supply pre-recorded MDs in 1997. — Retailers were unwilling to devote shelf space to pre-recorded MD albums because they feared that they could cannibalize music cassette sales and because the MD technology appeared to have gained a limited installed base in comparison to competing standards (e.g. Philips DCC).
TomTom GO	— Sales representatives — Professionals who drive different vehicles for work	Very positive: — Early adopters were particularly impressed by the high portability and ease of use of the device. — The positive reaction was also suggested by the precision of the incorporated satellite maps and the vocal instructions.	— Providers of digitalized maps — Organizations regulating access to GPS services	Very positive: — TomTom had secured support from Tele Atlas for the provision of digital maps well in advance of the commercialization of the GO. — The US Department of Defense gave all firms the opportunity to use the GPS system without particular restrictions and without applying a fee.

(*Continued*)

Table 3.4. (*Continued*)

Innovation	Early adopters	Early adopters acceptance	Key players of the adoption network	Adoption network acceptance
Sony Walkman	— Young men between 20 and 25 years old, particularly those fond of sport and outdoor activities	Very positive: — Early adopters were excited about the new concept of portable music and the near-CD quality of sound reproduction.	— Record labels that supply pre-recorded music in MC format	Very positive: — At the time when the Walkman was launched, the market for music cassettes was growing at significant annual rates; thus, players were open to endorsing any products that could boost sales of pre-recorded cassettes. This explains the support Walkman received from record labels and retailers.
RIM BlackBerry	— Chief Information Officers or Chief Financial Officers for whom the BlackBerry also represents a status symbol — Sales agents	Very positive: — According to a market research, the large majority of people who tried the BlackBerry said they could not live and work without it anymore.	— Mobile network carriers that allow the BlackBerry to work on their networks	Very positive: — RIM had already established in 1995 a number of commercial agreements with some of the main US carriers (e.g. BellSouth and Cantel) for one of its earlier products (a pager). This asset was critical for ensuring a rapid diffusion of the BlackBerry.

(*Continued*)

Table 3.4.   (*Continued*)

Innovation	Early adopters	Early adopters acceptance	Key players of the adoption network	Adoption network acceptance
PalmPilot	— Middle-aged computer-literate men, especially executives and professionals who travel a lot for work	Very positive: — Early adopters appreciated the ease of use of the machine and its handwriting recognition system. — The capability of the device to communicate with PC and Macintosh for exchanging information and updating data was perfectly working since the first units were released in the market.	— Developers of contents and applications — Manufacturers of complementary devices — Retailers and distributors who play an important role in educating customers about the new product	Very positive: — Many firms decided to supply complementary hardware devices that improved the Pilot's functionalities (e.g. Qualcomm, Kodak, Novatel Wireless). — Many software development firms supported the platform as well (e.g. Lotus, Peanut Press, Symantec). — Circuit City (one of the leading electronic retailers in the US) heavily sponsored the product's introduction and engaged in extensive customer education activities for it. This behavior can be explained considering that Palm took on the risk of the launch itself, signing a long-term, US$20 million agreement in favor of Circuit City.

(*Continued*)

Table 3.4. (*Continued*)

Innovation	Early adopters	Early adopters acceptance	Key players of the adoption network	Adoption network acceptance
Nintendo NES	— Young boys between 14 and 16 years old	Very positive: — Early adopters particularly appreciated the product's graphic capabilities and the entertaining quality of the games available on the market.	— Software companies that develop game titles for the console	Very positive: — The NES was able to raise a significant interest in the developers' community (e.g. Namco, Konami, Hudson, Capcom, Taito, Bandai) for the new product, through the establishment of very advantageous licensing agreements.
Apple iPod	— Macintosh users who love the Apple brand (the early adopters of the iPod were also Mac lovers because the first models could communicate only with computers featuring the latest version of the Mac OS operating system)	Very positive: — The early adopters accepted the new product with enthusiasm. They appreciated its technical characteristics, and also identified themselves with the lifestyle it was an icon of.	— Record labels	Very positive: — The iPod was able to reproduce music in a number of digital formats largely available on the market. Nevertheless, the approach adopted by Apple to make the most out of the iPod (i.e. combining it with the iTunes Music Store) required that record labels agreed to distribute their songs through the online system. Apple won the support of some of the major labels (e.g. Sony Music, BMG, EMI, Universal) by ensuring a high royalty rate (65%) on each song sold through iTunes.

types of limitations once introduced into the market. This is consistent with the model developed in the previous section of the chapter.

The collected information was also used to describe the decisions taken by the managers responsible for the new products launched along the dimensions reported in Table 3.1. Afterwards, I used pattern-matching and cross-case comparison techniques (Yin, 2004) to disclose any recurrent differences in the commercialization decisions of successful and unsuccessful systemic innovations, as well as of successful and unsuccessful radical innovations. This allowed me to identify a number of recurrent paradigmatic commercialization decisions that could be interpreted as being responsible for raising an extensive (or limited) support from the innovation's adoption network and a positive (or negative) attitude in its early adopters. The outcome of this analysis is described in detail in the following section.

3.4 Empirical Results

This section discusses how and why the approaches used to commercialize the 11 high-tech innovations considered in the research influenced the degree of support provided by the critical players of the adoption network and the post-purchase attitude developed by early adopters.

3.4.1 Commercialization decisions influencing adoption network acceptance

Comparing the commercialization of the successful and unsuccessful systemic innovations in the sample, a number of decisions taken along the dimensions listed in Table 3.1 have been unearthed that seem to explain the heterogeneous acceptance the innovations received in their adoption network. Table 3.5 provides a synthesis of these decisions.

3.4.1.1 Interfirm relationships

Our analysis indicates that obtaining the support from the critical members of an innovation's adoption network requires chiefly a careful administration of the interfirm relationships that are established before and during the commercialization process.

Table 3.5. Commercialization decisions improving the likelihood of a positive adoption network acceptance.

Variables	Decisions
Interfirm relationships	— The firm establishes long-term, strategic partnerships with the critical players of the adoption network to share with them the risks and costs that giving support to the innovation entails. — The firm allows its competitors to manufacture products based on the innovation's underlying technology (through out-licensing agreements). — The firm allows complementary product manufacturers (e.g. add-on or software developers) to access, at advantageous conditions, the innovation's underlying technology. — In the case of content-based innovations, the firm sells at a low price or free of charge the software authoring system to the community of developers.
Timing	— The long-term, strategic partnerships with the critical players of the adoption network are established earlier on in the commercialization process, before the new product diffuses in the bulk of its target market.
Targeting and positioning	— The innovation has a clear and unambiguous positioning in the market that favors convergence in the behavior of the adoption network's players.

The decision to prevent other companies (e.g. competitors, suppliers of complementary hardware and software) from manufacturing products based on the innovation's underlying technology is likely to be the first detrimental decision for the large-scale adoption of a high-technology innovation. This is due to the strong network externalities that high-tech markets, because of their tight interconnectedness, are currently experiencing (McDade *et al.*, 2002). Accordingly, letting the actors of the adoption network manufacture products based on the innovation's technology (e.g. through advantageous out-licensing agreements) increases the availability of complementary products and the chances that a potential adopter will choose to purchase the innovation. This in turn exponentially enhances the value of the innovation in the eyes of both subsequent adopters and the other members of the adoption network, in a self-reinforcing double-loop cycle (Schilling, 2003). The effects of this commercialization decision are very clear when comparing the case of the PalmPilot (whose OS operating system was released for free to all manufacturers of add-ons and software applications) with that of Sony Betamax (where Sony accepted to license the underlying technology to Zenith only more than one year after launch, when the incoming success of the VHS technology by JVC was already undisputable).

Another critical approach to win the support of the critical members of an adoption network is to enter into long-term, strategic partnerships with them. This allows them to share the risks and the costs they incur when supporting a systemic innovation (e.g. developing and manufacturing ad hoc, specialized, complementary devices or pieces of software). This is what Palm did, in 1996, when commercializing the Pilot: it decided to sign a US$20 million agreement with Circuit City to ensure adequate shelf space and customer education services for its new product. Similarly, Apple — to streamline the acceptance of the iPod and the associated iTunes Music Store service — was able to convince a number of record labels (e.g. Sony Music Entertainment, BMG, EMI, Universal and Warner) to endorse the new service provision model by ensuring a 65% compensation for each song sold through iTunes. In a similar vein, Nintendo invested heavily in order to obtain the full support for its NES from the most important game developers (e.g. Taito, Bandai, Capcom). This required the Japanese firm to grant above-average money compensation for each game sold. Sometimes, the innovating firm refuses to establish any partnerships with the members of the adoption network — or simply sets up arm's-length, commercial relationships with them — in order to maximize potential profits from the innovation. This is evident in the case of 3DO, which failed to establish any form of relationship with the developers of software titles and the manu-facturers of consoles for its new Interactive Multiplayer. A similar phenomenon is clear in the commercialization of the Betamax, where Sony refused to partner with video rental channels and film produc-ers (with the exception of Paramount Home Video, with which a joint venture was established).

A critical member of the adoption network for content-based innovations is the community of small and highly creative software and application developers. In order to secure their support, it is especially crucial to develop an easy-to-use software authoring kit that is made available for free or at a very low price. This is what Palm did when it released, for free, the application development kit for the Pilot. 3DO, on the other hand, decided to sell the author-ing system for the Interactive Multiplayer for several thousand dollars.

3.4.1.2 Timing

Besides the form of the interfirm relationships with the critical mem-bers of the adoption network, it seems that the timing with which they are established is important in determining the degree of support they ensure to the innovation. The analysis indicates that sometimes firms deliberately postpone the establishment of strategic partnerships with the adoption network on the assumption that, once the innova-tion has taken off in the market, its critical players will support it of their own accord. However, it often happens that, after an initial, unexpected growth of the new product's sales, the innovation never diffuses in the largest part of the target market. This is what happened in the commercialization of the MiniDisc, when Sony refused to part-ner with consumer electronics outlets (which played a critical role in ensuring a large availability of recorded music albums) under the belief that the new format would diffuse in the mass market anyway and, as a result, they would be forced to provide the required shelf space. This phenomenon is due to the fact that the bulk of a high-tech consumer innovation's target market is made up of people who resist new products and experience a high level of uncertainty when evaluating the opportunity to buy them. Although early adopters might be willing to purchase the new product despite it not being backed up by the critical members of the adoption network (because they are mainly attracted by the technical content and degree of sophistication of the innovation and are able to more objectively assess its advantages), this represents an important signal to later adopters of the value of the innovation, which helps reduce their resistance and customer uncertainty.

Therefore, although a high-tech innovation may experience an unexpected sales growth immediately after launch without support from the critical players of the adoption network, it is of paramount importance to rapidly secure this support through the establishment of long-term, strategic partnerships, if large-scale adoption is to be achieved. All firms whose innovations had experienced a relevant and rapid diffusion in the bulk of their target market started to work with the adoption network's critical players very early on. This is clear in the cases of PalmPilot, Nintendo NES and Apple iPod.

3.4.1.3 *Targeting and positioning*

Especially for content-based innovations, it seems that a firm succeeds more easily in orchestrating the behavior of the adoption network's players and in securing their support if the positioning of the new product is unambiguous. The experience of 3DO in the commercialization of the Interactive Multiplayer is paradigmatic in this respect. The new, revolutionary console always lacked a library of software titles that were able to fully exploit its graphic capabilities. This was partly due to its unclear positioning: the Multiplayer was sold as a gaming platform with advanced interactive, learning and educational capabilities, enabled by its CD-ROM support, that caused confusion in the developers' community about the exact applications required for its commercial success. On the contrary, the NES by Nintendo was unambiguously positioned as a gaming system, and the PalmPilot as a substitute for personal paper-based organizers.

3.4.2 Commercialization decisions influencing early adopters acceptance

Comparing the commercialization of the successful and unsuccessful radical innovations in the sample, a number of choices taken along the dimensions listed in Table 3.1 have been identified that appear to clarify the heterogeneous attitude the innovations generated in their early adopters. Table 3.6 provides a synthesis of these commercialization decisions.

3.4.2.1 Timing

It often happens that firms rush to market their high-tech innovations in an attempt to establish them as technological standards and to quickly recover from their R&D investments. This means that firms sometimes launch an incomplete product, with some functionalities not perfectly working, as a result of the acceleration of development and testing activities. This seems to have a very negative effect on the attitude developed by early adopters. Companies sometimes prefer shortening the time to market at the expense of product completeness on the assumption that the potential technical problems will not affect the purchase decision and the satisfaction of the average member of the target market. In doing so, they overlook that the innovation is adopted immediately after launch by those customer segments that are most sensitive to the new product's technical content and sophistication, and whose opinion about the new product is key in affecting subsequent purchases. This erroneous conduct is clear in the commercialization of the IBM PC Junior and the Apple Newton, while there is no sign of new product acceleration for the successful radical innovations in the sample (e.g. TomTom GO, Sony Walkman and RIM BlackBerry).

It should be noted that the negative impact of the launch of an incomplete product is exacerbated by a keenly anticipated pre-announcement campaign. It raises early adopters' expectations toward the innovation, who are then very disappointed when it reaches the market in an incomplete version, with very negative effects on the

Table 3.6. Commercialization decisions improving the likelihood of a positive early adopters acceptance.

Variables	Decisions
Timing	— The firm makes sure that development activities (including prototyping and beta testing) are complete before the innovation is introduced into the market. — The firm pre-announces the innovation early if it is sure that the new product at launch will have a complete configuration and will not lack any critical functionalities advertised during the pre-announcement campaign.
Targeting and positioning	— The firm proactively identifies, within the broad target market of the innovation, those niches and segments that have a compelling reason to purchase the new product and hence will buy it immediately after launch, well in advance of the average member of the target market.
Product	— The firm designs a configuration of the new product at launch including only those functionalities that are critical to satisfy the compelling reason to buy for the early adopters. — The firm makes sure that these functionalities work properly from the moment the first units of the new product are delivered to the market. — The configuration of the new product at launch includes a limited number of functionalities in addition to the innovation's core functions. This increases the likelihood that they will be perfectly working from the moment the first units are delivered to distribution channels. — There is no inconsistency between the configuration of the new product at launch and the characteristics advertised during the pre-announcement campaign.
Advertising and promotion	— The messages used to pre-announce the new product stress those characteristics of the innovation that will be available at launch and will be working perfectly.

attitude they develop toward the innovation. This happened with the Apple Newton, which was announced 18 months before the actual launch and was known as one of the most-hyped and most-postponed products for years. Similarly, the PC Junior was pre-announced about 12 months before the launch, thus explaining the curiosity, rumors and enthusiasm that accompanied the new product, which began to be labeled by analysts with the nickname "Peanut". Interestingly, IBM itself contributed to nurture these expectations, drawing a thick curtain of secrecy over the new product after having pre-announced it.

3.4.2.2 Targeting and positioning

The incapability to understand that an incomplete new product is likely to elicit a very negative reaction in the first market segments that adopt it is also due to a lack of proactive targeting of these early adopters. The firms in the sample that failed to raise a positive post-purchase attitude among early adopters did not specifically target the innovation at any specific market segments after launch. This is clear in the cases of Apple Newton and IBM PC Junior, which were aimed at a broadly defined market made up of mass consumers and families with children, respectively. It was only after the first months of sales that managers realized the new products were being purchased by people with a very different profile than the average target customer (executives and companies for sales force automation applications in the case of Apple Newton, and managers used to working with a traditional PC at the office who wanted to bring some work home in the case of IBM PC Junior). On the other hand, when commercializing the Walkman, Sony realized that it was going to be initially purchased by young men fond of sports and outdoor living, and that the near-CD quality of sound reproduction associated with advanced portability of the device was key in affecting their post-purchase attitude. Similarly, RIM targeted its BlackBerry immediately after launch to top executives (e.g. Chief Information Officers, Chief Financial Officers) and sales agents who had a compelling reason to receive e-mail messages in real time while traveling for work, and ensured that this functionality was working perfectly from a technical point of view.

3.4.2.3 Product

The aforementioned lack of targeting of the innovation's early adopters is also detrimental because it often prevents firms from devising a configuration of the whole product at launch that meets early adopters' expectations, which are usually very different from the intended average target customer's. For instance, the IBM PC Junior was not compatible with many of the applications available for the traditional PC, whereas the Apple Newton lacked connectivity with PC and Macintosh at launch. It is noteworthy and seemingly nonsensical that both IBM and Apple had sponsored these capabilities of the new products during the pre-announcement campaign, which exacerbates the negative effect of an inappropriate product configuration at launch on early adopters' satisfaction. This might be the result of an attempt to anticipate the launch of the innovation without a clear targeting of the early customers.

On the other hand, the successful innovations in the sample do not seem to have missed any critical functionalities to satisfy early adopters' expectations. How could this be achieved? The analysis suggests that an effective commercialization strategy should include a limited number of simple functionalities in the configuration of the new product at launch, designed to satisfy the compelling reason to purchase for early adopters. The product configuration is enriched with additional functionalities as long as the innovation diffuses in the less innovative segments of the target market. An essential prerequisite for successfully adopting this approach, which increases the likelihood that the new product will be complete at launch despite a firm's attempt to rush it to market, is a careful targeting of the innovation's early customers. This approach was, for instance, adopted by RIM in the commercialization of the BlackBerry. In order to improve the chances of satisfying the new product's early customers, RIM decided to design and launch a simplified version of the BlackBerry, called Desktop Redirector, that could work using as a mail server any PC or laptop and only featured the revolutionary "push" approach to e-mail delivery. Agenda, address book and synchronization with PC were added as long as the BlackBerry diffused in the market. On the contrary, Apple tried to include as many complex functionalities as possible in the first version of the Newton (e.g. infrared communication, advanced handwriting recognition, contact manager, organizer, synchronization with both PC and Macintosh, traditional and wireless phone connectivity), some of which were absent or did not function perfectly at launch, resulting in a very negative attitude among early adopters.

3.4.2.4 *Advertising and promotion*

The role of the pre-announcement campaign in influencing the post-purchase attitude of early adopters has already been discussed in this section of the chapter. In particular, it has emerged that an early pre-announcement of the new product generates great expectations in the innovation's early adopters. If the new product at launch fails to fulfill these expectations, because it is incomplete as a result of a rush to market or because it lacks some functionalities that are critical for early adopters, the latter turn out to be highly dissatisfied with the innovation, and their opinion about it freezes any further diffusion of the new product. Therefore, if a firm chooses to pre-announce a high-tech innovation, it must be sure to arrive on the market with a complete product having the few, critical functionalities necessary to satisfy the compelling reason to buy among early adopters. This is consistent with literature on new product pre-announcements (NPPAs), which indicates that pre-announcing and then missing introduction dates for new products is not detrimental *per se* in terms of customer acceptance. It becomes problematic only when the new product, once it reaches the market, fails to fulfill the expectations of early adopters nurtured by the pre-announcement campaign (Lilly and Walters, 1997). This is exactly what happened with the commercialization of the Apple Newton and the IBM PC Junior.

3.5 Conclusions

This chapter represents a first attempt to investigate the reasons why a large share of the innovations that ultimately reach the market do not experience a satisfactory diffusion and their sales are promptly discontinued. Starting from the premise that the diffusion of a new product needs to be appropriately managed (at least as properly as its development process), the chapter discusses on which levers and how managers should intervene with the aim to successfully administer the market acceptance of an innovation that has a given set of technical and functional characteristics, and that is launched within the framework of a given competitive and product strategy.

Focusing on consumer high-tech innovations, the chapter shows that the approaches used to bring a new product to market can influence the customer acceptance it experiences in two major ways: (1) by affecting the extent to which the critical players of the innovation's adoption network support the diffusion process of the new product; and (2) by influencing the attitude that the innovation's early adopters develop toward the new product after having purchased and used it. Acknowledging the heterogeneous nature of high-technology innovations, the chapter also explains that securing the support of the adoption network during the commercialization of the new product is particularly critical to ensure large-scale acceptance of systemic innovations, i.e. new products that necessitate significant readjustments of the other components of the system they are part of to be productively used. On the other hand, stimulating a positive post-purchase attitude from early adopters appears to be essential to ensure significant levels of diffusion of radical innovations, i.e. new products that considerably change behavior and consumption patterns in their target market. By an inductive, empirically based analysis of 11 high-tech consumer innovations, the chapter goes on to investigate which approaches can be employed during the commercialization and market launch of a new product in order to increase the chances of stimulating a positive post-purchase attitude from its early adopters and securing the support from the critical members of its adoption network. The main results of this analysis are synthesized in Tables 3.5 and 3.6.

The results of this chapter are believed to hold some relevant managerial implications. Firstly, they emphasize the importance of appropriately managing the market introduction and diffusion processes for high-technology innovations. The arguments developed in the chapter explain that the approaches used to bring a new product to market might be as important as its technical and functional content in determining the degree of customer acceptance that it experiences and, ultimately, its commercial performance. Furthermore, the chapter provides product and marketing managers working in high-technology markets with a framework to identify, on the basis of the characteristics of the innovation they are responsible for, which aspects of the commercialization strategy (those required to secure the support of the adoption network or those necessary to stimulate a positive attitude from early adopters) should be given higher priority to increase the chances of achieving large-scale diffusion. Considering that the commercialization and market launch of a new product is often the single costliest stage of the whole innovation process (Cooper and Kleinschmidt, 1988), this framework is likely to improve new product performance not only in terms of market acceptance (i.e. volumes, sales and market share), but also as far as profitability is concerned. Finally, product and marketing managers are given a set of recommendations (synthesized in Tables 3.5 and 3.6) about how some critical commercialization decisions should be taken so as to avoid mistakes that are precursors of unsatisfactory levels of diffusion. Interestingly, it appears that decisions concerning pricing and distribution strategy are not critical in affecting adoption network and early adopters acceptance of high-technology innovations.

By studying how the approaches used to introduce an innovation into the market might affect its diffusion and market acceptance, this chapter represents a first attempt to bridge the gap between innovation management and diffusion of innovation research. In particular, it broadens the scope of innovation management research to include, among the factors that might affect new product success, some variables related to the last stages (i.e. market introduction) of the innovation process — variables which have been relatively neglected by extant research so far. At the same time, it suggests how the scope of diffusion of innovation research could be widened to consider the role played by supply-side variables (i.e. endogenous factors controlled by the firm commercializing the innovation) in explaining new products' market acceptance. It is also hoped that the analysis presented in this chapter will stimulate future research able to overcome some of its limitations. Firstly, this chapter focuses on only two key factors that have the potential to affect customer acceptance of high-technology innovations and that can be controlled by the firm commercializing the new product. Further theoretical and empirical work will be needed to disclose other endogenous reasons underlying heterogeneous levels of diffusion for high-tech new products. Secondly, the chapter focuses on consumer product innovations. It would be interesting to investigate whether and to what extent the dynamics discussed above are able to explain different levels of customer acceptance in industrial markets and for service innovations. Finally, it would be worth studying how commercialization decisions influence the speed at which high-tech innovations diffuse into the market. This chapter focuses on the overall level of diffusion experienced by the new product, but looking at the pace with which it is adopted could be useful as well to explain success and failure, especially in winner-takes-all markets.

References

Alexander, D.L., Lynch, J.G. and Wang, Q. (2008). As times go by: do cold feet follow warm intention for really-new vs. incrementally-new products? *Journal of Marketing Research*, 45, 307–319.

Bayus, B.L. (1994). Are product life cycles really getting shorter? *Journal of Product Innovation Management*, 11(4), 300–308.

Beard, C. and Easingwood, C. (1996). New product launch — marketing actions and tactics for high-technology products. *Industrial Marketing Management*, 25, 87–103.

Bianchi, O. (2004). Why do some new services or products fail? *Journal of the Canadian Institute of Marketing*, 7(3), 2–4.

Borrus, M. and Zysman, J. (1997). Globalization with borders: the rise of Wintelism as the future of industrial competition. *Industry and Innovation*, 4(2), 141–166.

Burt, R.S. (1987). Social contagion and innovation: cohesion versus structural equivalence. *American Journal of Sociology*, 92(6), 1287–1335.

Calantone, R.G. and Montoya-Weiss, M.M. (1993). Product launch and follow-on. In: W. Souder and J.D. Sherman (eds.), *Managing New Technology Development*, New York: McGraw-Hill, pp. 217–248.

Chakravorti, B. (2003). *The Slow Pace of Fast Change: Bringing Innovation to Market in a Connected World*. Boston: Harvard Business School Press.

Chakravorti, B. (2004). The role of adoption networks in the success of innovation. *Technology in Society*, 26, 469–482.

Cierpicki, S., Wright, M. and Sharp, B. (2000). Managers' knowledge of marketing principles: the case of new product development. *Journal of Empirical Generalisations in Marketing Science*, 5, 771–790.

Cooper, R.G. and Kleinschmidt, E.J. (1987). New products: what separates winners from losers? *Journal of Product Innovation Management*, 4, 169–184.

Cooper, R.G. and Kleinschmidt, E.J. (1988). Resource allocation in the new product process. *Industrial Marketing Management*, 17(3), 249–262.

Czepiel, J.A. (1975). Patterns of interorganizational communications and the diffusion of a major technological innovation in a competitive industrial community. *Academy of Management Journal*, 18(1), 6–24.

Davies, A. (2004). Moving base into high-value integrated solutions: a value stream approach. *Industrial and Corporate Change*, 13(5), 727–756.

Davies, W. and Brush, K.E. (1997). High-tech industry marketing: the elements of a sophisticated global strategy. *Industrial Marketing Management*, 26, 1–13.

Deroïan, F. (2002). Formation of social networks and diffusion of innovations. *Research Policy*, 31, 835–846.

Easingwood, C. and Harrington, S. (2002). Launching and re-launching high technology products. *Technovation*, 22, 657–666.

Eisenhardt, K.M. and Graebner, M.E. (2007). Theory building from cases: opportunities and challenges. *Academy of Management Journal*, 50(1), 25–32.

Elton, J., Shah, B. and Voyzey, J. (2002). Intellectual property: partnering for profit. *McKinsey Quarterly*, 4, 58–67.

Frambach, R.T., Barkema, H.G., Noteboom, B. and Wedel, M. (1998). Adoption of a service innovation in a business market: an empirical test of supply-side variables. *Journal of Business Research*, 41, 161–174.

Geroski, P.A. (2000). Model of technology diffusion. *Research Policy*, 29, 603–625.

Golder, P.N. and Tellis, G.J. (1993). Pioneer advantage: marketing logic or marketing legend? *Journal of Marketing Research*, 30, 158–170.

Gottschalk, L.R. (1969). *Understanding History: A Primer of Historical Method.* New York: Knopf.

Gourville, J. (2006). Eager seller and stony buyers: understanding the psychology of new-product adoption. *Harvard Business Review*, 84(6), 98–106.

Hoeffler, S. (2003). Measuring preferences for really-new products. *Journal of Marketing Research*, 40, 406–420.

Hultink, E.J., Griffin, A., Hart, S. and Robben, H.S.J. (1997). Industrial new product launch strategies and product development performance. *Journal of Product Innovation Management*, 14, 243–257.

Hultink, E.J., Griffin, A., Robben, H.S.J. and Hart, S. (1998). In search of generic launch strategies for new products. *International Journal of Research in Marketing*, 15, 269–285.

Hultink, E.J., Hart, S., Robben, H.S.J. and Griffin, A. (2000). Launch decisions and new product success: an empirical comparison of consumer and industrial products. *Journal of Product Innovation Management*, 17(1), 5–23.

Hultink, E.J. and Robben, H.S.J. (1999). Launch strategy and new product performance: an empirical examination in the Netherlands. *Journal of Product Innovation Management*, 16(6), 545–556.

Kahneman, D., Knetsch, J.L. and Thaler, R.H. (1990). Experimental tests of the endowment effect and the Coase theorem. *Journal of Political Economy*, 98(6), 1324–1348.

Kahneman, D. and Tversky, A. (1979). Prospect theory: an analysis of decisions under risk. *Econometrica*, 47, 313–327.

Kleinschmidt, E.J. and Cooper, R.G. (1991). The impact of product innovativeness on performance. *Journal of Product Innovation Management*, 8, 240–251.

Leonard-Barton, D. (1985). Experts as negative opinion leaders in the diffusion of a technological innovation. *Journal of Consumer Research*, 11, 914–926.

Lichtenthaler, U. (2005). External commercialization of knowledge: review and research agenda. *International Journal of Management Reviews*, 7(4), 231–255.

Lichtenthaler, U. (2008). Open innovation in practice: an analysis of strategic approaches to technology transactions. *IEEE Transactions on Engineering Management*, 55(1), 148–157.

Lilly, B. and Walters, R. (1997). Toward a model of new product preannouncement timing. *Journal of Product Innovation Management*, 14(4), 4–20.

McDade, S.R., Olivia, T.A. and Pirsch, J.A. (2002). The organizational adoption of high-technology products "for use": effects of size, preferences, and radicalness of impact. *Industrial Marketing Management*, 31(5), 441–456.

Meldrum, M.J. (1995). Marketing high-tech products: the emerging themes. *European Journal of Marketing*, 29(10), 45–58.

Nevens, T.M., Summe, G.L. and Uttal, B. (1990). Commercializing technology: what the best companies do. *Harvard Business Review*, 68(4), 154–163.

Nevett, T. (1991). Historical investigation and the practice of marketing. *Journal of Marketing*, 55, 13–23.

Richins, M.L. (1984). Word of mouth communication as negative information. In: A.T.C. Kinnear (ed.), *Advances in Consumer Research*, Ann Arbor: Association for Consumer Research, pp. 697–702.

Rivette, D. and Kline, K.G. (2000). *Rembrandts in the Attic: Unlocking the Hidden Value of Patents*. Boston: Harvard Business School Press.

Rogers, E.M. (2003). *Diffusion of Innovations*. New York: Free Press.

Rohlfs, J.H. (2001). *Bandwagon Effects in High-Technology Industries*. Boston: The MIT Press.

Schilling, M.A. (2003). Technological leapfrogging: lessons from the U.S. video game console industry. *California Management Review*, 45(3), 6–32.

Schilling, M.A. (2005). *Strategic Management of Technological Innovation*. New York: McGraw-Hill.

Siggelkow, N. (2007). Persuasion with case studies. *Academy of Management Journal*, 50(1), 20–24.

Teece, D. (1984). Economic analysis and strategic management. *California Management Review*, 26(3), 87–110.

Turnbull, P.W. and Meenaghan, A. (1980). Diffusion of innovation and opinion leadership. *European Journal of Marketing*, 14(1), 3–32.

Van den Bulte, C. and Stremersch, S. (2004). Social contagion and income heterogeneity in new product diffusion: a meta-analytic test. *Marketing Science*, 23(4), 530–544.

Van der Panne, G., Van Beers, C. and Kleinknecht, A. (2003). Success and failure of innovation: a literature review. *International Journal of Innovation Management*, 7(3), 1–30.

Weber, R.P. (1990). *Basic Content Analysis*. Newbury Park: Sage.

Wind, J. and Mahajan, V. (1987). Marketing hype: a new perspective for new product research and introduction. *Journal of Product Innovation Management*, 4, 43–49.

Wolf, M. (2006). The world must get to grips with seismic economic shifts. *Financial Express*, February 7. Available at http://www.financialexpress-bd.com/.

Yin, R.K. (2004). *Case Study Research: Design and Methods*. Thousand Oaks, CA: Sage Publications.

Yoffie, D. (1997). *Competing in the Age of Digital Convergence*. Boston: Harvard Business School Press.

Chapter 4

Launch Strategies and New Product Success

Susan Hart and Nikolaos Tzokas

4.1 Introduction

Over more than 40 years of research on the factors influencing success and failure rates for new products have established that product advantage (uniqueness and competitive superiority) is probably the single most important consideration for new products. Uniqueness and competitive superiority, however, are defined in the eyes of the customer. Much too often firms forget that it is not enough to develop products and services which, on paper or in the technical jargon of designers, engineers, operations managers, accountants and even sales people and marketers, seem unique or superior to competitive ones. All of these views are important, but it is the perceptions of the customers that ultimately count for the innovation to be a success. In the words of Adam Smith — the point of production is consumption.

4.1.1 *Easy to say, hard to put into practice!*

How, then, can companies make sure that, when they introduce a new product or service, the targeted customers perceive it as unique and superior to competitive ones? The answer to this question directs attention to the whole of the new product/service development

(NPSD) process. Here, research has established the role that *profi-ciency* in the NPSD process plays. Such proficiency entails, among other things, customer involvement in the process and a well-planned and well-executed launch of the product in the marketplace.

In this chapter, we examine the factors a company should master in order to become proficient in the planning, development and execution of a successful launch for a new product or service. The significance of the launch is emphasized by the fact that, of all the stages in the NPSD process, the launch often absorbs the largest amount of managerial and financial resources. We will review the evidence accumulated through research, with an overall aim to provide an integrated perspective of the theoretical advances made in this field, acknowledge normative conclusions and highlight direc-tions for further research.

The chapter consists of three sections. The first section takes the view that, to better understand the new product launch, one needs to approach it as an integral part of the NPSD process as well as a collection of activities with significant links to the overall strategic posture of the firm. The thesis here is that, unless launch-related imperatives have permeated the whole NPSD process, there is the risk of significant ramifications not only for the product/service in ques-tion but for the firm as a whole. The second section looks in more detail on the activities that constitute the launch process and reports their interrelationships. Here, we deconstruct the launch decision-making process and identify the managerial and organizational factors that are necessary to realize an integrated process, the natural outcome of which is an effective and efficient launch of the product or service. The final section highlights some further areas where more research is needed, and directs attention to changes in the environ-ment that may require us to reconsider the ways we approach the launch stage of an NPSD process and the mechanisms we put in place to warrant sustainable performance. Overall, these three sections take us through a brief history of the field's development — from the pioneering works of Cooper (1979) and Crawford (1980), where launch was first clearly highlighted as a critical success factor; to the work of Hultink *et al.* (1998) and the works by Di Benedetto (1999),

Guiltinan (1999) and Hultink and Robben (1999) in the first special issue on the topic by the *Journal of Product Innovation Management* (*JPIM*); to later contributions which take a much more eclectic approach to the subject (e.g. Kleinschmidt *et al.* (2007) in the *JPIM* special issue on "global product innovation and launch").

4.2 Understanding and Positioning the Launch of New Products and Services

There is no doubt that launch is the "moment of truth" for any new product or service. It is the point where the product or service is made available to the market, and its value proposition communicated to the customers of the firm and the users of the product. In the NPSD literature, launch is presented as the penultimate stage in the NPSD process, followed only by the post-launch evaluation. It is widely acknowledged, however, that, despite its formal "position" in a multi-staged process, the fact of its success delineates and reflects the success or failure of the whole endeavor, thus making the launch stage an integral and uniquely important part of the NPSD process. According to Cooper (1994), a key requirement for success in NPSD is for the market launch plan to begin early in the new product development process. To appreciate this, one needs to remember that the stage-gate™ NPSD process put forward by Cooper, despite considerable criticism of its linear visual character, does incorporate the notion of continuous feedback loops and risk/uncertainty reduction based on the collection, dissemination and use of information as required by the tasks inherent in each stage and each gate.

For the launch plan to be put in place, one needs to collect significant market, competitive and general environment intelligence. Obviously, some of this information is collected continuously as part of the firm's management information systems, but it is the actuality of introducing the product or service to customers that drives the firm towards the collection of information which spans a wide spectrum of areas critical for the final success of the new product — information that needs to be collected throughout the process of developing the new product or service, and not just at the end. This requires an understanding of the position of the new product/service launch stage within the entire process, which is examined below.

4.2.1 New product/service launch context

Throughout the new product/service development process, the costs tend to increase, often exponentially, with each successive step in the process. While the earlier phases (idea generation, screening, concept testing) absorb considerable management time, they rarely call for any significant capital investment of the kind which will become necessary as the process moves into prototype development, physical testing and test marketing. Launch is another matter altogether. The level of investment is dramatically increased as purchases of the necessary plant and equipment to produce the product are made, sufficient inventories for responding to the initial demand are held, and advertising, promotional and sales efforts are implemented. The amount required will vary both absolutely and proportionately, depending on whether it is a product or service and on the nature of the market to be served (business-to-business or ultimate consumer). The commitment to launch a new product calls for significant financial investment on top of that which has already been made, known as the "sunk costs". The launch decision, i.e. the final "go/no-go" decision, needs to be made on the basis of the anticipated revenues to be earned relative to the total investment (comprising both the sunk costs and the projected launch costs). To argue that substantial sums have been invested to develop an idea to the point where launch must be considered and that these sums should not be thrown away is irrelevant. The guiding principle must always be not to throw good money after bad. In other words, if the past and necessary future investment cannot be recouped, any further investment should be stopped before the launch takes place. If, on the other hand, the considerations indicate a "go" decision, then a marketing plan must be devised to launch the product. Given this broader context, we will now review the various terms used by studies in order to select a particular definition for use throughout the rest of the chapter.

4.2.2 What is a product launch: defining terms

The "launch cycle" or "launch stage" describes those activities which take place after the conceptual and physical development of a new product is complete that are necessary to present the product to its target market and to begin to generate income from sales of the new product. These activities, which take place towards the "end" of the NPSD process, are referred to using a variety of terms in the NPSD literature: market entry, launch strategy, product launch, commercialization and introduction. Since this stage of the NPSD process is one of the most neglected, there are relatively few pertinent research studies that operationalize the precise activities and decisions. This means, therefore, that there are few empirically derived definitions of what a product launch encompasses.

A number of classic studies have defined and operationalized "entry strategy", a term generally used to cover the situation in which a strategic business unit begins to compete in a product market where it did not previously operate (Biggadike, 1979; Lambkin, 1988; Ryans, 1988). These studies focused on "market entry" in a number of contexts. Lilien and Yoon (1989), Urban *et al.* (1986) and Green and Ryans (1990) considered market entry within the context of new product development, whilst other studies focused on strategic entry into a new market (Biggadike, 1979; Lambkin, 1988; Lieberman and Montgomery, 1988) or market entry into international (export) markets (Anderson and Coughlan, 1987; Ryans, 1988). Although these definitions relate to situations other than the launch of a new product, the operationalizations used have been transferred to the situation faced by those executing a new product launch, for example, by Hultink *et al.* (2000).

4.3 The Ingredients of a Launch Strategy

A quick scan of the relevant literature shows that NPSD researchers have devoted considerable attention to the notion of NPSD strategy and the strategic management of the NPSD process. The pioneering works of Crawford (1980) and Booz, Allen & Hamilton (1982) outlined the need for a product innovation charter (PIC) and a strategic planning step in the NPSD process, respectively. Crawford (1980) introduced the PIC as a spin-off of the strategic planning process of firms. Its focus is the NPSD process, and it carries a "directional and activity mandate" (p. 4). The key parts of a typical PIC are outlined in Table 4.1.

The PIC was an important step in the development of a strategic approach to NPSD, as it outlined a number of important considerations that need to be taken into account by firms. Strategies here are defined as combinations of means (tactics, policies) and ends (goals, objectives, mission), and are reflected at three levels — corporate, competitive and functional — which inform each other (Porter, 1985; Mintzberg, 1978). In referring to the launch strategy, several authors have followed Biggadike's (1979) approach and distinguished between posture and marketing mix decisions, with posture reflecting strategic upfront decisions that are taken early in the NPSD process and are difficult to change, and marketing mix decisions reflecting the tactics used to accomplish the desired performance outcome of the

Table 4.1.   Outline of a PIC.

A. The target business arenas, defined:
   (1) by product type;
   (2) by end-user activity;
   (3) by technology; and
   (4) by intermediate or end-customer group.

B. The goals or objectives of product innovation activities, expressed in terms of:
   (1) the quantitative result to be achieved; and
   (2) special qualitative goals.

C. The program of activities to achieve the goals or objectives. It includes:
   (1) strengths to be exploited by the program;
   (2) weaknesses to avoid;
   (3) the source of innovation;
   (4) the degree of innovativeness sought; and
   (5) special conditions, restrictions or mandates.

Source: Based on Crawford (1980).

launch and which are easy to change if required. For the purposes of this chapter, we refer to launch strategy as the combination of strategic and tactical decisions and actions that delineate the context in which the new product and its business model will be developed and launched (i.e. what, why, where and when to launch), and the operational approach to be followed (i.e. how to launch).

Table 4.2 has been adapted from the work of Calantone and Di Benedetto (2007), and reports a large number of empirical, conceptual and review articles on the topic. Despite the importance of NPSD launch and the development of the market for new products, what is striking from this table is how few research teams have focused on this crucial — not to mention expensive — phase of the NPSD cycle.

4.3.1 Strategic launch decisions

Strategic launch decisions take place much earlier than the actual launch of the final product in the marketplace. Hultink *et al.* (1997) forwarded four categories of strategic decisions for launch, and assembled specific variables pertinent to each of the categories. These are shown in Table 4.3.

These variables provide a rich perspective of the strategic decisions that are directly related to the launch of a new product or service. Furthermore, as is the case with the different levels of a firm's strategy (i.e. corporate, competitive and functional), the innovation strategy of the firm should, in theory, drive the competitive, market and product launch strategies. However, it is interesting to note here that, whereas different combinations of strategic postures have been examined and will be reviewed later in this chapter, the interrelationships among these variables have yet to be examined in an NPSD environment.

4.3.1.1 Firm strategy

The way in which a firm chooses to operate in its markets has a profound effect on the choices that can be made during the launch phase of NPSD. For example, the company's image and reputation in the market (Hultink and Schoormans, 1995), along with its reputation

Table 4.2.   Launch strategy studies.

Author	Study type	Contents
Calantone and Montoya-Weiss (1994)	Review article	The launch plan, launch timing, launch strategies and control of the launch process
Saunders and Jobber (1994)	Empirical study (USA and UK)	Launch of replacement products and comparison of successful to unsuccessful launches
Hultink and Schoormans (1995)	Empirical study (the Netherlands)	Analysis of high-tech product launch decisions
Ottum (1996)	Review article	Issues and procedures for launching a consumer product
Stryker (1996)	Review article	Issues and procedures for launching a business product
Hultink et al. (1997)	Empirical study (UK)	Interactions between product lanuch decisions and performance outcomes; differentiation between strategic and tactical launch decisions
Hultink et al. (1997)	Empirical study (the Netherlands)	Relationship between launch strategies and performance outcomes; differentiation between strategic and tactical launch decisions
Hultink et al. (1998)	Empirical study (UK)	Categorization of generic new product launch strategies
Hultink and Hart (1998)	Empirical study (UK)	Comparison of launch strategies for high- and low-advantage new products
Robben (1998)	Empirical study (UK)	Categorization of generic new product launch strategies
Guiltinan (1999)	Conceptual paper	Launch tactics need to be aligned with perceptions of the new product's relative advantage and compatibility; relationship between strategy and tactics
Di Benedetto (1999)	Empirical study (North America)	Successful launches related to good execution of strategic, tactical and information-gathering activities

(*Continued*)

Table 4.2. (*Continued*)

Author	Study type	Contents
Hultink and Robben (1999)	Empirical study (the Netherlands)	Relationship between launch strategy and market acceptance as well as product performance for both consumer and industrial products
Bowersox *et al.* (1999)	Conceptual paper	Importance of logistics and supply chain relationships to successful launch; lean launch strategies based on response-based logistics
Hultink *et al.* (1999)	Empirical study (UK)	Consumer product launch decisions; relationship between launch decisions and performance outcomes
Hultink *et al.* (2000)	Empirical study (UK)	Comparison of consumer and industrial new product launch decisions; examination of launch support programs (e.g. advertising media)
Thoelke *et al.* (2001)	Case study (8 Dutch companies)	Strengths and weaknesses of launch strategies (differentiation, make-or-buy decision, launch of new feature, etc.)
Debruyne *et al.* (2002)	Empirical study (UK, USA, the Netherlands)	Competitive reactions to radical versus incremental new products are different; discussion of in which situations competitors are likely to react or not
Hultink and Langerak (2002)	Empirical study (the Netherlands)	Investigation of launch signals such as hostility, commitment and consequences, and the impact of these on the strength and speed of competitive reaction
Lee and O'Connor (2003)	Empirical study (USA)	Relationship between communication strategy and new product performance is moderated by the product's innovativeness

(*Continued*)

Table 4.2. (*Continued*)

Author	Study type	Contents
Langerak *et al.* (2004)	Empirical study (the Netherlands)	Relationship of market orientation to product advantage and to launch strategies and tactics
Nagle (2005)	Review article	The launch plan, launch phases, launch team and manager selection, launch and continuous improvement
Calantone *et al.* (2005)	Review article	Launch strategy, flexible supply chain, benefits of a lean launch, illustrations in two industries
Hsieh and Tsai (2007)	Empirical study (Taiwan)	Launch strategy, technological capability and social capital
Hsieh *et al.* (2008)	Empirical study (Taiwan)	Launch proficiency and market orientation as moderators of the product advantage–performance relationship

Source: Adapted from Calantone and Di Benedetto (2007).

Table 4.3. Strategic launch variables.

Product Strategy
Product innovativeness
Relative product newness
NPSD cycle time

Market Strategy
Breadth of segments served
Stage of product life cycle
Target market growth rate

Competitive Stance
Number of competitors
Product advantage

Firm Strategy
Innovation strategy and objectives
Driver
Timing strategy

Source: Hultink *et al.* (1997).

and experience in developing and launching new products, have been found to affect product launch (Johne and Snelson, 1988). These points are readily understood when considering the launch in the UK of Tia Lusso, a coffee and cream liqueur. The new product, developed to appeal to a younger audience than did traditional liqueurs, needed to reflect its developer, Allied Domecq, whose product range is known for stable, reputable brands. The new product, therefore, resonated similar brand values as its older sister, Tia Maria, in keeping with Allied Domecq's reputation, but it was updated to appeal to the younger segment.

Another firm factor that has an impact on product launch includes the extent to which an organization pursues technological leadership, technological imitation or cost reduction. Closely related to the extent of technological innovation pursued by the firm is the extent to which the firm is driven in its new product development by market or technological factors. These technology and market drivers of the new product program will also affect the rest of the launch mechanics, including the breadth of distribution, the media selected for marketing communications and the pricing level for introduction. The important element to retain from this discussion is to understand that the strategic position taken by the firm has a determining influence on much of the action details of a new product launch. For example, Nike is unlikely to develop a "me-too", cheap running shoe now that it has invested so much in sport shoe technology and in leading the field. Research by Hultink *et al.* (2000) showed that consumer firms often launch market-driven, incremental improvements, whilst industrial firms' new products are more often innovative and designed with performance-improvement or cost-reduction intentions. That being said, the nature of the markets into which the new products will eventually be launched also has a profound influence on the specifics of the launch. These are examined below.

4.3.1.2 *Market strategy*

Market strategy describes several issues: market maturity, segmentation and timing.

Market maturity

There is a greater likelihood of sales growth where a market is growing than where demand is static (Kohli and Jaworski, 1990; Narver and Slater, 1990). The association between high growth and success is not always clear-cut, however. In new markets, where growth might be expected to be high, innovators face a great deal of uncertainty (Moriarty and Kosnik, 1989). If uptake of the new product accelerates more quickly than expected, then product shortages may be encountered. If demand grows rapidly, the level of competitive entry might be higher than predicted, causing upheaval in the launch strategy. Empirical results paint an inconsistent picture, partly because of the way market growth is measured. One measure is the stage of the product market life cycle. In the chemical industry, for example, Cooper and Kleinschmidt (1993) found that products introduced in the introductory stage of the life cycle of a product market suffered a disproportionately high failure rate, whereas products entering markets in the early growth phase had a higher-than-average success rate; but for products launched in the growth, early maturity, maturity and decline stages, no difference in success and failure rates was found.

Segmentation

The market decisions that are pertinent to the launch strategy relate to the need to define the target market via segmentation. Once again, this decision should ideally have its roots early in the product development process, at the time of the initial definition of the strategy guiding the NPSD. Cooper (1984) highlighted different combinations, concluding that strategies which targeted high-potential-growth markets, together with those avoiding markets where competitors are dominant, were more successful. Underlying these strategies is the fundamental choice between attempting to sell the new product to everyone — undifferentiated marketing — and targeting the product to a specific group of customers who, it is felt, have a predisposition to the product's attributes. The specific launch decision relates to those market segments which will be the targets for new product sales. In other words, people (or organizations) have similar buying characteristics within segments, but are differentiated in these with respect to other segments. This classification of the total market allows companies to position and promote a new product to its optimum advantage. The task for those involved in launching new products is to find descriptors of the markets that are meaningful in that they classify potential buyers into groups which will respond differently to the launch strategy for the new products.

There is very little empirical evidence to suggest what might be an optimal way of segmenting the market for a new product, with attention turning from traditional market descriptors of a socio-demographic nature to the identification of "innovators" and concepts of "crossing the chasm" between the innovators and the early majority, or identifying those customers who make up "the tipping point".

Timing

Since the mid-1980s, growing attention has been given to the means of accelerating the development and launch of new products and reducing "time to market", thereby securing a competitive advantage.

While it is widely held that first-to-market products enjoy competitive advantages over later arrivals, several commentators have pursued contrary arguments. The advantages thought to accrue to early entrants include the acquisition of market knowledge, which allows fine-tuning and second-generation products to be introduced before competitors (Stigler, 1981), the freedom to charge a premium until competitive products are launched (Dumaine, 1989; Rosenau, 1990; Smith and Reinertsen, 1991), greater levels of profitability (Dumaine, 1989), the ability to create greater barriers to entry for potential competitive offerings (Bain, 1956; Biggadike, 1979) and enhanced market image due to being the technological leader. Even where advantages are not forwarded, the evidence of shortening product life cycles (Guveritz, 1983), increasing numbers of product introductions (Cordero, 1991) and intensifying levels of competition (Womack *et al.*, 1990) means that, in order to stay viable, companies may have to turn their attention toward moving more products to market faster. There are counterarguments, however; it is not clear, for example, that advantages of early entry are automatic due to the technological and market uncertainties inherent in the development of new products. These may allow later entrants to develop superior skills for the market being developed, at considerable expense, by the first movers, thereby allowing them to outplay the first movers with their own offering.

4.3.1.3 *Product strategy*

The key elements of product strategy that have been shown to affect new product performance include the level of newness (also called novelty or innovativeness) and product advantage.

Innovativeness/Newness/Novelty

Theoretically, the greater the degree of novelty, the lower the threat of early competitor response and the higher the need for precise targeting of potential early adopters. Conversely, the lower the degree of novelty, the more important the manipulation of the other variables in the marketing mix — price, distribution (place) and promotion.

Where a high degree of novelty is involved, higher levels of resistance to change can be anticipated and, usually, a slow build-up of demand over time as potential customers learn of the product's existence and switch to it from previously preferred products for which it is a substitute. In this case, a niche marketing strategy is likely to be most appropriate. Where a low degree of novelty is involved, the basic choice rests between a niche or a penetration strategy. Firms with limited resources will usually have no choice but to follow a niche strategy; whereas larger and better endowed/established firms may choose either a saturation approach (penetration strategy) by launching in all segments and regions simultaneously or a segment-by-segment, market-by-market controlled "roll-out" (a variant of the niche strategy).

Product advantage

Product advantage is defined as the outcome of the new product process, comprising the degree of unique benefits not previously available, the extent to which customer needs are better satisfied, the product's relative quality and innovativeness, and the extent to which the new product solves customer problems better (Cooper, 1979). Product advantage has consistently been shown to be a key differentiator between success and failure in the development of new products and services alike, although its relationship with other differentiators of success and failure in NPSD has not been the focus of investigation. The research study of Hultink and Hart (1998) found that the launch of products with a high level of advantage was different in numerous respects from the launch of products with a lower level of advantage. For example, high-advantage new products had more aggressive sales objectives, tended to be developed for early entry in high-growth markets and had a niche targeting strategy. Equally, products with high advantage were launched in a broader assortment, were supported by higher levels of promotion and distribution expenditures, used a broader mix of promotional types and adopted a skimming or "early return on investment (ROI)" pricing strategy. More products with high advantage used brand names and engaged promotional techniques associated with a "push" strategy, while products with low advantage tended to use customer promotion and new distributors more often.

4.3.1.4 *Competitive strategy*

Two issues relating to the competitive strategy of new product launch are particularly important: the competitive intensity of the market, and the reaction from competitors to the new product's launch.

Competitive intensity (number of competitors)

One aspect of the dynamics of market growth and the progress from introduction to decline is the level of competition experienced by companies. Lilien and Yoon (1989) studied the competitive structure of markets into which new products are launched, finding that ordinary new products fare better where the degree of competitiveness is low and where the number of competitors is small. Clearly, companies avoiding competitive markets have more space in which to develop their uniqueness.

Competitive reaction

Another element in the outcome of a product launch is the competitive reaction it provokes, since the latter can affect profitability, market share and market position. Heil and Walters (1993) investigated the factors that govern the strength of the competitive reaction to a new product, but few studies have specifically examined the impact of competitive reaction on new product success rates. A more recent study by Debruyne *et al.* (2002) showed that two thirds of new product launches meet competitive reaction, particularly where the new product is "really-new" and targeted at a specific niche. Moreover, they found that products launched into high-growth markets are not immune to competitive reaction. It is, therefore, vital to consider the competitive reaction and to recognize that this will have an influence on the extent of success for the new product and how quickly it arrives.

The key factor when taking these strategic launch issues into account is to recognize that, in most cases, they represent choices (either explicit or implicit) that will already have been made by the time it comes to making the actual decisions regarding how best to introduce the product into the market. Moreover, these choices are interrelated. The fact of a new product being highly innovative or "really-new" means that identifying the early adopters is crucial, considering the likely reaction of incumbent competitors is vital and, as we have seen above, there is likely to be resistance to change, so a niche segmentation strategy is indicated. More importantly, the combination of these strategic factors will also have an extremely strong influence on the tactics of the launch, and it is to these that the chapter now turns.

4.3.2 *Tactical launch decisions*

Tactical launch decisions reflect how the launch of a new product or service unfolds in the marketplace. They include the marketing actions or operations required to launch the product. One of the early attempts to map these decisions was made by Beard and Easingwood (1996). Table 4.4 illustrates their selection of launch tactics, which emerged from a study of 101 marketing actions that were used to launch new high-tech products. In addition, the sequence of activities in Table 4.4 reflects the authors' perspective that different tactics are taken at different points in time and, therefore, there may be a structural relationship amongst them.

Others have approached launch tactics as a simpler reflection of the marketing mix (e.g. Hultink *et al.*, 1997; Guiltinan, 1999).

4.3.2.1 *Product decisions*

Considerations regarding the new product itself include the positioning of the product, the choice of branding and the breadth of the product line (also called product assortment).

Table 4.4. Tactical launch decisions.

1. Market Preparation Tactics	2. Targeting Tactics
License the product technology	Target innovators
Supply to other equipment manufacturers	Target early adopters
Provide pre-launch information	Target late adopters
Create special distribution arrangements	Target existing customers
	Target competitors' customers
3. Positioning Tactics	**4. Market Attack Tactics**
Appeal to heavy users	Use opinion leaders
Emphasize exclusivity	Use reference sites
Emphasize a low price	Use educating methods
Emphasize technological superiority	Use a "winner" image
Emphasize a special application	Promote the product to dealers
Emphasize a safe bet (customer protection)	Lend or lease the product
	Promote to a special customer

Source: Beard and Easingwood (1996).

Positioning

Cooper (1993b) defines positioning as "how the product will be perceived by potential customers" (p. 240), and this perception is in relation to that of competitive product offerings. Crawford (1994) delineates two alternatives in positioning decisions. The first involves positioning the product in relation to its attributes (features, functions or benefits). The second involves using surrogate factors to position the product. Surrogate factors are those that imply the superiority of the new product over incumbent products, without specifying the reasons, using a number of devices such as endorsement, experience of the manufacturer and parentage.

Once again, there are few studies that have incorporated the positioning of products as a factor in the launch strategy, although this is logically linked to the notion of product uniqueness/advantage, which is such a powerful explanatory factor in new product success (Cooper, 1993b). It is generally agreed that, without a clear, concise statement of position, the chances of product success are reduced.

Branding

The second consideration regarding the product line launch relates to branding. Whilst branding may be thought of purely in terms of product identification, it is also a powerful positioning tool and is equally related to issues governing the choice of product assortment. Where identification is the only purpose, a combination of letters and models may well suffice. If the identification of the product is linked to the position of the product with respect to other products offered by the company, then the brand name may be used to communicate this relationship. In the case of a range of products, the brand name chosen will apply to the various models and versions of the product in the line. In the case of a strong company identity, the brand name chosen may echo its identity and image.

Breadth of the product line

The third consideration in product line decisions is the breadth of the line. The number of versions, models or variations of a product will depend on the strategic nature of the new development, i.e. whether the development is an addition to an existing line of products or a completely new line (or range) of products. In both cases, the question of cannibalization versus synergy must be addressed. There are synergistic effects to be gained from launching a wide range of products, particularly in terms of the advertising, promotion and distribution expenditures. On the other hand, the larger the range, the greater the potential for cannibalization, in which sales of the new product do not increase overall sales and profits of the product range, but rather replace existing sales and profits. The research of Hultink *et al.* (2000) showed that, for consumer and industrial goods alike, successful new products are introduced with a broader assortment.

4.3.2.2 *Pricing decisions*

The price of a new product at the time of launch is an integral element in its appeal (or lack of appeal). The price reflects its competitive positioning and may be a measure of the product's quality for consumers, and it is a key factor, along with sales volume, in the financial performance of the new product launch. The pricing decision for a new product not only involves the launch price, with its embedded discounts and promotional devices, but extends to the choice between skimming and penetrating, which is by nature a long-term choice. These strategies can be seen to relate to the demand curve. Where the demand curve is stable over time and where production costs decrease with increasing sales volume and experience effects, initial high prices may be followed by lower prices — price skimming — which in turn is followed by a penetration pricing strategy. Until recently, this strategy was advised as the most profitable route, especially for highly innovative products. Now, however, the tendency towards shorter life cycles and decreasing time lags between first movers and early "me-too" products has caused a re-think in pricing strategy for new products. Specifically, where a product's diffusion into the market is considered likely to follow the typical diffusion curve, there is an argument for employing penetration pricing to hinder competitive product launches and to benefit from increasing economies of scale as volume sales of the product increase along with diffusion. This view necessitates a longer-term perspective of the recovery of development costs.

In addition to the skim-or-penetrate choice, there are other questions about pricing: whether or not there are product range or line considerations, as with models of cars; and whether the pricing structure is to offer a single, comprehensive price, or whether this will be more diffuse to encourage rates of uptake. Introductory discounts are often necessary to motivate the sales force, distributors and end buyers of the new product. Again, these have an impact on reaching the break-even point, and the question of balance between market trial and acceptance and ROI must be maintained.

4.3.2.3 *Distribution decisions*

Distribution is crucial to the eventual acceptance and sales of a new product in the market, as it governs the availability of the new product to customers. It goes without saying that the distribution channels chosen must reflect the target market's buying behavior, and must allow for maximum availability to the target market. Not only does this imply achieving the desired level of stocking amongst the chosen distributors, but it also means meeting the stated objectives regarding the amount of shelf or store space given over to a new product. This clearly is a consideration impinging upon the advertising and promotional strategy, which is considered in the next section. Much trade promotion is aimed at convincing distributors to stock the product, and at gaining their support in terms of their own selling effort for the new product throughout and beyond the launch period. In addition, the distribution channels chosen may reinforce or dilute the intended message of the product's position in the marketplace. Thus, a product may benefit from extensive distribution if it is intended for mass markets, whereas selective or exclusive distribution will be more appropriate for products being aimed at differentiated or niche market segments. Besides the selectivity chosen for the distribution of the new product, the quality of the distribution will also help or hinder the intended positioning of the product. In particular, the role of distributors in providing customer services is a crucial aspect of positioning. It is generally recognized, however, that the task of promoting the product through the distribution channel is one which requires careful management; distributors must agree on their role. This will vary according to the power of the distributor in relation to the power of the manufacturer or seller of the new product. In fast moving consumer goods (FMCG) industries, for example, where the relative power of retailers is high, they will have their own rules and priorities for stocking and locating new products. Where the power of manufacturers is higher, as, for example, in office equipment, the manufacturer may have a larger role in negotiating the role of distributors. In either case, it is important that objectives are set for distribution (i.e. the task) so that this element of the marketing mix can be monitored effectively for the launch.

Finally, the move away from the supplier-dominant paradigm to the relationship paradigm in marketing means that it is crucial to establish mutually beneficial relationships with distributors, who provide the final link in the chain between the product and the market. If support from distributors is not adequate, it increases the likelihood that the product will not be available widely enough to optimize sales.

Very few studies have focused on the role of distribution choices in effective new product launches. The research by Hultink *et al.* (2000) showed that successful industrial and consumer new product launches invested heavily in distribution.

Sales force

For many launches, the extent to which distributors agree to support the new product is a function of effective personal selling. Cooper (1993a) contends that, for the majority of new products, decisions regarding the sales force will be straightforward. There is very little in the way of empirical research to confirm or infirm this view. Where the new product is aimed at a market already served by the company, the existing sales force will require training about the new product and sales management will be required to plan for the inclusion of the new product in call schedules and targets.

4.3.2.4 Promotion decisions

Promotion is taken to consist of all kinds of marketing communications, which include considering the extent to which communications are individualized or mass, sales promotion techniques and advertising. Each of these is dealt with below.

Personal and impersonal communications

As noted earlier, communication has a vital role to play throughout the buying process, from the initial creation of awareness of a new product's existence right through to the reduction of uncertainty concerning the rightness of the decision once a purchase has been made. Basically, communications fall into two categories, personal and impersonal, the use and importance of each of which vary according to the stage in the buying process which has been reached.

As the term implies, personal communications involve direct person-to-person contact and may be buyer- or seller-initiated, formal or informal in nature. Sending a salesman to call on a potential customer is an example of a formal, seller-initiated personal communication; asking a friend's opinion of Brand X is an informal, buyer-initiated communication. By contrast, impersonal communications involve the use of one of the media — print, broadcast, Internet and so on — and are the major province of advertising.

Non-personal media are usually most effective in establishing awareness and interest, while personal influence is necessary to move the members of an audience up the hierarchy of effects from desire to action. It has been found that personal influence is most effective in high-risk purchase situations, as, for example, in cases where the buyer is expending relatively large amounts of money, purchases infrequently and is unfamiliar with the product(s) under consideration; while mass or impersonal communication is most effective in the case of familiar, frequently purchased items of low unit value.

However, while the emphasis may be on one or the other form of communication, it is usual to find both forms employed together.

Even where this is not part of the seller's deliberate communication strategy, impersonal channels are almost invariably affected by the mediation of personal sources.

Furthermore, it is important to emphasize that the influence of word-of-mouth communication is equally as important in industrial markets as in consumer markets. Opinion leadership also operates in industrial markets and seems to be situation-specific.

Sales promotion

Although there is a comparative lack of attention given to promotion in the marketing literature, promotion is of great importance to marketing managers, particularly in new product launches. Promotional techniques include those aimed at intermediaries — retailers and wholesalers — and include discounts, training, point-of-sale material, direct mail, mail coupons, off-pack discounts and other incentive offerings. These are introduced to increase stocking by the chosen distributors and trial by end users. The proportion of the investment in promotion (and advertising, see below) that is given over to trade and consumers is linked to the extent to which the new product follows a "push" (intermediary-focused) or a "pull" (consumer-focused) strategy. Although there is not much empirical literature on which to draw when making normative statements regarding this division of resources, lower levels of awareness for the new product have been suggested as requiring a "pull", rather than a "push", strategy for advertising and promotion. The effect of promotion on the launch sales is often viewed as being short-term, with the result that promotion is considered to change the timing (but not the volume) of sales. In other words, promotional tools may shift the sales pattern from a steady, constant uptake to one where there is an immediate high volume followed by a period of low sales volume. Clearly, this means that the promotional activity must be planned within a longer, rather than a shorter, time horizon, and should ideally extend to the first few years of a new product's life.

Advertising

In contrast to sales promotion devices, advertising is a major subject of academic study in its own right. Summarizing the content and wisdom from research into advertising is a task well beyond the scope of the current chapter. However, in conjunction with sales promotion, advertising is a crucial element in the launch of a new product, and is also linked to the "push" versus "pull" dimension described above. Total advertising expenditures have been shown to impact on the performance of new product introductions (Lambkin, 1988; Biggadike, 1979), which is unsurprising given the role of advertising in positioning the product and creating awareness, interest and trial. The effect of the Internet, Web 2.0 and social networking is an observable phenomenon in terms of consumer products, although their effects have yet to be formally studied widely.

As was stated earlier, the launch strategy for a new product requires a mix of marketing ingredients whereby all elements work together to reinforce one another. Through the description of the launch decision considerations, we have pointed out the way in which decision variables interrelate. The next section discusses these relationships in greater detail.

4.4 The Interrelationships of the Launch Decisions

Already mentioned are the links between pricing and competitive positioning, and between market segmentation and product assortment; the interrelationships between promotion, advertising, sales force and distribution decisions; and the interdependence of product positioning, advertising, branding and distribution. Equally complex are the interconnections among segmentation, branding, product assortment and "push" versus "pull" strategies. Biggadike (1979) has considered the problems that arise from the attempt to take account of the interactions among these factors. One approach is to focus on each dimension individually, as done by Bain (1956); however, much of this contradicts marketing theory, which stresses the importance of the interactions amongst the marketing mix variables and high levels of integration.

Another approach is to recognize these interactions and attempt to identify internally consistent strategies. The observation that this approach was rare when Biggadike (1979) began his study holds true today, particularly in respect to new product launch strategies. Biggadike (1979) attempted to examine some of these interrelationships by performing a principal components analysis on 12 marketing mix variables in his study of market entry in corporate diversification. From this analysis, three types of entry strategy were posited. The first type of entry strategy is an aggressive entry strategy, which features high sales force, advertising and promotion expenditures, coupled with new channels of distribution, low prices and relative product quality. The second type of entry strategy combines a broad product line assortment with a wide focus in terms of customer types and numbers, and is labeled a breadth entry strategy. The third type of entry strategy features high price and quality and high levels of customer service, and is named a luxuriousness entry strategy. When related to performance, the breadth strategy performed better than the other two. Lambkin's (1988) study also found interrelationships among marketing mix variables (which she calls competitive strategy). Using analysis of variance t was found that pioneering businesses enter markets with broader product lines, more extensive distribution networks, higher levels of customer support, higher product quality and a larger production capacity than early followers or late entrants. The early followers spend less on marketing than the other two groups, and have inferior product quality and fewer customer services than pioneers; whist the late entrants do not portray any clear strategies. When related to the performance measure of market share, it was found that the pioneering strategy has the strongest impact on market share. These studies, which explored entry strategies in a wider context than product launch, go some way to confirming that elements of the marketing mix are interrelated. Common to both these studies are variables that are defined before the beginning of the launch cycle. Both, for example, include product quality as a variable; as noted above, product quality, advantage, positioning and target market selection are all present before the tactical launch decisions are taken.

The work of Hultink *et al.* (2000) specifically addresses the way in which these strategic and tactical decisions work together. In dealing with new consumer products, the work identified four types of launch: highly innovative new product launch; fast-to-market, innovative new product launch; "me-too" product launch; and incremental improvement launch. Each of these types combines strategic and tactical launch factors which are mutually reinforcing; and where the two levels do not serve each other, the launch strategy as a whole is less successful. The findings suggest that different patterns of combinations exist between strategic and tactical launch decisions, and that the success profiles of these different patterns vary. For example, the highly innovative new products and the fast-to-market new products both describe new products that are deemed to be high in advantage and innovativeness, but the market focus of the highly innovative ones was unclear in terms of the targeting strategy and the number of competitors faced. This backs up the notion that, for new consumer products, a company's drive for innovativeness and advantage must be accompanied by a concern for consumer and competitor perceptions. Without a clear idea of the targeting strategy for the new product, developers were not sure that any of its tactical decisions for getting the product to consumers was appropriate, thus explaining in part the mismatch between the strategic and tactical decisions taken for this group. Specifically, despite high advantage and innovativeness guiding the new products' strategy, the tactics of the launches included a promotional expenditure that was lower than competitors' and an unfocused pricing strategy, revealing a muddled presentation of the new products' potential benefits. On the other hand, the fast-to-market new products harmonized the innovation/advantage dimensions with a clear target market where there were no direct competitors, marrying these strategic factors with launch tactics which clearly positioned the new products in the consumers' mind and made the products widely available to them.

Conventional wisdom suggests that unique, innovative products should be launched using a price skimming strategy to recover costs, with an exclusive distribution strategy to encourage adoption by innovators. Once competitive offerings arrive on the market, the price can be lowered and distribution extended to capture more of the market. The fast-to-market new products departed from this norm with intensive (wide) distribution and higher promotional expenditures.

Put another way, the most successful type of new products, the fast-to-market innovations, demonstrates most (but not all) of the "classic" recommended actions for the launch of new innovative products. This means there is ample opportunity for future research in the field of new product and service launch. Moreover, there are issues regarding the anatomy of the launch of a new product that have been problematic in the past; one of these is marketing investment and is considered below.

Since strategic launch decisions are made early in the NPSD process, researchers recognized the fact that there may be a relationship between strategic and technical decisions in that strategic launch considerations drive the choice of launch tactics. This was confirmed by Hultink *et al.* (1997, 1998) in their studies of 1,022 new product launches by 622 firms from the Netherlands and the UK. These authors identified that the strategic decisions managers make about the product innovativeness and product newness (product strategy), the number of competitors and product life cycle (PLC) stage (market strategy), and the new product development (NPD) driver and five objectives (i.e. capitalizing on the existing market, expanding the product range, producing at a lower cost, erecting competitive barriers and increasing penetration) (firm strategy) are associated with later tactical decisions dictating the pricing strategy and relative price level (pricing tactics), branding and assortment breadth (product tactics), and the use of customer and sales force promotion (promotion tactics). This configuration reflected cases such as a small assortment of relatively less innovative, lower-priced new products, which were developed as a result of a market need and launched in a later stage of the PLC in a market with many competitors. The associated objectives for these products were expanding the product range, erecting barriers for competitors, and capitalizing on lower costs and on an existing market. In this case, a new brand name was developed for these products, alongside a penetration pricing approach and promotion aiming at both customers and the sales force.

However, the same authors found another combination of strategic and tactical launch decisions, showing that the launch of less innovative products (product strategy) in a market with few competitors (market strategy) with the objective to erect barriers to entry without establishing a foothold (firm strategy) was accompanied by increased customer promotion and TV advertising as well as high distribution expenditures aimed at current distribution channels.

Encouraged by the identified links between strategic and tactical decisions, Hultink *et al.* (1998) investigated the existence of any systematic configurations of strategic and tactical launch decisions, as well as their relative performance. The impetus to this investigation was the opportunity to offer strong managerial recommendations in case they identified systematic configurations of better performance. Launch strategies underpinning *innovative new products* reflected cases that launched completely new, relatively more innovative products, driven by technological capabilities and introduced in an early stage of the PLC with the objective to establish a foothold in a new market. Tactical launch decisions in these cases included a relatively broad product assortment as compared to competitors, a new brand name, new distribution channels with lower distribution expenditures and a price skimming strategy. *Offensive improvements* reflected launches of moderately new products in a market with few competitors with the objective of erecting competitive barriers. Tactical launch decisions involved a broad product assortment, current distribution channels, higher prices and the use of customer promotion and TV advertising. Finally, *defensive additions* reflected launches of market-driven, less innovative, reformulated new products introduced later in the PLC in a market with many competitors. The objectives here were to expand the product range, erect competitive barriers, increase penetration, produce existing products at a lower cost and capitalize on existing markets.

Overall, in terms of performance, offensive improvement launch strategies were the most successful, followed by the innovative new product launches and the defensive additions. Such differences in performance prompted Hultink *et al.* (2000) to go one step further by comparing and contrasting configurations of successful and unsuccessful product launches involving industrial and consumer new products. They were able to identify specific combinations of strategic and tactical decisions mostly associated with successful launches in either industrial or consumer new products (see Table 4.5).

Table 4.5. Strategic and tactical launch decisions for successful consumer and industrial products.

Successful consumer products	Successful industrial products
Strategic Decisions More innovative than competitive products Developed in 6 months to 3 years More often improvements Introduced in markets growing at 5–10% Introduced more often with the objective of entering an existing market, developing the company image, putting up barriers, using excess capacity, lowering the cost as much as possible and/or increasing market penetration	**Strategic Decisions** More innovative than competitive products Developed in 6 months to 1 year More often improvements Introduced in markets growing at >10% Introduced in the maturity phase and in markets with 1 to 3 competitors Introduced more often with the objective of entering an existing market, developing the company image, lowering the cost as much as possible and/or increasing market penetration
Tactical Decisions Introduced in a broader range More often a brand extension Introduced with a higher distribution expenditure than competitors Introduced at similar prices as competitors Used penetration pricing Used a higher promotion expenditure than competitors	**Tactical Decisions** Introduced in a broader range Introduced with a similar distribution expenditure as competitors Introduced with a similar promotion expenditure as competitors Introduced more often with print advertising and direct marketing methods

Source: Adapted from Hultink *et al.* (2000).

4.5 Conclusion

This chapter has reviewed the factors which have been identified to have a direct influence upon the success or failure of new product launches. It is clear from this review that the launch decision is a complex one and requires considerable information, skills and competence. Overall, it is a decision that requires attention early on in the NPSD process. This need for early attention to launch and its central role in the NPSD process are by no means a unique characteristic of a specific action of the firm or indeed a need simply felt during the NPSD process only. Instead, they reflect a very old, albeit still very relevant, challenge faced by firms: the challenge between exploration and exploitation. Sustainable success is the outcome of a firm's ability to innovate (explore) and market (exploit) new products and services successfully. Management gurus have gone as far as claiming that nothing else but innovation and marketing matter in an organization. The obvious importance of innovation and marketing needs to be addressed by considering that the competencies, skills and resources required by a firm to innovate are significantly different than those required for marketing these innovations.

Recently, there has been another wave of attention to this old conundrum in the management literature under the theme of the "ambidextrous" organization (Birkinshaw and Gibson, 2004). O'Reilly and Tushman (2004) introduced what they call the "ambidextrous organization" to describe the challenges facing many organizations, whereby they have to be able to exploit current products while simultaneously exploring the future. Looking at the example of Ciba Vision, a unit of the Swiss pharmaceutical company Ciba-Geigy (now Novartis), their article describes how Ciba Vision's management realized that radical new products were required to grow the company (and even to fend off decline) while continuing to make money from its more conventional portfolio of contact lens and eye care products. The decision was taken to launch six formal development projects aiming at revolutionary change, two in manufacturing processes and four in new products. Many smaller R&D projects aimed at ongoing product improvement were canceled to release cash for the more ambitious R&D imperatives. Traditional business sections were still able to pursue incremental innovations of their own, but the R&D budget was dedicated to the development of real breakthroughs. These projects were freed from the structures of the old organization and instead autonomous units for the new projects were developed, each with its own R&D, finance and marketing functions.

In addition to the organizational and structural issues, it is important to consider launch strategies under different environmental conditions too. In a recent study, Kleinschmidt *et al.* (2007) investigated NPD success in a global setting. Specifically, their study evaluated organizational NPD resources (the firm's global innovation culture, attitude to resource commitment, top-management involvement and NPD process formality), NPD process capabilities or routines for identifying and exploiting new product opportunities (global knowledge integration, NPD homework activities and launch preparation), and global NPD program performance. On the basis of 387 global NPD programs (in North America and Europe), the authors found that global knowledge integration, NPD homework activities and launch preparation play a significant role in global NPD program success.

We conclude this chapter by calling readers to reflect on these approaches as a means for delineating new directions for reflection and research on the launch strategies and tactics used by firms and their relevant success. In other words, we call for more research on how combinations of launch strategies and their eventual success or failure rates come out of specific organizational structures, specific management practices, and the accumulation and deployment of specific skills and competencies that promote their emergence and success in the marketplace nationally and internationally.

References

Anderson, E. and Coughlan, A.T. (1987). International market entry and expansion via independent or integrated channels of distribution. *Journal of Marketing*, 51(1), 71–82.

Bain, J. (1956). *Barriers to New Competition.* Cambridge, MA: Harvard University Press.

Beard, C. and Easingwood, C. (1996). New product launch in high-technology industries. *Industrial Marketing Management*, 25, 87–103.

Biggadike, E.R. (1979). *Corporate Diversification: Entry, Strategy and Performance.* Cambridge, MA: Harvard University Press.

Birkinshaw, J. and Gibson, C. (2004). Building ambidexterity into an organization. *Sloan Management Review*, 45(4), 47–55.

Booz, Allen & Hamilton. (1982). *New Product Management for the 1980s.* New York: Booz, Allen & Hamilton, Inc.

Bowersox, D.J., Stank, T.P. and Daugherty, P.J. (1999). Lean launch: managing product introduction risk through response-based logistics. *Journal of Product Innovation Management*, 16(6), 557–568.

Calantone, R. and Montoya-Weiss, M. (1994). Product launch and follow-on. In: W.E. Souder and J.D. Sherman (eds.), *Managing New Technology Development*, New York: McGraw-Hill, pp. 217–248.

Calantone, R.J. and Di Benedetto, C.A. (2007). Clustering product launches by price and launch strategy. *Journal of Business and Industrial Marketing*, 22, 4–19.

Calantone, R.J., Di Benedetto, C.A. and Stank, T.P. (2005). Managing the supply chain implications of launch. In: K.B. Kahn, G. Castellion and A. Griffin (eds.), *The PDMA Handbook of New Product Development*, 2nd ed., Hoboken, NJ: Wiley, pp. 466–478.

Cooper, A.C. (1993a). Challenges in predicting new firm performance. *Journal of Business Venturing*, 8, 241–253.

Cooper, R.G. (1979). The dimensions of industrial new product success and failure. *Journal of Marketing*, 43, 93–103.

Cooper, R.G. (1984). How new product strategies impact on performance. *Journal of Product Innovation Management*, 1(1), 5–18.

Cooper, R.G. (1993b). *Winning at New Products: Accelerating the Process from Idea to Launch.* Reading, MA: Addison-Wesley.

Cooper, R.G. (1994). Third-generation new product processes. *Journal of Product Innovation Management*, 11(1), 3–14.

Cooper, R.G. and Kleinschmidt, E.J. (1993). New product success in the chemical industry. *Industrial Marketing Management*, 22(2), 85–99.

Cordero, R. (1991). Managing for speed to avoid product obsolescence: a survey of techniques. *Journal of Product Innovation Management*, 8(4), 283–294.

Crawford, C.M. (1980). Defining the charter for product innovation. *Sloan Management Review*, Fall, 3–12.

Crawford, C.M. (1994). *New Product Management.* Homewood, IL: Richard D. Irwin.

Debruyne, M., Moenaert, R., Griffin, A., Hart, S., Hultink, E.J. and Robben, H. (2002). The impact of new product launch strategies on competitive reaction in industrial markets. *Journal of Product Innovation Management*, 19, 159–170.

Di Benedetto, C.A. (1999). Identifying the key success factors in new product launch. *Journal of Product Innovation Management*, 16(6), 530–544.

Dumaine, B. (1989). How managers can succeed through speed. *Fortune*, 119, 54–59.

Green, D.H. and Ryans, A.B. (1990). Entry strategies and market performance: causal modeling of a business simulation. *Journal of Product Innovation Management*, 7, 45–58.

Guiltinan, J.P. (1999). Launch strategy, launch tactics, and demand outcomes. *Journal of Product Innovation Management*, 16, 509–529.

Guveritz, S. (1983). Technology will shorten product life-cycles. *Business Marketing*, 12, 44–54.

Heil, O.P. and Walters, R.G. (1993). Explaining competitive reactions to new products: an empirical signaling study. *Journal of Product Innovation Management*, 10, 53–65.

Hsieh, M. and Tsai, K. (2007). Technological capability, social capital and the launch strategy for innovative products. *Industrial Marketing Management*, 36(4), 493–502.

Hsieh, M., Tsai, K. and Wang, J. (2008). The moderating effects of market orientation and launch proficiency on the product advantage–performance relationship. *Industrial Marketing Management*, 37(5), 580–592.

Hultink, E.J., Griffin, A., Hart, S. and Robben, H.S.J. (1997). Industrial new product launch strategies and product development performance. *Journal of Product Innovation Management*, 14(4), 243–257.

Hultink, E.J., Griffin, A., Robben, H.S.J. and Hart, S. (1998). In search of generic launch strategies for new products. *International Journal of Research in Marketing*, 15, 269–285.

Hultink, E.J. and Hart, S. (1998). The world's path to the better mousetrap: myth or reality? An empirical investigation into the launch strategies of high and low advantage new products. *European Journal of Innovation Management*, 1(3), 106–122.

Hultink, E.J., Hart, S., Robben, H.S.J. and Griffin, A. (1999). New consumer product launch: strategies and performance. *Journal of Strategic Marketing*, 7(3), 153–174.

Hultink, E.J., Hart, S., Robben, H.S.J. and Griffin, A. (2000). Launch decisions and new product success: an empirical comparison of consumer and industrial products. *Journal of Product Innovation Management*, 17, 5–23.

Hultink, E.J. and Langerak, F. (2002). Launch decisions and competitive reactions: an exploratory market signaling study. *Journal of Product Innovation Management*, 19(3), 199–212.

Hultink, E.J. and Robben, H.S.J. (1999). Launch strategy and new product performance: an empirical examination in the Netherlands. *Journal of Product Innovation Management*, 16, 545–556.

Hultink, E.J. and Schoormans, J.P.L. (1995). How to launch a high-tech product successfully: an analysis of marketing managers' strategy choices. *Journal of High Technology Management Research*, 6(2), 229–242.

Johne, F.A. and Snelson, P.A. (1988). Success factors in product innovation: a selective review of the literature. *Journal of Product Innovation Management*, 5, 114–128.

Kleinschmidt, E., de Brentani, U. and Salomo, S. (2007). Performance of global new product development programs: a resource-based view. *Journal of Product Innovation Management*, 24, 419–441.

Kohli, A.K. and Jaworski, B.J. (1990). Market orientation: the construct, research propositions and managerial implications. *Journal of Marketing*, 54, 1–18.

Lambkin, M. (1988). Order of entry and performance in new markets. *Strategic Management Journal*, 9, 127–140.

Langerak, F., Hultink, E.J. and Robben, H.S.J. (2004). The impact of market orientation, product advantage, and launch proficiency on new product performance and organizational performance. *Journal of Product Innovation Management*, 21(2), 79–94.

Lee, Y. and O'Connor, G.C. (2003). The impact of communication strategy on launching new products: the moderating role of product innovativeness. *Journal of Product Innovation Management*, 20(1), 4–21.

Lieberman, M.B. and Montgomery, D.B. (1988). First-mover advantages. *Strategic Management Journal*, 9, 41–58.

Lilien, G.L. and Yoon, E. (1989). Determinants of new industrial product performance: a strategic re-examination of the literature. *IEEE Transactions on Engineering Management*, 36(1), 3–10.

Mintzberg, H. (1978). Patterns in strategy formation. *Management Science*, 24(9), 934–948.

Moriarty, R.T. and Kosnik, T.J. (1989). High-tech marketing: concepts, continuity and change. *Sloan Management Review*, 30, 7–17.

Nagle, S. (2005). Managing new product and service launch. In: K.B. Kahn, G. Castellion and A. Griffin (eds.), *The PDMA Handbook of New Product Development*, 2nd ed., Hoboken, NJ: Wiley, pp. 455–465.

Narver, J.C. and Slater, S.F. (1990). The effect of market orientation on business profitability. *Journal of Marketing*, 54, 20–35.

O'Reilly, C. and Tushman, M.L. (2004). The ambidextrous organization. *Harvard Business Review*, 82, 1–9.

Ottum, B.D. (1996). Launching a new consumer product. In: M.D. Rosenau, A. Griffin, G. Castellion and N. Anscheutz (eds.), *The PDMA Handbook of New Product Development*, New York: Wiley, pp. 381–394.

Porter, M.E. (1985). Technology and competitive advantage. *Journal of Business Strategy*, 5, 60–78.

Robben, H.S.J. (1998). In search of generic launch strategies of new products. *International Journal of Research in Marketing*, 15, 269–286.

Rosenau, M.D. (1990). *Faster New Product Development: Getting the Right Products to Market Quickly*. New York: AMACOM.

Ryans, A.B. (1988). Strategic market entry factors and market share achievement in Japan. *Journal of International Business Studies*, 19, 389–409.

Saunders, J. and Jobber, D. (1994). Product replacement: strategies for simultaneous product deletion and launch. *Journal of Product Innovation Management*, 11(5), 433–450.

Smith, P.G. and Reinertsen, D.G. (1991). *Developing Products in Half the Time*. New York: Van Nostrand Reinhold.

Stigler, G. (1981). The economics of information. *Journal of Political Economy*, 69, 213–225.

Stryker, J.D. (1996). Launching a new business-to-business product. In: M.D. Rosenau, A. Griffin, G. Castellion and N. Anscheutz (eds.), *The PDMA Handbook of New Product Development*, New York: Wiley, pp. 363–380.

Thoelke, J.M., Hultink, E.J. and Robben, H.S.J. (2001). Launching new product features: a multiple case examination. *Journal of Product Innovation Management*, 18(1), 3–14.

Urban, G.L., Carter, T., Gaskin, S. and Mucha, Z. (1986). Market share rewards to pioneering brands: an empirical analysis and strategic implications. *Management Science*, 32(6), 645–659.

Womack, J.P., Jones, D.T. and Roos, D. (1990). *The Machine That Changed the World: The Story of Lean Production*. New York: Macmillan.

Chapter 5

Co-constructing the Brand and the Product

John K. Christiansen, Claus J. Varnes,
Birgitte Hollensen and Birgitte C. Blomberg

5.1 Introduction

Brands are formed by innovation and driven by new products, as
these provide a temporary competitive advantage (Kapferer, 2004;
Barney, 1991). Until this point, however, much research with respect
to brands and product development has evolved around brand and
line extensions with an emphasis on brand meanings perceived by
users (Uggla, 2004; Broniarczyk and Alba, 1994; Keller, 2003; Wee
and Ming, 2003; Grime *et al.*, 2002; Del Rio *et al.*, 2001; Meyvis and
Janiszewski, 2004; Glynn and Brodie, 1998; Reast, 2005). Most
significantly, the bulk of research has been directed towards determining the factors that contribute to the perceived and so-called "fit"
or similarity, and hence ultimate acceptance of the extension by
consumers, between the extension and the parent brand (Boush and
Loken, 1991; Gronhaug *et al.*, 2002; Park *et al.*, 1991; Dacin and
Smith, 1994; Zimmer and Bhat, 2004; Thorbjørnsen, 2005). Some
of this research has addressed the issue that consumer evaluations of
the brand and line extensions (or those types of new product development) tend to be inversely related to the similarity perceived in the
new extension. Furthermore, it has been suggested that the
extendibility of brand is a function of cognitive and affective processes

for both product class and brand-specific associations (Martin *et al.*, 2005). Other topics include brand equity (Myers, 2003; Chen, 2001; Delgado-Ballester and Munuera-Alemán, 2005; Pappu *et al.*, 2005; Keller and Sood, 2003; Pitta and Katsanis, 1995), brand value (Hupp and Powaga, 2004; Doyle, 2001; Jones, 2005; Munoz and Kumar, 2004), brand personality and image (Nandan, 2005; Phau and Lau, 2001; Wee, 2004; Martinez and de Chernatony, 2004; Freling and Forbes, 2005), brand loyalty (Gounaris and Stathakopoulos, 2004; Quester and Lim, 2003; Taylor *et al.*, 2004), and product and brand platforms (Sköld and Karlsson, 2007).

Thus, while much emphasis has been placed on the relationship between brands and products, so far only limited attention has been directed towards understanding the innovation process by which brands are formed (Kapferer, 2004). International textbooks on branding, like Kapferer's (2004) *The New Strategic Brand Management* and Aaker and Joachimsthaler's (2000) *Brand Leadership*, do not cover the aspect of branding vis-à-vis the process of product development. Similarly, textbooks on innovation management, like Tidd and Bessant's (2009) *Managing Innovation*, do not connect the notions of branding with their normative recommendations for successful management of product and service innovation. Only a few have investigated (e.g. Ambler and Styles, 1997; Blichfeldt, 2005; Jones and Tollin, 2008) or asked for analysis of (Montague, 1999; Jones and Tollin, 2008) the connection between these two seemingly separate yet interdependent concepts. This is the point of departure of this chapter.

As stated earlier, research on product development has focused on the development of new products and services, whereas research on marketing and branding has emphasized what types of line extensions to create. Neither has sought to explain how to integrate brand(s) and product development processes at an action-oriented level.

The remainder of this chapter is organized as follows. First, prior research on integrating branding and product and service development is discussed. This is followed by a review of the network process perspective used in our analysis. Subsequently, we discuss the concept of branding, including a presentation of Kapferer's (2004) identity prism. Next is a section on methodology, and an analysis of two cases based on the constructivist theory. Finally, we have a discussion on the findings, conclusions and implications for research and management.

5.2 Branding and the Product Development Process

Montague (1999) argued in a conceptual paper for the integration of brand and product development, as the brand holds the promise and the product holds the delivery. Blichfeldt (2005) found that management practices of line/brand extensions in the fast moving consumer goods (FMCG) companies investigated in her research did not correspond with existing theories on product development or with branding theories. This is so because it has been assumed that, if there are brand-related issues connected with the product development process, then these have resided within the launch stages of the process, i.e. at the end of the product development cycle (Ambler and Styles, 1997). Blichfeldt (2005) points to the need to consider branding issues *throughout* the process when developing brand extensions. In structured approaches to product development (e.g. Cooper, 2001), decisions on the marketing plan, for instance, are determined in the last phases of the product development process. If the key issues in product development projects are what to launch, when to launch and how to launch (Hultink *et al.*, 1997), then the key issues of branding also emerge around those processes.

Thus, some authors view branding and innovation from another perspective, whereby the brand is developed through the process of innovation and a continuous flow of innovations can drive the brand. This requires constant innovation processes to develop the brand (Kapferer, 2004). Saunders *et al.* (2005) try to identify the decision criteria used in the consumer packaged goods sector over the phases of product development. They report from a survey that "clearly identified brand strategy" and "brand fit" are among the factors which product development project managers report as important throughout the different phases. Bhat and Bowonder (2001), who stress the personality linked to every brand, support this line of reasoning. They endorse innovations to keep the "personality" active. Moreover, they claim that globalization has intensified the combination of innovation and branding to ensure an incessant customer dedication to the brand. In turn, Briggs (2004), on the North American-based Product Development Management Association (PDMA) website, advocates the need to recognize the brand as the starting point for every product development and labels this as brand-centered product development. He believes that the emotional brand experience should be the point of departure instead of the product's physical attributes. This is based on the view that products can be copied but the brand cannot, and that a valuable brand will endure in the customers' minds (see also Barney, 1991).

Schultz and Hatch (2003) regard product development as a means for closing the gap between the (intended) identities that companies aim to communicate and the image that customers perceive. Therefore, branding should not only be a strategic task but should also align the brand perception of employees and customers, since the internal culture should be reflected in the customers' image (Schultz and Hatch, 2003; Hatch and Schultz, 2008). Therefore, there will be three elements (identity, product and image) and the risk of two gaps: a gap between identity and product, and a gap between product and image. The company can have a product that does not reflect the company's culture, or a product that does not reflect the perceived image. The product can meet expectations only if *both* gaps are closed.

Finally, a new line of research (Jones and Tollin, 2008) is raising awareness about the need to analyze the role of marketing in relation to innovation. A study of the mental models of chief marketing executives showed that they seemed to be focused on either company products or corporate brands, and that the integration of these was not on their agenda (Jones and Tollin, 2008). These results are consistent with the findings of Blichfeldt (2005), who, from case studies of 14 FMCG companies, found that while some companies do incorporate brand thinking in the development of new products, there are others which deliberately do not pay attention to branding. A similar type of myopia is reflected in the observations of the innovation management literature, where Francis and Bessant (2005) note that managers are often focused on product innovation; while in the branding literature, Kapferer (2004) focuses on the branding aspect.

In conclusion, we may state that prior research is mostly conceptual, based on surveys or case studies on brand/product orientation. We have not identified studies that have investigated the microprocesses of innovation, trying to uncover how the brand performs and interacts with other actors in the process. Furthermore, the assumptions in prior research often presume clear demarcations between the innovative phase and the marketing and launch phases, and between the focal company and the external environment. However, these premises of divisions and structures in the innovation process might actually limit our understanding of the innovation process in practice (Christiansen and Varnes, 2007; Akrich *et al.*, 2002a), and especially our understanding of the complexities and dynamics of how brand and product become related during the innovation process.

5.3 The Network Process Perspective

The network process perspective was introduced to the product development domain (Christiansen and Varnes, 2007) as an approach to capture the dynamics and the fragility of the product development process. The network process perspective is derived from the actor-network theory (ANT) (Callon, 1986a; Callon, 1986b; Latour, 1991; Law, 1992a), and more recently from the works of Akrich *et al.* (2002a, 2002b) and Latour (2005). As the ANT is covered by an ever-growing and rather diverse set of different authors with different views, we found it relevant to derive a number of basic and fundamental characteristics and mechanisms and present these as a perspective. The network process perspective is based on a constructivist perspective (ANT). Consequently, the process of construction instead of the final structure, for instance, is of interest to this perspective. These assumptions have great bearing for understanding the marketplace (Christiansen *et al.*, 2008), among other issues, but also for branding which is the subject of this study. The network process perspective offers the understanding of identity as a network in which roles are continuously negotiated in dynamic relations and depend on who can successfully establish obligatory passage points. Here, "social" is understood as "nothing other than patterned networks of heterogeneous materials" (Law, 1992a, p. 381). Law (1992a) departs from an ontological and epistemological perspective where "[a]ctor-network theory assumes that social structure is not a noun but a verb" (p. 385). As a consequence, no distinction can be made between the object and the context, which implies that we cannot distinguish between a linear, structured approach on the one side and branding on the other. Thus, we need to understand how relations create actor-networks in product development, as human and non-human actors are producing the network. Actor-networks are constructed and are fragile, and consist of heterogeneous human and non-human actors:

> Thus analysis of ordering struggle is central to actor-network theory. The object is to explore and describe local processes of patterning, social orchestration, ordering, and resistance. In short, it is to explore the process that is often called translation, which generates ordering effects such as devices, agents, institutions, or organizations. . . . This, then, is the core of the actor-network approach: a concern with how actors and organizations mobilize, juxtapose, and hold together the bits and pieces out of which they are composed [Law, 1992b, pp. 5–6]
>
> In the absence of one ingredient the whole would break down. . . . These juxtapositions define the conditions of operation for the actor-world. In fact, it is from these juxtapositions that the actor-world draws its coherence, its consistency, and the structure of relationships that exists between the components that go to make it up. Without placing them in a network, these elements would be doomed. [Callon, 1986b, pp. 23, 30]

Spokespersons advocate and enroll other human and non-human actors into the network (Akrich *et al.*, 2002a) through obligatory passage points (Callon, 1986a) in interessement processes. Translation creates an actor-world consisting of different entities. It attaches characteristics to them by creating relationships between them in networks, which might be fragile (Latour, 1991). Translations speak for others, but in their own language. Each entity, however, is also a simplification of other entities behind that entity, and so forth. "The actor-world is the context which gives each entity its significance and defines its limitations. It does this by associating the entity to which it is linked" (Callon, 1986b).

In a network process perspective, marketing strategies are one among other non-human actors, and need to connect with other human and non-human actors in order to establish a stable network. Negotiations are needed to stabilize the network, and conflicts can arise during the processes. Networks can be challenged in numerous ways. Negotiations and conflicts between human and non-human actors in the network continually stabilize and de-stabilize the network. Therefore, brand identity too gets stabilized and de-stabilized, and this process continues well after the development has "ended" and the product has been launched into the marketplace. The brand needs spokespersons to talk for it, and it needs to be related and connected in order to influence the network that represents the outcome, e.g. a product with a certain identity.

The analytical perspective applied here helps us to recognize the significance of non-human actors, the importance of relationships and the interessement processes. In our ANT-inspired perspective as outlined in Table 5.1, branding could be said to be the outcome of fragile networks among heterogeneous actors.

Finally, ANT has introduced the notion of obligatory passage points (Callon, 1986a), which refer to some "must-meet" passages before the process and network can proceed. They get actors involved, and include interessement processes by which actors are translated into the network. Translations can be done by different means and processes, but often through a process starting with "problematization". One can regard the myriad of micro-decisions by the actors (e.g. those involved in a project) as attempts to align actors through four moments of translation: problematization, interessement, enrollment and spokespersons. These are highlighted below in our analysis of innovation processes. These moments of translation are active when framing an obligatory passage point, and address our first research question: *In establishing the network for the new product, what are the struggles of problematization, interessement, enrollment and spokespersons?*

5.4 Branding

The understanding of the brand and branding is different in the traditional linear perspective of the innovation process (Christiansen

Table 5.1. Differences between the linear perspective and the derived network process perspective vis-à-vis branding.

	Linear perspective	Network process perspective
Understanding of the brand	A manageable and stable component (a variable).	A dynamic component: brand*ing*.
How is brand identity established?	Through formal post-development/launch activities initiated by the marketing department.	Constructed through continuous negotiations between the actors in the network influencing the brand identity.
How is brand identity managed?	Brand identity is managed through marketing initiatives that the customers are exposed to. Marketing initiatives shape the brand identity. *The brand is designed and implemented.*	The brand surfaces after a struggle and is under negotiation. *The brand is constructed.*
Is brand identity stable?	Brand identity is always stable, since it is manageable.	The stability of the brand identity is related to the stability of the network.
Who influences brand identity?	Those who are involved in designing and executing marketing activities influence brand identity.	All actors in the network who constitute the brand and innovation processes influence the brand identity. These include human and non-human actors.

and Varnes, 2007) and in a network process perspective. The best-known definition of brand management from a linear product development perspective is the one from the American Marketing Association (AMA), where a brand is "[a] name, term, sign, symbol, or a combination of them, intended to identify the goods or services of either one seller or a group of sellers and to differentiate those goods or services from those of competitors" (AMA, 1960). This leans towards an understanding of the brand whereby the branding activities are related to the marketing activities in the launch phase. This is also the brand definition that several authors within marketing adhere to (Keller, 2003; Ambler and Styles, 1997; Aaker and Joachimsthaler, 2000).

There is sparse empirical research on branding in new product development processes (Ambler and Styles, 1997; Blichfeldt, 2005). However, brand understanding is gradually moving away from the perspective where the brand is not considered before the development has ended and the product is launched (Ambler and Styles, 1997), and is shifting towards a more relational view that fits into our network process perspective.

The brand identity prism (Kapferer, 2004) will be used to analyze the creation of brand during the observed processes (see Figure 5.1). The prism consists of six aspects: physical, personality, culture, relationships, reflection and self-image. The *physical* aspect is a combination of the apparent product and brand elements. The brand *personality* is created through communication, and shows what kind of person the product or service would be if it were human. The *culture* defines the basis for the product or service; not only is the culture enclosed in the product, but the product or service also communicates it. Brands are often interchanged between people, and will therefore also define the *relationships* that surround a product or service. The product or brand will also create a *reflection* of the type of person who purchases it. Lastly, the *self-image* is the target group's internal picture. These six aspects are assembled in the prism, and the status of each can range from weak to strong. The difference between a weak and a strong prism is that a strong prism will include meaningful words or phrases in all aspects and the different aspects will not

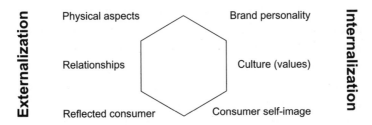

Figure 5.1. Brand identity prism derived from Kapferer (2004).

contain many repeated words or phrases. All of the aspects are inter-related and the sum of the aspects will create an essence that is an extract of the meaning (Kapferer, 2004).

Our understanding of the prism as well as of the brand is dynamic when we comprehend the innovation process in a constructivist perspective. As the word "brand*ing*" discloses, this process is ongoing (Hatch and Schultz, 2008). We perceive the process as a continuous negotiation of the brand identity, as the branding occurs constantly in the network. Thus, we regard the conceptualization of the brand as a dynamic process in which the brand identity is created through relationships that are negotiated in a network. The second research question then becomes: *How are the identity prisms of two product brands influenced by the innovation process?*

5.5 The Empirical Study

This study is explorative and focuses on how the relationship between products and brands emerges over time, how one influences the other, and how a stable outcome (result) is established. The dynamics are explored by analyzing the enrollment processes, negotiations and interessement in a constructivist perspective.

By employing an in-depth case analysis (Yin, 2003), four translation moments in the development of two products in two companies were analyzed. The choice of moments was based on three criteria: (1) the moment had to be described as a tension that had a critical impact on the innovation process by the participants; (2) the moment had to be mentioned (cross-referenced) by several respondents; and (3) the moment had to have an effect on one or more aspects of the brand identity prism. In-depth interviews were used to uncover underlying attitudes, motivations and emotions (Malhotra and Birks, 2006).

Triangulated evidence (Yin, 2003) from various data sources was collected for the purpose of this study, based on interviews, written documentation and observations gained through continued close interaction with both companies for several years. Thirteen interviews were conducted with participants from the studied innovation processes as members of management meeting decision groups, steering committee members and project team members. The interviews lasted from one-and-a-half to two-and-a-half hours each. They were guided by a semi-structured questionnaire that was split into four themes according to the network process theory applied here. During the interview, visual tools as well as a laddering technique were employed. This ensured an insight into the respondents' understanding of the product development process, and made it possible to map the product brand identity prisms. All respondents were not selected beforehand, but were identified as the network was followed and key actors identified (Latour, 2005). This validates the point that additional interviews would not have added positive effects to understand the networks (Strauss and Corbin, 1998). Moreover, various written company and project documentation was collected. Finally, two of the researchers had been employed in the companies while two others had prior knowledge of the companies from other projects, which improved the context understanding in the research team.

Some insights and knowledge can best, and sometimes only, be produced by in-depth studies or ethnographic-type studies (Van Maanen, 1996) — this is especially true for phenomena related to the social world (Flyvbjerg, 2001). Using methods like surveys surely can provide the basis for generalizations across large samples, but those kinds of studies are "trapped in retrospective explanation" building (Akrich *et al.*, 2002a, p. 191). Also, as discussed earlier, prior studies on the mental models and branding (Jones and Tollin, 2008) or on the roles of different criteria during the product development process (Saunders *et al.*, 2005) uncover interesting aspects and are valid in their own right, but are not able to describe the activities, processes and struggles that human and non-human actors encounter during the process. As the strength of generalization and the ability to uncover interesting phenomena from research are grounded on an objectivistic perspective (such as surveys) and can be questioned (Flyvbjerg, 2001), we here apply an approach that adds to "a theory of innovation which is closer to the actors and their experiences" (Akrich *et al.*, 2002a, p. 191). Furthermore, as our chosen theoretical perspective implies the acceptance of heterogeneity and the establishment of networks among heterogeneous human and non-human actors (Law, 1992a), the possibility of generalizations across multiple heterogeneous sets is rather distant. It simply becomes less evident, or probably impossible, to transfer one observation from a specific location and network to another different locality. However, these restrictions from within our chosen theoretical perspective will not make it impossible for us to provide some conclusions, but the generalizations on those and transferability to other cases in time and space have to be treated with great care.

The selection of cases within the theoretical perspective is about the identification of situations and processes that can produce new insights (Flyvbjerg, 2001) based on close studies of activities and access to different networks (Callon, 1991), rather than the belief that a perfect sample exists from which wide-ranging generalizations can be drawn. The two cases in this chapter were thus chosen for three reasons. First, they represent large international companies (aspiring to become global), with a defined marketing and brand strategy as well as a structured and managed approach to product development. Thus, they had a number of features and structures that are recommended in many normative writings on the management of product development and branding. Second, they gave wide access to the research team in terms of possibilities for observations, interviews and access to internal documents, which is an important prerequisite for this type of research. Finally, the research team has strong background information on both cases, as several team members had been involved with both companies for several years in different ways.

5.6 Case Analysis: Medico

Medico is a global firm that operates in the medical care industry. The company is active in three different product areas, one of which is ostomy where a project is studied here. Medico's headquarters and its central R&D are located in Denmark. The company exports products to more than 65 countries. Production facilities are located in the USA, China and Europe, and the company employs more than 7,000 people. Medico is one of the few larger firms that operate in this market.

The company has a formal, structured product development process, with phases and gates that have been used for more than 13 years and are updated frequently to match needs. The marketing department is involved throughout the product development process, as the firm employs a cross-functional approach to product development. Marketing is assigned different important roles throughout the process. This is done in the first phase by adding consumer knowledge obtained from research; next, by participating in the concept development and product design, and implementing the whole marketing mix in a test market; and lastly, by rolling the product out to international markets. The concept of branding is addressed in the concept development phase; otherwise, branding considerations are not mentioned in the structured process model. However, as gleaned from interviews and anecdotal evidence, in Medico branding considerations do not normally take place until the end of product development and just before launch. At this stage, clinical tests are important, but it is also critical as to how to promote the new product to customers and relate it to the existing brands by considering product design and packaging.

In 2000, the management of Medico decided to start the development of a new generation of stoma bags. The adhesive was to be improved with a new technology to bring additional value to the product. Users would benefit in terms of security when using the stoma bag. The first analysis focuses on two critical incidents in the innovation process of the new stoma bag in Medico: the non-woven fabric and the foil.

5.6.1 *Medico 1: non-woven fabric*

5.6.1.1 *Problematization*

The project participants identified the first critical incident as that around the negotiation of a new non-woven fabric to cover the bag. The project group was enthusiastic about incorporating the non-woven fabric, as it was considered to provide a new unique selling proposition (USP) in the marketing campaign and would outdo other competing products. The non-woven fabric was unique due to its features. However, it was not originally designed for the medical industry. The supplier representatives referred directly to their CEO and were excited at the prospect of entering a new industry such as Medico's, but the CEO of the supplying company already had many customers from other industries; he was therefore critical in his choice of new customers and continuously focused on opportunity costs and short-term profit. The actors from within Medico wanted to know whether non-woven fabric could be a part of the project. This was the obligatory passage point by which the project group had to interest and enroll the various human and non-human actors to establish and stabilize the network. This was imperative as the supplier was the only one who could manufacture this fabric. There were several obstacles to successfully interest and enroll the actors, as illustrated in Figure 5.2.

Figure 5.2 illustrates that the project group should avoid that non-woven fabric would want to be a part of other products, that the representatives would obtain superior offers from other customers, and that the CEO of the supplying company would insist on short-term profits. Medico could not offer as fast short-term profits as the nappy industry, which was the supplier's primary market, but could ensure a long-term commitment and an opportunity of entering a new market: the market for medical devices.

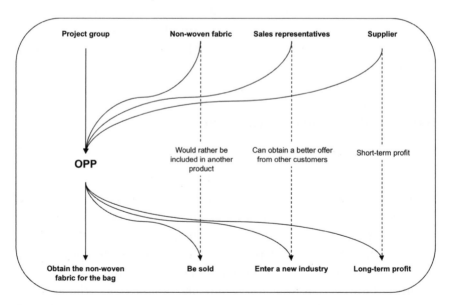

Figure 5.2.   Interessement challenges for the project group with the non-woven fabric.

5.6.1.2 Devices of interessement

Different devices of interessement were employed in the negotiations with the actors. The project group attempted to persuade the chief representative of the supplier by stressing the high potential profits from entering the lucrative market for medical devices. Medico also invested in an embossing mill at the cost of US$1 million, demonstrating its commitment. Moreover, the project team conducted tests of the non-woven fabric to prove the quality, features and effects of the fabric towards Medico, and to interest the non-woven fabric itself.

5.6.1.3 Enrollment

The interessement had a positive effect on some of the actors in the obligatory passage point. The non-woven fabric was enrolled after successful tests and could therefore be a part of the stoma bag. The representatives were enrolled since they became convinced of the opportunities in entering a new and valuable industry. The CEO of the supplier, however, was not successfully interested and effectively resisted enrollment into the obligatory passage point. He was not convinced of the potential long-term profit; instead, he was interested in the short-term profit provided by the nappy industry. This led to the breakdown of the obligatory passage point and the network around it, and the new stoma bag was not provided with this type of fabric, disabling a USP.

5.6.1.4 Spokespersons

The project group spoke on behalf of non-woven fabric through the use of the tests and the embossing mill, both of which showed successful utilization. The sales representatives were supposed to talk on behalf of the CEO; nevertheless, the project group later learnt that the CEO did not legitimize the representatives as the CEO rejected the agreements that had been settled in prior meetings.

5.6.2 *Medico 2: foil*

5.6.2.1 *Problematization*

The second moment of the same innovation process concerns the properties of the foil in the stoma bag. The foil, which is to be removed before application, comes with a cutting guide that the end user draws on to adjust the size of the hole to the size of the stoma before putting the adhesive onto the body. End users and nurses knew about unmet needs and possible improvements that could be included. An external design company had visual knowledge and creative solutions; however, they did not possess the same market knowledge and values as Medico, which made it difficult for them to design in correspondence with the Medico brand values. The Danish Society for the Visually Impaired is a public institution that serves those who are visually handicapped. Medico's production plant played an important role by declaring what was possible to manufacture. The steering committee was the interface between the project group and the management meeting group, and vetted the recommendations before passing them on. It also decided how much autonomy the project group was provided with. The management meeting group was formally in charge of resources devoted to the different projects and took the "go/kill" decisions. All of the involved actors provided suggestions for the improvement of the design and usefulness of the foil. Figure 5.3 illustrates the obstacles for ensuring stabilization of the network and successful interessement through the obligatory passage point which would produce a new foil.

Figure 5.3 illustrates the struggles facing the project group to keep the end users and nurses from feeling unsafe with Medico; the design company from being contracted by another company; the Danish Society for the Visually Impaired and the production plant from engaging in other tasks; the steering committee from revoking the project group's autonomy; and the management meeting group from withholding the necessary resources.

5.6.2.2 *Devices of interessement*

The project group used different interessement devices to stabilize the network around the foil. Medico employed user surveys, interviews

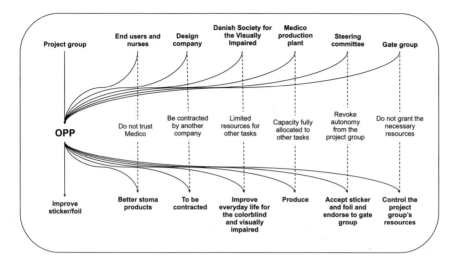

Figure 5.3. Interessement challenges for the project group with the foil.

and product testing to engage the end users and nurses regarding the new product. The design company was interested with lucrative contracts to explore, learn and observe Medico values. As a member of the project team happened to live close to the office of the Danish Society for the Visually Impaired, he suggested contacting the Society in order to get their experts' views on the cutting guide. Since the foil had to be manufactured in Medico's own plant, the project team was in continuous dialog with the plant to ensure that the machines could produce the new foil. The design of the foil had to be endorsed by the steering committee, which was advising the management meeting group. Since the management meeting group controlled the project team resources, the latter presented its ideas, plans and progress to the steering committee.

5.6.2.3 *Enrollment*

The project group successfully enrolled the end users and nurses to participate in the activities. Their suggestions regarding the design of the foil were helpful in that it was realized that the lines on the cutting guide were difficult to see. The design company also used the input from the surveys and their interpretation of the Medico values while designing the foil. In the process, it was suggested that the Medico logo should be printed on the foil. While this was not a part of the original design, the project group, the steering committee and the management meeting group accepted it. The project team ensured the participation of the Danish Society for the Visually Impaired in the surveys. The Society's input was taken into consideration while deciding the color combination of the cutting guide on the foil: dark writing on a white background, which catered to the need for contrasts for the visually impaired. The production team was also brought on board and helped with the final design of the foil. The project group brought in the steering committee and the management meeting group. Thus, all actors were enrolled into the network, which was thereby stabilized around the design of the foil.

5.6.2.4 *Spokespersons*

Several spokespersons were involved, but no one spoke strongly on behalf of the company brand. The recommendations and suggestions of the different actors were taken into consideration and influenced the final product. At no point were the spokespersons contradicted by their respective allies.

5.6.3 *Effects on the identity prism of the Medico processes*

Apart from influencing the physical appearance of the product, the moments of translation also influenced the overall brand identity. The analyses revealed no explicit branding considerations, but showed how the brand identity was informally and unconsciously negotiated throughout the product development. Based on the brand identity prism formulated by Kapferer (2004), the brand identity was analyzed for the developed stoma bag. All six aspects of brand identity (physical, personality, culture, relationships, reflection and self-image) were mapped before and after the translation moments. This is illustrated in Figure 5.4.

The breakdown of negotiations and, therefore, of the obligatory passage point with the supplier of the non-woven fabric had a negative

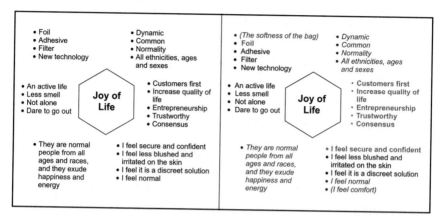

Figure 5.4. The brand identity prism before and after the process. The left box illustrates the intended or desired outcomes, while the right box illustrates the realized outcomes of the process. The bold points indicate positive contributions to the brand identity. The italicized points indicate a negative impact or weakening of the brand identity, and the parentheses around italicized points illustrate the impact of a breakdown of a part of the network.

impact on the brand identity. A softer stoma bag could have contributed positively to the physical aspect of the brand identity. There would also have been a positive effect on the self-image, as the stoma bag could have been more comfortable for the end user. The foil, however, had positive effects on the brand identity. Improvements in the cutting guide and the printing of the Medico logo on the foil improved the physical aspect of the product. Moreover, following the company values, the project team took into account the views and experiences of end users and nurses to improve the product. The company logo on the product made it easier for end users and nurses to identify the foil, which strengthened the cultural aspect but diminished the investment in the product brand. While the logo on the foil benefited the corporate brand, the marketing platform was built up around the new product brand. This meant that the positive effects of the marketing platform were not fully exploited, which resulted in a weaker brand identity in terms of brand personality, consumer reflection and consumer self-image. In the end, the foil only reflected Medico's (corporate) values and not those of the product or the attempted new subbrand.

Overall, the network in four out of six aspects was stable at the time of the interviews. Some features for the physical and cultural aspects were still being negotiated. The brand essence for the product was found to be "joy of life".

5.7 Case Analysis: Window

Window is a global manufacturer of windows. With production facilities in 10 countries and subsidiaries in 40 countries, the company employs around 9,500 people. The company's headquarters and product development are located in Denmark. Window officially employs a structured innovation approach in which different functional areas participate in cross-functional teams. The model includes initial stages of gathering information and developing ideas, where consumer needs and market surveys are analyzed and new concepts based on these needs and surveys are developed. Markets are segmented and potentials are calculated for each segment. This is done in cooperation with the different sales companies in their respective countries. Additionally, the company has developed a forum for collecting ideas that can be accessed by everyone, and employees are encouraged to submit ideas on future products and improvements. A roadmap of new products is completed once a year.

During the product development process, representatives from the communication and marketing department become a part of the project group and engage in discussions regarding the product design and branding. However, no marketing function is formally integrated into the development phase. Only at the end of the product development stage is marketing formally involved, i.e. when the product is to be marketed just before the launch phase. At this point, the marketing department is made responsible for the commercial launch initiatives. Even though Window is conscious and aware of its brand and its value, branding issues are not explicitly addressed in the company product development model. Likewise, a design policy is also absent in the product development model.

In 2003, the company acquired an American manufacturer of sun tunnels: a skylight that can bring sunlight into small rooms where there is no possibility for installing a regular window. Sun tunnels were already widely sold in the US and Australia, where the product originated. However, since Window wanted to sell the sun tunnels in Europe, it had to develop the product as some features were not considered marketable in Europe. It decided to adjust the light shaft and the roof components. This case includes two critical incidents in the innovation process: the gray frame and the diffuser.

5.7.1 Window 1: gray frame

5.7.1.1 Problematization

The first moment involved negotiations about the color of the window frame: a special tone of gray, which is regularly used by the company for most of its frames. The steering committee believed that this special gray tone on the sun tunnel would reinforce the positive associations that people have with the company. The gray tone is used on all Window products so as to ensure that the brand can be easily recognized. The Department of Discovery and Radical Development initiated the sun tunnel project, but was concerned that it might compromise the value of Window's corporate brand as being focused on windows. The Department for Evolutionary Development took over the project and made minor corrections to the design. The marketing department presented knowledge about the markets and consumers, and participated in the decision regarding the choice of color due to branding and sales reasons. The Department for Evolutionary Development counseled two experienced employees from the plastic and metal production unit regarding the choice of material.

The suppliers were responsible for delivering the material and dyeing the frame. If they succeeded, they would secure a long-term profit. Window was already using the polyurethane (PUR) material in some of its products and, therefore, it was a known technology. However, it had to be ensured that this material could be colored the correct tone of gray and could fulfill the demands relating to price and tests. Unlike PUR, plastic was not a known technology; other than this, the same conditions applied. The goal of the steering committee was to ensure that all actors would be interested in the idea of constructing a window frame that could be dyed a special tone of gray for the sun tunnel. Figure 5.5 shows that the actors had to overcome several obstacles before they could be successfully enrolled into the project.

Figure 5.5 shows that both PUR and plastic could be opposed to being dyed gray. The supplier of the material could fail to color the material. The production department could fail to find a suitable supplier for the material. The marketing department could claim that the gray tone would be unmarketable or would not fit the existing product program. The Department for Evolutionary Development could prepare their drawings and papers without color. The Department of Discovery and Radical Development could be opposed to the color gray. Finally, the special tone of gray could change during testing. It was necessary for the steering committee to successfully manage the interessement of the heterogeneous human

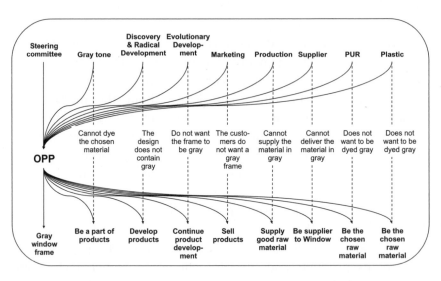

Figure 5.5.   Interessement challenges for the gray color.

and non-human actors, overcome the obstacles and conflicts, and establish a successful translation through the obligatory passage point.

5.7.1.2 *Devices of interessement*

The steering committee used several devices for the interessement. The internal departments were interested in the quality of the product. PUR and plastic were interested by the possibility of being the raw material used for the sun tunnels. Devices of interessement consisted of the tests and prices of the PUR and plastic so that they could show their worth. The supplier of the material was interested by the possibility to sign a long-term contract as the supplier of the raw material of a completely new category.

5.7.1.3 *Enrollment*

The internal actors were successfully enrolled into the network: they wanted the frame to be gray. PUR was chosen over plastic, since its documentation and performance were better. The construction department used the test results, experience and pricing knowledge to make this decision. As per the wishes of the steering committee, the department ordered PUR in the gray tone from the supplier and the latter began its development. Unfortunately, the supplier was not successful as tests showed that the material could not hold the gray tone in sunlight. Even as it kept trying, after six attempts the steering committee decided to stop the supplier and the frame ended up being black. The PUR and the gray tone were thus not enrolled successfully, and the network around the gray frame broke down.

5.7.1.4 *Spokespersons*

The spokespersons represented a wide range of concerns. Two spokespersons did not represent valid claims and were not successfully enrolled: the representative from the marketing department, and the supplier representing PUR. The latter actor insisted that PUR could be dyed gray. However, since this did not happen, it became clear that

180   *J. K. Christiansen et al.*

the supplier was not a legitimized spokesperson. As for the marketing representative, the individual was underrepresented compared with other departments and had little authority to take market-related decisions. Furthermore, the marketing actor did not successfully speak on behalf of branding in the process.

5.7.2 Window 2: diffuser

5.7.2.1 Problematization

The second moment of translation in the Window case concerns the diffuser. It was initially argued that Window would obtain economies of scale and save costs by having the diffuser delivered from China to both the subsidiary in the USA and the Danish parent corporation. The American subsidiary would be the point of contact with the Chinese supplier. The involvement of the Department for Evolutionary Development would be minimal, since it only needed to verify the quality of the diffuser through some built-in tests. The American subsidiary was responsible for the production and quality of the diffuser. It hired an American company to handle the contact (and contract) with the Chinese supplier. Two employees from that company identified a Chinese supplier who would deliver the diffuser. The diffuser was designed by a mutual design team from Denmark and the USA, and consisted of two acrylic plates that were glued together. The steering committee had to ensure that all actors successfully passed the obligatory passage point.

Figure 5.6 illustrates the challenges that the steering committee faced. First, it had to make sure that the Department for Evolutionary Development did not oppose a delivery from China; second, that the American subsidiary did not refuse to cooperate with the headquarters; third, that the American company found a Chinese manufacturer; fourth, that the Chinese supplier did not accept another offer and could meet quality requirements; and finally, that the diffuser passed the tests and could be delivered on time.

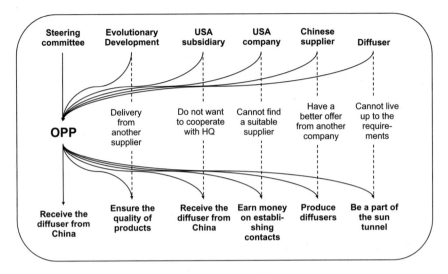

Figure 5.6. Interessement challenges for the diffuser.

5.7.2.2 *Devices of interessement*

The steering committee put devices of interessement into use to interest the actors. Dialog and negotiations were used to interest the actors. To interest the diffuser itself, different tests of the device were undertaken. The interessement of the USA-based subsidiary was only partly successful, as it passed on the job to another company, adding another actor to the network. Negotiations and formal contracts by proxy were used towards the Chinese supplier.

5.7.2.3 *Enrollment*

All of the actors were enrolled into the network vis-à-vis receiving the diffuser from China. Unfortunately, the diffuser did not meet the quality standards. Several units in the first shipment were damaged or of poor quality when arriving at Window, and employees had to repair the units so that they could be delivered with the rest of the components of the sun tunnel. The steering committee thereby made the network stable again. As the situation was not acceptable, the steering committee took over the contract with the Chinese supplier from the

American subsidiary, and introduced the Chinese Window subsidiary as mediator between the headquarters and the Chinese supplier. This changed the network such that the American subsidiary and the American company were excluded from the network.

5.7.2.4 *Spokespersons*

The spokesperson for the diffuser was initially the Department for Evolutionary Development, but later the steering committee took on that role, as it was decided that the diffuser was acceptable as a product and fitted into the Window brand (even with a black frame) but that quality had to be improved. The spokesperson for the Chinese supplier changed quite a few times. First, it was represented by the American company, then by the American subsidiary, and finally by the Chinese subsidiary. However, the rest of the spokespersons were stable during the process. The Window brand did have spokespersons from the marketing department, but they did not appear to be very central in the network although their concerns were not neglected.

5.7.3 *Effects on the identity prism of the Window processes*

The processes had a significant influence on the brand identity of the sun tunnel. In this case too, the data revealed no formal branding processes, but branding concerns were addressed during the processes and both translation moments. Figure 5.7 illustrates how the processes and the new network affected the brand identity.

The outcome that the frame was black instead of gray negatively influenced recognition of the product as being a part of the Window product portfolio. Therefore, the end users did not attach any association to the Window brand, which would have been the case had the frame been gray. This had a negative effect on the cultural aspect. At the same time, the gray tone could have been a part of the physical aspect, which did not happen. For the same reason, the color black had a negative impact. On the other hand, some expressed the opinion that the sun tunnel did not need to communicate the same

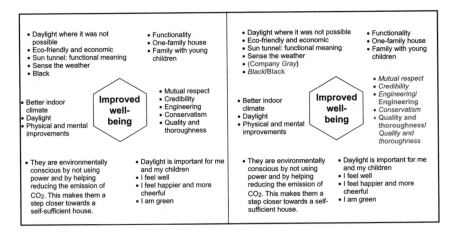

Figure 5.7. The brand identity prism as intended (left) and the actual outcome of the Window product development processes (right).

message as the other products. If this were true, then the black color would actually be a benefit for the brand identity and Window would be able to differentiate the product. In fact, one idea presented during the development process was that the sun tunnel should be presented as a new and different line of products. The end users were never exposed to the quality problems with the diffusers, since Window repaired and ensured the quality of all the damaged diffusers before they entered the market. Thus, no end user received a product that was not quality-assured, which positively affected some of the aspects in the culture: the value of solid engineering, the attention to quality and the thoroughness feature of Window products. One of the aspects, culture, was still being negotiated and was therefore not stable. The brand essence was identified as "improved well-being".

5.8 Discussion

Understanding the innovation process from a network process perspective makes it possible to explore the relationship between brand, product and innovation processes. It shows the constant negotiations and struggles between actors regarding the various components of the product, including brand identity. Therefore, brand identity cannot be perceived as a stable and manageable aspect of the product, nor can it be seen as an established entity subsequent to the innovation process. Brand identity is molded through constant negotiations between the human and non-human actors. The outcome is a co-created brand.

Although the network process perspective departs from ANT (which is rather reluctant to generalize, given that events and networks are specific and not considered stable *per se*, as the relationships between heterogeneous human and non-human actors can shift or be replaced, or as new actors can enter and connect or make new networks), we are nevertheless bold enough to list the two cases discussed above on different dimensions, as shown in Table 5.2.

Medico has a defined brand strategy, while Window works with some implicit assumptions and regards the color gray as one of its brand features (besides the value of engineering and quality). In Medico, the marketing function participated in the product development process, but the marketing actors were not able to place themselves as central in the new network, and the outcome was a somewhat weakened brand identity when measured with the Kapferer (2004) prism. Technical issues with the non-woven fabric came to dominate the final phases in the Medico case, and the branding issues never became an issue with a "loud" or influential spokesperson.

In Window's case, it seems that technical challenges also came to dominate the network establishment. The marketing spokespersons did let themselves become enrolled without strong resistance when the brand was threatened, but the marketing department was not present or represented in the second critical incident of the product development phase. When deciding the final network that represented the outcome, technical issues and quality concerns came to dominate, and a unique feature of the brand (i.e. the gray color) was removed from the product.

Although in both cases the brands were represented by spokespersons from the marketing departments, these spokespersons were not always able to actively defend the established brands. When seen from the brand perspective, the outcomes of the product development

Table 5.2.   Summary of the two cases.

	Medico	Window
Branding strategy as related to the structured company product development process	Branding strategy is part of the structured approach for management of innovation in the concept development phase and prior to the launch of new products.	There is no formal branding strategy approach to product development. A tradition of using gray color on products exists.
Brand translations (outcomes of the process)	The brand essence "joy of life" was strengthened, by a new advanced foil, on the cultural facets, but weakened on the facets of consumer reflection and brand personality as the obligatory passage point of the non-woven fabric was unsuccessful.	The interessement of gray color was not successful, which especially weakened the cultural dimensions of brand identity. The Chinese supplier was successfully enrolled, but compromised quality standards.
Impact on the marketing function as an actor	Although marketing was formally represented in the gate group, many other heterogeneous actors spoke on behalf of users. Marketing did not place itself as central in the new product network that was produced.	The Department of Discovery and Radical Development and the marketing function spoke for the gray color. But, the known technology of PUR came to dominate and the gray color was excluded. Marketing was not represented in the second obligatory passage point. Marketing did not place itself as a strong actor.
Features that became focal concerns (and actors) in the new stabilized product	The supplier representatives were illegitimate spokespersons overturned by another actor, and the non-woven fabric could not be enrolled or enable a successful obligatory passage point. New legitimate spokespersons for users were enrolled in developing the foil.	The sun proved to be a treacherous actor in establishing the gray color on the sun tunnel frame. Other actors spoke on behalf of the Chinese supplier, eventually excluding the American contacts.

processes seemed haphazard in both cases. On the other hand, it could be argued in both cases that the brand — as a non-human actor — was producing conflicts, which made it impossible to create stable networks with those technical solutions (other non-human actors) that seemed to be available as viable solutions here. The brand, in its more or less perfect shape and definition, had to be changed or at least modified in order to allow the two processes to successfully pass the obligatory passage points and produce new products.

The analysis further demonstrates that activities not only during but also before launch influence the branding of products. Structured approaches have been suggested as a solution (Veryzer and Borja de Mozota, 2005) when branding and product development should be integrated, but our observations indicate that these have a limited effect on the strength and direction of the brand identity network.

Kapferer (1992) identifies six components in brand identity: physical, personality, culture, relationships, reflection and self-image. He proposes that brand identities can be either weak or strong. By understanding brand*ing* to mean all of those components in a network of relations connected through an obligatory passage point, this chapter has exposed the dynamics of these brand identities, their interrelatedness, and how they can become strong and weak in the same process. The analysis reveals that the designed product and the brand are both moldable and are co-constructed in the process. Deviations from existing brand values and norms are easily fabricated as struggles and new actors enter the stage.

Schultz and Hatch (2003) were concerned about the "gap" between the corporate identity and the performance of the product, but the analyses presented here propose that brand identity is co-produced with the product and therefore needs to be understood in a more dynamic perspective as a continuous negotiation. Finally, but not least, the network process perspective has added a new perspective to the four paradigms of brand management proposed by Louro and Cunha (2001).

This analysis indicates that there is great potential to increase our understanding of the relationship between innovation processes and brand and branding, but we have to shift towards a more dynamic view of the innovation processes.

5.9 Conclusion

There were two objectives and two research questions that we wanted to investigate. The first research question was related to the challenges that can be observed while creating the network for a new product by successfully passing the obligatory passage points. We can conclude that struggles certainly did occur during the four moments of translation in the two cases. These struggles concerned human and non-human actors on a wide range of issues, which included the enrollment of a new fabric; the enrollment of a new supplier; the reluctance of end users and nurses to trust the company; a busy production plant; the ability of a steering committee to support the project direction; the lack of resources from the gate group; the reluctance of a plastic material to be dyed in the right color; the sun being tough on a new material; a supplier who could not deliver the right material; a subsidiary that struggled for independence from the headquarters; a supplier that could leave the project at a critical time; and parts of products that might or might not have had the right quality.

The second research question was concerned with how the identity prisms of two product brands were influenced, and the answer is that it was not easy for the marketing function to defend or strengthen the existing brand during the process. Both cases demonstrated that the new networks and products (outcomes) represented a strengthened brand identity on some dimensions, while other dimensions were weakened during the processes, as shown in Figures 5.4 and 5.7.

How do brand and product development processes interact? Using our network process perspective derived from the ANT, we have been able to demonstrate the interactive nature and the co-creation of products and brands. The outcomes are co-created during complex processes amongst the heterogeneous actors who are involved in the process in several (sometimes unexpected) ways, as nurses, consultants, woven fabrics, reluctant plastic and suppliers from

China (among others) need to be aligned and interessed, and made stable. The fragile nature of the processes has become clearer through this analysis; and the importance of spokespersons, interessement, conflicts and struggles with human and non-human actors in the translation processes has become evident.

How do brands and branding strategies influence product development, and do branding strategies facilitate or impede the development process? In both cases, the spokespersons from marketing tried to defend the brand identity, but were unsuccessful in placing themselves and the brand as central actors in the process and in the new network. Marketing and brand identity were two among many other human and non-human actors. This means that the brand identity in both cases became de-coupled or loosely coupled to the innovation process, and that made it possible to come up with new technical superior solutions. However, these were not aligned with the present branding strategies in any of the companies — that would require much work.

If marketing and branding experts want to influence and defend potentially strong brands, there is much to learn from these two cases. However, the recommendations can be summarized into two points: first, a clear idea and definition of what the brand and the branding strategies are; and second, an active involvement during the processes in order to influence the creation of new networks by speaking actively on behalf of the brand.

Another implication is the need to be aware of the potential changes and modifications to the brand during the innovation processes, and that branding aspects need to be considered as an integrated part of the whole innovation process. The innovation processes might actually innovate the brand to new and interesting places. The examples presented here might also indicate why some firms are more consistent in their branding efforts than others, as their innovation processes might have integrated brand issues along the process and internalized the values into norm systems influencing the myriad of micro-decisions taken, but never sure not to be challenged or be translated in new unforeseen ways.

Further studies of the micro-processes based on the network process perspective, or ethnographic-inspired studies based on good access to companies and potentially real-time observations, could add to our knowledge on these issues.

Acknowledgments

We would like to thank our colleagues at the Department of Operations Management, Copenhagen Business School, for their critical comments and suggestions during the ongoing series of seminars. Our thanks also go out to the participants of the 15th International Product Development Conference held in Hamburg, June 2008, who stimulated us to continue the research.

References

Aaker, D.A. and Joachimsthaler, E. (2000). *Brand Leadership*. London: Free Press.

Akrich, M., Callon, M. and Latour, B. (2002a). The key to success in innovation. Part I: the art of interessement. *International Journal of Innovation Management*, 6(2), 187–206.

Akrich, M., Callon, M. and Latour, B. (2002b). The key to success in innovation. Part II: the art of choosing good spokespersons. *International Journal of Innovation Management*, 6(2), 207–225.

Ambler, T. and Styles, C. (1997). Brand development versus new product development: toward a process model of extension decisions. *Journal of Product & Brand Management*, 6(4), 222–234.

American Marketing Association (AMA). (1960). *Marketing Definitions: A Glossary of Marketing Terms*. Chicago: AMA.

Barney, J. (1991). Firm resources and sustained competitive advantage. *Journal of Management*, 17(1), 99–120.

Bhat, B. and Bowonder, B. (2001). Innovation as an enhancer of brand personality: globalization experience of Titan Industries. *Creativity and Innovation Management*, 10(1), 26–39.

Blichfeldt, B.S. (2005). On the development of brand and line extensions. *Journal of Brand Management*, 12(3), 177–190.

Boush, D.M. and Loken, B. (1991). A process-tracing study of brand extension evaluation. *Journal of Marketing Research*, 28(1), 16–28.

Briggs, H. (2004). The value of integrating the brand experience into the product development process. Available at http://www.pdma.org/visions/oct04/product development-practices.html/.

Broniarczyk, S.M. and Alba, J.W. (1994). The importance of the brand in brand extension. *Journal of Marketing Research*, 31(2), 214–228.

Callon, M. (1986a). Some elements of a sociology of translation: domestication of the scallops and the fishermen of St Brieuc Bay. In: J. Law (ed.), *Power, Action and Belief: A New Sociology of Knowledge?*, London: Routledge, pp. 196–223.

Callon, M. (1986b). The sociology of an actor-network: the case of the electric vehicle. In: M. Callon, J. Law and A. Rip (eds.), *Mapping the Dynamics of Science and Technology*, London: Macmillan, pp. 19–34.

Callon, M. (1991). Techno-economic networks and irreversibility. In: J. Law (ed.), *A Sociology of Monsters: Essays of Power, Technology and Domination*, London: Routledge, pp. 132–165.

Chen, A. (2001). Using free association to examine the relationship between the characteristics of brand associations and brand equity. *Journal of Product & Brand Management*, 10(7), 439–451.

Christiansen, J.K., Lefevre, S., Varnes, C.J. and Wolf, A. (2008). How market perceptions influence knowledge strategies on user involvement. In: K. Tollin and A. Carù (eds.), *Strategic Market Creation: A New Perspective on Marketing and Innovation Management*, Chippenham: John Wiley & Sons, pp. 285–312.

Christiansen, J.K. and Varnes, C.J. (2007). Making decisions on innovation: meetings or networks? *Creativity and Innovation Management Journal*, 16(3), 282–298.

Cooper, R.G. (2001). *Winning at New Products: Accelerating the Process from Idea to Launch*, 3rd ed. Reading, MA: Perseus Books Group.

Dacin, P.A. and Smith, D.C. (1994). The effect of brand portfolio characteristics on consumer evaluations of brand extensions. *Journal of Marketing Research*, 31(2), 229–242.

Del Rio, A.B., Vázquez, R. and Iglesias, V. (2001). The role of the brand name in obtaining differential advantages. *Journal of Product & Brand Management*, 10(7), 452–465.

Delgado-Ballester, E. and Munuera-Alemán, J.L. (2005). Does brand trust matter to brand equity? *Journal of Product & Brand Management*, 14(3), 187–196.

Doyle, P. (2001). Building value-based branding strategies. *Journal of Strategic Marketing*, 9(4), 255–268.

Flyvbjerg, B. (2001). *Making Social Science Matter*. Cambridge: Cambridge University Press.

Francis, D. and Bessant, J. (2005). Targeting innovation and implications for capability development. *Technovation*, 25, 171–183.

Freling, T.H. and Forbes, L.P. (2005). An empirical analysis of the brand personality effect. *Journal of Product & Brand Management*, 14(7), 404–413.

Glynn, M.S. and Brodie, R.J. (1998). The importance of brand-specific associations in brand extension: further empirical results. *Journal of Product & Brand Management*, 7(6), 509–518.

Gounaris, S. and Stathakopoulos, V. (2004). Antecedents and consequences of brand loyalty: an empirical study. *Journal of Brand Management*, 11(4), 283–306.

Grime, I., Diamantopoulus, A. and Smith, G. (2002). Consumer evaluations of extensions and their effects on the core brand: key issues and research propositions. *European Journal of Marketing*, 36, 1415–1438.

Gronhaug, K., Hem, L. and Lines, R. (2002). Exploring the impact of product category risk and consumer knowledge in brand extensions. *Journal of Brand Management*, 9, 463–476.

Hatch, M.J. and Schultz, M. (2008). *Taking Brand Initiative: How Companies Can Align Strategy, Culture and Identity Through Corporate Branding*. San Francisco: Jossey-Bass.

Hultink, E.J., Griffin, A., Hart, S. and Robben, H.S. (1997). Industrial new product launch strategies and product development performance. *Journal of Product Innovation Management*, 14(4), 243–257.

Hupp, O. and Powaga, K. (2004). Using consumer attitudes to value brands: evaluation of the financial value of brands. *Journal of Advertising Research*, 44(3), 225–231.

Jones, R. (2005). Finding sources of brand value: developing a stakeholder model of brand equity. *Journal of Brand Management*, 13(1), 10–32.

Jones, R. and Tollin, K. (2008). Marketing's role for firms' renewal and innovation capability. In: K. Tollin and A. Carù (eds.), *Strategic Market Creation: A New Perspective on Marketing and Innovation Management*, Chippenham: John Wiley & Sons, pp. 124–157.

Kapferer, J.N. (1992). *Strategic Brand Management: Creating and Sustaining Brand Equity Long Term*. London: Kogan Page.

Kapferer, J.N. (2004). *The New Strategic Brand Management: Creating and Sustaining Brand Equity Long Term*, 3rd ed. London: Kogan Page.

Keller, K.L. (2003). *Strategic Brand Management: Building, Measuring, and Managing Brand Equity*. Upper Saddle River, NJ: Prentice Hall.

Keller, K.L. and Sood, S. (2003). Brand equity dilution. *MIT Sloan Management Review*, 45(1), 12–15.

Latour, B. (1991). Technology is society made durable. In: J. Law (ed.), *A Sociology of Monsters: Essays of Power, Technology and Domination*, London: Routledge, pp. 103–131.

Latour, B. (2005). *Reassembling the Social*. Oxford: Oxford University Press.

Law, J. (1992a). Notes on the theory of the actor-network: ordering, strategy, and heterogeneity. *Systemic Practice and Action Research*, 5(4), 379–393.

Law, J. (1992b). Notes on the theory of the actor network: ordering, strategy and heterogeneity. Published by the Centre for Science Studies, Lancaster University,

UK. Available at http://www.comp.lancs.ac.uk/sociology/papers/Law-Notes-on-ANT.pdf/.

Louro, M.J. and Cunha, P.V. (2001). Brand management paradigms. *Journal of Marketing Management*, 17(7/8), 849–875.

Malhotra, N.K. and Birks, D.F. (2006). *Marketing Research: An Applied Orientation*. London: Prentice Hall.

Martin, I.M., Stewart, D.W. and Matta, S. (2005). Branding strategies, marketing communication, and perceived brand meaning: the transfer of purposive, goal-oriented brand meaning to brand extensions. *Journal of the Academy of Marketing Science*, 33(3), 275–294.

Martinez, E. and de Chernatony, L. (2004). The effect of brand extension strategies upon brand image. *Journal of Consumer Marketing*, 21(1), 39–50.

Meyvis, T. and Janiszewski, C. (2004). When are broader brands stronger brands? An accessibility perspective on the success of brand extensions. *Journal of Consumer Research*, 31(2), 346–357.

Montague, M. (1999). Integrating the product + brand experience. *Design Management Journal*, 10(2), 17–23.

Munoz, T. and Kumar, S. (2004). Brand metrics: gauging and linking brands with business performance. *Journal of Brand Management*, 11(5), 381–387.

Myers, C.A. (2003). Managing brand equity: a look at the impact of attributes. *Journal of Product & Brand Management*, 12(1), 39–52.

Nandan, S. (2005). An exploration of the brand identity–brand image linkage: a communications perspective. *Journal of Brand Management*, 12(4), 264–278.

Pappu, R., Quester, P.G. and Cooksey, R.W. (2005). Consumer-based brand equity: improving the measurement — empirical evidence. *Journal of Product & Brand Management*, 14(3), 142–154.

Park, C.W., Milberg, S. and Lawson, R. (1991). Evaluation of brand extensions: the role of product feature similarity and brand concept consistency. *Journal of Consumer Research*, 18(2), 185–193.

Phau, I. and Lau, K.C. (2001). Brand personality and consumer self-expression: single or dual carriageway? *Journal of Brand Management*, 8(6), 428–444.

Pitta, D.A. and Katsanis, L.P. (1995). Understanding brand equity for successful brand extension. *Journal of Consumer Marketing*, 12(4), 51–64.

Quester, P. and Lim, A.L. (2003). Product involvement/brand loyalty: is there a link? *Journal of Product & Brand Management*, 12(1), 22–38.

Reast, J.D. (2005). Brand trust and brand extension acceptance: the relationship. *Journal of Product & Brand Management*, 14(1), 4–13.

Saunders, J., Wong, V., Stagg, C., Mar, M. and Fontan, S. (2005). How screening criteria change during brand development. *Journal of Product & Brand Management*, 14(4), 239–249.

Schultz, M. and Hatch, M.J. (2003). The cycles of corporate branding: the case of LEGO Company. *California Management Review*, 46(1), 6–26.

Sköld, M. and Karlsson, C. (2007). Multibranded platform development: a corporate strategy with multimanagerial challenges. *Journal of Product Innovation Management*, 24, 554–566.

Strauss, A.L. and Corbin, J. (1998). *Basics of Qualitative Research: Techniques and Procedures for Developing Grounded Theory*, 2nd ed. Thousand Oaks, CA: Sage Publications.

Taylor, S.A., Celuch, K. and Goodwin, S. (2004). The importance of brand equity to customer loyalty. *Journal of Product & Brand Management*, 13(4), 217–227.

Thorbjørnsen, H. (2005). Brand extensions: brand concept congruency and feed-back effects revisited. *Journal of Product & Brand Management*, 14(4), 250–257.

Tidd, J. and Bessant, J. (2009). *Managing Innovation: Integrating Technological, Market and Organizational Change*. Chichester: Wiley.

Uggla, H. (2004). The brand association base: a conceptual model for strategically leveraging partner brand equity. *Journal of Brand Management*, 12(2), 105–123.

Van Maanen, J. (1996). Ethnography. In: A. Kuper and J. Kuper (eds.), *The Social Science Encyclopedia*, 2nd ed., London: Routledge, pp. 263–265.

Veryzer, R.W. and Borja de Mozota, B. (2005). The impact of user-oriented design on new product development: an examination of fundamental relationships. *Journal of Product Innovation Management*, 22(2), 128–143.

Wee, T.T.T. (2004). Extending human personality to brands: the stability factor. *Journal of Brand Management*, 11(4), 317–330.

Wee, T.T.T. and Ming, M.C.H. (2003). Leveraging on symbolic values and meanings in branding. *Journal of Brand Management*, 10(3), 208–218.

Yin, R.K. (2003). *Case Study Research: Design and Methods*. Thousand Oaks, CA: Sage Publications.

Zimmer, M.R. and Bhat, S. (2004). The reciprocal effects of extension quality and fit on parent brand attitude. *Journal of Product & Brand Management*, 13(1), 37–46.

Chapter 6

Understanding Consumer Responses to Innovations

Qing Wang

6.1 Introduction

By combining business examples with prior theories and recent empirical findings, this chapter will examine several important issues in understanding consumer responses to innovations. These issues are summarized in the following questions:

(1) Why do consumers respond to new technologies/products differently (Section 6.2)?

(2) What stages do consumers go through to adopt an innovation (Section 6.3)?

(3) Why is it difficult to measure consumer adoption intentions for really-new products (Section 6.4)?

(4) Why do some users achieve greater usage and consumption satisfaction than others from the newly acquired products (Section 6.5)?

To find an answer to the first question, one has to take into consideration both consumer-related characteristics and innovation-related characteristics. Consumer-related characteristics include demographics, lifestyle, personality traits, knowledge and expertise, and so on. Innovation-related characteristics include new benefits and costs, usefulness and ease of use, etc. The former helps explain why different consumers may respond to the same innovation differently. For example, consumers with a strong environmental awareness are likely to respond more favorably to solar energy panels than consumers whose environmental awareness is weak or non-existent. The latter helps explain why a consumer prefers one innovation to another. For example, a consumer is likely to prefer an innovation that is well designed and easy to use than one that is more difficult to use.

Next, to answer the second question, one needs to have some knowledge of the cognitive and affective processes involved in consumer decision making. This process has been oversimplified in previous research on innovation management. A fuller picture of the factors that influence consumers' decision making for innovation adoption will be provided in the relevant section of this chapter.

The third question centers on the definition and nature of product newness. In this chapter, product newness is defined from the perspective of consumers instead of that of producers. It will be shown that product newness has both positive and negative impacts on consumers' adoption intention. This view is supported by strong empirical evidence and represents an important departure from the traditional approaches to innovation management research, where newness is defined from a producer's perspective and is considered predominantly a positive characteristic. However, the findings show that the perceived newness of a product can in fact negatively affect consumers' adoption intention of the product. Some theoretical explanations will be offered for this finding.

Finally, the literature on innovation adoption has so far focused on how consumers think about new products before they acquire them (Gatignon and Robertson, 1985). According to Rogers (2003), only about 0.2% of studies within the diffusion-of-innovation paradigm have been devoted to consumer behavior after the technology has been acquired. There is little knowledge of what drives the extent of consumption and the use of a new product after purchase. The fourth question addresses this critical gap, and investigates the drivers and the consequences of new product usage.

The objective of this chapter is to explore the above issues from theoretical, empirical and managerial perspectives. The managerial perspective is the key to answer the "so what" question. Put differently, how can managers, marketers and government agents do a better job given these theories and empirical findings? Firstly, the issue of consumer-related characteristics and innovation-related characteristics will be discussed to understand why consumers respond to new technologies/products differently.

6.2 Innovation-Related Characteristics and Consumer-Related Characteristics

According to Rogers (2003), diffusion is the "process by which an innovation is communicated through certain channels over time among the members of a social system". This is an overarching definition of diffusion, under which diffusion can be studied from many different angles: from the perspective of the consumer who buys and uses new technological products or services (e.g. home broadband service); from the perspective of the business which adopts new technologies (e.g. a commercial airliner purchasing new airplanes); or from the perspective of the government, which aims to benefit society as a whole (e.g. the issue of Internet access for low-income families or people in remote areas). This chapter will study innovation diffusion primarily from the consumers' and the business' perspectives, particularly the perspective of consumers as it is underresearched in the area of innovation management.

A recent example of successful innovation is the Google search engine, which is known as one of the world's best brands through word of mouth. Google's success can be examined from both the consumers' perspective and the business' perspective by asking the question, "What innovative characteristics does Google have that have made it such a phenomenal success?" From the consumers' perspective, the innovation characteristics include its superior functionality as the ultimate answer machine with its laser-like focus. This "machine" not only provides the benefits of accuracy, reliability and ease of use, but is also cost-free. From the business' perspective, Google provides advertisements that are highly targeted, subtle, effective and useful. Additionally, it offers search services for corporate partners such as

Yahoo, Virgin and Sony. It is important to note that these innovative characteristics are enabled by Google's cutting-edge PageRank search technology. Therefore, Google is diffused simultaneously to consumers as well as to business users, whereby the performances of Google in these two customer segments are highly interdependent.

Another successful example of groundbreaking innovation is the emergence of blogs. Similar to our analysis of Google, we can examine blogs' success as a new online medium from both the consumers' perspective and the business' perspective and explore the unique innovative characteristics of blogs. A blog is a social networking site and a digital community for consumers. It creates a model of consumer collaboration. For companies, blogs have the potential to become the next important means of marketing communication through "consumer-generated" advertising (Deighton and Kornfeld, 2007). This will create new challenges and opportunities for marketers in terms of how to influence and participate in the social world of consumers.

Despite the potential of blogs to revolutionize both the way people communicate and the way companies carry out marketing communication and advertising, like all new technologies, some questions remain. For example, is blogging too complex to learn? What are the relative advantages of blogs compared to traditional websites or other types of social networking? These questions will help us understand the technical superiority of a new technology. However, to predict how "big" a new technology is likely to become, one should also understand the consumer-related characteristics and the dynamics among potential adopters. For example, what is the profile of the bloggers? Are bloggers very different from non-bloggers? Can bloggers influence non-bloggers and vice versa? These questions will help clarify the commercial potential of a new technology.

Innovations like the Google search engine and blogs have the potential to change the competitive business landscape. Companies that understand the impact of such new technologies are likely to dominate the industry and the future marketplace. However, as we have learned from many past failures, innovations are costly to develop and many have failed to deliver on their promises. Numerous studies have been carried out to explore the success or failure factors for innovation (e.g. Urban *et al.*, 1996). However, the majority of these studies have focused on factors influencing the process of new product development; relatively few studies have explored factors influencing the process of new product adoption, such as the relationship between innovation-related characteristics and consumer-related characteristics.

Much research on innovation-related characteristics in marketing originates from the "characteristics" approach suggested by Lancaster (1966, 1971, 1990), such as the laddering methods (Reynolds and Gutman, 1988) and the association pattern technique (Ter Hofstede *et al.*, 1998). This approach sees products as describable by a vector of characteristics, at least some of which are, in principle, measurable. For example, the quality of cars can be measured by top speed and acceleration, space, fuel consumption, safety standards, etc. (von Tunzelmann and Wang, 2007). The "quality ladder" amounts to arranging this vector of characteristics on an ascending scale as one proceeds upmarket (e.g. Grossman and Helpman, 1991). However, such quality ladders may be difficult to rank, as consumers are heterogeneous in their preferences and characteristics. The same product characteristics might have different effects on consumers with different characteristics. For example, it is found that the inclusion of novel attributes such as Alpine Class fill for a down jacket dramatically affects customers' preferences for premium-priced brands (Carpenter *et al.*, 1994), but not for other brands.

A number of consumer-related characteristics are found to be critical for new product adoption, such as consumer innovativeness and lifestyle. Rogers (2003) defines consumer innovativeness as "the degree to which an individual is relatively early in adopting new ideas than other members of a social system". He measures consumer innovativeness by the behavioral profiles of different adopters. These include socioeconomic status, personality variables, and communication behavior. For example, innovators are defined as venturesome; they are resourceful, knowledgeable and risk-seeking. Early adopters are defined as respectable; they are opinion leaders with sound judgment and a responsible attitude. Next, the early majority are defined as deliberate; they are cautious but positive. The late majority are defined as skeptical; they have limited resources and avoid uncertainty. Finally, laggards are defined as traditional; they are local and isolated, and the past is their main reference point. Another definition of consumer innovativeness, proposed by Hirschman (1980), is "the degree to which an individual makes innovation decisions independently of the communicated experience of others" and "the desire to seek out information about innovations". Two dimensions are used to measure consumer innovativeness, namely, consumer independent judgment making (CIJM) and consumer novelty seeking (CNS).

Consumer lifestyle is also found to significantly influence consumer responses to innovations (see Zhu et al., 2009). Lifestyle as a criterion has been adopted broadly by companies to segment their markets and position their new products. For example, Motorola, Inc. introduced a series of portable cellular phones for consumers with different lifestyles in 1996. In 2006, Standard Chartered launched a new lifestyle credit card specially tailored to young professionals with adventurous and outgoing lifestyles. New product attributes can be divided into functional attributes (those concerning the functional qualities of the product) and hedonic attributes (those delivering hedonic benefits) (Snelders and Schoormans, 2001). For example, "punctuality" is a functional attribute of an alarm clock, while "elegance" is a hedonic attribute. Consumers with different lifestyles tend to prefer different new product characteristics.

According to Kivetz and Simonson (2002), functional attributes are conceptually related to necessities and hedonic attributes are conceptually related to luxuries. Similarly, Berry (1994) proposes a "principle of precedence" to argue that there is a moral obligation to fulfill needs first before looking to fulfill luxuries. Thus, the relative importance of functional versus hedonic product attributes changes as one "moves up" economically and socially. In other words, for some consumers, having additional new product characteristics enables them to extract greater utility from the product and hence greater satisfaction; for some others, adding new product characteristics may be undesirable, pointless and hence a waste of time and money (see Thompson et al., 2005).

Having discussed the implications of the relationship between innovation-related and consumer-related characteristics for innovation adoption, the next section will discuss the stages that consumers typically go through when they adopt an innovation.

6.3 Consumer Adoption Process of Innovations

As we have already discussed, superior products are characterized not only by technological superiority, but also by marketing superiority. For consumers, technological properties are complex and "cold". In order for a new technological product to be accepted by the majority of consumers, it needs to connect with people at an emotional level. In other words, superior products combine both technological advantages (through innovations or patents) and an emotional link with consumers (through successful branding). For example, Microsoft uses the slogan "Your Potential, Our Passion" to convey both technical superiority and an emotional connection with consumers. Other examples include Toyota's slogan "Oh, What a Feeling!"; Viagra's advertising runs "Makes Me Feel Like Myself Again"; and Gillette claims that it is "The Best a Man Can Get". Branding strategy such as this helps build consumers' belief in the brand, which in turn positively influences their attitude towards the brand and eventually their adoption intention.

Belief and attitude are the key psychological attributes of consumers. They are a person's consistent favorable or unfavorable evaluations and tendencies towards an object or idea. The process of a consumer's innovation decision begins with belief, through to attitude, intention, and finally to purchase and use. Specifically, consumers go through five stages in their innovation-decision process:

- Knowledge: an individual learns of the innovation's existence and gains some understanding of how it functions;
- Persuasion: an individual forms a favorable or unfavorable attitude toward the innovation;
- Decision: an individual engages in activities that lead to a choice to either adopt or reject the innovation;

- Implementation: an individual puts the innovation into use; and
- Confirmation: an individual seeks reinforcement of the innovation decision that has already been made after being exposed to additional information, initial use or trial.

It would be untruthful to say that this process is a solely rational process. In reality, this process is far more obtuse. When consumers make decisions about a purchase, they may use shortcuts; they may use feelings rather than reason. Most importantly, they often do not know why they make the decisions they make, although they may justify their decisions with retrospect. For example, why do people prefer bottled water to tap water despite knowing that both have very similar contents? Perhaps subconsciously water is a purifying ritual; it goes beyond the basic function of quenching thirst to the spiritual function of cleansing one's body and mind, and bottled water fits in with this spiritual function of water better than tap water does.

The example of water illustrates that a product has human-like qualities that people can associate with emotionally. Technological products are not just functional; they provide emotional satisfaction as well. For example, a mobile phone was advertised by Sony Ericsson as connecting people and showing two beautiful babies from different parts of the world embracing. The key message is that a Sony Ericsson mobile phone connects people. In contrast, Motorola's mobile phone advertisements showed an eagle spreading its wings and flying high in the sky. The key message here is that a Motorola phone gives you freedom. Very different images are being used to market the same product by targeting different emotional needs. These messages that tap into people's inner desires are powerful persuaders that move consumers from one stage to the next in their innovation-decision process.

Different individuals move through this process at different speeds, influenced by a number of factors such as their innovativeness or lifestyle and advertising messages, as already discussed. It was also shown earlier that innovation-related characteristics may not be appreciated by all consumers, as their needs are different. The next section will discuss further as to why some products, if they are perceived as "really-new" by the consumer, may in fact put consumers off buying them.

6.4 Product Newness and the "Curse of Innovation"

Various definitions exist for what makes a product "really-new", focusing on chronological, technological or psychological newness. Booz, Allen & Hamilton (1982) distinguishes products that are "new to the market" from those that are "new to the firm". Goldenberg *et al.* (2001) find that moderately-new-to-market products are more successful than really-new products.

Consumer researchers have focused on the negative aspect of newness, i.e. the psychological newness. This negative effect of psychological newness on innovation adoption derives from the inapplicability of existing category knowledge to understand the new product (Moreau *et al.*, 2001; Wood and Lynch, 2002). Hoeffler (2003) argued that, compared to incrementally-new products, really-new products make consumers uncertain of their ability to estimate their consumption utility prior to purchase; and that, for really-new products compared to incrementally-new products, consumers perceive:

- greater ability to do things that one cannot easily do with existing ways;
- greater uncertainty about their benefits;
- greater uncertainty about cost-benefit tradeoffs; and
- greater need to change one's behavior in order to attain the potential benefits.

By this definition, psychological newness is not a matter of chronological age. For instance, streaming TV and flat-screen plasma TV were introduced at roughly the same time in 1997. However, a longitudinal study of real consumers of 22 new communication and entertainment products by Alexander *et al.* (2008) showed that streaming TV is perceived as higher in psychological newness by those who have never owned but plan to acquire one in the near future.

This is because it allows consumers to do new things, but the benefits and cost-benefit tradeoffs are uncertain, and significant behavioral change is required to enjoy the benefits. On the other hand, the benefits of flat-screen plasma TV are relatively certain and consumers do not think they will have to change their behavior to enjoy the benefits.

Other examples of really-new products at the time of their introduction into the market include computed tomography (CT) scanners, digital cameras, genetically modified (GM) food, Segway scooters, Dryel (a home dry cleaning device), 3G mobile phones and so on. The Segway scooter was hyped by sophisticated investors such as Jeff Bezos of Amazon.com. Steve Jobs predicted that cities would be built to accommodate the computer-controlled, self-balancing human transporter, and John Doerr predicted that Segway would make its first billion dollars faster than any company in history. The Segway scooter was released for sale in 2002, but by the summer of 2004, less than 10,000 units had been sold (Foust, 2006). Segway's experience typifies the issues firms face in marketing really-new products and in measuring demand. Like many firms launching technologically new products, Segway failed to consider how hard it would be for consumers to estimate how useful a really-new product would be for them. When the CT scanner was first invented by EMI, specialists estimated a miniscule market size, but failed to understand the potential and entirely new benefits that this really-new product was about to offer. The CT scanner went on to revolutionize the healthcare sector worldwide.

For companies, measuring market demand for this type of product is difficult. This is because traditional market research techniques that rely on consumers' recall of past experience with similar products cannot be reliably applied, as consumers have no previous experience or knowledge with a really-new product. New techniques such as mental simulation and analogical thinking are required to more accurately measure preferences under an accelerated new product learning environment (see Urban *et al.*, 1996).

An added difficulty in measuring the demand for really-new products is the in-built biases of both the consumers and the companies. To make matters worse, they are biased in opposite directions. As we have already discussed, the adoption of such an innovation often requires significant behavioral change. However, consumers tend to psychologically overweigh what they are being asked to give up (i.e. the benefit of the current status quo) relative to what they will get (i.e. the benefit of the new alternative). In contrast, developers tend to psychologically overweigh the benefit of their innovation relative to the benefit of the current alternative. The result is a clash of perspectives, i.e. the so-called "curse of innovation" (see Gourville, 2005).

Such a problem can be explained using the prospect theory (Kahneman and Tversky, 1979). This theory states that the benefits being given up will loom larger than the benefits to be gained by a factor of two or three. Similarly, the new costs encountered will loom larger than the old costs now avoided. For example, Dryel was a really-new product developed by Procter & Gamble. It was launched in September 1999 as a radical at-home alternative to dry cleaning. However, despite the new benefits of cheap and convenient dry cleaning that it promised to deliver, there existed much natural fear and skepticism associated with this "new to the world" category and sales were extremely disappointing in the first few years. Based upon key consumer insights, the company launched a major campaign named "Habits" (indicating the breaking up of the deeply seeded dry cleaning habit) to educate consumers on the functional benefits and relevance of Dryel as well as to ease their fears.

Moreover, this tendency to underweigh the new benefits and overweigh the new costs of really-new products is exacerbated by the passage of time. In a study by Wang *et al.* (2008) on the adoption intention of an entirely new mobile feedback service, participants were given a description of the new service and were then asked to evaluate the service for possible adoption. Half of the participants were assigned a near-term condition (i.e. "Imagine you will have the new service available to use tomorrow."), and the other half were assigned a distant-time condition (i.e. "Imagine you will have the new service available to use in six months' time."). In both conditions, participants were asked to evaluate the new service in terms of benefit and cost. However, it turned out that the weightings they gave to these two elements changed with the time frame of possible adoption: benefits mattered more when consumers thought of possible adoption in the future, whereas cost mattered more when consumers thought of possible adoption tomorrow. Put differently, as it gets closer to crunch time (i.e. the purchase), the perceived new benefits of a new product become less important as a factor, whereas the perceived costs of the new product become a salient factor in consumers' adoption decision.

With regard to the temporal distance and psychological newness, Alexander *et al.* (2008) found that not only were consumers less likely to form purchase intentions for really-new products than for incrementally-new products; among those consumers who had formed an intention to buy a really-new product, fewer of them would actually follow through on their intentions than those consumers who had formed an intention to buy an incrementally-new product. This greater dropout rate for really-new products compared to that for incrementally-new products can be explained using temporal construal theory (Liberman and Trope, 1998; Trope and Liberman, 2000). Compared to incrementally-new products, really-new products are higher in desirability but lower in feasibility (because significant change in behavior is necessary to attain the potential benefits). Construal theory states that people represent temporally distant actions in terms of their abstract, high-level considerations, i.e. their desirability. They represent more near-term actions in terms of their concrete, low-level considerations, i.e. their feasibility. In other words, the high desirability of really-new products becomes less important as the purchase draws near, whereas the low feasibility of really-new products becomes a salient factor when the time comes to buy the new product, thus resulting in a lower follow-through rate for really-new products than for incrementally-new products.

In this section, the negative effect of perceived product newness has been discussed. At the same time, it is important to note that perceived product newness also has a number of positive effects on adoption intention. In particular, product newness was found to be positively correlated to the amount of word of mouth (WOM) generated by consumers (Moldovan *et al.*, 2006). It was found that perceived product newness or originality increases consumers' willingness to exchange information about the product (the amount of WOM), and that WOM decreases over time as consumers get used to the product and it no longer appears to be novel or original. The challenge for managers thus lies in the ability to best utilize the positive effects of perceived newness, whilst avoiding or reducing the negative effects of perceived newness. For example, WOM induced by perceived newness may be used as an effective way to raise consumers' awareness of and trust in the new product before the new product launch (i.e. in a temporal distance), while also positioning the new product closer to an existing category (e.g. position the digital camera closer to the analog camera) when the new product is introduced into the market.

WOM is often discussed in the social context of new product diffusion (see Arndt, 1967; Herr *et al.*, 1991). Since new product adoption is characterized by high perceived uncertainty, individuals considering such adoption often seek advice and information from their social networks to assist them in their evaluation of the new product's benefits, features and costs. Additionally, positive product WOM is a major consequence of consumption satisfaction (Anderson, 1998). The next section will discuss factors influencing the consumption experience and the extent of usage of new technological products after the purchase.

6.5 Consumption Experience and Usage

Consumers spend heavily on technology, yet little is known about what drives the extent of their usage over time and their consumption experience. The success of an innovation ultimately depends on consumers' acceptance and sufficient use of that innovation — not necessarily the easiest thing for firms to ensure. Customers who buy a product and use it less than expected will be less inclined to invest further in the technology (Farley *et al.*, 1987). Many consumers, for example, buy the latest consumer technology products, encounter difficulty using them, and then stash them in the back of closets and drawers, pass them on to friends, or sell them to others through online sites like eBay.com and Craigslist.org (Hafner, 2003). A quick search of consumer technology product listings on eBay one afternoon in mid-March 2009 found nearly 60,000 listings for products described as "like new", and nearly 19,000 listings for products described as having been used little or not at all. For the firms behind these products, having a product that is purchased but not used as expected will lead to negative WOM, which will dampen others' purchases (Anderson, 1998; Moldovan *et al.*, 2006).

The link between consumption experience and usage can be studied from both cognitive and affective perspectives. From a cognitive perspective, initial users of a particular new technological product may feel that they have developed non-transferable, product-specific skills. Having invested time and energy to become competent in one technological consumer product, consumers may want to capitalize on the product-specific skills by further increasing the usage level of that product (Hoch and Deighton, 1989). From an affective perspective, the experience of early use of technologically new products evokes both positive and negative emotions in consumers that significantly influence their evaluation of the product and intention for further use (Wood and Moreau, 2006; Mick and Fournier, 1998).

Many factors may affect a customer's satisfaction with their consumption experience. Wood and Moreau (2006) show that 48% of potential digital camera buyers delayed purchase because of perceived usage difficulty, and that 30% of home networking products were returned because of actual usage difficulty. If consumers are not able to use a new purchase as much as they would have liked due to usage difficulties, they will be discouraged in future adoption, thus slowing down the diffusion process. Additionally, when using new technologies, consumers experience many emotions. Exploratory research conducted by Mick and Fournier (1998) indicates that consumers' responses to technological products may be characterized by paradoxes, e.g. control/chaos and freedom/enslavement. The conflict and ambivalence precipitated by paradoxes lead, in turn, to anxiety and stress.

In an empirical study, Wang *et al.* (2010) found that one's initial goal orientation leads individuals to follow two distinct usage paths: one toward increasing usage, and the other toward decreasing usage or even disuse. Specifically, because individuals with an approach goal orientation perceive the new product use as a challenge, this construal is likely to generate excitement, encourage affective and cognitive investment, and facilitate great concentration and task absorption during product use. In contrast, people with an avoidance goal orientation perceive the new product as fearful or a threat; this construal in turn elicits anxiety and encourages great self-protective withdrawal of affective and cognitive resources from further product use.

Additionally, because new and technologically complex products are characterized by high uncertainty about the value of new benefits, consumers will likely encounter unexpected joys, frustrations and surprises when they start using the product. Wang *et al.* (2010) found that individuals with an avoidance goal orientation tend to focus on the negative aspects of product-relevant information, likely generating negative emotional responses. Individuals with an approach goal orientation, on the other hand, focus on the positive aspects of product-relevant information, likely generating positive emotional responses. Moreover, positive and negative emotional responses such as surprises are found to be correlated respectively to positive and negative WOM recommendations to others. The implication of these findings for companies is that they must have measures in place in their after-sales service to effectively deal with consumers' negative affects generated from their consumption experience, in order to avoid damage to the company brand or reputation and to create a more positive overall experience for customers. In addition, marketing communication may be tailored to trigger a stronger approach goal orientation mindset among customers in order to encourage greater product use after the purchase.

6.6 Conclusions

This chapter has discussed several important and relevant issues concerning consumer responses to innovations. The important relationship between innovation-related characteristics and consumer-related characteristics for innovation adoption has been examined. It has been shown that superior products combine both technological advantages, gained through innovations or patents, and an emotional link with consumers through successful branding. It has been confirmed that different individuals move through the innovation adoption process at different speeds, influenced by factors such as their innovativeness or lifestyle and marketing communication messages. The negative effect of psychological newness on innovation adoption was examined, and several examples of really-new products were provided. Really-new products are characterized by high psychological newness, i.e. the inapplicability of existing category knowledge to understand the new products. Problems with forecasting and measuring really-new products have, in many instances, resulted in innovation failures. A number of specific causes for the difficulties in measuring consumer demand were investigated, and these include the in-built biases of both consumers and producers in their evaluation of the new product benefits and costs as well as the effect of temporal construal on consumers' adoption intention. The positive effect of perceived product newness on innovation adoption was also noted in relation to its effect on WOM communication. Finally, the importance of the consumption experience for innovation adoption, and the link between consumption experience and the extent of usage, was discussed. The importance of consumption experience is twofold: it allows consumers to extract utility from the product they have purchased; and it results in either consumption satisfaction or disappointment, which in turn influences their future adoption intention and the adoption intention of those around them through WOM communication.

Several important managerial implications have been derived from this chapter. These include matching consumer lifestyle with new product characteristics (Section 6.2); designing brand strategy to combine both technical superiority and emotional appeal (Section 6.3); measuring and positioning really-new products effectively (Section 6.4); and using marketing communication to stimulate greater product use (Section 6.5).

References

Alexander, D.L., Lynch, J.G. Jr. and Wang, Q. (2008). As time goes by: do cold feet follow warm intentions for really new versus incrementally new products? *Journal of Marketing Research*, 45(3), 307–319.

Anderson, E.W. (1998). Customer satisfaction and word of mouth. *Journal of Service Research*, 1(1), 5–17.

Arndt, J. (1967). Role of product-related conversations in the diffusion of a new product. *Journal of Marketing Research*, 4(3), 291–295.

Berry, C.J. (1994). *The Idea of Luxury*. Cambridge: Cambridge University Press.

Booz, Allen & Hamilton. (1982). *New Product Management for the 1980s*. New York: Booz, Allen & Hamilton, Inc.

Carpenter, G.S., Glazer, R. and Nakamoto, K. (1994). Meaningful brands from meaningless differentiation: the dependence on irrelevant attributes. *Journal of Marketing Research*, 31(3), 339–350.

Deighton, J.A. and Kornfeld, L. (2007). Digital interactivity: unanticipated consequences for markets, marketing and consumers. HBS Working Papers. Available at http://www.hbs.edu/research/pdf/08-017.pdf/.

Farley, J.U., Kahn, B., Lehmann, D.R. and Moore, W.L. (1987). Modeling the choice to automate. *Sloan Management Review*, 28(2), 5–15.

Foust, J. (2006). Of Segways and space. Available at http://www.thespacereview.com/article/636/1/ (accessed June 5, 2006).

Gatignon, H. and Robertson, T. (1985). A propositional inventory for new diffusion research. *Journal of Consumer Research*, 11(4), 849–867.

Goldenberg, J., Lehmann, D.R. and Mazurski, D. (2001). The idea itself and the circumstances of its emergence as predictors of new product success. *Management Science*, 47(1), 69–84.

Gourville, J. (2005). The curse of innovation: why innovative new products fail. MSI Working Paper No. 05-117.

Grossman, G.M. and Helpman, E. (1991). *Innovation and Growth in the Global Economy*. Cambridge, MA: MIT Press.

Hafner, K. (2003). Seductive electronic gadgets are soon forgotten. *The New York Times*, October 15, p. C2.

Herr, P.M., Kardes, F.R. and Kim, J. (1991). Effects of word-of-mouth and product-attribute information on persuasion: an accessibility-diagnosticity perspective. *Journal of Consumer Research*, 17(4), 454–462.

Hirschman, E.C. (1980). Innovativeness, novelty seeking, and consumer creativity. *Journal of Consumer Research*, 7(3), 283–295.

Hoch, S.J. and Deighton, J. (1989). Managing what consumers learn from experience. *Journal of Marketing*, 53(2), 1–20.

Hoeffler, S. (2003). Measuring preferences for really new products. *Journal of Marketing Research*, 40(4), 406–420.

Kahneman, D. and Tversky, A. (1979). Prospect theory: an analysis of decision under risk. *Econometrica*, 47(2), 263–291.

Kivetz, R. and Simonson, I. (2002). Earning the right to indulge: effort as determinant of customer preferences towards frequency program rewards. *Journal of Marketing Research*, 39(2), 155–169.

Lancaster, K.J. (1966). A new approach to consumer theory. *Journal of Political Economy*, 74, 132–157.

Lancaster, K.J. (1971). *Consumer Demand: A New Approach.* New York: Columbia University Press.

Lancaster, K.J. (1990). The economics of product variety: a survey. *Marketing Science*, 9(3), 189–206.

Liberman, N. and Trope, Y. (1998). The role of feasibility and desirability considerations in near and distant future decisions: a test of temporal construal theory. *Journal of Personality and Social Psychology*, 75(1), 5–18.

Mick, D.G. and Fournier, S. (1998). Paradoxes of technology: consumer cognizance, emotions, and coping strategies. *Journal of Consumer Research*, 25(2), 123–143.

Moldovan, S., Goldenberg, J. and Chattopadhyay, A. (2006). What drives word-of-mouth? The roles of product originality and usefulness. MSI Working Paper No. 06-111.

Moreau, C.P., Lehmann, D.R. and Markman, A.B. (2001). Entrenched knowledge structures and consumer response to new products. *Journal of Marketing Research*, 38(1), 14–29.

Reynolds, T.J. and Gutman, J. (1988). Laddering theory: methods, analysis and interpretation. *Journal of Advertising Research*, 28(February/March), 11–31.

Rogers, E.M. (2003). *Diffusion of Innovations.* New York: Simon & Schuster.

Snelders, D. and Schoormans, J.P.L. (2001). The relation between concrete and abstract attributes. In: *European Marketing Academy 30th Conference Proceedings, Bergen, Norway*, pp. 1–6.

Ter Hofstede, F., Audenaert, A., Steenkamp, J.B.E. and Wedel, M. (1998). An investigation into the association pattern technique as a quantitative approach to measuring means-end chains. *International Journal of Research in Marketing*, 15(1), 37–50.

Thompson, D.V., Hamilton, R.W. and Rust, R.T. (2005). Feature fatigue: when product capabilities become too much of a good thing. *Journal of Marketing Research*, 42(4), 431–442.

Trope, Y. and Liberman, N. (2000). Temporal construal and time-dependent changes in preferences. *Journal of Personality and Social Psychology*, 79(6), 876–889.

Urban, G.L., Weinberg, B.D. and Hauser, J.R. (1996). Premarket forecasting of really-new products. *Journal of Marketing*, 60(1), 47–60.

von Tunzelmann, G.N. and Wang, Q. (2007). Capability and production theory. *Structural Change and Economic Dynamics*, 18, 192–211.

Wang, Q., Alexander, D.L. and Lynch, J.G. Jr. (2010). After the box has been opened: the antecedents and consequences of new product usage and the moderating effects of product knowledge and perceived newness. To appear in *Advances in Consumer Research*, 36.

Wang, Q., Dacko, S. and Gad, M. (2008). Factors influencing consumers' evaluation and adoption intention of really-new products or services: prior knowledge, innovativeness and timing of product evaluation. *Advances in Consumer Research*, 35, 416–422.

Wood, S.L. and Lynch, J.G. Jr. (2002). Prior knowledge and complacency in new product learning. *Journal of Consumer Research*, 29(3), 416–426.

Wood, S.L. and Moreau, C.P. (2006). From fear to loathing? How emotion influences the evaluation and early use of innovations. *Journal of Marketing*, 70(3), 44–57.

Zhu, H., Wang, Q., Yan, L. and Wu, G. (2009). Are consumers what they consume? Linking lifestyle segmentation to product attributes: an exploratory study of the Chinese mobile phone market. *Journal of Marketing Management*, 25(3–4), 295–314.

Chapter 7

Developing Technical and Market Standards for Innovations

Davide Chiaroni and Vittorio Chiesa

7.1 Introduction

A "standard" is a set of characteristics, quantities or requirements that defines the features of a product, process, service, interface or material (Breitenberger, 1987). Standards can be set (David, 1987) with the aim of (1) identifying and defining in a unique way a product, process, service or material (*reference* standard); (2) ensuring that products, systems or services satisfy at least certain defined characteristics (*minimum quality* standard); or (3) ensuring that a component or subsystem can successfully be incorporated and be interoperable with other constituents of a larger system of closely specified inputs and outputs (*interface* or *compatibility* standard).

In the last 50 years, the number of standards and of organizations supporting standard-setting processes has experienced a dramatic increase in a wide number of industries. The reason for this increase can be searched into evolutionary economy theory (Funk, 2009). Most industries, and particularly those where innovations are based on the development of new technologies, underwent in the last few decades a gradual evolution from an integral to a modular structure for products and processes (Sanchez and Mahoney, 1996; Sanchez and Collins, 1999). This modular configuration of products brought with it market modularity (Christensen and Raynor, 2003) or network markets (Besen and Farrell, 1994), i.e. the presence of a variety of actors involved in single stages of the product development process and where users like to buy different products that are compatible with each other and with those bought by others (Mangematin and Callon, 1995). Technical and market standards (particularly those concerning interface and compatibility between different components and processes) represent a key issue in this evolutionary process, allowing for "a tightly integrated hierarchy" to be supplanted by a "loosely coupled" network of actors assuming a variety of configurations (Schilling and Steensma, 2001; Orton and Weick, 1990).

Setting a standard requires an agreement between at least some of the actors involved — buyer and seller, manufacturer and user, government and industry or users, retailer and manufacturer and users, or any other possible combination (Spivak and Brenner, 2001) — who have to adhere in their activities and interactions to the specifications set by the standard. This agreement can be forced by the presence of an entity (either public or private) or enforced by the government with regulatory power (*de jure* standard), or can be reached through a process involving interactions of different actors on the market (*de facto* standard) (Axelrod *et al.*, 1995; Besen, 1992; Besen and Farrell, 1994; David and Greenstein, 1990; David and Steinmueller, 1994; Ehrnberg and Jacobsson, 1997; Faraoni, 1997; Greenstein, 1997; Lehr, 1996; Malerba and Orsenigo, 1997).

This chapter focuses on *de facto* standards, as (1) none of the actors involved has the regulatory power of setting the standard, and therefore each actor has the chance to play an active role in the standardization process; (2) the agreement between the different actors can be the result of the action of a single dominant firm imposing its standard through exerting its market power, or of fierce standardization wars, or in other cases of a process where competitors agree on a common standard before introducing a new technology on the market; and (3) they are usually the result of a dynamic and interactive process. In other words, if a *de jure* standard is the result of the action of a single entity empowered with the regulatory power, for a *de facto* standard firms in the industry actively participate in the standard-setting process by potentially adopting different strategies and managing a number of complex interactions with other actors. In particular, the chapter studies the process of setting a *de facto* standard by investigating (1) the different strategies implemented by the actors involved in the process; and (2) the dynamics of their interactions from the inception of the technology upon which the standard is based until it hits the market.

The chapter is organized as follows. Section 7.2 revises the literature on standard setting. Section 7.3 describes the empirical setting used for the study, and the results are then presented and discussed at length in Section 7.4. Finally, Section 7.5 draws some conclusions and provides suggestions for future research.

7.2 Standard Setting: A Literature Review

Several contributions in literature have studied *de facto* standardization and the strategies companies may adopt to actively participate in the standardization process.

A first stream of literature discusses the role of network externalities (Besen and Farrell, 1994; Katz and Shapiro, 1985; Lehr, 1996; Greenstein, 1997; Faraoni, 1997; Besen, 1992; David, 1992; Langlois and Robertson, 1992; Liebowitz and Margolis, 1994; Kogut *et al.*, 1995) in triggering the process of standard setting. Network externalities can be divided into two-way externalities and one-way externalities (Osterberg and Thomson, 1998). A typical example of the former is that of fax machines. If only one user owns a fax machine, there is not any real value deriving from the ownership; but if a second machine arrives on the market, the first owner increases its benefits as he/she can then send and receive faxes. Each additional machine will increase the benefits for all of the previous owners. One-way externalities are well represented by the example of credit cards. In such a case, it is necessary to further distinguish between two different categories of users: payers and payees. The value the payers expect to derive depends directly on the increase in the number of payees and only indirectly on the increase in the number of payers; for payees, the opposite is true. Hence, the externalities are only one-way because each character in the market has a well-defined role and his/her benefits depend only on the behavior of the other category of

218   *D. Chiaroni and V. Chiesa*

characters, having himself/herself very few possibilities of influencing the payoff.

In any case, firms operating in industries where network external-ities are in place would benefit from the presence of a single common standard, and particularly of an interface standard, allowing all users' products to be interoperable among each other. This increases the value for users deriving from the ownership and the efficiency of eco-nomic activity (Tassey, 2000). Indeed, if competing technologies (or eventually standards) are in place, the value for a user is limited and proportional to the number of other users (i.e. the so-called "installed base") adopting the same technology.

The effect of network externalities in triggering the setting of a standard is even greater when, as for example in the multimedia industry, users must use complementary products (e.g. audio and video storage devices for audio and video players) or invest heavily in product-specific learning in order to use a product effectively (Katz and Shapiro, 1985). In those industries (like in multimedia) where network externalities play a relevant role, the need for a *de facto* stan-dard emerges (Lehr, 1996). Even in such cases, however, there could be contextual conditions that do not lead to the setting of a common standard on the market and that allow several non-compatible tech-nologies to co-exist. This happens, for example, when rather separate market segments are present and comprise enough users to allow single-segment, specialized firms gaining remarkable profits. In video game consoles, the three competing technologies developed by Microsoft, Sony and Nintendo in reality mainly address different mar-ket segments of web gamers, young gamers and adult gamers, respectively.

A second stream of literature relevant for this chapter deals with the strategies followed by firms aiming at actively participating in a *de facto* standard setting process (Katz and Shapiro, 1985, 1994; David, 1987; Jorde and Teece, 1990; Weiss and Sirbu, 1990; Axelrod *et al.*, 1995; Grindley, 1995; Doz and Hamel, 1998; Shapiro and Varian, 1999; Toth, 2001). Even if different authors may use differ-ent terms (and with different degrees of detail) for identifying standard-setting strategies, it is possible to summarize literature contributions into the following classifications:

- Stand-alone strategies, where firms promote their own proprietary technologies as a standard;
- Collaboration strategies, where firms enter into an alliance or coalition to develop and promote a standard; and
- SDO strategy, where firms promote (or enter) a voluntary organization — standards development organization (SDO)[1] — constituted by almost all major industry players (and eventually user groups) that is aimed at setting a common standard mediating among different interests.

In all cases, the firm succeeds only if its proposed standard gains a large installed base of customers to create sufficient network externalities (David and Greenstein, 1990). Other actors in the industry will adopt the proposed technology only if the installed base is large enough, and the "bandwagon" of adoption may or is expected to lock out competing technologies (Katz and Shapiro, 1985; Farrell and Saloner, 1986).

Each of the above strategies (stand-alone, collaboration, SDO) has received a lot of attention in the literature. A summary of their pros and cons is presented below.

7.2.1 *Stand-alone strategy*

When a firm possesses enough competencies and resources or exerts a dominant power over an industry (Katz and Shapiro, 1985; Farrell and Saloner, 1986), it may attempt a stand-alone standardization strategy. There are two main reasons that can lead firms to choose a

---

[1] SDOs — in the meaning used in this chapter — are organizations not entitled with a governmental regulatory power (as, for example, is the case of the International Organization for Standardization (ISO)), but rather have received such power directly from the actors of the industry who contributed to their creation.

stand-alone standard-setting strategy: (1) it allows a strict control over the technology, thus maximizing *ceteris paribus* the appropriability of rents generated by the new product/system or process (Teece, 1986; David, 1992; Grindley and Toker, 1993; Ehrnberg and Jacobsson, 1997); and (2) it may significantly speed up the timing of introduction of the standard (David and Greenstein, 1990; Vesey, 1991; David and Steinmueller, 1994; Bailetti and Callahan, 1995; McWilliams and Zilberman, 1996; Von Braun, 1997), avoiding the delay related to negotiation that is usually afforded because of the long bargaining activity among potential partners.

It is, however, a matter of evidence that the attempt to achieve stand-alone standardization can also have strong disadvantages (David, 1992). First of all, it requires the firm to invest autonomously a great amount of resources in a risky process. Second, it could divert important resources from the core aspects of the technology in an attempt to develop all of the complementary assets and provide the complementary goods needed for a successful standardization (Utterback, 1982, 1994; Teece, 1998). Finally, stand-alone standardization could also increase the inertia of the market. Indeed, potential users, fearing an opportunistic behavior of the firm, could be reluctant in acquiring the technology, thus reducing the overall size of the market.

7.2.2 Collaboration strategy

Alternatively to the stand-alone strategy, a firm willing to pursue a *de facto* standard may look for some form of cooperation with competitors, suppliers, customers or other actors in the industry who could offer resources relevant to the standard-setting process. Some authors (see, for example, Axelrod *et al.*, 1995) suggest distinguishing the standard-setting process into two phases: (1) a development phase, where technical requirements and features are defined to solve compatibility problems; and (2) a sponsoring phase, where products adhering to the now-defined standard are actually marketed. In the first phase, a firm may search for "developing collaborations", with the aim of supporting the definition of technological issues; whereas in the second phase, "sponsoring collaborations" are needed with the aim of fostering (against competing standards) the market penetration of the standard through achieving the largest installed base and therefore exploiting the highest network externalities.

The two typologies of collaboration require different resources and competences, and hence different partners have to be involved (Chiesa and Toletti, 2003). In developing collaborations, as well as in technological collaborations, firms search for (1) reducing the risks and costs of both the technological development phase and the standardization process; (2) accessing more skills and competences, particularly those related to complementary products or components, to make simpler the achievement of a suitable standard; and (3) pre-empting similar actions from competitors and, at least to a certain degree, locking partnering firms to the proposed standard in a potential "standards war" on the market (Gallagher and Seung, 2002).

In sponsoring collaborations, on the contrary, the main driver is the search for increasing the market power necessary to impose the standard once it has been developed. This may happen either (1) directly, i.e. a firm that does not have a large market share may join with some competitors, forming sponsoring collaborations, in order to increase the installed base and, hence, the probability of success of the standard; or (2) indirectly, i.e. collaborations may also improve the credibility to users. In network markets (in which the value for both vendors and users increases as the number of adopters rises), users may fear opportunistic behavior by producers and may therefore delay the purchase of the product until a common *de facto* standard is defined. If more firms participate in a coalition, the risk of opportunistic behavior (i.e. of a "standards war" after the introduction of the product into the market) is significantly lowered. In fact, once the standard hits the market, each firm participating in the sponsoring coalition will start competing with the others with its own products to gain the largest market share. Therefore, if the sponsoring coalition involves a large number of firms, fierce competition is expected on the market, thus helping to maintain low prices and preventing the risk that a single firm will increase prices at will to exploit a monopolistic rent over the standard (Jeanneret and Verdierc, 1996; Wood and Brown, 1998).

Collaboration strategies, however, also have several disadvantages. First of all, particularly in the development phase, firms are exposed to the risk of opportunistic behavior of partners about standard development activities (Axelrod *et al.*, 1995), thus potentially reducing the positive effect of sharing R&D costs and risks over multiple firms. Moreover, particularly if close rivals are members of the same consortium, firms may be involved in fierce price competition on the market after the adoption of the standard. In other words, firms are exposed to the risk that close rivals may gain a competitive advantage at their own expense (Weiss and Sirbu, 1990).

7.2.3 *SDO strategy*

The creation of SDOs (Farrell and Saloner, 1986; David and Steinmueller, 1994; Shapiro and Varian, 1999) for setting a *de facto* standard in a given industry can be seen as an extreme form of collaboration strategy, where the coalition comprises almost all of the key players in the industry, thus ensuring access to the needed resources and competences and achieving enough market power to impose the standard on the market. The aim of SDOs is to avoid competition between different standards (which is unavoidable when different, competing coalitions support their own technologies) through the definition of a common proposal on which all actors of the market can agree. There are different reasons for the formation of SDOs: (1) they reduce the risks and costs of the standard-setting process by spreading them over a large number of firms; (2) they allow the greatest possible enlargement of the installed base, hence favoring the diffusion of the standard and increasing the chances of success of the standard-setting process; and (3) they reduce the risk of an inadequate or delayed development of the market due to users' reluctance in purchasing non-standardized products.

However, the strategy of creating an SDO is the exact opposite of pursuing a stand-alone strategy. It has as disadvantages the low degree of control that can be exerted over the technology by the proposing firms and the potential delay in the introduction of the standard into the market due to the length of negotiations among partners.

In a *de facto* standard setting process, the choice about which standardization strategy to adopt is a key issue, as even the firm's survival is challenged if the strategy fails (David and Greenstein, 1990; Chiesa *et al.*, 1998). As a matter of fact, the loser of the standardization race loses the first-mover advantage (i.e. the benefits of a temporary monopolistic power), and has to spend additional (and potentially relevant) resources in order to bridge the technological and knowledge gap with the winner (Cohen *et al.*, 1996; Tellis and Golder, 1996; Bryman, 1997; Chung, 1999). Furthermore, the loser has to compete within the boundaries defined by the competitor who imposed its standard.

7.3 The Empirical Study: *de facto* Standards in the Multimedia Industry

The study of the process of setting a *de facto* standard is based on eight in-depth case studies of standard-setting processes in the multimedia industry (see Table 7.1). Case study research has been selected because, as suggested by a number of scholars, this is in fact a very powerful method for building a rich understanding of complex phenomena (Eisenhardt, 1989), like standard-setting processes, that requires the capability to answer "how" and "why" questions (Yin, 2003). The aim of this study is to investigate the "how", i.e. through which strategies and interactions different actors participate in the standard-setting process, and the "why", i.e. understanding the dynamics of and the reasons for such choices. Multiple case studies are then appropriate when attempting to externally validate findings through cross-case comparisons (Eisenhardt, 1989). Therefore, they typically yield more robust, generalizable and testable interpretations of a phenomenon than single case study research.

The choice of the multimedia industry requires a two-fold explanation. On the one hand, selecting a single (even if wide) industry allowed us to compare different cases without controlling for industry-specific factors, thus further increasing the robustness of interpretations on the standard-setting process. On the other hand, the multimedia industry is a very suitable environment for studying the standard-setting process of *de facto* standards as it is a complex and challenging environment

Table 7.1. Empirical setting.

Case	Time period	Standards available	Main firms involved	Key points	Result
Videocassette recorder (VCR)	1956–1977	VHS, Betamax	Matsushita, JVC, Sony	A war of standards emerged over the format of VCRs between Sony (with its standard Betamax) and Matsushita and JVC (with VHS). The former attempted to impose its standard on its own, whereas Matsushita and JVC promoted a number of licensing agreements with other producers to rapidly increase the market penetration of VHS.	Both standards reached the market. However, within a few years VHS gained the lion's share of the installed base, thus becoming the *de facto* standard for VCRs.
Compact disc (CD)	1976–1980	Pre-market technologies developed separately by Philips and Sony, and one standard available	Philips, Sony	Philips and Sony agreed in defining a compromise standard (CD) for the next generation of audio data storage devices before entering into the market.	Once marketed, the CD standard gained the strong support of large content providers like Columbia and PolyGram.

(Continued)

Table 7.1. (*Continued*)

Case	Time period	Standards available	Main firms involved	Key points	Result
Operating system software for personal computers (PCs)	1979–1982	MS-DOS, Macintosh	Microsoft, IBM, Apple	Apple attempted to impose on its own a standard (Macintosh) for PCs. Microsoft reacted quickly and, with its MS-DOS, gained the support of IBM, which at that time was leading the PC industry. The sponsoring by IBM convinced users that MS-DOS would be largely diffused in the market.	MS-DOS became the *de facto* standard for PC operating systems.
Instruction set architecture for personal computers (PCs)	1991–1993	Advanced Computing Environment (ACE), 32-bit instruction set architecture	Compaq, DEC, Microsoft, Intel	In an attempt to oppose the diffusion of Intel's 32-bit PC architecture, about 250 firms, led by Compaq and DEC, established a consortium named the Advanced Computing Environment (ACE). The aim of the consortium was to impose a new *de facto* standard based on RISC instruction.	The ACE consortium, due to its size and the heterogeneity of actors involved, was not able to mediate among the different interests and dissolved within a few years.

(*Continued*)

Table 7.1.   (*Continued*)

Case	Time period	Standards available	Main firms involved	Key points	Result
Digital audio tape	1990–1996	Digital Compact Cassette (DCC), MiniDisc	Sony, Philips, Matsushita	Philips and Matsushita developed the DCC system, targeted as a replacement for Philips' analog cassette audio tape system. In the meantime, Sony also developed a competing standard (MiniDisc) based on magneto-optical technologies. Once both reached the market, the two competing standards were hampered by large record companies that refused to participate in later sponsoring alliances.	Both standards resulted in market failure, never reaching an adequate installed base. A few years later, the advent of DVD closed the window of opportunity for digital audio tapes.

(*Continued*)

Table 7.1. (*Continued*)

Case	Time period	Standards available	Main firms involved	Key points	Result
56k modem	1995–1998	X2, K56flex	USRobotics/ 3Com, Rockwell, Lucent, Motorola	USRobotics/3Com, at that time the market leader in analog modems, launched a new standard (X2) for ensuring a higher connection speed (56kb per second). Immediately after the introduction of X2, Rockwell, Lucent and Motorola developed a competing solution (K56flex).	The adverse reaction of the market to the presence of competing standards forced promoting firms to reach a compromise. The agreement was reached by the mediation of the International Telecommunication Union (ITU).

(*Continued*)

Table 7.1. (*Continued*)

Case	Time period	Standards available	Main firms involved	Key points	Result
DVD	1994–1996	MultiMediaCD (MMCD), SuperDisc (SD)	Sony, Philips, Toshiba, Matsushita	The need for a new device for audio and video data with higher storing capacity than CD forced the emergence of two competing standards. Sony and Philips, gaining the support of equipment and device manufacturers, developed a new technology named MultiMediaCD (MMCD). Matsushita and Toshiba, at the opposite end, proposed as a standard the new SuperDisc (SD) technology, with the support of Time Warner and major movie makers.	The competing standards solutions encountered strong reluctance upon market introduction. In 1995, IBM wrote a letter to the "rivals" suggesting a compromise. The coalitions merged into the Digital Versatile Disc (DVD) Forum. A new standard, named DVD, was created and marketed in 1996.

(*Continued*)

Table 7.1. (*Continued*)

Case	Time period	Standards available	Main firms involved	Key points	Result
High-definition DVD	2002–2008	HD DVD, Blu-ray	Sony, Philips, Toshiba, Matsushita	Two coalitions emerged from the failure of the DVD Forum and, led respectively by Sony–Philips and Toshiba–Matsushita, attempted to impose their own standards (Blu-ray and HD DVD) for large audio, video and data storage devices to be used particularly for recording and reproducing movies with digital quality. The coalitions involved a huge number of actors in the industry, ranging from content providers and equipment manufacturers to software firms and retail distributors.	Sony and Philips (Blu-ray) finally won the "standards war" by creating a stronger and wider network of partners.

characterized by (1) high turbulence (Fine, 2000) and high speed of technological innovation; (2) a huge number of actors; and (3) a high degree of modularity, i.e. a huge number of potential points of interaction between different actors.

The analysis is mainly based on 20 interviews with 17 top managers who were directly involved in the definition of strategies for standard setting in their own firms. Interviewed managers belonged to the following firms: IBM, Intel, Lucent, Matsushita, Microsoft, Motorola, Philips, Sony, Toshiba and USRobotics/3Com, most of which were involved in more than one standard-setting process (see Table 7.1). Different interviews were performed in each firm of the sample for each standard-setting process undertaken by the firm and, when possible, different managers were interviewed in regards to the same standard-setting process in order to take into account the points of view of different people. The interviews lasted an average of about two hours each and were based on an open questionnaire that provided the framework for discussion, leaving at the same time the possibility to follow hints offered by the interviewees. The aim of the interviews was to understand (1) the strategies chosen by each firm in each standard-setting process; (2) the reasons for their success or failure, i.e. the key issues perceived in their implementation; and (3) the evolution of such strategies over time, following the development and sponsoring of the standard.

Secondary information was also collected in the form of company reports and project documentation. These provided the researchers with background information about the selected cases, especially the strategies and their evolution over the years. Above all, secondary information sources were integrated, in a triangulation process, with data drawn from the direct interviews in order to ensure information validity (Yin, 2003).

The cases of the 56k modem, DVD and high-definition DVD are presented here (see Tables 7.2 and 7.3, and Figure 7.1) with the aim of providing the reader with more details on the different strategies (and their evolution) of the firms involved in setting a *de facto* standard in the multimedia industry. The overall results of the empirical investigation are discussed in Section 7.4.

Table 7.2. The standard-setting process of the 56k modem.

Industry dynamics	Strategies of key players	
	USRobotics/3Com	Rockwell
1995: The 28.8k modem is the *de facto* standard in the emerging Internet industry. The demand for a higher connection speed, however, clearly emerges.	Starts a stand-alone development of a new technology for ensuring a higher connection speed (56kb per second). The new technology for modems is called X2.	
1996: The market for modems grows significantly.	Completes the development of the X2 technology in collaboration with Texas Instruments. Announces to the market the introduction of the new X2 modem and the willingness to impose it as a standard.	Starts to develop a new technology, named K56flex, in collaboration with Motorola and Lucent Technologies. Enlarges its network to include sponsoring firms like Hayes, Ascend and other Internet service providers (ISPs). The network calls itself the Open 56K Forum.

(*Continued*)

Table 7.2.   (Continued)

| Industry dynamics | Strategies of key players | |
	USRobotics/3Com	Rockwell
1997: The market demonstrates not to appreciate the contemporary presence of two competing standards. The demand significantly underperforms even cautious forecasts.	Attracts relevant sponsoring firms for the X2 technology. Among them are IBM, HP, NEC and ISPs like AOL. The mediation is overseen by the International Telecommunication Union, an international consortium including all major industry players. The resulting standard (56k) is, however, more similar (roughly 70%) to X2.	Promotes a compromise with the competing networks led by USRobotics.
1998: The demand starts growing more consistently, even if not as expected.	Invests in productive and distribution capacity, showing a great confidence in the development of the market. Continues to enlarge the network of alliances, including more ISPs.	Resists on the market with a relatively marginal positioning. Motorola, Ascend, Diamond and Hayes leave the market.

Source: Adapted from Chiesa and Toletti (2003).

Table 7.3.   The standard-setting process of DVD and high-definition DVD.

Industry dynamics	Strategies of key players	
	Sony–Philips	Toshiba–Matsushita
1994: The main Hollywood studios appoint a commission in order to define the guidelines for the production of movies that will be stored on a new generation of CDs.	Develop a new technology, named MultiMediaCD (MMCD), based on the original single-layer architecture of CD and with a storage capacity of 3.7 GB. Gain the support of major equipment and device manufacturers, as the MMCD architecture (being closer to traditional CD) requires only slight modifications to existing plants.	Develop a new technology, named SuperDisc (SD), based on a new architecture joining together two discs (dual-layer disc) and with a storage capacity of 5 GB. Gain the support of Time Warner and major movie makers, partly due to a foreseeable higher storage capacity than MMCD.
1995–1996: Competing standards encounter a strong reluctance at market introduction. SD is threatened by a shortage of playback devices, whereas MMCD suffers from a potential shortage of content (i.e. movies). IBM (together with Apple, HP, Compaq, Intel and Microsoft) writes a letter to the "rivals" suggesting a compromise.	The two rival groups announce their merge into a unique group, named the Digital Versatile Disc (DVD) Forum. A new standard named DVD, based on SD architecture and on MMCD data storage technology, is created with an initial storage capacity of 4.7 GB. The first DVD players and the first personal computers with DVD players appear in 1996, while the massive technology launch begins in 1997.	

(*Continued*)

Table 7.3.   (*Continued*)

Strategies of key players		
Industry dynamics	Sony–Philips	Toshiba–Matsushita

2000:

A high-definition (HD) technology emerges for producing and recording movies with superior audio and video quality. A movie in high definition generates about five times as much digital data as the same movie saved on the first-generation DVD format.

A conflict arises in the DVD Forum, failing to reach a consensus on how to adapt DVD to the new requirements.

2002–2005:

After the failure to compromise on a new standard within the DVD Forum, the introduction of the new high-definition DVD is delayed, whereas market interest for the new standard increases significantly over time.

Leave the DVD Forum, together with Pioneer, Samsung and Hitachi, creating the Blu-ray Founders group. Blu-ray is a completely innovative technology, employing a special blue-violet laser with a very small wavelength and using track pitches (the space between two tracks) of 65 μm. As a result, storage capacity reaches 50 GB.

Enlarge the network of partners for Blu-ray, including Dell and Apple, and later (in 2004) also 20th Century Fox and Walt Disney Pictures and Television.

Present to the DVD Forum (or rather, to its remaining partners), together with NEC and Microsoft, the HD DVD standard. In the HD DVD, data are recorded with a blue laser on supports that have the same size as the traditional DVD and that can reach a storage capacity of 30 GB.

Enlarge the network of partners for the HD DVD, including Intel and later (in 2003) also Universal and Paramount.

(*Continued*)

Table 7.3. (*Continued*)

Industry dynamics	Strategies of key players	
	Sony–Philips	Toshiba–Matsushita
2006–2008: HD DVD and Blu-ray first reach the market in 2006. Only from 2007, however, does the market (particularly for movies) grow at a significant rate.	Sign an agreement with Blockbuster, one of the largest retail distributors of DVDs (both for movies and for console games). Strengthen the relationships with producers of devices, particularly with LG Electronics.	In 2008, after losing consistent market share in the movie and console markets, announce to abandon the production of HD DVD, adopting the Blu-ray standard.

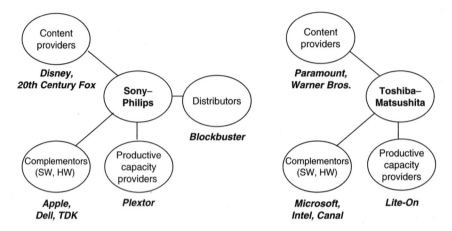

Figure 7.1. Competing coalitions in the standard-setting process of high-definition DVD.

7.4 Strategies for Standard Setting in the Multimedia Industry

7.4.1 *Pros and cons of fundamental strategies for standard setting*

Evidence collected through the case studies allowed us to analyze different strategies of key players in the process of setting *de facto* standards in the multimedia industry. The following results can be highlighted.

7.4.1.1 *Stand-alone strategy*

It appears clearly that stand-alone strategies are extremely difficult (if even viable) to be pursued in the multimedia industry. USRobotics in 1995 tried a stand-alone strategy to impose its own standard (X2) for the 56k modem on the market, but the sudden and at that time unforeseen emergence of a competing technology (K56flex) — developed by a consortium consisting of Rockwell, Motorola and Lucent — prevented USRobotics from reaching a dominant position in the market with its new technology. The struggle between the two standards ended in 1998 through the intervention of an SDO but significantly delayed the introduction of the standard, thus reducing the window of opportunity for exploiting the market potential of the new standard. The same happened in the early 1980s when the attempt by Apple to impose its own standard (Macintosh) for personal computers failed against the Microsoft–IBM alliance, which in fact succeeded in imposing the MS-DOS as a standard for PC operating system software. The quick start of the standard-setting process that was allowed for Apple by its in-house production facilities of all the complementary products (e.g. software, printers and other external devices) was later overcome by the Microsoft–IBM alliance, which was better able to follow the extraordinary growth of the PC market by leveraging its externalized production and a stronger distribution chain. The ability to "catch" the market's growth by creating a network of firms supporting the standard-setting process was also at the foundation of the success in the late 1970s of VHS, developed by JVC and Matsushita, over Betamax whose developer (Sony) attempted to impose the standard by choosing a stand-alone strategy.

The failure of stand-alone strategies can be explained in light of the interviews with managers of firms involved in the above standard-setting processes. Indeed, in order to succeed, a stand-alone strategy requires the presence of three conditions:

- The availability, within the boundaries of the firm, of all the technological skills and competences needed for developing the new standard;
- The availability of complementary assets (Abernathy and Utterback, 1982; Teece, 1986; Tushman and Anderson, 1986), such as competitive manufacturing, distribution, marketing and after-sales support services, for ensuring the diffusion of the standard in the market and a quick reach of a dominant position over the installed base; and
- A high appropriability of the standard for preventing the potential entrance of fast followers (Langerak and Hultink, 2005) with competing technological solutions.

The presence of these conditions is rather rare (or even impossible) in the multimedia industry which, as already mentioned, is characterized by (1) high technological complexity and high product modularity, making it almost impossible for a single firm to master all of the needed skills and competences for developing a new standard on its own; (2) a large number of actors, both in upstream and downstream activities, making rather rare the integration of all activities within the boundaries of a firm and hence requiring the firm to deal with external specialized actors for accessing needed complementary assets (Funk, 2003); and (3) high speed in technological development, reducing the effect of appropriability regimes. These characteristics are now even more evident than they were a few decades ago, thus further reducing the chances of success for firms willing to adopt a stand-alone strategy.

7.4.1.2 *Collaboration strategy*

As far as collaboration strategies are concerned, empirical evidence suggests that developing and sponsoring collaborations — i.e. those mirroring the different phases of the standard-setting process — can hardly be distinguished. Indeed, only in early cases, as for example in the VCR and PC operating system software or in CD and digital audio tape, is it possible to clearly separate the two phases. In the process of setting a standard for CD, for example, Sony and Philips both developed their own proprietary technologies using their traditional supplier networks. When in the late 1970s Sony and Philips started searching for sponsoring partners to introduce their respective technologies into the market, they had to face the resistance of content providers (and particularly of large record companies like Columbia and PolyGram) who were willing to prevent a "standards war" like the one between VHS and Betamax that was in place in the video market segment just a few years before. Sony and Philips then decided to jointly develop and define a common CD standard. This agreement persuaded Columbia and PolyGram to support the CD, providing a rich catalog of music titles to sponsor the diffusion of the new standard. The strong mutual trust among involved firms, along with their huge resources and market power, eventually made the launch of the CD standard a big success. Similarly, in the case of the digital audio tape, Sony (with its MiniDisc) and the development alliance between Philips and Matsushita (with the Digital Compact Cassette) both attempted to replace traditional magnetic tapes with a new digital device. Once they reached the market in 1995, the two competing standards were hampered by large record companies that were not involved in the development phase and that refused to participate in later sponsoring alliances. Both MiniDisc and DCC eventually resulted in failure, never reaching an adequate installed base before the window of opportunity closed with the advent of DVD.

Since the early 1990s, on the contrary, standard-setting processes in the multimedia industry have been pursued through more complex networks of partnering actors where development and sponsoring activities have overlapped more and more. In the standard-setting process for the 56k modem, it took less than six months from the initial development of the K56flex technology, coordinated by Rockwell in alliance with Motorola and Lucent, to the enlargement of the consortium to include Hayes, Ascend and other Internet service providers (ISPs) for sponsoring the future diffusion of the new technology, which at that time was still under development. The overlapping between the development and sponsoring phases is even more evident in the case of DVD, where the two competing standards, MultiMediaCD (MMCD) and SuperDisc (SD), were concurrently developed and supported by coalitions led respectively by Sony–Philips (with the support of major equipment and device manufacturers like Ricoh and Verbatim) and by Toshiba–Matsushita (with the support of Time Warner and other movie makers). In the next generation of high-definition DVD, Sony, Philips, Pioneer, Samsung and Hitachi formed the Blu-ray Disc Association (including also Dell, Apple, 20th Century Fox, Walt Disney Pictures and Television, Sony Pictures and later on the dealer Blockbuster) in opposition to the HD DVD standard proposed by Toshiba and Matsushita (with the support of NEC, Microsoft, Intel, Time Warner, Universal and Paramount).

Interviewed managers clearly identified two reasons for such a shift towards the creation of more complex networks for simultaneously developing and sponsoring the new standard:

(1) The turbulence of the multimedia industry that has significantly increased in the last two decades, and the consequent reduction of products' and standards' life cycle time (Fine, 2000), forcing firms which are willing to impose a new standard to simultaneously manage the development and sponsoring phases; and
(2) The increased size and complexity of the value network (Christensen and Raynor, 2003) surrounding products in the multimedia industry, requiring the firm to consider the claims of all actors in the network since the beginning of the development phase.

Creating and managing such networks, however, is a rather difficult task. A successful collaboration strategy requires:

• The ability to reach a technological compromise that minimizes the "sacrifices" for partnering firms (Jorde and Teece, 1990). Collaborations may involve firms that have just developed their own technology or whose assets are better suited to a certain technological solution (as was the case for MMCD, which gained the approval of equipment manufacturers as it was based on the original single-layer architecture of CD). These firms will effectively support the new standard only if the expected returns clearly exceed the switching costs they would incur for adhering to the new standard;
• A high level of trust and a low rivalry between partners. Each firm aims at increasing its own competitive position relative to that of competitors. Therefore, it could be expected that if the number of direct rivals in the alliance is high, the level of trust and the chances of reaching an effective compromise on a common standard are low. In other words, firms should avoid involving in the coalition close rivals, i.e. firms with similar market segmentation profiles that possess similar technical and market skills and assets (Axelrod *et al.*, 1995);

- A high representativeness of actors in the value network (Christensen and Raynor, 2003). In this respect, firms willing to lead a coalition for setting a standard have to firstly identify the key nodes of the network, i.e. those actors whose contribution is relevant to the value perceived by users. For example, in the case of high-definition DVD, Blu-ray ultimately won the standardization war by gaining the support of Blockbuster, one of the strongest retail distributors in the US market. The contribution of Blockbuster to the perceived value of users resides in the fact that they can find in an easier way, i.e. closer to their homes, products adopting the Blu-ray standard; and
- A high market power of the coalition. The chances of imposing a *de facto* standard, particularly when competing networks are in place, increase with the market power of the coalition supporting a given standard. The term "market power" refers to the absolute size of partners, or to the importance of their brands in the target market, or to the strength of their complementary assets like production capacity or distributive channels.

7.4.1.3   *SDO strategy*

SDOs emerge as an alternative solution for imposing a *de facto* standard when the presence of competing coalitions with a well-balanced power leads to a stalemate in the market. This solution was adopted in the case of the 56k modem once the coalition led by Rockwell decided to join the effort of the opposing alliance of USRobotics through the mediation of the International Telecommunication Union (ITU). The same happened in DVD where, after the intervention of IBM (and other major PC manufacturers) in 1995, the coalitions led by Sony–Philips and Toshiba–Matsushita reached a compromise: to use the EFM technology (adopted in MMCD) for data storage on a dual-layer disc architecture (i.e. that of SD). The compromise was enacted by the creation of an SDO, the DVD Forum, including all actors of the two competing coalitions. The attempt to create an SDO was, on the contrary (but consistent with the premise), a failure in the case of instruction set architectures for personal computers. In less than a year, about 250 firms joined an SDO, the Advanced Computing Environment (ACE), created to impose a new *de facto* standard based on the RISC instruction set in opposition to the strengthening of Wintelism (Borrus and Zysman, 1997), i.e. solutions based on Microsoft's proprietary software (Windows) and Intel's chips. The ACE was unable to mediate among the numerous different interests, with dissenter groups continuously forming that refused to agree on a standard. Obviously, the ACE missed the presence of a key player like Intel (whereas Microsoft participated sporadically in work groups).

The critical success factors of an SDO strategy for standard setting in the multimedia industry, according to interviewed managers, can be summarized as follows:

- A high level of commitment from all participants. Indeed, in highly turbulent environments like the multimedia industry, the effectiveness of an SDO is highly related to its ability to quickly reach a compromise solution. Long-lasting negotiations, being the consequence of low commitment, bring SDOs to failure, as single participants (or subgroups) may find it more effective to risk a stand-alone or a collaboration strategy rather than waiting for the SDO until the window of opportunity for the new technology closes. For example, the DVD Forum, after successfully and quickly agreeing in 1995 on the first generation of DVD, lost the commitment of its participants for the second (high-definition) generation of DVD, who delayed the work of the organization and later abandoned it; and
- A high degree of compatibility among the existing technologies. By definition, an SDO comprises close rivals that are expected to start a fierce competition among themselves once the decision about the common standard to be adopted is taken. If the transition from pre-standard proprietary technologies to the agreed standard involves high switching costs for some of the firms and low switching costs for the others (i.e. if existing technologies are significantly different from each other), the reaching of a final compromise within the SDO is expected to be hampered (Axelrod *et al.*, 1995).

7.4.2 Towards a paradigmatic process of de facto standard setting

It is fairly evident that the process of standard setting, as discussed above, is characterized by relevant dynamics. These dynamics in part are obviously due to the high turbulence and complexity of the multimedia industry, but in part also reflect the evolution of the strategic choices of firms in response to the actions of their competitors. Although there are many differences between cases studied, it seems possible to draft a common path of evolution that may represent a paradigmatic process of how to set a *de facto* standard in the multimedia industry.

This paradigmatic process can be summarized as follows. The process starts by constituting a relatively small consortium of partnering firms with high technological commonalities and/or with a positive track record of past relationships that increases trust among partners. This is particularly evident in the case of DVD, where Sony and Philips as well as Toshiba and Matsushita had already shared their efforts for setting previous standards, as in the cases of CD and VCR. The reason for establishing a relatively small consortium resides in the fact that there is a period of ferment at the very beginning of a standard-setting process, like for any technological discontinuity, when alternative technologies compete within each consortium to emerge as the proposed standard in a context of high technological and market uncertainty (Stuart, 2000). In such a period of ferment, firms tend to reduce the risk of potential technological spillovers or of opportunistic behavior by addressing only a relatively limited number of trusted partners.

Once the bulk of the new standard technology has been developed, standard setters move very quickly to expand their network to include key actors in the industry's value network (Christensen and Raynor, 2003). Indeed, once the specifications behind the standard are open for pushing its adoption within the industry, the initial competitive advantage based on technological knowledge is potentially destroyed and has to be overcome by new competitive advantages in complementary assets (Funk, 2003). In this case, the larger the size of the consortium (i.e. its market power), the larger the chance to achieve a dominant position in the installed base and therefore the chance to win the standardization war. In the case of the 56k modem, a key role was played by the ISPs, who were in fact the direct interface with final users. Similarly, in the case of high-definition DVD, content providers on one side and distributors on the other side controlled the key complementary assets for favoring the adoption of the Blu-ray standard by users.

When a coalition wins a "standards war", *ceteris paribus*, firms constituting that coalition maximize their profit out of the standard. On the one hand, the establishment of a *de facto* standard allows for a more stable development and growth of the market (David, 1987). On the other hand, firms in rival coalitions that adhere to the new standard need to incur usually high switching costs and eventually experience a delay in the access to the market.

Therefore, only when a dominant position cannot be reasonably reached by any of the competing coalitions, like in the case of the 56k modem, can SDOs find their justification in searching for a compromise solution. This results, however, in a reduction of potential profits for participating firms and can therefore be considered only as a "residual" solution, a second best after admitting that direct competition would have ended "at par". Indeed, once the possibility for a new technological discontinuity emerges, like in the case of the high-definition DVD, the process restarts around a consortium of firms unhooking themselves from the SDO.

Although this process has only been observed in a few cases, according to the authors, it may represent an interesting insight into the dynamics of standard-setting strategies.

7.5 Conclusions

This chapter has reported the results of eight in-depth case studies on the process of setting *de facto* standards in the multimedia industry, ranging from the case of the VCR in the early 1960s to the high-definition DVD in the early 2000s. First of all, it investigated the different strategies implemented by firms involved in the process, and discussed at length their pros and cons in light of the experience of interviewed managers. Stand-alone strategies are rather rare, as they are extremely difficult to pursue in the multimedia industry. Firms willing to impose a new standard in the industry mostly adopt a collaboration strategy, taking the lead in complex networks of partnering actors who potentially cover all of the nodes of the value network surrounding the new standard and where development and sponsoring activities are increasingly overlapping. In this respect, it is rather difficult to apply the traditional distinction between standard development and sponsoring collaborations to the multimedia industry. SDOs emerge as a "residual" solution for mediating different interests in cases where the presence of competing coalitions leads to a stalemate in the market.

Furthermore, this chapter investigated the dynamics of the standard-setting process, from the inception of the technology upon which the standard is based until it hits the market, and has drafted a paradigmatic process of setting a *de facto* standard. The process starts around a bulk of trusted partners, who bring to the consortium both key technological competences and the perspectives of critical actors of the value network surrounding the products where the standard applies. The consortium then rapidly expands to include other actors with the aim of gaining a dominant position within the installed base, i.e. of ensuring the highest chances of success for the new standard. Only when this expansion is contrasted by the presence of one or more rival consortia with similar market power does an SDO emerge to compose, at least temporarily, different interests into a common standard. The process, however, restarts when a new opportunity appears for technological discontinuity.

Further research (and a larger sample) is needed to assess the results presented in this chapter, particularly those related to the dynamics of the standard-setting processes. Nevertheless, it contributes to posing the problem and offers some hints for further study in this area. Another interesting avenue for further research concerns the replication of this study in other industries (e.g. mobile communication and financial services), maybe starting with those that have characteristics (in terms of the turbulence of the business environment and technological intensity) similar to the multimedia industry.

References

Abernathy, W. and Utterback, J.M. (1982). Patterns of industrial innovation. In: M. Tushman and W. Moore (eds.), *Readings in the Management of Innovation*, Boston: Pitman, pp. 97–108.

Axelrod, R., Mitchell, W., Thomas, R.E., Bennet, D.S. and Bruderer, E. (1995). Coalition formation in standard-setting alliances. *Management Science*, 41(9), 1493–1508.

Bailetti, A.J. and Callahan, J.R. (1995). Managing consistency between product development and public standards evolution. *Research Policy*, 24, 913–931.

Besen, S.M. (1992). AM versus FM: the battle of the bands. *Industrial and Corporate Change*, 1(2), 375–396.

Besen, S.M. and Farrell, J. (1994). Choosing how to compete: strategies and tactics in standardization. *Journal of Economic Perspectives*, 8(2), 117–131.

Borrus, M. and Zysman, J. (1997). Globalization with borders: the rise of Wintelism as the future of industrial competition. *Industry and Innovation*, 4(2), 141–166.

Breitenberger, M. (1987). The ABCs of standard-related activities in the United States. Prepared for the National Bureau of Standards, US Department of Commerce.

Bryman, A. (1997). Animating the pioneer versus late entrant debate: an historical case study. *Journal of Management Studies*, 34(3), 415–438.

Chiesa, V., Manzini, R. and Toletti, G. (1998). Alliances in standard-setting. Presented at The R&D Management Conference, Avila, Spain, September 30–October 2.

Chiesa, V. and Toletti, G. (2003). Standard-setting strategies in the multimedia sector. *International Journal of Innovation Management*, 7(3), 1–28.

Christensen, C.M. and Raynor, M.E. (2003). *The Innovator's Solution: Creating and Sustaining Successful Growth*. Boston: Harvard Business School Press.

Chung, C.H. (1999). Balancing the two dimensions of time for time-based competition. *Journal of Managerial Issues*, 11(3), 299–314.

Cohen, M.A., Eliashberg, J. and Ho, T.H. (1996). New product development: the performance and time-to-market tradeoff. *Management Science*, 42(2), 173–186.

David, P.A. (1987). Some new standards for the economics of standardization in the information age. In: P. Dasgupta and P. Stoneman (eds.), *Economic Policy and Technological Performance*, Cambridge: Cambridge University Press, pp. 206–239.

David, P.A. (1992). Heroes, herds and hysteresis in technological history: Thomas Edison and "the battle of the systems" reconsidered. *Industrial and Corporate Change*, 1(1), 129–180.

David, P.A. and Greenstein, S. (1990). The economics of compatibility standards: an introduction to recent research. *Economics of Innovation and New Technology*, 1, 3–41.

David, P.A. and Steinmueller, W.E. (1994). Economics of compatibility standards and competition in telecommunication networks. *Information Economics and Policy*, 6, 217–241.

Doz, Y.L. and Hamel, G. (1998). *Alliance Advantage: The Act of Creating Value Through Partnering*. Boston: Harvard Business School Press.

Ehrnberg, E. and Jacobsson, S. (1997). Indicators of discontinuous technological change: an exploratory study of two discontinuities in the machine tool industry. *R&D Management*, 27(2), 107–126.

Eisenhardt, K.M. (1989). Building theories from case study research. *Academy of Management Review*, 14(4), 532–550.

Faraoni, M. (1997). Standard tecnologici e decisioni di impresa. *Economia & Management*, 5, 69–79.

Farrell, J. and Gallini, N.Y. (1988). Second-sourcing as a commitment: monopoly incentives to attract competition. *Quarterly Journal of Economics*, 103, 673–693.

Farrell, J. and Saloner, G. (1986). Installed base and compatibility: innovation, product preannouncements and predation. *American Economic Review*, 76, 940–955.

Fine, C.H. (2000). Clockspeed-based strategies for supply chain design. *Production and Operations Management*, 9(3), 213–221.

Funk, J.L. (2003). Standards, dominant designs and preferential acquisition of complementary assets through slight information advantage. *Research Policy*, 32, 1325–1341.

Funk, J.L. (2009). The co-evolution of technology and methods of standard setting: the case of the mobile phone industry. *Journal of Evolutionary Economy*, 19, 73–93.

Gallagher, S. and Seung, H.P. (2002). Innovation and competition in standard-based industries: a historical analysis of the U.S. home video game market. *IEEE Transactions on Engineering Management*, 49(1), 67–82.

Greenstein, S.M. (1997). Lock-in and the costs of switching mainframe computer vendors: what do buyers see? *Industrial and Corporate Change*, 6(2), 247–273.

Grindley, P. (1995). *Standards Strategy and Policy: Cases and Stories*. Oxford: Oxford University Press.

Grindley, P. and Toker, S. (1993). Regulators, markets and standards coordination: policy lessons from Telepoint. *Economics of Innovation and New Technologies*, 2, 319–342.

Jeanneret, M.H. and Verdierc, T. (1996). Standardization and protection in a vertical differentiation model. *European Journal of Political Economy*, 12(2), 253–271.

Jorde, T.M. and Teece, D.J. (1990). Innovation and co-operation: implications for competition and antitrust. *Journal of Economic Perspectives*, 4(3), 75–96.

Katz, M.L. and Shapiro, C. (1985). Network externalities, competition, and compatibility. *American Economic Review*, 75(3), 424–440.

Katz, M.L. and Shapiro, C. (1994). Systems competition and network effects. *Journal of Economic Perspectives*, 8(2), 93–115.

Kogut, B., Walker, G. and Kim, D.J. (1995). Co-operation and entry induction as an extension of technological rivalry. *Research Policy*, 24, 77–95.

Langerak, F. and Hultink, E.J. (2005). The impact of new product development acceleration approaches on speed and profitability: lessons for pioneers and fast followers. *IEEE Transactions on Engineering Management*, 52(1), 30–42.

Langlois, R.N. and Robertson, P.L. (1992). Networks and innovation in a modular system: lessons from the microcomputer and stereo component industries. *Research Policy*, 21, 297–313.

Lehr, W. (1996). Compatibility standards and industry competition: two case studies. *Economics of Innovation and New Technologies*, 4, 97–112.

Liebowitz, S.J. and Margolis, S.E. (1994). Network externality: an uncommon tragedy. *Journal of Economic Perspectives*, 8(2), 133–150.

Malerba, F. and Orsenigo, L. (1997). Technological regimes and sectoral patterns of innovative activities. *Industrial and Corporate Change*, 6(1), 83–117.

Mangematin, V. and Callon, M. (1995). Technological competition, strategies of the firms and the choice of the first users: the case of road guidance technologies. *Research Policy*, 24, 441–458.

McWilliams, B. and Zilberman, D. (1996). Time of technology adoption and learning by using. *Economics of Innovation and New Technology*, 4, 139–154.

Orton, D. and Weick, K.E. (1990). Loosely coupled systems: a reconceptualization. *Academy of Management Review*, 15(2), 203–223.

Osterberg, W.P. and Thomson, J.B. (1998). Network externalities: the catch-22 of retail payments innovations. *Economic Commentary (Cleveland)*, February 15, pp. 1–5.

Sanchez, R. and Collins, R.P. (1999). Competing in modular markets. Research Working Paper Series, International Institute for Management Development.

Sanchez, R. and Mahoney, J.T. (1996). Modularity, flexibility, and knowledge management in product and organization design. *Strategic Management Journal*, 17(Winter Special Issue), 63–76.

Schilling, M.A. and Steensma, H.K. (2001). The use of modular organizational forms: an industry-level analysis. *Academy of Management Journal*, 44(6), 1149–1168.

Shapiro, C. and Varian, H. (1999). *Information Rules.* Oxford: Oxford University Press.

Spivak, S.M. and Brenner, F.C. (2001). *Standardization Essentials: Principles and Practices.* New York: Marcel Dekker.

Stuart, T.E. (2000). Interorganizational alliances and the performance of firms: a study of growth and innovation rates in a high-technology industry. *Strategic Management Journal*, 21(8), 791–811.

Tassey, G. (2000). Standardization in technology-based markets. *Research Policy*, 29, 587–602.

Teece, D.J. (1986). Profiting from technological innovation: implications for integration, collaboration, licensing and public policy. *Research Policy*, 15, 285–305.

Teece, D.J. (1998). Capturing value from knowledge assets: the new economy, markets for know-how, and intangible assets. *California Management Review*, 40(3), 55–79.

Tellis, G.J. and Golder, P.N. (1996). First to market, first to fail? Real causes of enduring market leadership. *Sloan Management Review*, 37(2), 65–75.

Toth, R.B. (2001). The U.S. standardization system: a new perspective. In: S.M. Spivak and F.C. Brenner (eds.), *Standardization Essentials: Principles and Practices*, New York: Marcel Dekker, pp. 131–148.

Tushman, M.L. and Anderson, P. (1986). Technological discontinuities and organizational environments. *Administrative Science Quarterly*, 31(3), 439–465.

Utterback, J.M. (1982). Innovation in industry and the diffusion of technology. In: M. Tushman and W. Moore (eds.), *Readings in the Management of Innovation*, Boston: Pitman, pp. 29–41.

Utterback, J.M. (1994). *Mastering the Dynamics of Innovation*. Boston: Harvard Business School Press.

Vesey, J.T. (1991). The new competitors: they think in terms of speed to market. *Academy of Management Executive*, 5(2), 23–33.

Von Braun, C.F. (1997). *The Innovation War*. Upper Saddle River, NJ: Prentice Hall.

Weiss, M.B.H. and Sirbu, M. (1990). Technological choice in voluntary standards committees: an empirical analysis. *Economics of Innovation and New Technology*, 1, 111–133.

Wood, S.C. and Brown, G.S. (1998). Commercializing nascent technology: the case of laser diodes at Sony. *Journal of Product Innovation Management*, 15, 167–183.

Yin, R.K. (2003). *Case Study Research: Design and Methods*. Thousand Oaks, CA: Sage Publications.

Part II

Sector-Specific Dynamics
of Diffusion

Chapter 8

Diffusion of Pharmaceutical Innovations in Health Systems

Rifat A. Atun, Ipek Gurol-Urganci
and Desmond Sheridan

8.1 Introduction

Sustained improvements in health depend on the uptake and diffusion of innovative technologies (Cutler and McClellan, 2001). The World Health Organization estimates that half of all the gains in global health between 1952 and 1992 resulted from access to better medicines, diagnostics and application of new knowledge; the remaining gains were due to income improvements and better education (World Health Organization, 1999).

Given the importance of innovations to sustained improvements in health, governments should create a favorable environment for innovation. The creation of such an environment depends on a sound understanding of the innovation process, the factors which encourage or hinder innovation, and the goals and objectives of health systems. Partial understanding of the innovation process, the factors which influence the uptake and diffusion of innovations, and the goals and objectives of health systems may lead to the development of policies and regulations that hinder the innovation process as well as the uptake and diffusion of innovations.

This chapter provides an overview of innovation models, how these have evolved over time and the consequences of partial understanding of the innovation process. We describe health system goals and objectives, and argue why it is important to understand these when formulating regulatory interventions. We present a summary of a systematic review of empirical studies that explore how broad and health-system-specific regulations influence the adoption and diffusion of innovative technologies (in this case, innovative medicines) in health systems. The chapter concludes with a discussion of the findings and policy implications of these.

8.2 Innovation Models

In his review of innovation models, Tidd (2006; see also Tidd and Bessant, 2009) notes the shortcomings of early models of innovation that consider the innovation process to be linear, driven by "technology push" (i.e. a sequence of related R&D initiatives that lead to the development of a new product or process and eventual adoption in the marketplace) or "market pull" (i.e. solutions which are generated in response to a market signal that a new intervention is needed to address a problem). These linear "pull" and "push" models do not adequately capture the nature of the innovation process and the innovation ecosystems within which these innovations occur.

More recent models of innovation look at the innovation process as a whole, and identify that the innovation process is dynamic, discontinuous, incremental, interdependent and highly influenced by a number of factors (e.g. a network of actors, availability of resources, incentive systems and constraints). Using these more recent models and viewing innovation from a more holistic lens, it is possible to see how policies based on a partial view of the innovation process can adversely affect innovation. For example, a partial view that focuses on "technology push" alone may encourage investments in R&D that lead to outputs not valued (or needed) by users. On the other hand, a partial view that focuses on "market pull" alone may lead to the development of products or services that the market wants but risks detachment from technological development, with consequent risks of erosion of competitiveness and technological leapfrogging. Focusing on the "pull" and "push" interaction alone may result in undue emphasis on the early stages of the innovation and an R&D base that has difficulty in translating new discoveries into applicable therapies, as the development of reward systems which encourage the adoption and diffusion of innovations may be overlooked. The creation of an enabling environment which encourages the adoption and diffusion of innovations is critically important to ensure that innovators are appropriately rewarded.

A further problem with the predominant innovation models is that they tend to be generic rather than domain-focused. The innovation process in life sciences, and particularly in the biopharmaceutical sector, has a number of distinctive features that are unique to this knowledge-intensive domain. For example, the biopharma sector is characterized by lengthy product life cycles (on average, it takes 12 years of R&D before a new chemical entity (NCE) is launched to market), high risk due to a high attrition rate in R&D (on average, only one in 100 NCEs that go into development make it to market), high development costs (estimated to be over US$800 million for a product (DiMasi *et al.*, 2003)), high levels of government regulation, multiple stakeholders involved in decision making, and market failure when regulation is inappropriate or partial. Another important feature of the innovation process in the biopharma sector is the "bench-to-bedside" interaction. The ability of physicians to work across a wide range of scientific fields both in the laboratory and at patients' bedsides enables continuous innovation, as new technologies and solutions are developed incrementally over many years during which the effects of existing innovations on the health status of users are observed and solutions incrementally enhanced to address the problems identified (Sheridan, 2006). Understanding these unique features of the innovation process in the life sciences and biopharma sector is therefore critically important.

8.3 Health System Goals and Objectives

The goals of health systems are to improve the level and distribution
of good health, to provide an adequate level of financial risk protection, and to ensure that users are satisfied with the services they
receive. Health systems should deliver effective services and technologies in an efficient manner, but also be equitable and responsive
to user needs. Equity, efficiency, effectiveness and choice objectives
must all be balanced to reflect society's preferences and priorities.
These priorities will differ in different countries, as societal preferences and value systems vary. For instance, the US, with a more
libertarian orientation, emphasizes individual choice; while in many
European countries, equity is an overarching societal objective. In
order to achieve these health system goals and objectives, governments
should encourage the adoption and diffusion of health-improving
innovations and mechanisms that efficiently allocate resources to the
most cost-effective interventions.

A health system is composed of interacting elements that include:

(1) Financing (how the funds are collected and pooled);
(2) Resource allocation and provider payment systems (how the
     pooled funds and other available resources, such as human
     resources, capital investment or equipment, are allocated, and
     the mechanisms and methods used for paying health service
     providers);
(3) Stewardship and organizational arrangements (the policy and
     regulatory environment, and the structural arrangements for
     purchasers, providers and market regulators); and
(4) Service provision (services the health sector provides as distinct
     from the structures within which these services are provided)
     (Atun *et al.*, 2007b).

Policy makers manage these elements through regulations
and incentives to achieve health system objectives and goals. These
elements interact such that changes in one element influence
the functioning of others, creating a complex dynamic system. This

interaction affects the way rules, norms and enforcement mechanisms are implemented to generate system responses. As with the behavior of other complex systems, these responses may not be easy to predict and may indeed be counterintuitive (Atun *et al.*, 2005) — sometimes leading to the opposite effect to the change that was intended. For example, a regulatory intervention aimed at rationing novel technologies or services to reduce costs and improve efficiency may adversely affect equity or effectiveness and indeed increase the overall cost of the health system, if a reduction in service or technology access in one part of the system causes increased utilization of services in other parts. Hence, there is a need for more holistic approaches to policy making, with careful examination of the possible impact of regulatory interventions on system objectives (Atun and Menabde, 2008).

8.4 How Regulation Influences the Diffusion of Innovations in Health Systems

The influence of regulation on the uptake and diffusion of innovations can be explored through a prism of new innovative drugs. In the pharmaceutical sector, an innovation is defined as a technological advance leading to the creation of a new drug or one that enhances the therapeutic value of an existing drug (Wilsdon and Nitsche, 2004). Diffusion occurs when "an innovation is communicated through certain channels over time among the members of a social system" (Rogers, 2005).

Earlier reviews which have explored the diffusion of innovations in service organizations identified that empirical studies in this area were limited in number and narrow in scope, focusing on single factors but not taking into account how broad contextual and health system factors influence the adoption and diffusion process (Greenhalgh *et al.*, 2005). This methodological shortcoming is important because innovations in health systems are influenced by factors such as the compatibility of the innovation with the system, the value added by the innovation in comparison with existing products (Ruof *et al.*, 2002), the institutional or political context within which the innovation is introduced, budgetary constraints and clinicians' behavior (Ferlie *et al.*, 2000; Fitzgerald *et al.*, 2003). Building on earlier reviews, we undertook a systematic review of 389 studies that fulfilled our quality criteria for inclusion (from 74,981 published articles identified). These studies explored how the characteristics of an innovation, the behavior of individual and organizational adopters, the communication process (amongst adopters), factors relating to the health system, and factors relating to the broad context influence the adoption and diffusion of innovative medicines.

We analyzed how the changes in health system elements (financing, resource allocation, provider payment systems, organizational structure and service provision) and regulatory changes influence the uptake and diffusion of innovative medicines (Atun *et al.*, 2005). Both new molecular entities (drugs with active ingredients that have not yet been approved by authorities) and drugs which provide incremental therapeutic advances on active ingredients that have already been approved for market use were considered. These advances might include enhanced compliance, improved safety profiles and new benefits to patient subgroups. A detailed review and the methodology are described elsewhere (Atun and Gurol-Urganci, 2006).

An analysis of diffusion patterns for a new therapeutic class of drugs in 15 countries showed that developing countries[1] had lower diffusion speeds than developed countries. Diffusion speeds were positively associated with per capita health expenditure and negatively associated with price levels (Desiraju *et al.*, 2004).

Many countries have introduced cost containment policies for pharmaceuticals (such as reference pricing, limits on the number of prescriptions, withdrawal of reimbursement, cost sharing, budgetary restrictions, drug delisting and restrictive drug formularies) to change the behavior of physicians and patients. These are explored in what follows.

---

[1]As defined by the World Bank, the per capita income level in developing countries is less than US$9,076 (see World Bank Development Prospects Group, 2002).

8.4.1 *Price regulation*

8.4.1.1 *Direct price controls*

Price controls involve setting fixed pharmaceutical prices. New innovative drugs, even those that are first-in-class, are less likely to be introduced in countries with strong price controls, and if launched the market introduction is delayed (Brouwers *et al.*, 2004; Danzon *et al.*, 2005; Kyle, 2006a). Firms are less likely to launch their products in other markets following launches in price-controlled markets (Kyle, 2006b). Pharmaceutical price controls reduce incentives for research-based firms to develop innovative products (Calfee, 2000, 2001) and may lead to both short- and long-term welfare losses, the magnitudes of which are affected by the price level set and the price elasticity of demand (Vogel, 2004).

8.4.1.2 *Profit controls*

There is limited empirical evidence regarding the effects of profit controls as regulatory mechanisms (Earl-Slater, 1997). Profit controls introduced in Spain in the late 1980s were criticized because they did not lead to reduction in costs and were subsequently abandoned (Darba, 2003). The Pharmaceutical Pricing Regulation Scheme (which sets a maximum profit level for pharmaceutical firms, while allowing them to set launch prices for new medicines) used in the UK — when compared with other approaches — has helped reduce the growth of drug expenditures, enabled annual savings in drug budgets, and created a stable regulatory environment which encourages high levels of R&D investment (Burstall, 1997).

8.4.1.3 *Reference pricing*

Reference pricing (RP) is designed to work as a cost containment tool by imposing a maximum reimbursable price to an insured patient for a given class of pharmaceutical products. It affects the pricing behavior of pharmaceutical firms, which adjust the prices of their branded and generic products in order to preserve access to the reimbursement market and to protect insured persons from additional out-of-pocket expenses (Ellison et al., 1997; Lopez-Casasnovas and Puig-Junoy, 2000; Pavcnik, 2000). Although many countries have introduced RP schemes over the last two decades, most studies which explore the impact of such schemes are anecdotal and descriptive, while the empirically based studies on the subject have been criticized for their methodological shortcomings (Puig-Junoy, 2005). Most of the studies published in peer-reviewed journals that explore RP look at narrow measures, such as changes in aggregate expenditure and utilization, without analyzing the impact that these changes have on the health status of patients (Schneeweiss et al., 1998).

After RP was first introduced in Germany in 1989, the total number of prescriptions initially declined and the market share of generic medicines increased. Expenditure on pharmaceuticals declined due to the changed prescribing behavior of doctors, lower prices and increased patient charges (Lopez-Casasnovas and Puig-Junoy, 2000). But after this initial decline, expenditures began to rise, mainly because of the limited impact on prescribing volumes (Giuliani et al., 1998). This pattern continues in Germany today.

In the Netherlands, RP led to an initial price reduction of branded medicines, but the creation of a guaranteed reimbursement ceiling resulted in generic drug producers increasing their prices to the guaranteed level. Although the market share of generics increased in the 1990s, total savings for the health service were much lower than expected (Koopmanschap and Rutten, 2003). Within one year of introducing RP in Sweden, savings were achieved as the average price of drugs affected by the policy declined by 19% and their market share fell by 3% (Ljungkvist et al., 1997). However, the entry of new drugs to the market was significantly deterred. This led to higher prices which counterbalanced the cost savings achieved (Lundkvist, 2002), and as a result both Norway and Sweden abandoned RP (Mrazek and Mossialos, 2004).

In Italy, RP resulted in an average decline of 7% in prices (Fattore and Jommi, 1998) and estimated annual savings of 1.6% in total drug expenditures (Rocchi et al., 2004). Adoption of the RP scheme in Andalusia, Spain, failed to achieve the expected consumer price competition (Puig-Junoy, 2004), and savings were less than those realized by other cost containment policies, such as wholesale- and pharmacist-margin reductions and negative lists (Darba, 2003). In Europe, therefore, savings resulting from RP have fallen far short of the levels expected, and this has prompted many European countries to introduce additional cost containment measures (Dickson and Redwood, 1998).

In 1995, the Canadian province of British Columbia introduced RP for five therapeutic classes of drugs. Substitutions with lower-cost alternatives led to initial cost savings (Hazlet and Blough, 2002; Marshall *et al.*, 2002; Schneeweiss *et al.*, 2002b, 2003; Grootendorst *et al.*, 2005), but the initial rapid fall in the number of prescriptions was not sustained (Grootendorst *et al.*, 2001). RP appeared to decrease compliance among low-income persons (Schneeweiss *et al.*, 2002b) and reduced the utilization of innovative drugs, but also reduced outpatient visits by these patients (Hazlet and Blough, 2002). When higher-cost prescriptions were replaced by lower-cost substitutes in one study, the rate of physician visits increased while no changes were observed in the hospital utilization patterns (Schneeweiss *et al.*, 2003) — findings confirmed by another study which found no significant change in health service utilization or outcomes (Schneeweiss *et al.*, 2002c). In British Columbia, cost savings resulting from RP were attributed to reduced drug utilization and cost shifting to patients, rather than to actual changes in drug prices (Schneeweiss *et al.*, 2004).

In Australia and New Zealand, the growth rate of drug expenditures declined (Ioannides-Demos *et al.*, 2002) after the introduction of RP. However, the extent to which this can be attributed to RP is difficult to determine, as the scheme was accompanied by other regulatory changes in the health system (Lopez-Casasnovas and Puig-Junoy, 2000).

In the US, the introduction of RP has been resisted because of fears that it may adversely affect patients (Kanavos and Reinhardt, 2003). Drawing on the experience in Germany, the Netherlands and New Zealand, Danzon and Ketcham (2003) concluded that RP in the US Medicare program would disproportionately affect innovative, "on-patent" products and discourage R&D investment, which over time could disrupt the supply of new innovative drugs and erode US competitiveness in pharmaceuticals.

8.5 Cross-Country Price Differentials and Parallel Trade

A comparison of pharmaceutical prices between countries shows drug prices to be higher in Japan than in the US, which in turn are 6–33% higher than the average prices in Canada, Chile, France, Germany, Italy, Mexico and the UK. It is not just prices that vary. Delayed introduction and low initial utilization levels mean that the consumption of innovative medicines in Canada, France, Germany and the UK is about 50% lower than in the US (Danzon and Furukuwa, 2003).

In the European Union (EU), there is no single market for medicines, and price differentials amongst the EU countries have resulted in arbitrage and parallel trade, with leakage of medicines from low-price countries (e.g. Greece) to high-price countries (e.g. UK). In Sweden, within three years of accession to the EU, parallel imports accounted for 16% of the sales of the top 50 products. On average, the prices of drugs subject to competition decreased by 12–19% (Ganslandt and Maskus, 2004) due to the market entry of a large number of firms. Most of the profits from parallel trade accrue to "middle men" rather than to end users or innovators, and this acts to discourage research investment (Kanavos and Costa-Font, 2005). Thus, Szymanski and Valletti (2005) showed that, in industries with high R&D investment, parallel trade reduces incentives to invest and the positive welfare effects of parallel trade diminish.

8.5.1 *Generic entry and price competition*

An analysis of seven countries (the US, the UK, Canada and Germany vs. France, Italy and Japan) confirmed that generic price competition is significantly and negatively associated with the degree of regulation in health systems (Danzon and Chao, 2000). In general, the entry of generics negatively affects the diffusion of innovative drugs, but the extent of impact varies depending on the regulatory environment (Bae, 1997). In less regulated systems such as the US, patent expiry is followed by a rapid market penetration by competing generics and a sharp decline in the price of patented medicines. In systems which administer prices, such as Italy and France, patent expiry results in a more gradual change.

In the US, the growth of managed care and regulatory policies which encourage or mandate generic substitution have led to a rapid expansion of the market share for generic drugs (Kane and Saltman, 1997). Similarly, in the UK, selective reimbursement lists, indicative drug budgets, initiatives to change prescribing behavior and the use of generic names when training medical students have led to a rapid uptake of generics and a decline in the use of off-patent drugs (Burstall, 1997). Increased prescribing of generics was also observed in the Netherlands, where a government-led educational campaign targeted physicians to change their prescribing patterns (Kanavos and Mossialos, 1999).

8.5.2 *Health technology assessment*

Health technology assessment (HTA) examines the short- and long-term clinical, economic and social consequences of the application or use of a particular technology (Draborg *et al.*, 2005). HTA uses economic evaluation to assess whether technologies that have been proven to be safe and efficacious are also cost-effective for the purchaser. This approach, often referred to as a "fourth hurdle" (Freemantle, 1999), is being increasingly used in Europe, North America, Australia and New Zealand to aid priority setting in health systems and to inform reimbursement decisions for new drugs and technologies (Oliver *et al.*, 2004; Hivon *et al.*, 2005).

In the EU, economic evaluation studies are being more widely adopted to assess the cost-effectiveness of drugs and in deciding whether new drugs should be approved for reimbursement. However, these studies seem to have a limited and varied influence on decision making. Thus, in England, where the National Institute for Health and Clinical Excellence (NICE) recommends which of the licensed drugs should be used in the National Health Service (NHS) and issues guidelines on their use, the implementation of these recommendations varies by provider unit and by topic (Sheldon et al., 2004). Typically, new drugs not approved by NICE are not reimbursed and are not prescribed in the NHS. Conversely, the issuance of NICE guidance on the use of a new class of medicines and approval by health authorities for reimbursement (Mace and Taylor, 2003) do not guarantee their use in clinical practice.

8.6 Changes in Health System Financing

8.6.1 Effect of health insurance

Studies in the US demonstrate that health insurance coverage increases the use of medicines (Leibowitz et al., 1985; Hillman et al., 1999; Lyles and Palumbo, 1999; Danzon and Pauly, 2002; Berndt, 2005). In contrast, lack of insurance coverage restricts access to essential treatment (Blustein, 2000), reduces the utilization of prescription drugs (Cunningham, 2002), and hinders the uptake and diffusion of innovations. This is true even where there is a demonstrable need for and physician awareness of the benefits of the innovative drug (Griffiths et al., 1994). Compared to established participants, new enrollees in an insurance plan utilize more pharmaceuticals, particularly expensive and innovative ones (Stuart et al., 1991; Stuart and Coulson, 1993; Gianfrancesco et al., 1994). Medicare enrollees having private prescription drug coverage tend to use newer innovative medicines, compared with enrollees who have no such coverage (Seddon et al., 2001; Lichtenberg, 2002).

8.6.2 Cost sharing

Cost sharing adversely influences the aggregate demand for prescriptions and the utilization of medicines (Lavers, 1989; Harris et al., 1990; Hurley, 1991; Ryan and Birch, 1991; Dustan et al., 1992; Huttin, 1994; Gerdtham, 1996; Johnson et al., 1997; Adams, 2001).

It also leads to a decline in the utilization of essential drugs (Stuart, 1998; Fortess *et al.*, 2001; Schneeweiss *et al.*, 2002a), reduces compliance (Dor, 2004), and increases adverse health events (Tamblyn *et al.*, 2001), particularly for poor patients and those with chronic illnesses (Lexchin and Grootendorst, 2004; Stuart and Zacker, 1999). With cost sharing, the decline in utilization of medicines essential for serious medical conditions is small, as long as out-of-pocket spending is not large (Pilote *et al.*, 2002) and patients' sensitivity to such charges is low (Carrin and Hanvoravongchai, 2003). However, it is unclear from these studies whether cost sharing has a differential effect on innovative and established drugs.

8.6.3 *Drug budgets and prescribing limits*

In general, drug budgets adversely affect the uptake and diffusion of innovative medicines by encouraging the use of generic low-cost (rather than cost-effective) drugs (Bradlow and Coulter, 1993; Maxwell *et al.*, 1993; Von der Schulenburg, 1994) and delaying the introduction of new innovative drugs (Le Pen, 2003). The health effects of prescribing changes due to restricted drug budgets have not been adequately studied, but drug budgets do not always lead to cost savings. Indeed, experience suggests that the number of prescriptions or health expenditure may actually increase (Schoffski and Graf von der Schulenburg, 1997; Schwermann *et al.*, 2003), especially if there are no incentives to prescribe efficiently and effectively (McGuire and Litt, 2003).

Restricting or withdrawing reimbursement for drugs leads to reduced prescribing, substitution of newer drugs with older ones, and increased referral of patients to parts of the health system where these drugs may be accessed (Huttin and Andral, 2000). All of this has a net result of increased overall prescribing and expenditure (Soumerai, 1990; Ross-Degnan *et al.*, 1993). For example, limiting the number of prescriptions for patients with chronic illness can lead to a rapid decline in the utilization of medicines, along with an increase in more costly hospitalizations and use of outpatient services (Soumerai *et al.*, 1987, 1991, 1994). However, as the studies examined used changes in aggregate utilization levels as endpoints, the differential impact of these policies on the uptake of innovative medicines is not clear.

8.7 Organizational Changes

A number of studies have explored the impact of new organizational forms on prescribing patterns (i.e. changes in the prescribing volume, unit cost of prescribing and prescribing of generic medicines).

8.7.1 *General practice fundholding in the UK*

General practice (GP) fundholding was introduced in England in 1989 as part of health reforms aimed at improving the efficiency and responsiveness of the health system. These reforms led to a separation of the planning and purchasing functions from service provision; but also gave GPs the option to have budgets for management, medicines and diagnostic tests, and for purchasing services from hospitals. GPs had an economic incentive to use these budgets efficiently, since they could retain savings for investment in their practices.

Given similar budgets for medicines, GP fundholders reduced both the overall annual cost of prescribing (Bradlow and Coulter, 1993) and the rate of increase in prescribing costs more than non-fundholders did (Wilson *et al.*, 1996, 1997). Savings were achieved through a simultaneous reduction in prescribing volume and cost of per item prescribed (Wilson *et al.*, 1995), increased prescribing of generic medicines (Rafferty *et al.*, 1997), and reduced prescribing volume combined with higher unit cost per prescription (Maxwell *et al.*, 1993). Fundholding GPs used therapeutic substitution and therapeutic conservatism to contain prescribing costs. There was no evidence, however, that they were slower than non-fundholding GPs in taking up innovative medicines (Wilson *et al.*, 1999). Savings associated with the GP fundholding schemes were observed only in the early years; within three to four years of joining the scheme, the prescribing patterns of fundholding GPs converged with those of non-fundholding practices (Stewart-Brown *et al.*, 1995; Harris and

Scrivener, 1996; Rafferty *et al.*, 1997; Whynes *et al.*, 1997). Changes in prescribing behavior were observed in non-fundholding GPs that were given economic incentives and targets to reduce prescribing costs (Bateman *et al.*, 1996).

A major shortcoming of these studies is that none of them assessed the impact of fundholding on the quality of prescribing or on the uptake and diffusion of innovative medicines.

8.7.2 *Managed care in the US*

Managed care — characterized by integrated financing and delivery of services, fixed health care budgets, shift of services from hospitals to ambulatory care, rebates from a manufacturer for inclusion and utilization of its drugs in the formulary, and a number of mechanisms to control health care costs — was introduced in response to rapidly rising health care costs, and has become the dominant mode of health care financing and delivery in the US.

The overall impact of managed care on the cost and utilization of medicines is mixed (Hurley *et al.*, 1989; Schoenman *et al.*, 1997). But, there are no empirical studies which have explored how managed care influences the quality of prescribing relative to innovative medicines, health outcomes and wider economic benefits. Managed care has increased the price elasticity of on-patent medicines (Danzon, 1999). The use of these medicines by managed care organizations (MCOs) does not appear to differ from fee-for-service plans, because new innovative medicines satisfy previously unmet needs and are perceived to help reduce total health care costs (even at the cost of some increase in drug expenditure) (Chernew *et al.*, 1997). Furthermore, contracts between MCOs and manufacturers that incorporate discounts and rebates enable the use of innovative medicines (Murray and Deardorff, 1998). With expanded coverage, managed care may lead to an increased use of new innovative medicines by improving patient access (Weiner *et al.*, 1991), lowering out-of-pocket payments, and enabling greater use of prescription medicines (Davis *et al.*, 1999).

8.8 Service Provision

Medical services cannot be viewed in isolation. Instead, they should be viewed as a network of interrelated activities where interventions in one part of the system result in changes in the use of other parts. Improved access to innovative medicines generally decreases hospitalization rates and overall health care expenditures.

8.8.1 *Disease management*

Disease management requires integrated management of chronic illnesses to improve the efficiency, quality and effectiveness of care. This can enhance patient safety, improve health outcomes and achieve economic benefits, provided that it allows an appropriate uptake of innovative medicines that help to reduce hospitalizations (Sclar *et al.*, 1994; Armstrong and Langley, 1996).

8.8.2 *Formularies*

Formularies define a "basket of drugs" for reimbursement, and are used in most countries as a policy tool to control costs and influence demand (Jacobzone, 2005). The effectiveness of formularies in controlling drug costs is not universal, but instead varies by country and by therapeutic group (Huskamp, 2003). High degrees of restriction limit access to innovative medicines, increase health care utilization and decrease incentives for innovation, all without containing costs (Goodwin, 2003) especially over the long term.

In the US, patients who live in states with closed Medicaid formularies have significantly restricted access to new innovative drugs, including first-in-class drugs (Grabowski, 1988). Conversely, when restrictive formularies are disallowed, access to innovative medicines increases (Walser *et al.*, 1996). For example, in the case of patients who are mentally ill, open access led to a rapid uptake of innovative medicines and an increase in drug costs; but overall health expenditure declined due to reduced nursing home use and enhanced equity, as racial disparities in treatment access were eliminated (McCombs *et al.*, 2004). Medicaid's removal of drug formulary restrictions has led to an increase in the number of prescriptions, physician visits and outpatient visits per person, along with a decline in the number of inpatient hospital admissions (Kozma *et al.*, 1990).

8.9 Discussions and Conclusions

Multiple interacting factors influence the uptake and diffusion of drugs, but no studies have yet explored how regulatory and health system elements interact to collectively influence the uptake and diffusion of innovative medicines. A few studies have analyzed how particular regulations aimed at containing costs influence the prices, utilization and expenditure of medicines. However, the impact of these measures on the diffusion of innovative medicines has not been adequately explored. To date, those studies which have explored the effect of regulatory interventions on the uptake and diffusion of medicines have relied on aggregate measures, such as the volume of medications prescribed and the expenditure for drugs, without analyzing the impact on total health expenditures. Furthermore, by focusing exclusively on efficiency, these studies have not adequately explored the impact of regulatory interventions on other health system goals and objectives, such as health outcomes, user satisfaction, effectiveness, equity and patient choice. They underscore the dangers of a partial understanding of innovation and the adverse consequences of regulatory interventions that do not take a holistic view of innovation and health delivery.

Many cost containment policies have consequences beyond drug budgets alone. Strong price regulation adversely affects access to innovation, as innovative medicines are less likely to be launched first in countries that strongly regulate drug prices; it may also lead to welfare losses in the short and the long run by reducing incentives for research-based firms to invest in R&D to develop innovative products. RP and restrictive formularies negatively affect the uptake and diffusion of innovative medicines. RP especially affects the diffusion of on-patent medicines by forcing down their prices, thereby diminishing the incentive for research-led firms to invest in R&D. Although RP can achieve short-term savings for drug budgets, these savings are not sustained, and health expenditure may actually increase as many patients whose medicines are switched to lower-cost substitutes because of RP may stop their treatment and experience worsening health outcomes.

HTA is being used more widely in developed countries to aid priority setting and to inform reimbursement decisions for new drugs and technologies. However, few studies have rigorously examined the effect of HTA on the uptake and diffusion of innovations. Long delays during the assessment of new and innovative drugs restrict or excessively delay access to them. As HTA is applied very early in a product's life cycle, before there is an opportunity to use the drug in the target population, it inadequately captures the benefits offered by those medicines and creates a disadvantage for innovations whose benefits are delayed.

This demonstrates the risks of partial understanding of the innovation process in the life sciences, as HTA functions as a cost containment tool (rather than as a mechanism used to increase the adoption and diffusion of effective technologies), reducing opportunities for innovations. A recent pan-European study comparing patient access to cancer drugs concluded that delays in HTAs (such as those undertaken by NICE) negatively affected patient care by further delaying the availability of licensed new innovative medicines (Wilking and Jonsson, 2005). There are concerns that the recently established Institute for Quality and Efficiency in Health Care in Germany (Institut für Qualität und Wirtschaftlichkeit im Gesundheitswesen (IQWiG)) may lower the incentives to introduce innovations into the German market and may act as a barrier to the uptake of innovative medicines. Both IQWiG and NICE require cost-effectiveness analysis before a new innovation is made available to patients (Von der Schulenburg, 2006).

This approach has several weaknesses as far as the innovation process is concerned:

(1) The true benefit of new drugs is often not apparent until long after their introduction;

(2) Reliance on limited data from clinical trials and economic models to assess likely cost-effectiveness may be misleading;

(3) A major element of drug innovation results from clinical experience following the launch of the prototype of a new drug class, which cannot be foreseen or predicted; and

(4) HTA has the potential to impact not only the diffusion of a particular medicine, but also the innovation process and the financial mechanisms that generated it as well as potential future innovations that may result from post-launch clinical experience of its use. This approach to HTA appears to contradict the main impetus of European science policies, which seek to encourage the development of a knowledge-based economy through R&D and investment in patents (Atun *et al.*, 2007a).

Hence, we witness a unique feature of the life sciences sector in Europe: while seeking to promote R&D in this area through community-supported research programs, health policies that encourage HTA and cost containment discourage the introduction of new innovative medicines for use (Von der Schulenburg, 2006).

Other policies aimed at cost containment (such as therapeutic substitution and cost sharing) can adversely influence the diffusion of new medicines and, by reducing the demand for necessary drugs, can lead to high levels of adverse health events and higher overall health system costs, because savings achieved from cost-sharing policies may be outstripped by higher outpatient use and greater hospitalization. In contrast, expansion of health insurance coverage leads to an increase in the utilization of pharmaceuticals. But lack of health insurance and reduced coverage create substantial barriers to the uptake and diffusion of innovative pharmaceuticals, deter the use of necessary medicines and undermine equity. Poorer segments of the population, namely, the elderly and the chronically ill, would disproportionately bear the brunt of these polices.

Although disease management programs may result in higher pharmaceutical costs, an appropriate increase in the uptake of innovative medicines leads to fewer hospitalizations, improved quality of care, and therefore overall cost savings and improved health outcomes.

In conclusion, there are major gaps in the evidence base needed to inform policy on the uptake and diffusion of new medicines. Studies that explore how changes in the regulatory environment and health system elements influence the uptake of drugs are too narrow in scope. Most of them focus on narrow efficiency measures (such as aggregate utilization of drugs or pharmaceutical expenditures), but fail to adequately explore the impact of these changes on the uptake of innovative medicines and innovation systems, as well as on other health system objectives such as equity, effectiveness and choice. These narrow approaches reflect a partial understanding of the innovation process in the biopharmaceutical sector and the complexities of translating new knowledge into new medicines.

This review confirms the need for decision makers to adopt a more holistic approach to policy making and regulation. The potential impact of these policies and regulations on health system goals and objectives should be explored carefully. Decision makers must look beyond narrow efficiency measures in one part of the health system (such as pharmaceutical budgets), and consider the impact of health policies on the health system as a whole and on innovation systems in the biopharma sector.

References

Adams, A.S. (2001). The case for a Medicare drug coverage benefit: a critical review of the empirical evidence. *Annual Review of Public Health*, 22, 49–61.

Armstrong, E.P. and Langley, P.C. (1996). Disease management programs. *American Journal of Health System Pharmacy*, 53(1), 53–58.

Atun, R.A. and Gurol-Urganci, I. (2006). Factors influencing the uptake and diffusion of pharmaceutical innovations: a systematic review. Tanaka Business School Discussion Paper, Imperial College London.

Atun, R.A., Harvey, I. and Wild, J. (2007a). Innovation, patents and economic growth. *International Journal of Innovation Management*, 11(2), 279–297.

Atun, R.A., Kyratsis, I., Jelic, G., Rados-Malicbegovic, D. and Gurol-Urganci, I. (2007b). Diffusion of complex health innovations — implementation of primary care reforms in Bosnia and Herzegovina. *Health Policy and Planning*, 22(1), 28–39.

Atun, R.A., McKee, M., Drobniewski, F. and Coker, R. (2005). Analysis of how the health systems context shapes responses to the control of human immunodeficiency virus: case-studies from the Russian Federation. *Bulletin of the World Health Organization*, 83(10), 730–738.

Atun, R.A. and Menabde, N. (2008). Health systems and systems thinking. In: R.J. Coker, R.A. Atun and M. McKee (eds.), *Health Systems and the Challenge of Communicable Diseases: Experiences from Europe and Latin America*, Maidenhead, Berkshire: Open University Press, pp. 121–120.

Bae, J.P. (1997). Drug patent expirations and the speed of generic entry. *Health Services Research*, 32(1), 87–101.

Bateman, D.N., Campbell, M., Donaldson, L.J., Roberts, S.J. and Smith, J.M. (1996). A prescribing incentive scheme for non-fundholding general practices: an observational study. *British Medical Journal*, 313(7056), 535–538.

Berndt, E. (2005). The U.S. pharmaceutical industry: why major growth in times of cost containment? *Health Affairs*, 20(2), 100–114.

Blustein, J. (2000). Drug coverage and drug purchases by Medicare beneficiaries with hypertension. *Health Affairs*, 19(2), 219–230.

Bradlow, J. and Coulter, A. (1993). Effect of fundholding and indicative prescribing schemes on general practitioners' prescribing costs. *British Medical Journal*, 307(6913), 1186–1189.

Brouwers, C.A., Silverstein, M.B. and Wolff, T. (2004). *Adverse Consequences of OECD Government Interventions in Pharmaceutical Markets on the U.S. Economy and Consumer*. BCG White Paper.

Burstall, M.L. (1997). The management of the cost and utilisation of pharmaceuticals in the United Kingdom. *Health Policy*, 41(Suppl), S27–S43.

Calfee, J.E. (2000). The increasing necessity for market-based pharmaceutical prices. *Pharmacoeconomics*, 18(Suppl 1), 47–57.

Calfee, J.E. (2001). Pharmaceutical price controls and patient welfare. *Annals of Internal Medicine*, 134(11), 1060–1064.

Carrin, G. and Hanvoravongchai, P. (2003). Provider payments and patient charges as policy tools for cost-containment: how successful are they in high-income countries? *Human Resources for Health*, 1(6), 1–10.

Chernew, M., Fendrick, A.M. and Hirth, R.A. (1997). Managed care and medical technology: implications for cost growth. *Health Affairs*, 16(2), 196–206.

Cunningham, P.J. (2002). Prescription drug access: not just a Medicare problem. Center for Studying Health System Change Issue Brief No. 51.

Cutler, D.M. and McClellan, M. (2001). Is technological change in medicine worth it? *Health Affairs*, 20(5), 11–29.

Danzon, P.M. (1999). The pharmaceutical industry. Available at http://encyclo.findlaw.com/5880book.pdf/.

Danzon, P.M. and Chao, L.W. (2000). Cross-national price differences for pharmaceuticals: how large, and why? *Journal of Health Economics*, 19(2), 159–195.

Danzon, P.M. and Furukuwa, M. (2003). Prices and availability of pharmaceuticals: evidence from nine countries. *Health Affairs*, Web Exclusive (October), W3-521–W3-536.

Danzon, P.M. and Ketcham, J.D. (2003). Reference pricing of pharmaceuticals for Medicare: evidence from Germany, the Netherlands and New Zealand. NBER Working Paper No. 10007.

Danzon, P.M. and Pauly, M.V. (2002). Health insurance and the growth of pharmaceutical expenditures. *Journal of Law and Economics*, 45, 587–613.

Danzon, P.M., Wang, R.Y. and Wang, L. (2005). The impact of price regulation on the launch delay of new drugs: evidence from twenty-five major markets in the 1990s. *Health Economics*, 14, 269–292.

Darba, J. (2003). Pharmaceutical expenditure in Spain: evolution and cost containment measures during 1998–2001. *European Journal of Health Economics*, 4(3), 151–157.

Davis, M., Poisal, J., Chulis, G., Zarabozo, C. and Cooper, B. (1999). Prescription drug coverage, utilization, and spending among Medicare beneficiaries. *Health Affairs*, 18(1), 231–243.

Desiraju, R., Nair, H. and Chintagunta, P. (2004). Diffusion of new pharmaceutical drugs in developing and developed nations. *International Journal of Research in Marketing*, 21(4), 341–357.

Dickson, M. and Redwood, H. (1998). Pharmaceutical reference prices: how do they work in practice? *Pharmacoeconomics*, 14(5), 471–479.

DiMasi, J., Hansen, R. and Grabowski, H. (2003). The price of innovation: new estimates of drug development costs. *Journal of Health Economics*, 22(2), 151–185.

Dor, A. (2004). Does cost sharing affect compliance? NBER Working Paper No. 10738.

Draborg, E., Gyrd-Hansen, D., Poulsen, P.B. and Horder, M. (2005). International comparison of the definition and the practical application of health technology assessment. *International Journal of Technology Assessment in Health Care*, 21(1), 89–95.

Dustan, H.P., Caplan, L.R., Curry, C.L., De Leon, A.C. Jr., Douglas, F.L., Frishman, W., Hill, M.N., Washington, R.L., Steigerwalt, S. and Shulman, N.B. (1992). Report of the Task Force on the Availability of Cardiovascular Drugs to the Medically Indigent. *Circulation*, 85(2), 849–860.

Earl-Slater, A. (1997). Regulating the price of the UK's drugs: second thoughts after the government's first report. *British Medical Journal*, 314(7077), 365–368.

Ellison, S.F., Cockburn, I., Griliches, Z. and Hausman, J. (1997). Characteristics of demand for pharmaceutical products: an examination of four cephalosporins. *RAND Journal of Economics*, 28(3), 426–446.

Fattore, G. and Jommi, C. (1998). The new pharmaceutical policy in Italy. *Health Policy*, 46(1), 21–41.

Ferlie, E., Fitzgerald, L. and Wood, M. (2000). Getting evidence into clinical practice: an organisational behavior perspective. *Journal of Health Services Research and Policy*, 5(2), 96–102.

Fitzgerald, L., Ferlie, E. and Hawkins, C. (2003). Innovation in healthcare: how does credible evidence influence professionals? *Health and Social Care in the Community*, 11(3), 219–228.

Fortess, E.E., Soumerai, S.B., McLaughlin, T.J. and Ross-Degnan, D. (2001). Utilization of essential medications by vulnerable older people after a drug benefit cap: importance of mental disorders, chronic pain, and practice setting. *Journal of American Geriatric Society*, 49(6), 793–797.

Freemantle, N. (1999). Does the UK National Health Service need a fourth hurdle for pharmaceutical reimbursement to encourage the more efficient prescribing of pharmaceuticals? *Health Policy*, 46(3), 255–265.

Ganslandt, M. and Maskus, K.E. (2004). Parallel imports and the pricing of pharmaceutical products: evidence from the European Union. *Journal of Health Economics*, 23(5), 1035–1057.

Gerdtham, U.G. (1996). The impact of user charges on the consumption of drugs: empirical evidence and economic implications. *Pharmacoeconomics*, 9(6), 478–483.

Gianfrancesco, F.D., Baines, A.P. and Richards, D. (1994). Utilization effects of prescription drug benefits in an aging population. *Health Care Financing Review*, 15(3), 113–126.

Giuliani, G., Selke, G. and Garattini, L. (1998). The German experience in reference pricing. *Health Policy*, 44(1), 73–85.

Goodwin, F.K. (2003). Impact of formularies on clinical innovation. *Journal of Clinical Psychiatry*, 64(Suppl 17), 11–14.

Grabowski, H. (1988). Medicaid patients' access to new drugs. *Health Affairs*, 7(5), 102–114.

Greenhalgh, T., Robert, G., Bate, P., Macfarlane, F. and Kyriakidou, O. (2005). *Diffusion of Innovations in Health Service Organisations: A Systematic Literature Review*. Oxford: Blackwell.

Griffiths, R.I., Powe, N.R., Greer, J., de Lissovoy, G., Anderson, G.F., Whelton, P.K., Watson, A.J. and Eggers, P.W. (1994). A review of the first year of Medicare coverage of erythropoietin. *Health Care Financing Review*, 15(3), 83–102.

Grootendorst, P.V., Dolovich, L.R., O'Brien, B.J., Holbrook, A.M. and Levy, A.R. (2001). Impact of reference-based pricing of nitrates on the use and costs of anti-anginal drugs. *Canadian Medical Association Journal*, 165(8), 1011–1019.

Grootendorst, P.V., Marshall, J.K., Holbrook, A.M., Dolovich, L.R., O'Brien, B.J. and Levy, A.R. (2005). The impact of reference pricing of nonsteroidal anti-inflammatory agents on the use and costs of analgesic drugs. *Health Services Research*, 40(5 Pt 1), 1297–1317.

Harris, B.L., Stergachis, A. and Ried, L.D. (1990). The effect of drug co-payments on utilization and cost of pharmaceuticals in a health maintenance organization. *Medical Care*, 28(10), 907–917.

Harris, C.M. and Scrivener, G. (1996). Fundholders' prescribing costs: the first five years. *British Medical Journal*, 313(7071), 1531–1534.

Hazlet, T.K. and Blough, D.K. (2002). Health services utilization with reference drug pricing of histamine(2) receptor antagonists in British Columbia elderly. *Medical Care*, 40(8), 640–649.

Hillman, A.L., Pauly, M.V., Escarce, J.J., Ripley, K., Gaynor, M., Clouse, J. and Ross, R. (1999). Financial incentives and drug spending in managed care. *Health Affairs*, 18(2), 189–200.

Hivon, M., Lehoux, P., Denis, J.L. and Tailliez, S. (2005). Use of health technology assessment in decision making: coresponsibility of users and producers? *International Journal of Technology Assessment in Health Care*, 21(2), 268–275.

Hurley, J. (1991). The effects of co-payments within drug reimbursement programs. *Canadian Public Policy*, 17(4), 473–489.

Hurley, R.E., Paul, J.E. and Freund, D.A. (1989). Going into gatekeeping: an empirical assessment. *QRB Quality Review Bulletin*, 15(10), 306–314.

Huskamp, H.A. (2003). Managing psychotropic drug costs: will formularies work? *Health Affairs*, 22(5), 84–96.

Huttin, C. (1994). The use of prescription charges. *Health Policy*, 27(1), 53–73.

Huttin, C. and Andral, J. (2000). How the reimbursement system may influence physicians' decisions: results from focus groups interviews in France. *Health Policy*, 54(2), 67–86.

Ioannides-Demos, L.L., Ibrahim, J.E. and McNeil, J.J. (2002). Reference-based pricing schemes: effect on pharmaceutical expenditure, resource utilisation and health outcomes. *Pharmacoeconomics*, 20(9), 577–591.

Jacobzone, S. (2005). Pharmaceutical policies in OECD countries: reconciling social and industrial goals. OECD Labour Market and Social Policy Occasional Paper No. 40.

Johnson, R.E., Goodman, M.J., Hornbrook, M.C. and Eldredge, M.B. (1997). The impact of increasing patient prescription drug cost sharing on therapeutic classes of drugs received and on the health status of elderly HMO members. *Health Services Research*, 32(1), 103–122.

Kanavos, P. and Costa-Font, J. (2005). Pharmaceutical parallel trade in Europe: stakeholder and competition effects. *Economic Policy*, 20(44), 753–798.

Kanavos, P. and Mossialos, E. (1999). Outstanding regulatory aspects in the European pharmaceutical market. *Pharmacoeconomics*, 15(6), 519–533.

Kanavos, P. and Reinhardt, U. (2003). Reference pricing for drugs: is it compatible with U.S. health care? *Health Affairs*, 22(3), 16–30.

Kane, N.M. and Saltman, R.B. (1997). Comparative experience in home care and pharmaceutical policy. *Health Policy*, 41(Suppl), S1–S7.

Koopmanschap, M.A. and Rutten, F.F. (2003). The drug budget silo mentality: the Dutch case. *Value in Health*, 6(Suppl 1), S46–S51.

Kozma, C.M., Reeder, C.E. and Lingle, E.W. (1990). Expanding Medicaid drug formulary coverage: effects on utilization of related services. *Medical Care*, 28(10), 963–977.

Kyle, M. (2006a). Pharmaceutical price controls and entry strategies. *Review of Economics and Statistics*, 89(1), 88–99.

Kyle, M. (2006b). The role of firm characteristics in pharmaceutical product launches. *RAND Journal of Economics*, 37(3), 602–618.

Lavers, R.J. (1989). Prescription charges, the demand for prescriptions and morbidity. *Applied Economics*, 21(8), 1043–1052.

Le Pen, C. (2003). The drug budget silo mentality: the French case. *Value in Health*, 6(Suppl 1), S10–S19.

Leibowitz, A., Manning, W.G. and Newhouse, J.P. (1985). The demand for prescription drugs as a function of cost-sharing. *Social Science & Medicine*, 21(10), 1063–1069.

Lexchin, J. and Grootendorst, P. (2004). Effects of prescription drug user fees on drug and health services use and on health status in vulnerable populations: a systematic review of the evidence. *International Journal of Health Services*, 34(1), 101–122.

Lichtenberg, F. (2002). Benefits and costs of newer drugs: an update. NBER Working Paper No. 8996.

Ljungkvist, M.O., Andersson, D. and Gunnarsson, B. (1997). Cost and utilisation of pharmaceuticals in Sweden. *Health Policy*, 41(Suppl 1), S55–S69.

Lopez-Casasnovas, G. and Puig-Junoy, J. (2000). Review of the literature on reference pricing. *Health Policy*, 54(2), 87–123.

Lundkvist, J. (2002). Pricing and reimbursement of drugs in Sweden. *European Journal of Health Economics*, 3(1), 66–70.

Lyles, A. and Palumbo, F.B. (1999). The effect of managed care on prescription drug costs and benefits. *Pharmacoeconomics*, 15(2), 129–140.

Mace, S. and Taylor, D. (2003). Adherence to NICE guidance for the use of anti-cholinesterases. *Disease Management & Health Outcomes*, 11(2), 129–137.

Marshall, J.K., Grootendorst, P.V., O'Brien, B.J., Dolovich, L.R., Holbrook, A.M. and Levy, A.R. (2002). Impact of reference-based pricing for histamine-2 receptor antagonists and restricted access for proton pump inhibitors in British Columbia. *Canadian Medical Association Journal*, 166(13), 1655–1662.

Maxwell, M., Heaney, D., Howie, J.G.R. and Noble, S. (1993). General practice fundholding: observations on prescribing patterns and costs using the defined daily dose method. *British Medical Journal*, 307(6913), 1190–1194.

McCombs, J.S., Mulani, P. and Gibson, P.J. (2004). Open access to innovative drugs: treatment substitutions or treatment expansion? *Health Care Financing Review*, 25(3), 35–53.

McGuire, A. and Litt, M. (2003). UK budgetary systems and new health-care technologies. *Value in Health*, 6(Suppl 1), S64–S73.

Mrazek, M.F. and Mossialos, E. (2004). Regulating pharmaceutical prices in the European Union. In: E. Mossialos, T. Walley and M.F. Mrazek (eds.), *Regulating Pharmaceuticals in Europe: Striving for Efficiency, Equity and Quality*, Maidenhead, Berkshire: Open University Press, pp. 114–129.

Murray, M.D. and Deardorff, F.W. (1998). Does managed care fuel pharmaceutical industry growth? *Pharmacoeconomics*, 14(4), 341–348.

Oliver, A., Mossialos, E. and Robinson, R. (2004). Health technology assessment and its influence on health-care priority setting. *International Journal of Technology Assessment in Health Care*, 20(1), 1–10.

Pavcnik, N. (2000). Do pharmaceutical prices respond to insurance? NBER Working Paper No. 7865.

Pilote, L., Beck, C., Richard, H. and Eisenberg, M.J. (2002). The effects of cost-sharing on essential drug prescriptions, utilization of medical care and outcomes after acute myocardial infarction in elderly patients. *Canadian Medical Association Journal*, 167(3), 246–252.

Puig-Junoy, J. (2004). Incentives and pharmaceutical reimbursement reforms in Spain. *Health Policy*, 67(2), 149–165.

Puig-Junoy, J. (2005). What is required to evaluate the impact of pharmaceutical reference pricing? *Applied Health Economics and Health Policy*, 4(2), 87–98.

Rafferty, T., Wilson-Davis, K. and McGavock, H. (1997). How has fundholding in Northern Ireland affected prescribing patterns? A longitudinal study. *British Medical Journal*, 315(7101), 166–170.

Rocchi, F., Addis, A. and Martini, N. (2004). Current national initiatives about drug policies and cost control in Europe: the Italy example. *Journal of Ambulatory Care Management*, 27(2), 127–131.

Rogers, E.M. (2005). *Diffusion of Innovations*. New York: Free Press.

Ross-Degnan, D., Soumerai, S.B., Fortess, E.E. and Gurwitz, J.H. (1993). Examining product risk in context: market withdrawal of zomepirac as a case study. *Journal of American Medical Association*, 270(16), 1937–1942.

Ruof, J., Mittendorf, T., Pirk, O. and von der Schulenburg, J.M. (2002). Diffusion of innovations: treatment of Alzheimer's disease in Germany. *Health Policy*, 60(1), 59–66.

Ryan, M. and Birch, S. (1991). Charging for health care: evidence on the utilisation of NHS prescribed drugs. *Social Science & Medicine*, 33(6), 681–687.

Schneeweiss, S., Dormuth, C., Grootendorst, P., Soumerai, S.B. and Maclure, M. (2004). Net health plan savings from reference pricing for angiotensin-converting enzyme inhibitors in elderly British Columbia residents. *Medical Care*, 42(7), 653–660.

Schneeweiss, S., Maclure, M. and Soumerai, S.B. (2002a). Prescription duration after drug copay changes in older people: methodological aspects. *Journal of American Geriatric Society*, 50(3), 521–525.

Schneeweiss, S., Schoffski, O. and Selke, G.W. (1998). What is Germany's experience on reference based drug pricing and the etiology of adverse health outcomes or substitution? *Health Policy*, 44(3), 253–260.

Schneeweiss, S., Soumerai, S.B., Glynn, R.J., Maclure, M., Dormuth, C. and Walker, A.M. (2002b). Impact of reference-based pricing for angiotensin-converting enzyme inhibitors on drug utilization. *Canadian Medical Association Journal,* 166(6), 737–745.

Schneeweiss, S., Soumerai, S.B., Maclure, M., Dormuth, C., Walker, A.M. and Glynn, R.J. (2003). Clinical and economic consequences of reference pricing for dihydropyridine calcium channel blockers. *Clinical Pharmacology and Therapeutics,* 74(4), 388–400.

Schneeweiss, S., Walker, A.M., Glynn, R.J., Maclure, M., Dormuth, C. and Soumerai, S.B. (2002c). Outcomes of reference pricing for angiotensin-converting–enzyme inhibitors. *New England Journal of Medicine,* 346(11), 822–829.

Schoenman, J.A., Evans, W.N. and Schur, C.L. (1997). Primary care case management for Medicaid recipients: evaluation of the Maryland Access to Care program. *Inquiry,* 34(2), 155–170.

Schoffski, O. and Graf von der Schulenburg, J.M. (1997). Unintended effects of a cost-containment policy: results of a natural experiment in Germany. *Social Science & Medicine,* 45(10), 1537–1539.

Schwermann, T., Greiner, W. and Von der Schulenburg, J.M. (2003). Using disease management and market reforms to address the adverse economic effects of drug budgets and price and reimbursement regulations in Germany. *Value in Health,* 6(Suppl 1), S20–S30.

Sclar, D.A., Robison, L.M., Skaer, T.L., Legg, R.F., Nemec, N.L., Galin, R.S., Hughes, T.E. and Buesching, D.P. (1994). Antidepressant pharmacotherapy: economic outcomes in a health maintenance organization. *Clinical Therapeutics,* 16(4), 715–730.

Seddon, M.E., Ayanian, J.Z., Landrum, M.B., Cleary, P.D., Peterson, E.A., Gahart, M.T. and McNeil, B.J. (2001). Quality of ambulatory care after myocardial infarction among Medicare patients by type of insurance and region. *American Journal of Medicine,* 111(1), 24–32.

Sheldon, T.A., Cullum, N., Dawson, D., Lankshear, A., Lowson, K., Watt, I., West, P., Wright, D. and Wright, J. (2004). What's the evidence that NICE guidance has been implemented? Results from a national evaluation using time series analysis, audit of patients' notes, and interviews. *British Medical Journal,* 329(7473), 999–1004.

Sheridan, D. (2006). Development and innovation in cardiovascular medicine. Imperial College London Discussion Paper.

Soumerai, S.B. (1990). Withdrawing payment for nonscientific drug therapy: intended and unexpected effects of a large-scale natural experiment. *Journal of American Medical Association,* 263(6), 831–839.

Soumerai, S.B., Avorn, J., Ross-Degnan, D. and Gortmaker, S. (1987). Payment restrictions for prescription drugs under Medicaid: effects on therapy, cost, and equity. *New England Journal of Medicine,* 317(9), 550–556.

Soumerai, S.B., McLaughlin, T.J., Ross-Degnan, D., Casteris, C.S. and Bollini, P. (1994). Effects of a limit on Medicaid drug-reimbursement benefits on the use of psychotropic agents and acute mental health services by patients with schizophrenia. *New England Journal of Medicine*, 331(10), 650–655.

Soumerai, S.B., Ross-Degnan, D., Avorn, J., McLaughlin, T. and Choodnovskiy, I. (1991). Effects of Medicaid drug-payment limits on admission to hospitals and nursing homes. *New England Journal of Medicine*, 325(15), 1072–1077.

Stewart-Brown, S., Surender, R., Bradlow, J., Coulter, A. and Doll, H. (1995). The effects of fundholding in general practice on prescribing habits three years after introduction of the scheme. *British Medical Journal*, 311(7019), 1543–1547.

Stuart, B. (1998). Ability to pay and the decision to medicate. *Medical Care*, 36(2), 202–211.

Stuart, B., Ahern, F., Rabatin, V. and Johnson, A. (1991). Patterns of outpatient prescription drug use among Pennsylvania elderly. *Health Care Financing Review*, 12(3), 61–72.

Stuart, B. and Coulson, N.E. (1993). Dynamic aspects of prescription drug use in an elderly population. *Health Services Research*, 28(2), 237–264.

Stuart, B. and Zacker, C. (1999). Who bears the burden of Medicaid drug copayment policies? *Health Affairs*, 18(2), 201–212.

Szymanski, S. and Valletti, T. (2005). Parallel trade, price discrimination, investment and price caps. *Economic Policy*, 20(44), 705–749.

Tamblyn, R., Laprise, R., Hanley, J.A., Abrahamowicz, M., Scott, S., Mayo, N., Hurley, J., Grad, R., Latimer, E., Perreault, R., McLeod, P., Huang, A., Larochelle, P. and Mallet, L. (2001). Adverse events associated with prescription drug cost-sharing among poor and elderly persons. *Journal of American Medical Association*, 285(4), 421–429.

Tidd, J. (2006). *From Knowledge Management to Strategic Competence: Measuring Technological, Market and Organizational Innovation*. London: Imperial College Press.

Tidd, J. and Bessant, J. (2009). *Managing Innovation: Integrating Technological, Market and Organizational Change*, 4th ed. Chichester: Wiley.

Vogel, R.J. (2004). Pharmaceutical pricing, price controls, and their effects on pharmaceutical sales and research and development expenditures in the European Union. *Clinical Therapeutics*, 26(8), 1327–1340.

Von der Schulenburg, J.M. (1994). The German health care system at the crossroads. *Health Economics*, 3(5), 301–303.

Von der Schulenburg, J.M. (2006). The regulatory environment for pharmaceutical innovation in Europe. Imperial College London Discussion Paper.

Walser, B.L., Ross-Degnan, D. and Soumerai, S.B. (1996). Do open formularies increase access to clinically useful drugs? *Health Affairs*, 15(3), 95–109.

Weiner, J.P., Lyles, A., Steinwachs, D.M. and Hall, K.C. (1991). Impact of managed care on prescription drug use. *Health Affairs*, 10(1), 140–154.

Whynes, D.K., Heron, T. and Avery, A.J. (1997). Prescribing cost savings by GP fundholders: long-term or short-term? *Health Economics*, 6(2), 209–211.

Wilking, N. and Jonsson, B. (2005). *A Pan-European Comparison Regarding Patient Access to Cancer Drugs*. Report by the Karolinska Institute and the Stockholm School of Economics, Stockholm, Sweden.

Wilsdon, T. and Nitsche, R. (2004). *Innovations in the Pharmaceutical Sector*. Available at http://pharmacos.eudra.org/F2/pharmacos/docs/Doc2004/nov/EU%20 Pharma%20Innovation_25-11-04.pdf/. Charles River Associates ENTR/03/28.

Wilson, R.P., Buchan, I. and Walley, T. (1995). Alterations in prescribing by general practitioner fundholders: an observational study. *British Medical Journal*, 311(7016), 1347–1350.

Wilson, R.P., Hatcher, J., Barton, S. and Walley, T. (1996). Influences of practice characteristics on prescribing in fundholding and non-fundholding general practices: an observational study. *British Medical Journal*, 313(7057), 595–599.

Wilson, R.P., Hatcher, J., Barton, S. and Walley, T. (1997). General practice fundholders' prescribing savings in one region of the United Kingdom, 1991–1994. *Health Policy*, 42(1), 29–37.

Wilson, R.P., Hatcher, J., Barton, S. and Walley, T. (1999). Therapeutic substitution and therapeutic conservatism as cost-containment strategies in primary care: a study of fundholders and non-fundholders. *British Journal of General Practice*, 49(443), 431–435.

World Bank Development Prospects Group. (2002). *Global Economic Prospects and the Developing Countries 2002*. Washington, D.C.: The World Bank.

World Health Organization. (1999). *The World Health Report 1999*. Geneva: WHO.

Chapter 9

Diffusion of Telecommunications Technologies: A Study of Mobile Telephony

Wen-Lin Chu, Xielin Liu and Feng-Shang Wu

9.1 Introduction

Telecommunications technology has evolved from wireline to wireless, and enables seamless communication without time or location constraints. The ability to communicate with individuals who are constantly moving has evolved remarkably since 1897, when Guglielmo Marconi first demonstrated the ability of radio to provide continuous contact with ships sailing the English Channel. However, the wireless communications era did not arrive until highly reliable, miniature, solid-state radio frequency hardware was developed in the 1970s (Rappaport, 2002). Mobile (cellular) telephony, which was an innovation in telecommunications technology over fixed-line telephony, experienced very rapid diffusion due to rapid deployment and low cost. Mobile telephony boomed during the 1990s as the costs of services gradually fell. The number of global mobile telephone subscribers reached 1.2 billion in 2002, for the first time exceeding the number of fixed-line subscribers (1.1 billion). By the end of 2008, there were over three times as many mobile telephone subscriptions (4.1 billion) as fixed-line telephone subscriptions (1.3 billion) (ITU, 2009). Mobile telephony has thus become the dominant telecommunications service globally. The rapid diffusion of mobile telephony has attracted considerable academic interest, and is an important topic in the study of innovation diffusion.

The diffusion of mobile telephony, like that of other innovations (Rogers, 2003), exhibits an S-shaped adoption curve over time. Empirical studies have examined the impetuses driving the diffusion using growth models. For example, Gruber and Verboven (2001a), who applied the logistic model to study mobile communication diffusion in 15 EU countries, determined that technology and competition are significant determinants of mobile diffusion. Rouvinen (2006) utilized the Gompertz model to compare the speeds of mobile communication diffusion between developed and developing countries. Rouvinen demonstrated that diffusion occurs faster in late entrants than early entrants. Sundqvist et al. (2005) applied the Bass model to identify the years in which mobile communication services were adopted in 25 countries. They demonstrated that national wealth is positively associated with early adoption of mobile communication services. As empirical data for mobile telephony diffusion accumulate, a synthetic roadmap is needed for both application and research.

This study synthesizes the main findings of mobile telephony diffusion in terms of diffusion models and factors affecting the diffusion rate. The remainder of this study is organized as follows. Section 9.2 reviews the terminology and models for diffusion of technological change. Section 9.3 compares the mechanisms of diffusion models used to analyze mobile telephony. Section 9.4 presents the regarding drivers of the diffusion rate of mobile telephony. Next, Section 9.5 gives the implications of these data. Finally, Section 9.6 concludes this study.

9.2 Diffusion of Technological Change

The diffusion of new technologies is typically an S-shaped process, and the diffusion rate generally varies markedly (Mansfield, 1961). Studies investigating the diffusion of technological change are abundant. These studies have analyzed the diffusion of technological change from various perspectives. Numerous terms and deterministic models have been proposed to explain the diffusion. For example, Mansfield (1961) emphasized the importance of the imitation rate, i.e. the bandwagon effect: "Where the profitability of using the innovation is very difficult to estimate, the mere fact that a large proportion of its competitors have introduced it may prompt a firm to consider it more favorably." Mansfield (1961) asserted that the full economic impact of a technological innovation does not occur until the imitation process is well underway. Fisher and Pry (1971) viewed technological advances as a set of substitution processes. They contended that many technological advances can be considered competitive substitutions of one method of satisfying a need for another, and that "the fractional rate of fractional substitution of new for old is proportional to the remaining amount of the old left to be substituted." Geroski (2000) contended, "If a new technology really is a significant improvement over existing technology, it is important to ask why some firms shift over to it more slowly than other firms. Possibly the most obvious explanation is that they just find out about the new technology later than other firms do." He analogized the information flow for the perception of new technology to an epidemic, and combined two communication sources — central source (broadcasting) and word of mouth — to develop his mixed information model for technology diffusion.

Moreover, Bass (1969) combined models of the purchasing behaviors of innovators and imitators, two customer categories, for consumer durables in his far-reaching Bass diffusion model for new product growth. Lekvall and Wahlbin (1973) distinguished between external (sources outside a set of prospective adopters, e.g. mass media advertising) and internal (interaction among members of a social system) influences in communicating an innovation. They determined that the relative strength of these two influences is not likely the same from one case to another, but rather varies according to the character of the innovation.

Notably, the effects of such imitative behavior, the substitution process, word-of-mouth information and internal influence on diffusion share a common mathematical formulation; whereas the effects of innovative behavior, broadcasting information and external influence on diffusion share another common mathematical formulation. Mahajan and Peterson (1985) found that, despite the broad application of diffusion models in various innovation scenarios, a paucity of information exists regarding their commonalities and differences. They utilized external and internal influences to integrate models of innovation diffusion, and generated a common mathematical formulation for discussing the similarities and differences among diffusion models. Table 9.1 summarizes the studies investigating the terminology and mathematical formulations for innovation diffusion. Mahajan and Peterson (1985) categorized the popular Gompertz (replacing $K - N$ with $\ln K - \ln N$) and logistic models as internal-influence models, and the Bass model as a mixed-influence model.

Table 9.1. Mathematical formulations and terminology for diffusion.

Category	External-influence model	Internal-influence model	Mixed-influence model
Mathematical formulation (Mahajan and Peterson, 1985)	$\dfrac{dN}{dt} = a(K - N)$ (Exponential function)	$\dfrac{dN}{dt} = bN(K - N)$ (Logistic function)	$\dfrac{dN}{dt} = (a + bN)(K - N)$
Terminology Mansfield (1961)		Rate of imitation	
Bass (1969)	Innovative behavior	Imitative behavior	Innovative and imitative behaviors
Fisher and Pry (1971)		Substitution process	
Lekvall and Wahlbin (1973)	External influence (sources outside a set of prospective adopters, e.g. mass media advertising)	Internal influence (interaction among members of a social system)	External and internal influences
Geroski (2000)	Central source/ broadcasting information	Word-of-mouth information	Mixed information source model

Note: N is the number of adopters at time t; K is the number of adopters at equilibrium, i.e. the maximum number of adopters; and a and b are constants.

9.3 Diffusion Models

Applying a diffusion model analogy is a common step in analyzing innovation diffusion. Numerous studies have attempted to fit the adoption of specific products, ranging from television sets to new drugs, to the S-curve. Mathematical techniques usually achieve a fairly good fit with historical data, but generic adoption models have not proven sufficiently robust (Tidd and Bessant, 2009). Meade and Islam (2006), in their review of the literature for modeling and forecasting innovation diffusion, found that, despite the wealth of research, few research questions have been fully resolved. Only deselected models, which are clearly inferior, have been reported. In a performance comparison of 17 models for forecasting the development of telecommunications markets in 15 different countries, the logistic and Gompertz models outperformed relatively more complex models (Meade and Islam, 1995). Moreover, Meade and Islam (2001) contended that a reasonable initial set of candidate models includes the Gompertz, logistic and Bass models, which are the three most widely used models in diffusion studies of telecommunications.

9.3.1 *Models and applications*

The Gompertz, logistic and Bass models are the three most popular models in diffusion studies of mobile telephony. Although all three present S-shaped contours, their dynamics differ. The mechanisms of the Gompertz, logistic and Bass models as well as their applications are as follows.

9.3.1.1 *Gompertz model*

The Gompertz model, a refinement of the demographic model presented by Malthus, is expressed as

$$\frac{dN}{dt} = rN \ln \frac{K}{N} \text{ or } \frac{dN/dt}{N} = r(\ln K - \ln N), \qquad (9.1)$$

where N is the number of adopters at time t; r is the growth rate; and K is the number of adopters at equilibrium, i.e. the maximum number of adopters. According to the Gompertz model, for a given number of adopters (N), the growth of adopters (dN/dt) is positively associated with the difference between the natural logarithm of the maximum number of adopters (ln K) and the natural logarithm of the given number of adopters (ln N).

An investigation by Chow (1967) on computer demand in the United States suggested that the Gompertz model provides a better explanation for demand than the logistic model does. The empirical results in that study are an important reference for diffusion studies considering adoption of the Gompertz model (e.g. Rouvinen, 2006). The Gompertz model is also commonly applied in studies examining the diffusion of the Internet (e.g. Kiiski and Pohjola, 2002).

9.3.1.2 *Logistic model*

The logistic model, which was also initially presented in demographic growth studies, is expressed as

$$\frac{dN}{dt} = rN\left(1 - \frac{N}{K}\right) \text{ or } \frac{dN/dt}{K-N} = \frac{r}{K}N, \qquad (9.2)$$

where N is the number of adopters at time t; r is the growth rate; and K is the number of adopters at equilibrium, i.e. the maximum number of adopters. In the logistic model, for a given number of adopters (N), the growth of adopters (dN/dt) is positively related to the percentage of adopter growth space (($K - N)/K$).

The logistic model is frequently applied to diffusion studies of mobile telephony. Griliches (1957) applied the model in a convincing explanation of hybrid corn technology adoption in the United States. These empirical results were referenced in many subsequent diffusion studies that evaluated the logistic model (e.g. Gruber and Verboven, 2001a, 2001b; Frank, 2004; Liikanen *et al.*, 2004; Botelho and Pinto, 2004; Jang *et al.*, 2005; Lee and Cho, 2007).

Moreover, telecommunications are the most natural example of network externalities (Shy, 2001). Telecommunications demand is heavily affected by the number of consumers connected to the same network. Equation (9.2) also signifies that the number of non-adopters ($K - N$) who later become adopters (dN/dt) is proportional to the number of adopters (N) with a coefficient of r/K. Assuming that the adoption decisions of non-adopters are positively related to the utility they receive, Equation (9.2) matches the definition of network externalities. Restated, the utility that a user derives from consuming a good is positively associated with the number of other agents consuming it, i.e. the demand-side economies of scale (Katz and Shapiro, 1985, 1986), or "the value to each telephone subscriber depends on the number of other people on the network" (Farrell and Saloner, 1986).

9.3.1.3 *Bass model*

In contrast to the five categories of adopters developed by Rogers (1962), the Bass model, which was developed for sales forecasting, employs two categories: innovators and imitators. Bass (1969) argued, "The probability that an initial purchase will be made at t given that no purchase has yet been made is a linear function of the number of previous buyers." This statement is reformulated as

$$\frac{f(t)}{1 - F(t)} = p + qF(t), \qquad (9.3)$$

where $f(t)$ is the likelihood of adoption at time t, $F(t)$ is adoption at time t as a percentage of ultimate potential adoption, p is the innovation coefficient, and q is the imitation coefficient. Equation (9.3) can be rearranged as

$$\frac{dN/dt}{K - N} = p + q\frac{N}{K}, \qquad (9.4)$$

where K is the number of adopters at equilibrium, i.e. the maximum number of adopters; and N, which equals $KF(t)$, is the total number of adopters in the $(0,t)$ interval.

Bass (1969) successfully forecasted peak sales of color TVs in 1968 using his model. His results provide an important reference for diffusion studies considering adopting this model (e.g. Dekimpe *et al.*, 1998; Sundqvist *et al.*, 2005).

9.3.2 Comparison of dynamics

Selecting a growth curve that best matches the underlying dynamics of the diffusion process is crucial (Martino, 1993). Equations (9.1), (9.2) and (9.4) for the Gompertz, logistic and Bass models, respectively, can be rewritten as follows for comparison:

$$\frac{dN}{dt} = rN(\ln K - \ln N)$$

$$\approx r(K - N) \text{ when } N \geq \frac{K}{2}. \qquad \text{(Gompertz)} \quad (9.5)$$

$$\frac{dN}{dt} = \frac{r}{K} N(K - N). \qquad \text{(Logistic)} \quad (9.6)$$

$$\frac{dN}{dt} = p(K - N) + \frac{q}{K} N(K - N). \qquad \text{(Bass)} \quad (9.7)$$

9.3.2.1 Gompertz model vs. logistic model

Both the Gompertz and logistic models can be classified as internal-influence models, as they are governed by the social interaction between prior adopters (N) and potential adopters ($\ln K - \ln N$ for Gompertz; $K - N$ for logistic) in the social system with the formulation of $N(\ln K - \ln N)$ and $N(K - N)$ as seen in Equations (9.5) and (9.6), respectively (Mahajan and Peterson, 1985) — namely, imitation or word of mouth (Table 9.1). However, at the late stage of diffusion (i.e. after the diffusion curve has passed the inflection point), the slopes for the Gompertz and logistic models are $r(K - N)$ (approximated by Taylor series expansion of $\ln(K/N)$) and $rN(K - N)/K$, respectively. That is, when the number of adopters (N) is large, the Gompertz curve is a function of non-adopters ($K - N$) only, whereas the logistic curve remains a function of both adopters and non-adopters ($N(K - N)$) (Martino, 1993). Therefore, if one diffusion process weakly correlates with the number of adopters when the diffusion process slows down (e.g. diffusion passes the inflection point), the Gompertz model outperforms the logistic model in depicting this diffusion process. However, if one diffusion process still strongly correlates with the number of adopters when the diffusion process slows down, the logistic model outperforms the Gompertz model in depicting this diffusion process. According to the network externalities, the decisions of non-adopters to adopt depend on the current number of adopters. The dynamics of the logistic model assume the existence of network externalities throughout the entire diffusion process.

Moreover, the Gompertz curve is asymmetrical, while that of the logistic model is symmetrical. If the maximum number of adopters is K, the inflection points of the asymmetrical Gompertz curve and the symmetrical logistic curve are at $0.368K$ and $0.5K$, respectively.

9.3.2.2 *Logistic model vs. Bass model*

The main difference between the logistic and Bass models (Equations (9.6) and (9.7), respectively) is that the effect of external influence (interaction outside the set of prospective adopters, e.g. mass media advertising) (Lekvall and Wahlbin, 1973) — namely, the effect of adoption behavior by innovators (Bass, 1969) or central source (broadcasting) information (Geroski, 2000) — is considered in the Bass model, whereas the logistic model only considers internal effects (Table 9.1). However, if the innovation coefficient (p) of the Bass model (Equation (9.7)) is negligible, the imitation coefficient (q) of the Bass model is the same as the growth rate (r) of the logistic model (Equation (9.6)). The two equations, Equations (9.6) and (9.7), thus become identical. Restated, if the innovation effect of the Bass model is so small that only the imitation effect of the

Bass model is significant, then the Bass model degenerates into the logistic model.

9.3.2.3 Representative sample: China

The Gompertz, logistic and Bass models have their own principles and advantages. No criteria have been presented for the selection of diffusion models for a studied population. To reduce the randomness and increase the reliability of model selection, Liu et al. (2008), based on data for mobile telephone subscribers in China during 1986–2007, compared annual performance in the fitness and forecasting ability of the Gompertz, logistic and Bass models to determine which model is most appropriate for analyzing mobile telephony growth in China. The three-year forecasting performance of each model was tested by root mean square error (RMSE) and mean absolute percentage error (MAPE) measures, adjusted from Meade and Islam (1995).

Liu et al. (2008) found that the Gompertz model, with the minimum accumulated RMSE, outperformed in the analysis of mobile telephony growth in China. Moreover, the RMSE performance of the logistic model was comparable to that of the Bass model. All innovation coefficients (p) of the Bass model were small ($1.7e-8$–$4.5e-5$), whereas the imitation coefficients (q) of the Bass model were comparable to the growth rates (r) of the logistic model (0.548–1.03). In other words, the Bass model revealed a small innovation effect on mobile telephony diffusion data in China, and only the imitation effect of the Bass model was significant. Thus, the Bass model degenerated into the logistic model.

Forecasting is a major aim of modeling (Meade, 1984), especially for undersaturated markets. The number of mobile subscribers in China reached 550 million in 2007, accounting for almost one out of five mobile subscriptions in the entire world (ITU, 2009). However, mobile telephony penetration (including Personal Handy-phone System (PHS) subscribers) was only 47.6% in China in 2007. China, then, is the mobile telephony market with the greatest growth

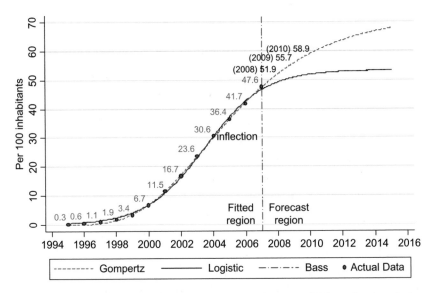

Figure 9.1.   Penetration of mobile telephony in China: model fit and extrapolation. The curves of the logistic and Bass models overlap. *Source*: Liu *et al.* (2008).

potential. To forecast the future growth of mobile telephony in China, the curve of the Gompertz model was extrapolated to forecast market growth for 2008–2010. The forecasted mobile telephony penetrations (including PHS subscribers) for 2008, 2009 and 2010 were 51.9%, 55.7% and 58.9%, respectively (Figure 9.1). According to data released by the Ministry of Industry and Information Technology (MIIT) of the People's Republic of China, the number of mobile telephone subscribers (including PHS subscribers) was 7.1e+08 at the end of 2008, accounting for 53.6% penetration. Therefore, the forecasting accuracy of mobile telephony penetration in China in 2008 using the Gompertz model reached as high as 95%.

According to the dynamics of the Gompertz model, the success of the Gompertz model in depicting mobile telephony diffusion in China means that the future diffusion of mobile telephony correlates with the decision characteristics of non-adopters rather than with network externalities.

9.4 Drivers of Diffusion Rate

Although mobile telephony diffusion can be depicted as an S-curve, the penetration and the slope — i.e. the diffusion rate — of the S-curve for each economy differs. Figure 9.2 displays the penetration curves of mobile telephony in 15 randomly selected economies, including Brazil, Canada, China, France, Finland, Germany, India, Italy, Japan, Korea, Russia, Sweden, Taiwan, the UK and the USA. Table 9.2 lists the penetration, prepaid ratio, population and GDP of each economy listed in Figure 9.2. By the end of 2007, mobile subscriptions had reached close to, on average, 50% worldwide, 100% in developed countries and 39% in developing countries (ITU, 2009). Indeed, "Amongst the developing regions, Africa continues to have the highest mobile growth rate (32% in 2006/2007) and mobile penetration has risen from just one in 50 people at the beginning of this century to over one fourth of the population today" (ITU, 2009, p. 3).

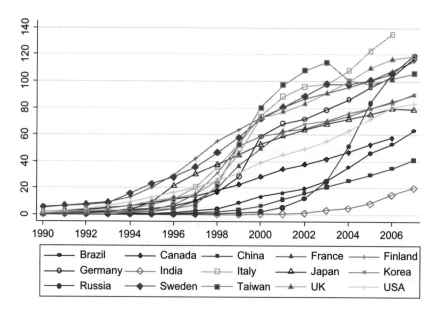

Figure 9.2.   Penetrations (%) of mobile telephony in 15 economies. *Source*: ITU (2008).

Table 9.2. Penetration, prepaid ratio, population and GDP in 15 economies.

Economy	Penetration (%)	Prepaid ratio (%)			Population (million)	GDP per capita (USD)
	2006	2004	2005	2006	2006	2006
Brazil	53	80	81	81	189	5,742
Canada	58	22	22	NA	33	39,314
China	42	21	20	NA	1,324	2,022
Finland	108	5	7	7	5	39,828
France	85	38	37	35	61	37,020
Germany	104	49	49	47	83	35,422
India	15	66	80	NA	1,120	762
Italy	135	91	92	94	58	31,802
Japan	79	3	3	2	128	34,264
Korea	84	NA	NA	NA	48	18,395
Russia	106	NA	NA	70	143	6,923
Sweden	106	53	51	49	9	43,190
Taiwan	102	16	11	11	23	15,978
UK	117	67	66	65	60	40,238
USA	80	10	11	NA	301	44,063

Source: ITU (2008).

The diffusion rate is a major topic in mobile telephony diffusion. Studies indicate that rapid diffusion occurs in late entrants (Ganesh *et al.*, 1997; Rouvinen, 2006; Takada and Jain, 1991). Studies of the diffusion rate have focused primarily on its drivers/determinants, which include technological innovation, deregulation and market competition, economic conditions, and distinctions between substitutive and complementary services. Table 9.3 lists several relevant studies, the diffusion model adopted by each, and their key findings related to the drivers of the diffusion rate.

Six key factors affecting the diffusion rate of mobile telephony are described below.

9.4.1 *Deregulation/market competition*

The theoretical and empirical literature has documented the importance of deregulation/market competition in mobile telephony

Table 9.3. Literature on mobile telephony diffusion.

Study	Model	No. of countries	Period	Factor[a]	Main Findings — Others
Dekimpe et al. (1998)	Bass	184	1979–1992		• The critical factors explaining diffusion patterns across countries are population and adoption ceiling.
Gruber and Verboven (2001a)	Logistic	15 (EU)	1984–1997	DIG, CMP, FIX[b]	• The CMP effect is smaller than the DIG effect. • Countries that were late in granting licenses revealed a significant but slow catch-up effect. • GDP is insignificant.
Gruber and Verboven (2001b)	Logistic	140	1981–1997	CMP	• Reliable conclusions for the effects of DIG on diffusion are currently unavailable.
Frank (2004)	Logistic	1 (Finland)	1981–1998	GDP	• Wireless network coverage is positively related to the number of potential adopters. • The model accurately predicted actual figures for 1999. • DIG and FIX are insignificant.

(Continued)

Table 9.3.   (*Continued*)

Study	Model	No. of countries	Period	Factor[a]	Main Findings — Others
Liikanen *et al.* (2004)	Logistic	80	1992–1998		• Positive within-generation network effects are identified. • First-generation or 1G (second-generation or 2G) mobile telephony is positively (negatively) associated with 2G (1G) diffusion.
Sundqvist *et al.* (2005)	Bass	25	1981–2000	GDP	• National wealth and cultural similarity to an innovation center are positively related to early adoption of mobile communications. • Late, uncertainty-avoiding adopters have a large imitation coefficient.
Jang *et al.* (2005)	Logistic	30	1980–2001	CMP, DIG, FIX[b]	• Significant differences in the S-curve spread are largely due to differences in the magnitudes of network externality coefficients. • GDP is insignificant.

(*Continued*)

Table 9.3. (*Continued*)

Study	Model	No. of countries	Period	Factor[a]	Main Findings — Others
Rouvinen (2006)	Gompertz	200	1992–2000	CMP	• The speed of diffusion does not significantly differ between developed and developing countries. • Late entrants exhibit rapid diffusion.
Lee and Cho (2007)	Logistic, autoregressive moving average (ARMA)	1 (Korea)	1984–2002	FIX[b], GDP	• The logistic model has a better fit to data than the ARMA (2,1) model does. • DIG is insignificant.

[a] Significant factors in the diffusion growth rate include service deregulation/market competition (CMP), digital technology/technological innovation (DIG), fixed network/telephone lines (FIX) and gross domestic production per capita (GDP).
[b] Significant with a negative coefficient.

diffusion (e.g. Gruber and Verboven, 2001a, 2001b; Jang *et al.*, 2005; Rouvinen, 2006). Competition forces an incumbent operator to reduce its tariffs in order to avoid losing customers to competitors. Gruber and Verboven (2001b) also observed that "introducing competition has a strong and immediate impact on diffusion."

Although telecommunications reforms to introduce market competition and facilitate diffusion are common in mobile telephony, their processes and outcomes are variable. For example, among the BRIC (Brazil, Russia, India and China) economies, both Brazil and Russia are beneficiaries of foreign investment and market competition (see Maciel *et al.* (2006) and Dobrovolskaya and Saluena (2004), respectively) and had mobile telephony penetrations of 63% and 119%, respectively, in 2007. Although India was one of the first developing countries during the mid-1980s to launch telecommunications sector reforms, few changes were introduced during the first decade (Petrazzini, 1996). However, market-oriented regulation to promote competition is now playing a major role in stimulating demand in India, causing rapid falls in tariffs. The subscriber base growth of mobile telephony in India ranks among the highest worldwide (Singh, 2008). Mobile telephony penetration in India reached 20% in 2007. The mobile telephony sector in China is run by a duopoly, and has not opened to foreign operators. Mobile telephony penetration in China reached 48% in 2007.

9.4.1.1 *Representative sample: Taiwan*

The penetration of mobile telephony exceeded 100% in only two economies in 2002, of which Taiwan — with a penetration of 108% — was the higher of the two. The other economy was Luxembourg with a penetration of 106% (ITU, 2008). In 1998, deregulation/market competition significantly accelerated mobile telephony diffusion in Taiwan (Chu and Wu, 2008). Two competition safeguard measures exerted by the telecommunications authority to reduce the interconnection fees between private mobile operators and the monopolized fixed-line operator were also critical factors that pushed the diffusion of mobile telephony in Taiwan. The first reduction occurred in

October 1998, when the interconnection fee was reduced to 1.15
TWD (Taiwan Dollar) per minute from 1.6 TWD per minute previously, amounting to a 28% reduction. The second reduction happened
in October 1999, when the interconnection fee was reduced again to
0.96 TWD per minute from 1.15 TWD per minute previously, representing a 17% reduction (DGT, 2000). Figure 9.3 compares the price
reductions and penetration related to mobile telephony in Taiwan.
The price of mobile telephony was 225.37 TWD per minute in 1998
(the first year in which private operators entered the market). In 1999
(the year in which the effect of the first reduction of interconnection
fees in October 1998 was included), the price of mobile telephony
was 105.82 TWD per minute, half that of 1998. In 2000 (the year in
which the effect of the second reduction of interconnection fees in
October 1999 was included), the price of mobile telephony was 9.87
TWD per minute, which was just one tenth of that in 1999.

The intervention by Taiwanese telecommunications regulators
in the interconnection fees charged by the monopoly state-owned

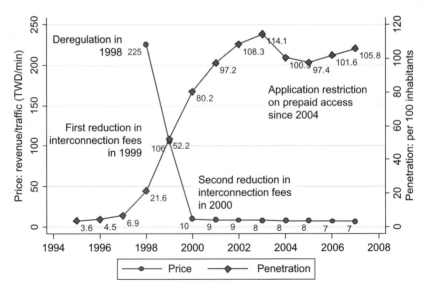

Figure 9.3.   Price vs. penetration of mobile telephony in Taiwan. Price before 1998
is unavailable. *Source*: National Communications Commission, Taiwan.

fixed-line operator and private mobile operators successfully acceler-ated mobile telephony diffusion in Taiwan to make the island a world leader, and has set a strong example of the usefulness of regulatory intervention for correcting market imperfections and boosting mar-ket competition in mobile telephony.

9.4.2 Handset prices

The handset is the major hardware cost item considered by non-adopters when deciding whether to adopt mobile telephony. Reduced handset costs due to the competition from low-cost domestic hand-set manufacturers have been a significant impetus to the diffusion of mobile telephony in China (Liu *et al.*, 2008).

The influence of decreased handset costs on mobile telephony dif-fusion is sometimes discussed together with the influence of market competition. For example, following deregulation, market competi-tion in mobile telephony in Taiwan immediately became so intense that handsets became virtually free for customers who subscribed to an operator and made the required minimum monthly payments (Chu and Wu, 2008).

9.4.3 Prepaid access

The advantages of prepaid features for mobile phone operators are avoiding credit risk and acquiring new customers at minimal cost. Meanwhile, the advantages to customers are avoiding the credit dis-qualification problems in postpaid services and benefiting from the commoditization of prepaid mobile phone services.

The availability of prepaid schemes is a key driver of mobile telephony growth in developing countries. For example, ease of access for individuals without a credit history is a major factor in the popularity of prepaid schemes in Africa (Minges, 1999). In China, commodity-like prepaid services meet the needs of migrating people, and the launch of prepaid services has significantly affected the dif-fusion of mobile telephony (Liu *et al.*, 2008). Moreover, the abnormal downward trend in mobile telephony penetration in

Taiwan in 2004 and 2005 (Figure 9.3) was due to the legal restrictions on the prepaid cards that were implemented to reduce fraud
and deception by users taking advantage of the anonymity offered
by prepaid services (DGT, 2005, 2006).

The popularity of prepaid services also underpins the rapid growth
of mobile telephony in Russia, which has the highest mobile telephony
penetration (119% in 2007) of the BRIC countries (Figure 9.2 and
Table 9.2). One characteristic feature of the Russian mobile telephony
market is the very large prepaid segment of the total number of mobile
phone users. The prepaid subscriber ratio in 2003 was 47% in Russia
(Dobrovolskaya and Saluena, 2004) and reached 90% by the end of
2007 (Kosowska, 2008).

9.4.4 *Technological innovation*

The first mobile cellular system utilized analog technology. The
evolution of mobile cellular systems to adopt digital technology was a
major technological innovation. Digital technology can overcome
the inefficiency in the frequency usage of analog technology, which
considerably limits subscriber expansion. Moreover, digital technology also offers additional functions such as the flexibility to transmit
mixed signals (voice and data) and digital encryption for privacy.

Previous studies have obtained inconsistent findings regarding
how mobile system digitization affects mobile telephony diffusion.
For example, the 15-state EU study by Gruber and Verboven (2001a)
demonstrated that the effect of digital technology was not only significant, but also exceeded that of market competition; however, Lee
and Cho (2007) examined Korean mobile telephony diffusion and
found that the digitization of mobile systems was insignificant (see
Table 9.3). Liu *et al.* (2008) and Chu and Wu (2008) also reported
no direct correlation between the digitization of mobile systems and
mobile telephony diffusion in China and Taiwan, respectively.

The International Telecommunication Union provides an explanation for this dilemma: " The success of mobile [telephony] has been a
triumph of technology married with marketing" (ITU, 1999). Restated,
without marketing, technological innovation alone is insufficient.

For example, Taiwan introduced the digital mobile system in 1996, two years before market competition was allowed in 1998. There was no marketing of mobile telephony by the monopoly state-owned operator. Moreover, mobile telephony tariffs remained much higher than those of fixed-line telephony. Extravagant functions alone enabled by advanced digital technology were not sufficiently attractive to promote the adoption of mobile telephony (see Figure 9.3).

9.4.5 *Economic conditions*

National economic conditions are often represented by the gross domestic product (GDP) in empirical studies of mobile telephony. Although studies have identified a correlation between GDP per capita and telephones per capita (Forestier *et al.*, 2002), previous studies have yielded inconsistent results regarding whether or not GDP per capita influences mobile telephony diffusion. For example, Gruber and Verboven (2001a) examined mobile telephony diffusion in 15 EU countries and found that the influence of GDP is insignificant (see Table 9.3). The GDP is also insignificant in China (Liu *et al.*, 2008) and Taiwan (Chu and Wu, 2008). However, a 25-country study of mobile telephone adoption by Sundqvist *et al.* (2005) indicated that GDP is a significant factor. The GDP is also significant in Korea (Lee and Cho, 2007; see also Table 9.3).

9.4.6 *Fixed-line telephony*

Mobile telephony was initially considered as complementary to fixed-line telephony in developed countries, but as a substitute for fixed-line telephony in developing countries (ITU, 1999). Empirical studies exhibit a diverse range of opinions. Numerous studies have also found that mobile telephony expansion occurs at the expense of fixed-line telephony in many countries, for example, South Korea, Portugal, Eastern Europe, the OECD countries, the USA and Africa (Hodge, 2005). However, Liu *et al.* (2008) reported that mobile telephony complements, rather than substitutes for, fixed-line telephony in China, a developing country. Moreover, Hamilton (2003) found that mobile and fixed-line telephony can shift between being substitutes or complements, depending on the context. Hodge (2005) argued, in the context of household behavior, that lower-income households treat mobile telephony as a substitute for fixed-line telephony, whereas higher-income households treat the two as complementary. Rodini *et al.* (2003) demonstrated that the substitutability of fixed-line and mobile telephony depends on the cross-price elasticity between the two.

A clear shift has occurred from fixed-line to mobile telephony, especially since the turn of the century. In contrast to the growth in mobile telephony, fixed-line telephony has experienced nearly no growth in the last decade. Indeed, fixed-line global penetration has been stagnating at just under 20% for the last few years. While the number of fixed telephone lines is falling in many developed countries, it tends to show very small growth rates in developing countries, where penetration rates stand at 14% (ITU, 2009).

9.5 Implications

9.5.1 *Diffusion model*

"Diffusion is the process by which an innovation is communicated through certain channels over time among the members of a social system" (Rogers, 2003). "Thus, diffusion is a communication process in which adopters persuade those who have not yet adopted to adopt" (Valente, 1995). Therefore, the process of diffusion of innovations can usually be characterized by an internal-influence (interaction between members of a social system) model or a mixed-influence model, which analyzes a combination of internal influence with external influence (interaction outside a set of prospective adopters). The Gompertz and logistic models are internal-influence models, whereas the Bass model is a mixed-influence model (Table 9.1).

Model selection is a case-dependent process (Meade and Islam, 2001). For example, in a performance comparison of the Gompertz, logistic and Bass models, Kim and Kim (2004) argued that the Bass model is most appropriate for mobile telephony diffusion in Korea, whereas Chu and Wu (2008) found that the logistic model adequately explains mobile telephony diffusion in Taiwan. Liu *et al.* (2008) demonstrated that the Gompertz model accurately depicts mobile telephony diffusion in China.

Moreover, the advent of curve fitting software packages enables an excellent "fit" for each curve (Martino, 1993). Selecting a model based simply on minor differences in the fit between curves is inadequate. Different models may achieve an identical fit, as was the case in the application of the logistic and Bass models to China (Liu *et al.*, 2008; see also Figure 9.1). Therefore, forecasting performance assessment, in which an effective complementary method is combined with the holdback sample method (Meade and Islam, 2001), should be carefully considered when selecting the diffusion model.

Additionally, unless they are modified, the growth curves cannot reflect market fluctuations caused by economic factors (Meade, 1984). Forecasters should be alert to significant policy changes, e.g. opening of markets, in the studied environment.

9.5.2 Drivers of diffusion rate

Telecommunications have long been considered essential to national competitiveness as the importance of mobile telephony increases in the current business environment. Mobile telephony penetrations vary among economies. Mobile telephony penetration was over 50% in 98 economies in 2006 (ITU, 2008), so others still have growth potential. Factors such as market competition (tariff reduction), low-cost handsets and prepaid access have contributed to the low-end market demand and are crucial to the rapid diffusion of mobile telephony. The abundant empirical works about impetuses to the diffusion rate of mobile telephony provide a useful reference for policy makers when deciding how to prioritize the acceleration of mobile telephony diffusion.

Although telecommunications reforms to introduce market competition and facilitate diffusion are common in mobile telephony, their processes and outcomes are variable. Modes of regulatory reform are governed by specific configurations of interest groups, production profiles, institutions and/or ideas (Vogel, 1997). For instance, commitments associated with bilateral negotiations with the European Union and the United States regarding World Trade Organization (WTO) accession were the main impetuses to the opening of the telecommunications market in Taiwan. The commitment to measures for reducing interconnection fees between the state-owned fixed-line operator and private mobile operators was critical to completing bilateral negotiations with the United States (CNA, 1998). Moreover, mobile telephony penetration in Taiwan fell in 2004 and 2005 (Figure 9.3) due to the introduction of limitations on applying for mobile phone prepaid cards in order to reduce fraud (DGT, 2005, 2006). However, the overall fraud did not decline[1]; instead, fraud was committed using other means.[2] Restated, these strict measures to prevent fraud were ineffective and had the negative side effect of reducing mobile telephony penetration. Hence, policy makers should consider the direct relationship between aims and means in their own specific circumstances before presenting measures to encourage or inhibit access to mobile telephony.

9.6 Conclusions

This study has synthesized the literature on mobile telephony diffusion in terms of diffusion models and impetuses to the diffusion rate. The main findings are summarized below:

(1) Telecommunications are the most natural example of network externalities (Shy, 2001). The logistic model, resembling the mathematical formula for network externalities, is popular in

[1] The total numbers of fraud offences each year in 2002–2006 were 26,397 (2002), 37,191 (2003), 40,001 (2004), 43,181 (2005) and 41,485 (2006) (data source: Ministry of the Interior, Taiwan).
[2] The numbers of fraud offences committed by Short Message Service (SMS) each year during 2005–2007 were 2,013 (2005), 434 (2006) and 215 (2007) (data source: Ministry of the Interior, Taiwan).

diffusion studies of mobile telephony and can be classified as an internal-influence (interaction among members of a social system) model.

(2) Besides taking into account internal influence, the Bass model also incorporates the external influence effect (interaction outside a set of prospective adopters) of diffusion. However, if the external influence effect is negligible, the performance of the Bass model will be identical to that of the logistic model. That is, the Bass model degenerates into the logistic model, as has been proven using data on mobile telephony diffusion in China.

(3) Like the logistic model, the Gompertz model is also classified as an internal-influence model. However, while the logistic model still correlates with network externalities during the late stages of diffusion, the Gompertz model does not. Moreover, the Gompertz model has been found to be the most appropriate model for depicting mobile telephony diffusion in China, where the number of mobile telephone subscribers reached 550 million in 2007.

(4) Market competition is commonly considered the proxy of tariff reduction. Handset prices represent the hardware cost associated with adopting mobile telephony. Commodity-like prepaid access helps users avoid credit disqualification problems, and enables operators to easily and cheaply acquire new customers. All of these three items are common drivers of the mobile telephony diffusion rate.

(5) Empirical works reveal inconsistent effects of both technological innovation (digitalization of mobile systems) and economic conditions (GDP) on the mobile telephony diffusion rate. These effects depend on other factors such as marketing, tariffs, etc.

(6) The shift from fixed-line to mobile telephony has been considerable.

Evidence of the diffusion of mobile telephony, the most common telecommunication technology, provides a reference for predicting the future diffusion path and for accelerating the adoption of mobile telephony and other emerging telecommunication technologies.

Moreover, the Gompertz model outperforms the logistic model in depicting mobile telephony diffusion in both China and India (Singh, 2008), both of which are populous countries. Further investigation is recommended for more populous countries to understand whether any correlation exists between model selection and population size.

References

Bass, F.M. (1969). A new product growth model for consumer durables. *Management Science*, 15, 215–227.

Botelho, A. and Pinto, L. (2004). The diffusion of cellular phones in Portugal. *Telecommunications Policy*, 28, 427–437.

Central News Agency (CNA). (1998). News release — US–Taiwan WTO bilateral negotiation: service sector (in Chinese). February 21. Available at http://www.cna.com.tw/.

Chow, G.C. (1967). Technological change and the demand for computers. *American Economic Review*, 57(5), 1117–1130.

Chu, W. and Wu, F. (2008). Diffusion of mobile communications: a Taiwanese case study. Paper presented at the 37th Annual Meeting of the Western Decision Sciences Institute (WDSI), March, San Diego, USA.

Dekimpe, M.G., Parker, P.M. and Sarvary, M. (1998). Staged estimation of international diffusion models. *Technological Forecasting and Social Change*, 57, 105–132.

Directorate General of Telecommunications (DGT). (2000). *DGT Annual Report 1999* (in Chinese). Taipei, Taiwan.

Directorate General of Telecommunications (DGT). (2005). *DGT Annual Report 2004* (in Chinese). Taipei, Taiwan.

Directorate General of Telecommunications (DGT). (2006). *DGT Annual Report 2005* (in Chinese). Taipei, Taiwan.

Dobrovolskaya, N. and Saluena, A. (2004). *Development of Russian Mobile Communications*. Publication 9, Northern Dimension Research Centre, Lappeenranta University of Technology, Lappeenranta, Finland.

Farrell, J. and Saloner, G. (1986). Installed base and compatibility: innovation, product preannouncements, and predation. *American Economic Review*, 76(5), 940–955.

Fisher, J.C. and Pry, R.H. (1971). A simple substitution model of technological change. *Technological Forecasting and Social Change*, 3, 75–88.

Forestier, E., Grace, J. and Kenny, C. (2002). Can information and communication technologies be pro-poor? *Telecommunications Policy*, 26, 623–646.

Frank, L.D. (2004). An analysis of the economic situation on modeling and forecasting the diffusion of wireless communications in Finland. *Technological Forecasting and Social Change*, 71, 391–403.

Ganesh, J., Kumar, V. and Subramaniam, V. (1997). Learning effect in multinational diffusion of consumer durables: an exploratory investigation. *Academy of Marketing Science*, 25(3), 214–228.

Geroski, P.A. (2000). Models of technology diffusion. *Research Policy*, 29, 603–625.

Griliches, Z. (1957). Hybrid corn: an exploration in the economics of technological change. *Econometrica*, 25(4), 501–522.

Gruber, H. and Verboven, F. (2001a). The diffusion of mobile telecommunications services in the European Union. *European Economic Review*, 45, 577–588.

Gruber, H. and Verboven, F. (2001b). The evolution of markets under entry and standards regulation: the case of global mobile telecommunications. *International Journal of Industrial Organization*, 19, 1189–1212.

Hamilton, J. (2003). Are main lines and mobile phones substitutes or complements? Evidence from Africa. *Telecommunications Policy*, 27, 109–133.

Hodge, J. (2005). Tariff structures and access substitution of mobile cellular for fixed line in South Africa. *Telecommunications Policy*, 29, 493–505.

International Telecommunication Union (ITU). (1999). *World Telecommunication Development Report 1999: Mobile Cellular*. Geneva, Switzerland.

International Telecommunication Union (ITU). (2008). *World Telecommunication/ICT Indicators 2007*. Geneva, Switzerland.

International Telecommunication Union (ITU). (2009). *Measuring the Information Society — The ICT Development Index*. Geneva, Switzerland.

Jang, S., Dai, S. and Sung, S. (2005). The pattern and externality effect of diffusion of mobile telecommunications: the case of the OECD and Taiwan. *Information Economics and Policy*, 17, 133–148.

Katz, M.L. and Shapiro, C. (1985). Network externalities, competition, and compatibility. *American Economic Review*, 75(3), 424–440.

Katz, M.L. and Shapiro, C. (1986). Technology adoption in the presence of network externalities. *Journal of Political Economy*, 94(4), 822–841.

Kiiski, S. and Pohjola, M. (2002). Cross-country diffusion of the Internet. *Information Economics and Policy*, 14, 297–310.

Kim, M. and Kim, H. (2004). Innovation diffusion of telecommunications: general patterns, diffusion clusters and differences by technological attribute. *International Journal of Innovation Management*, 8(2), 223–241.

Kosowska, E. (2008). Russia's mobile telephony market still on course for steady growth. Available at http://www.itandtelecompoland.com/.

Lee, M. and Cho, Y. (2007). The diffusion of mobile telecommunications services in Korea. *Applied Economics Letters*, 14, 477–481.

Lekvall, P. and Wahlbin, C. (1973). A study of some assumptions underlying innovation diffusion functions. *Swedish Journal of Economics*, 75, 362–377.

Liikanen, J., Stoneman, P. and Toivanen, O. (2004). Intergenerational effects in the diffusion of new technology: the case of mobile phones. *International Journal of Industrial Organization*, 22, 1137–1154.

Liu, X., Wu, F. and Chu, W. (2008). Innovation diffusion: adoption of mobile telephony in China. In: *Proceedings of the 1st International Society for Professional Innovation Management (ISPIM) Innovation Symposium, December, Singapore.*

Maciel, M., Whalley, J. and Meer, R. (2006). Foreign investment and consolidation in the Brazilian mobile telecommunications market. *Info: The Journal of Policy, Regulation and Strategy for Telecommunications, Information and Media*, 8(3), 60–77.

Mahajan, V. and Peterson, R. (1985). *Models for Innovation Diffusion*. Beverly Hills, CA: Sage Publications.

Mansfield, E. (1961). Technical change and the rate of imitation. *Econometrica*, 29(4), 741–766.

Martino, J.P. (1993). *Technological Forecasting for Decision Making*, 3rd ed. New York: McGraw-Hill.

Meade, N. (1984). The use of growth curves in forecasting market development — a review and appraisal. *Journal of Forecasting*, 3(4), 429–451.

Meade, N. and Islam, T. (1995). Forecasting with growth curves: an empirical comparison. *International Journal of Forecasting*, 11, 199–215.

Meade, N. and Islam, T. (2001). Forecasting the diffusion of innovations: implications for time series extrapolation. In: J.S. Armstrong (ed.), *Principles of Forecasting: A Handbook for Researchers and Practitioners*, Norwell, MA: Kluwer Academic Publishers, pp. 577–595.

Meade, N. and Islam, T. (2006). Modeling and forecasting the diffusion of innovation — a 25-year review. *International Journal of Forecasting*, 22, 519–545.

Minges, M. (1999). Mobile cellular communications in the Southern African region. *Telecommunications Policy*, 23, 585–593.

Petrazzini, B. (1996). Telecommunications policy in India: the political underpinning of reform. *Telecommunications Policy*, 20(1), 39–51.

Rappaport, T. (2002). *Wireless Communications: Principles and Practice*, 2nd ed. Upper Saddle River, NJ: Prentice Hall.

Rodini, M., Ward, M.R. and Woroch, G.A. (2003). Going mobile: substitutability between fixed and mobile access. *Telecommunications Policy*, 27, 457–476.

Rogers, E.M. (1962). *Diffusion of Innovations*. New York: The Free Press.

Rogers, E.M. (2003). *Diffusion of Innovations*, 5th ed. New York: The Free Press.

Rouvinen, P. (2006). Diffusion of digital mobile telephony: are developing countries different? *Telecommunications Policy*, 30, 46–63.

Shy, O. (2001). *The Economics of Network Industries*. Cambridge: Cambridge University Press.

Singh, S. (2008). The diffusion of mobile phones in India. *Telecommunications Policy*, 32, 642–651.

Sundqvist, S., Frank, L. and Puumalainen, K. (2005). The effects of country characteristics, culture similarity and adoption timing on the diffusion of wireless communications. *Journal of Business Research*, 58, 107–110.

Takada, H. and Jain, D. (1991). Cross-national analysis of diffusion of consumer durable goods in Pacific Rim countries. *Journal of Marketing*, 55(2), 48–54.

Tidd, J. and Bessant, J. (2009). *Managing Innovation: Integrating Technological, Market and Organizational Change*. West Sussex, UK: John Wiley & Sons.

Valente, T. (1995). *Network Models of the Diffusion of Innovations*. Cresskill, NJ: Hampton Press.

Vogel, S. (1997). International games with national rules: how regulation shapes competition in 'global' markets. *Journal of Public Policy*, 17(2), 169–193.

Chapter 10

Diffusion of Environmental Products and Services — Towards an Institutions-Theoretic Framework: Comparing Solar Photovoltaic (PV) Diffusion Patterns in Japan and the US

Kwok L. Shum and Chihiro Watanabe

10.1 Introduction

This chapter studies and compares the actual historical data for solar photovoltaic (PV) installation in Japan and the US, and proposes two deployment models to account for the differences. Deployment, along with research, development and demonstration, constitutes what is known as the RD3[1] — as coined by the President's Council of Advisors on Science and Technology (PCAST), US — innovative chain of a new technology.

Japan deploys photovoltaics (PV) with a focus on the utility grid-tied, small-scale PV system niche (over 90% of which is a standardized residential rooftop PV system) using a highly integrated value chain. This seems to draw upon Japan's strong manufacturing culture and

---

[1] RD3 = Research, Development, Demonstration and Deployment.

the associated social technology and institutions for supplier-dominated innovations. The US deploys PV as a broadly defined innovation emphasizing user-oriented customization in both on- and off-grid residential and industrial applications, using small independent and intermediary system integrators. Empirical analysis of the diffusion patterns in the grid-tied small system category in both contexts suggests that Japan's institutions seem to match its mass deployment strategy, while the US' combination of fragmented industry structure and diversified deployment gives rise to a complex diffusion pattern calling for continual institutional innovation or co-evolution. Our research therefore highlights that the diffusion of environmental products and services — or, in general, technical change — is not an autonomous process and has strong institutional underpinnings.[2] Some potential future extensions regarding utilities for this model will be highlighted.

According to Joseph Schumpeter (1939), the process of technical change consists of its invention, innovation and diffusion. While much innovation literature is focused on the generation and R&D of new technologies, it is only when such new technologies are diffused and widely utilized in an economy that their benefits can be fully reaped. Diffusion also allows technology's interaction with users for its continual improvement. As a result, the diffusion of technology plays a critical and active role in the technical change process.

New energy technology, such as renewable energy, and its uptake and diffusion can be considered an important component for the transition to a sustainable energy system contributing to broader environmental and energy security. As global environmental issues and energy resource scarcity emerge, the importance of renewable energy such as solar PV is ever-increasing. Yet, the introduction of solar PV to the existing fossil fuel energy regime faces different types of barriers due to the carbon lock-in (Unruh, 2000) that has arisen through a combination of systematic forces which perpetuate the fossil fuel-based infrastructure, including physical, social and informational elements. These barriers put renewable energy at an economic, regulatory and

---

[2] In this vein, Paul David has suggested the notion of institutions as a "technology for technical change" (Arora et al., 2006).

institutional disadvantage relative to the incumbent forms of energy supply.

In general, the diffusion of new technologies is not autonomous and is subject to institutional effects. Different types of technologies or technical change[3] need different types of accompanying institutional change. A big systemic change in technology, such as a change in the techno-economic paradigm, tends to provoke correspondingly big changes in institutions; conversely, some institutional innovations are particularly favorable to the introduction and diffusion of new technologies (Freeman, 1992). Perez (1983) has suggested that technologies and institutions co-evolve together so that such a mutual adjustment will lead to a good "match" between institutions and technologies for the latter's uptake and widespread utilization in the economy.

This chapter attempts to construct a theoretical and empirical framework for such a match theory in the context of the deployment or commercialization of a new energy technology. We draw upon Nelson and Sampat's (2001) notion of a physical and social technology to represent how a technology is deployed and the institutions for its deployment, respectively. A fundamental premise is that renewable energy such as solar PV represents a new user-oriented and decentralized energy-generation paradigm that is substantially different from the existing fossil fuel-based, supplier-oriented and centralized energy-generation regime. Solar PV is basically a general-purpose energy technology or a broadly defined innovation that is customizable to different local conditions and application requirements.

All designed solar PV systems need to be "put together" via a system integration process at the user site. This system integration need not be undertaken by PV system component manufacturers such as solar cell and module manufacturers. In fact, such integration can be undertaken by third-party independent project companies and system integrators. The diffusion of solar PV is therefore especially

---

[3] See, for example, Freeman (1992) on the four categories of technical change: incremental innovation, radical innovation, systems of technology and the techno-economic paradigm.

subject to how the system integration is done: either by component manufacturers or by intermediary system integrators situated between PV system component manufacturers and end users. These two different scenarios can be summarized in terms of the structure of the PV value chain from component manufacturers to the system end users. Different combinations of how this general technology is deployed and the value chain structure for its deployment will give rise to different diffusion patterns of a particular application utilizing this generic energy technology principle.

We studied and compared the actual historical data for solar PV installation in Japan and the US, and propose two deployment models to account for the differences. Japan deploys PV with a focus on the utility grid-tied, small-scale PV system niche (more than 90% of which is a standardized residential rooftop PV system) using an integrated PV value chain. This seems to draw upon Japan's strong manufacturing culture and the associated social technology and institutions for supplier-dominated innovations. The US, on the other hand, deploys PV as a broadly defined innovation using a customization strategy with diversified applications, but with a fragmented value chain consisting of component manufacturers, small independent intermediary system integrators, etc. These two deployment models can therefore be classified in terms of two dimensions: the focus of deployment focus and the integrity of the value chain for deployment. A focused deployment using an integrated value chain collectively constitutes a *closed* model of deployment, whereas a diversified deployment using a fragmented value chain can be conceptualized as an *open* model of deployment (Shum and Watanabe, 2006a).

Empirically, we used the probit diffusion model (Davies, 1979; Kodama, 1995) to analyze the PV installation patterns in the utility grid-tied small system category. Our findings appear to be able to discriminate between simple and complex diffusion patterns of this category of application in the context of the different deployment models. An evolutionary-theoretic account of technological diffusion (Lissoni and Metcalfe, 1994) is offered as a basis for interpreting such differences in diffusion patterns. On top of this, our attempt is to propose a theory of match or fit (Tidd, 2001) between how a technology is productized (the physical technology) and the institutions for its deployment (the social technology) in terms of the diffusion analysis results.

The rest of the chapter is organized as follows. Section 10.2 reviews the deployment statistics of PV in Japan and the US using data sources from the International Energy Agency (IEA). Section 10.3 summarizes relevant theories of the social aspect of technical change. Section 10.4 provides a diffusion framework for elucidating or interpreting the joint effects of the social technology and how a physical technology is deployed on the latter's diffusion. The final section presents the conclusions and offers possible future research directions.

10.2 Different PV Deployment Strategies

A review of the historical solar PV installation data in Japan and the US shows a marked contrast. According to the IEA (2003),[4] Japan's cumulative PV installation is three times that of the US. In the specific category of the utility grid-tied small PV residential system, Japan's cumulative installation is almost eight times that of the US, despite the fact that Japan has only one tenth of the building-integrated photovoltaics (BIPV) area potential (roof + facade) of that of the US. Existing studies on renewable energy policy have mostly focused on subsidies or financial-based instruments and incentives to compensate for the market distortion facing renewable energy technologies. However, a more fundamental issue is the economics of the production of renewable energy. The economics of a PV system are determined by the cost of its constituent components, such as the solar cell module (Watanabe *et al.*, 2002) and other balance of system (BOS)[5] components plus the installation

---

[4] At the time of writing (September 2007), national PV installation statistics provided by the IEA website were only available up until the year 2003.

[5] BOS refers to the PV hardware components (other than the solar cell) and includes an inverter, two-way net meters and other installation accessories. They jointly account for ~35–40% of the cost of a PV generation system. As a rough estimate, the construction cost carries about 10–15% of the total system cost. The combination of how PV is deployed and the choice of social technology will have the most impact on learning in the system installation cost and the transaction costs.

cost — collectively known as the system cost. The most relevant characteristic of these two cost components is that the economy of production of the module is subject to mass production learning and exhibits global spillover, while production learning of system integration is among diverse integration projects and is local in nature (Wene, 2000).

A small PV system, whether on or off the grid, while bearing the nature of a consumer electric appliance, is basically a small project that needs extensive on-site integration and installation work. Standardization in design, installation and interconnection (if applicable) will greatly optimize *ex post* transaction and installation costs. During the period of 1992–2003, Japan focused on productizing PV as a grid-tied, small-scale PV system (over 90% of which was a standardized residential rooftop system) accounting for over 90% of its overall cumulative PV installation. On the other hand, the US has productized PV as a broadly defined innovation or general-purpose technology, customizing the technology to end user-oriented requirements as both on- and off-grid small systems[6] for residential and commercial applications.

While the term "productizing" is used interchangeably with "deployment", productizing can be interpreted in light of more formal arguments in innovation management. According to Dosi (1988), the solution for most technological problems (e.g. designing a machine with certain performance characteristics, improving the efficiency of a production input, etc.) implies the use of pieces of knowledge of various sorts. Some elements represent a widely applicable understanding such as direct scientific knowledge or pervasive applicative principles, examples of which are mechanics, electromagnetism, optical principles or, as in this case, solar PV. Some other pieces of knowledge are specific to particular applications — in our case, to the experience of the producer or system integrators needed to put together a functioning system. The knowledge structure of an

---

[6] Besides small system, the IEA has also defined another category of PV application known as grid-tied centralized power plant (like the conventional fossil fuel-based power plant).

innovation can also be seen as articulated vs. tacit and public vs. private. Articulated knowledge is written down in considerable detail in manuals and articles, and is taught in schools. Tacit knowledge is mainly learned through practices and practical examples, such as the elements needed to be a "good engineer" or a "good designer" (Dosi, 1988, p. 224), and has more to do with the formulation of a problem than the brute force application of a principle. In activities aimed at technological innovation, a shared use of highly selected scientific and technological knowledge is coupled with the use and development of specific and often partly private (application-specific) heuristics and capabilities.

Productizing[7] can be seen as those engineering activities that are involved in the adaptation of the generic PV principle to particular application problems. However, since the generic principle is embodied in a solar PV cell supplied by module manufacturers and the actual system integration may involve independent system integrators, productizing PV needs to draw upon the different sources of knowledge distributed across these two groups of suppliers and needs to be concerned with their coordination or the "productionization"[8] aspect. In other words, deploying or productizing PV not only draws upon public and application-specific knowledge, but should also consider the production implication of how module suppliers and system integrators are to be coordinated. It is the primary argument of this chapter that different deployment models have not only adopted different deployment focuses, but have also coordinated these two groups of suppliers or sources of knowledge differently in terms of the different value chain structures observed.

It is conceivable that different institutional arrangements are necessary for the success of each of these deployment strategies. Empirically, different degrees of success can be measured in terms of learning in *system integration cost*. In addition, such differences will

---

[7] Productizing in the context of the PV sector is implicitly suggested by Serchuk and Singh (1998), as they advocated a "product" pathway to PV.
[8] We thank an anonymous reviewer for this suggestion.

also give rise to different diffusion patterns, mediated by the different industrial organization structure in the PV system integration sector in each country. We therefore briefly review each country's PV industry structure as background for further investigation.

10.2.1 Japan

As of the fiscal year (FY) 2003, cumulative PV installation in Japan reached 860 MWp, of which over 700 MWp was installed in the grid-connected small PV system category[9] (the grid-connected distributed category in Figure 10.1).

As mentioned in Section 10.1, Japan has adopted a mass deployment strategy to productize the PV technology, focusing on grid-tied, small-scale PV (residential) application. This draws upon Japan's

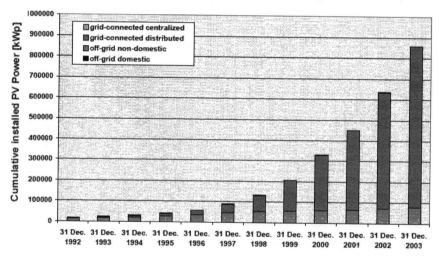

Figure 10.1. Japanese historical PV installation data by category: a mass deployment approach (IEA, 2003).[10]

---

[9] Within this category of grid-tied small systems, approximately 623 MWp was installed as a relatively standardized residential rooftop PV system, which can be regarded as an electric appliance as suggested by Dr. Yukinori Kuwano, President of the Photovoltaic Power Generation Technology Research Association.

[10] http://www.oja-services.nl/iea-pvps/countries/index.htm/.

excellence in manufacturing technology (Watanabe and Kondo, 2003) featuring total quality control (TQC), just-in-time (JIT), *kaizen* and other organizational innovations such as *keiretsu* or closed networks of interlocking suppliers. Within these closed networks, implicit transaction rules among related entities and specific communication languages are developed to coordinate product development. In fact,[11] a special condition of the Japanese PV industry is the fact that a few large companies internalize the whole PV value chain (or at least large portions of it), offering solar cells, modules, BOS components, system integration, financing and maintenance, etc. Many houses in Japan are prefabricated, i.e. construction companies use standardized building components; this is favorable for the integration of solar modules. Solar cell manufacturers therefore have either bought or forged strategic alliances with housing or construction companies, leading to vertical integrated entities. The integration of the PV system at an early stage in the planning of prefabricated and mass-manufactured houses offers the chance for a significant price reduction of PV systems compared to individually built houses or retrofit projects. The pre-installation and mass fabrication of homes in Japan enables manufacturers to limit actual installation work of the PV system on the building site, leading to considerable savings. The vertical integrated infrastructure in the PV industry (Figure 10.2) is thus very conducive to the mass production approach of productizing PV technology in Japan for a specific standard application.

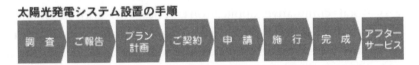

Figure 10.2. An integrated PV value chain within a firm boundary in the PV industry in Japan. Step 1, site inspection; step 2, report; step 3, project proposal and planning; step 4, the contracting process; step 5, applications; step 6, project execution; step 7, completion and commissioning; step 8, follow-up. *Source*: Sekisui Ltd, Japan.

---

[11] The rest of this subsection draws heavily upon Jager-Waldau (2004).

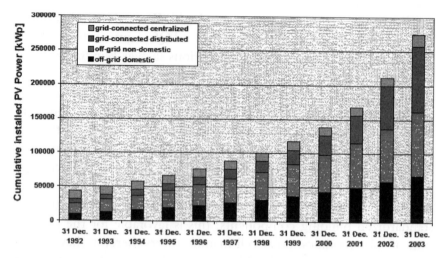

Figure 10.3. USA historical PV installation data by category: a diversified deployment approach (IEA, 2003).

10.2.2 USA

On the other hand, as of FY 2003, cumulative PV installation in the US reached 275.2 MWp, of which approximately 95.6 MWp was installed as a grid-connected distributed application (Figure 10.3). In fact, USA PV installation in the small systems category (exclusive of on-grid centralized application) is well split among off-grid domestic, off-grid non-domestic and on-grid distributed applications. However, the PV market has been dominated by off-grid applications (about 60% of total cumulative application). These off-grid installations include remote residential power, industrial applications, telecommunications and infrastructure (such as highway and pipeline lighting or buoys). These applications are competitive, since costly grid extension is avoided. The drawback is that these applications are mostly non-standardized and system integration is on a project-by-project basis, thus rendering any type of systemic learning impossible as is usually the case for user-oriented innovations in renewable energy (Ornetzeder and Rohracher, 2006).

10.2.3 *PV value chain issue*

Section 10.2.2 describes the deployment focus, or the lack of it, in the US model. In addition, a long history of PV spending on R&D to bring down the cost of PV cells and modules has created an industry that is focused primarily on component manufacturing in the US. As a result, the majority of engineers employed in the PV industry in the US are engaged in technology development rather than product development. A large percentage of PV system sales to final customers flows through small system integrators who assemble custom systems for individual customers. According to Paul Maycock (2005) of PV Systems in the US, in 2005 about 105 MW of PV power was installed by 100 system integrators in the US, many of which were "mom and pop stores". This market structure is highly fragmented and necessitates a large value-added component to each system, adding more than 50% of the final per-kilowatt cost of PV in many end-use applications. That is, many different firms participate in the PV value chain and each requires an acceptable profit margin, thus raising the price of the final product substantially. More importantly, this market structure insulates primary manufacturers from PV customers. It keeps the markets small because each small company lacks the economies of scale of the large integrated manufacturers. The small companies serving end-use markets do not have the resources to manufacture or further innovate upon standardized PV products that serve whole market segments rather than just a few customers (Ingersoll *et al.,* 2000).

As a result, one of the most conspicuous differences between the Japanese and US PV industries can be seen not only in terms of the diversity of applications, but also in terms of the value chain structure which brings these applications to the market. It is argued in this chapter that these combined differences will sustain different diffusion patterns of solar PV in the specific category of utility grid-tied small systems. This perspective can be generalized into the hypothesis that an effective deployment of new technology is contingent upon both the institutional arrangements and how the technology is actually productized, in terms of focus or diversification. A more effective deployment may be interpreted as a better match between the two, leading to better performance such as a greater extent of diffusion. Before we analyze the diffusion patterns, we need to resort to theoretical frameworks that conceptualize the holistic nature of technology, namely, its technical and social components. A particularly useful one for our purpose is that of Nelson and Sampat (2001).

10.3 The Systemic (Social) Nature of Technology

The deployment models above are characterized in terms of the diversity of deployment and the structure of the value chain used for deployment. These dual perspectives can be collapsed into the physical and social technology framework (Nelson and Sampat, 2001), which will be reviewed next to aid our theoretical development.[12]

10.3.1 Social technology and physical technology

Nelson and Sampat (2001), in trying to make sense of institutions as a factor shaping economic performance, conceptualized technology as consisting of both social and physical aspects. Their focus was to associate growth as being driven by technical change and institutions. Their line of inquiry, therefore, was on how institutions shape technical change and vice versa — a notion they termed "co-evolution".

Physical technology is inextricably connected with particular machinery and other specialized inputs that are employed; they are embodied in the "production function" in neo-classical economics. In the current context of our discussion, physical technology refers to the implementation of the physical principle of PV. This may involve the system architecture, components, installation, maintenance, etc.; and it requires the input of system integrators, component suppliers and even project financiers or other market players. Different solar PV

[12] Other similar frameworks include that of Fleck (2000), which was reviewed in Shum and Watanabe (2007).

applications will necessitate different system architectures. A standard utility grid-tied, small-scale residential system will have a different architecture/layout than that of a system which is not connected to the grid. Deploying PV with an emphasis on the diversity of applications or customization will lead to a proliferation of one-off system architectures with different physical components. In general, the diversity approach will lead to an oversupply of product variants (Geroski, 2003) and the industry will take a longer time to arrive at a dominant standard or architecture compared to a focused approach. Overall, deployment focus will influence the stabilization of the architectural aspect of the physical technology.

Social technology, on the other hand, is a concept that elaborates the carrying out of the physical technology, recognizing the multi-party interactions involved in the operation of most physical technologies that sometimes go on within a firm and sometimes between firms. In the case of solar PV, social technology refers to a social organization of the different market players cited above to finance, build and even operate a PV system. Within a firm, the M-form of organizing a multi-product company can be interpreted as a social technology. Among firms and in the context of joint R&D, a consortium composed of coordinating member firms' research efforts can be seen as a social technology of joint research and development.

Social technologies[13] therefore define the productive pathway for doing things, and define low-transaction-cost ways of doing things that involve coordinated human interaction. Different system architectures in the physical technology domain will have an implication on the choice of social or coordination technology for the carrying out of the physical technology. The optimal social technology for a modular architecture may be different from that for an integral architecture. Even for a given system architecture in the physical technology domain, there may be alternative ways of organizing the production processes to coordinate module suppliers and system

---

[13] These also include forms of business organizations, management practices, market mechanisms and structures, public policies, legal and regulatory structures, etc.

integrators. The differences of PV deployment models in Japan and the US can be partly attributed to such differently organized PV value chains.

As a result, the invisible social technology enters the story in terms of how it enables the implementation or development of physical technologies. However, the influence is not only one-way: prevailing social technologies or institutions can also strongly influence the way physical technologies evolve. It is more complete to think of social and physical technologies as co-evolving. In general, productive routines can be seen as consisting of both physical and social technology components.[14] In a more refined study, Nelson (2003) proposed that these two components which make up a technology have different evolution dynamics. This is an important reference point, as will be evident later, in interpreting the results of diffusion pattern analysis.

10.3.2 *The nature of a physical technology*

One practical way to think about or conceptualize physical technology that relates to our discussion of social technology is in terms of the *role of users*[15] in carrying out or developing the physical technology. There is now an emerging literature in innovation management theory and technical changes whereby users are playing an increasingly active role in the innovation process. Notions such as co-development, co-invention (Bresnahan and Greenstein, 1997), user-oriented innovations and user–producer interaction (Lundvall, 1988) all capture, in one way or another, this democratization of the innovation process (von Hippel, 2005). We can, in general, classify different physical technologies along a continuum of the degree of user participation.

---

[14] According to Nelson and Sampat (2001), the physical technology is a recipe that is anonymous regarding any division of labor, while the social technology refers to the division of labor plus a mode of coordination.

[15] See the *International Journal of Innovation Management*, Vol. 12, No. 3, September 2008, for a collection of articles concerning participatory innovation.

For product technologies such as TV, automobile and other manufactured items, the technologies are embodied in hardware and the product features are dominated by the suppliers or producers. Operational efficiency as well as attempts to leverage both cost and quality are critical to operations. We can roughly call this category of technology "manufactured technology". Another generic category of physical technology is known as "information technology", the product features of which are formed during the course of interaction with institutional systems. Users, based on a common or standardized interface, jointly develop product features with suppliers of technologies. Interoperability and network externality are the quintessential characteristics of information technology. What are the implications of the choice of social technology in order to carry out such different physical technologies as manufactured technology and information technology, which feature different amounts of user involvement in the technology or product development process?

For manufactured technology, Japanese companies are widely regarded as the most successful. These manufacturers intensively developed products using their own in-house technology, since customers were more interested in the quality of products than in the compatibility among products from different manufacturers. For quality assurance and cost control, firms used in-house procurement of manufacturing parts or relied on a closed network of long-term *keiretsu* suppliers for intensive horizontal coordination. They also developed an individual and specific communication language that consequently excluded entities outside of this closed network. This social technology of *keiretsu*[16] for implementing manufactured technology greatly facilitated information sharing among closed members and aided management initiatives such as TQC, JIT and *kaizen* (continual incremental improvement).

---

[16] *Keiretsu* is also a vital component of the lean manufacturing paradigm. Here, we only want to highlight *keiretsu* as a critical social technology that coordinates various interactions to implement the cost- and quality-driven manufactured technology.

In contrast, information technology has brought about open systems. The US culture of heterogeneity has proved to be much readier to embrace this physical technology. The open system paradigm or modular product system (Aoki, 2001) depends upon a network of module suppliers coordinated by a standardized digital interface, rather than relying upon a group of close suppliers leveraging on tacit knowledge. Due to the flexible nature of this physical technology, it allows easy customization (by recombining or mixing and matching different modules) to different applications in different contexts. One prototypical manifestation of this open paradigm is the Wintel platform for PC-based applications: numerous software applications have been developed for different applications based on the same platform.[17]

Kodama (2000) has said that information technology seems to have its own way of generating new business models or *use systems* as it diffuses into the user community. This is due to the fact that, based upon an industry standard, independent developers can develop specific applications or pursue decentralized innovations, leading to the self-propagation of this generic industry standard or information technology platform. This type of open coordination based on a common standard interface is drastically different from the closed Japanese *keiretsu* social technology to produce high-quality manufactured items at reduced cost and waste.

It is worth mentioning that, while manufactured technology usually leverages upon conventional economies of mass production such as dynamic learning by doing, information technology features a different, dynamic economy of scope or cross-learning (Shum, 2003; Shum and Watanabe, 2004) among different customized derivative applications based upon a common platform or interface. The optimal social technology that is chosen to implement these different physical technologies should therefore reflect how these two different modes or mechanisms of production learning come about. Specifically, in the case of information technology, platform suppliers such as Intel or Microsoft organize training programs and developer forums to

---

[17] At the time of writing, Microsoft had developed yet another platform for applications software development for robot-based applications.

facilitate exchanges of best practices or lessons learned among third-party independent developers. Without such mechanisms, cross-interaction or spillover learning will be undersupplied. Developer forums are therefore a critical social technology, as is vertical integration for manufactured technology, to organize a production organization for platform- or standard-based information technology.

10.4 A Technology Diffusion Framework to Understand the Differences in PV Deployment Models

Our objective now is to understand the implications of different value chain structures — or, broadly defining, social technologies — coupled with different PV deployment strategies in each national context on the dynamics of technology diffusion. We investigated the set of historical installation data for the grid-tied small PV system category as a percentage of the cumulative PV installation in each country. Table 10.1 shows the normalized numbers. It is very important to emphasize that the time series in the table does not represent the

Table 10.1. Normalized installation pattern (%) for the utility grid-tied small PV system category (IEA, 2003; and authors' own calculation).

	Japan	US
1992	0.06	—
1993	0.09	—
1994	0.16	0.14
1995	0.249	0.145
1996	0.343	0.143
1997	0.472	0.155
1998	0.582	0.158
1999	0.714	0.179
2000	0.79	0.202
2001	0.846	0.242
2002	0.88	0.299
2003	0.904	0.3473

percentage of grid-tied small PV system category diffusion with respect to the potential market size of that category, as is done in the traditional diffusion analysis. We need to consider the normalized ratio tabulated because we want to investigate the build-up in the grid-tied small PV system category that is driven not by the expansion of the overall PV system market in each country, but *only* by the inherent diffusion dynamics in that particular category. This is similar in spirit to the fact that adoption analysis requires an unchanging population of potential adopters (Kodama, 1995, p. 251). Put differently, the normalization will factor out the effect of overall market expansion on the innate diffusion dynamics of the grid-tied small PV system.

10.4.1 *Diffusion analysis of Japan's data*

From Table 10.1, Japan's percentage is increasing monotonically. This is a kind of regularity condition in order for logistic analysis to be applied to this set of data. Now, our objective is to characterize this time series of normalized or "reduced" diffusion dynamics in the grid-tied small PV system category, and to hypothesize it as being the joint effects of (1) a social technology of the integrated PV value chain in Japan and (2) a mass deployment focus upon this category.

The logistic analysis of Japan's data is shown as follows:

$$\log\left(\frac{m_t}{n - m_t}\right) = -1.330 + 0.204t, \text{ where } t = -28.662 \text{ or } 32.383.$$

$$\text{Adjusted } R^2 = 0.989.$$

Here, m_t are the individual entries in Table 10.1, and $n = 1$ because the maximum of m_t is unity. As can be seen, the adjusted R^2 is extremely high, and the regression coefficients all have high t-values. On this basis, we can identify the conventional logistic as the diffusion path that best characterizes the progression of the ratio of the cumulative installation of the small grid-tied PV system to overall cumulative PV installation in Japan, or the normalized diffusion dynamics of this category of PV application.

It is worthwhile to recapitulate that the conventional logistic assumes a word-of-mouth communication process, resulting in an epidemic process with less emphasis on institutional or behavioral aspects of diffusion (Geroski, 2000). In addition, it is important to note that previous studies (Kodama, 2000; Watanabe *et al.*, 2003) of the diffusion of mass-manufactured commoditized items also concur that the diffusion of such items fits the conventional logistic curve better than any other alternative diffusion models. Our empirical analysis therefore suggests that, under the integrated PV value chain, along with a sharp deployment focus and other associated government policies, the grid-tied small PV system category is productized or commercialized like a mass-manufactured technology in Japan.

10.4.2 *Diffusion analysis of US data*

We performed the same logistic analysis on the US data tabulated in Table 10.1 or shown in Figure 10.4. The corresponding results are shown as follows:

$$\log\left(\frac{m_t}{n - m_t}\right) = -0.929 + 0.056t, \quad \text{where } t = -17.827 \text{ or } 7.515.$$

$$\text{Adjusted } R^2 = 0.86.$$

This set of data does not seem to fit the single logistic as well as that of Japan's. The adjusted R^2 is 0.86 and the significance is less. If we use the case of Japan as a comparative base, the US results suggest that a diversified PV deployment approach, coupled with a very fragmented industry structure in the PV system integration sector, results in a non-conventional diffusion pattern in the grid-tied small PV system category. This implies that the diffusion is not information-based.

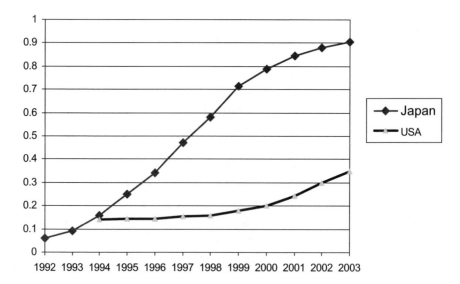

Figure 10.4. Plotting the data in Table 10.1.

To further characterize the US data, we adopted Davies' (1979) and Alderman and Davies' (1990) technology diffusion model and hypothesized that normalized or reduced diffusion patterns in the grid-tied small PV system category in the US may follow one of two different patterns: that of a *simple innovation* or of a *complex innovation*.

The Davies model belongs to a class of diffusion models known as equilibrium-based diffusion models (Davies, 1979; Lissoni and Metcalfe, 1994; Kodama, 1995; Geroski, 2000).[18] These are conceptualized to capture the decision-making or behavioral aspect of innovation (such as durable goods) adoption. This vantage point differs greatly from the conventional logistic curve or epidemic models,

---

[18] Note that there is a class of disequilibrium (or evolutionary) models that stresses how ordered patterns of diffusion may emerge from apparently irrational behaviors (Lissoni and Metcalfe, 1994). Cabral (2006) reported that equilibrium-based diffusion models incorporating network externality will lead to multiple diffusion paths, giving the diffusion of technology a catastrophic flavor.

which abstract from differences in the goals, characteristics or actions of individual members of the adopting population and instead focus on the diffusion of information in a simple, tractable, non-strategic setting.

The Davies model assumes the *heterogeneity* of agents (individuals[19]) in terms of the distribution of income or another characteristic relevant to the adoption of the innovation across the adopting population. An agent bases their adoption decision upon the relationship between their own income and a critical or threshold income. They will adopt the innovation if and only if their income is greater than their individual threshold; this threshold may depend on either the price of the innovation under consideration or the agent's own personal characteristics. All agents whose incomes are greater than their personal critical incomes are observed to adopt the innovation under consideration. As time passes, those who have not yet adopted the innovation may reverse their decision either because their incomes increase or because their critical threshold incomes decrease. If the incomes and the threshold incomes (which are different for different adopters) are log-normally distributed over the population, and the means of the two distributions grow and decline at a constant rate, respectively, such that more agents will meet their threshold and thus adopt the innovation, an S-shaped curve or sigmoid diffusion curve will be generated (Lissoni and Metcalfe, 1994).

It must be understood that this refined microeconomic adoption decision process at the agent level, when aggregated across the agents in the population, represents yet another mechanism to generate a sigmoid-shaped technology diffusion curve at the industry or economy level. Newer developments in this framework include those capturing the stochastic or uncertain nature of innovation adoption in the decision-making process using a real options approach (Stoneman and Toivanen, 2006; Stoneman, 2002).

---

[19] For firms as agents, the adoption variable may be in terms of their size, which can be treated as a proxy of their resourcefulness or other innovation assimilation capacities.

This refined approach to technology diffusion, while somewhat simplified, allows us to discern how *ex post* improvement of the innovation will influence the decision-making environment or the objective of the agents and hence the diffusion pattern of the innovation. Intuitively, a simple innovation, as mentioned before, experiences major improvements in the early years but fewer thereafter. On the other hand, a complex innovation has room for sustained improvement for many years after the first commercial introduction. These conspicuously different *ex post* improvement dynamics can be registered in the just-elaborated agent-level decision-making model in terms of the dynamics of threshold (Davies, 1979, pp. 69–70; Kodama, 1995, pp. 261–262). At the aggregate level, this should sketch out different diffusion patterns for the respective types or complexities of innovations. A simple innovation will have a cumulative log-normal pattern, while a complex innovation will sustain a cumulative normal time path. Visually, the former is a positively skewed diffusion curve, while the latter exhibits a symmetrical pattern (Kodama, 1995, p. 263).

It is important to note that the sources of *ex post* improvement of the innovations are not specified. In fact, these can be purely technical or institutional, the latter referring to, for instance, a better information environment that will minimize search cost, transaction cost, etc. for the adoption of innovations. The setup of equilibrium-based diffusion models, such as a probit model, is general enough to admit alternative profit-maximizing regimes as a decision-making rationale that captures the constraint placed on maximizing due to imperfect information and the fact that search involves non-trivial costs (Davies, 1979, p. 67). In the context of this chapter, different social technologies used in the implementation of a given physical technology will pose different decision-making environments for the adopters of the grid-tied small PV system category (PV appliance) and hence result in different adoption dynamics. In other words, the complexity of a technology, to potential adopters, is not solely defined by its physical characteristics but is also determined by the social technology implementing its productization, both of which jointly influence adopters' perceptions (Rogers, 2003).

A more prescriptive stance, as is proposed in this chapter, is that different PV deployment strategies (diversified vs. focused), combined with different social technologies (fragmented vs. vertical integration), result in different adoption environments for agents. Some combinations achieve a better match between physical and social technologies, and may make it easier for the adopter's bounded cognitive ability to understand new innovations and their potential, thus speeding up adoption. This is how a theory of contingent match or fit (Tidd, 2001) between innovations and institutions for the dissemination of the former can be proposed and empirically verified from the diffusion patterns.

Technically, we followed Alderman and Davies (1990). We probit-transformed[20] the US data according to the following transformation: Φ^{-1} $(m_t/n) = a + b \log t$ for simple innovations and Φ^{-1} $(m_t/n) = a + bt$ for complex innovations, where Φ is the probit operator and the arguments operated upon are listed in Table 10.1. The probit-transformed data are shown in Figure 10.5.

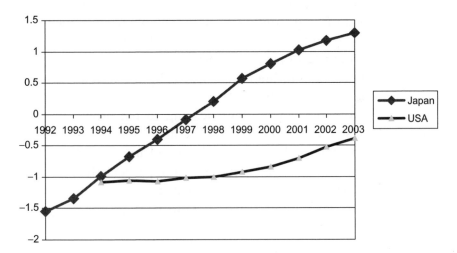

Figure 10.5. Transformed data from Table 10.1 by the probit operator.

---

[20] We must make a provision here that the log-normal distribution assumptions of the characteristics of the relevant PV adopting population for the grid-tied small PV system category are fulfilled.

10.4.3 Analysis of the US pattern

For simple innovation patterns,

$$\Phi^{-1}\left(\frac{m_t}{n}\right) = -1.257 + 0.263\log t, \quad \text{where } t = -10.452 \text{ or } 3.268.$$

$$\text{Adjusted } R^2 = 0.577.$$

For complex innovation patterns,

$$\Phi^{-1}\left(\frac{m_t}{n}\right) = -1.273 + 0.075t, \quad \text{where } t = -19.828 \text{ or } 7.249.$$

$$\text{Adjusted } R^2 = 0.851.$$

We can therefore conclude that the US data set fits better as a complex innovation pattern, which is cumulative normal. It features a slow take-off compared to that of Japan's simple logistics for the grid-tied small PV system category. The gradual build-up may need to be sustained through continual social technology adjustments or institutional co-evolution (Kodama, 1995).[21] The US pattern therefore departs from that of Japan, and may be due to the US deploying PV as an "information technology" (Watanabe *et al.*, 2003) type of physical technology. This strategy emphasizes user-oriented requirements across different applications, leading to the proliferation of one-of-a-kind system designs and architectures. Due to a social technology of fragmented value chains of intermediary and independent system integrators, these combinations are not particularly conducive to the productization of a given single category of PV application, unless there are institutions (such as industry standards or system

---

[21] Kodama (1995) compared the installation and utilization patterns of computers in Japan's prefectural governments during the 1960s and 1970s. A particular advantage of Kodama's data is that he could interpret the delay in utilizing the personal computer in certain categories of prefectural government jobs as being due to those jobs called for institutional adjustments, compared to other jobs which were rather independent or stand-alone in nature.

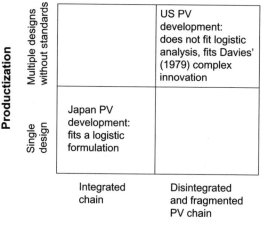

Figure 10.6. A summarizing two-by-two matrix depicting the effects of different combinations of social technology and physical technology upon the diffusion pattern of the specific grid-tied, small-scale PV system category (PV appliance).[22]

integrator training programs) that facilitate significant cross-learning (Shum, 2003) or spillover learning among designs and independent system integrators. These conspicuous differences between the countries' deployment strategies and social technologies used to implement such deployment, leading to this divergence in diffusion patterns in a specific category of application, are summarized in Figure 10.6.

10.5 Discussion, Conclusion and Future Works

10.5.1 *Discussion*

One of the most important conclusions from the above analysis is that the US' solar PV normalized installation pattern in the specific category

---

[22] There are also refined analyses of intermediate cases in some European contexts available from the authors upon request.

of grid-tied, small-scale systems follows a complex innovation pattern. This may be due to its diversified approach and fragmented value chain, yet without a social technology that facilitates learning among these designs and independent system installers and integrators. This section attempts to interpret this finding in light of an evolutionary perspective of diffusion, and to give a more concrete meaning of social technology adjustment or institutional co-evolution.

Recent evolutionary theory (Lissoni and Metcalfe, 1994) has suggested opening the "black box" and re-interpreting the epidemic approach to broaden the word-of-mouth interagent communication process to include a wide class of evolutionary processes and institutional arrangements sustaining the dynamics of diffusion. These additional factors include:

(1) Vertical and horizontal subcontracting relationships or other interfirm relationships;
(2) Cooperation, exchange or movement of skilled labor to motivate spillover learning;
(3) Technology standardization as an infrastructure for continual product innovation;
(4) Consortium policy leading to the generation of new technologies in the pre-competitive stage; and
(5) A network of designers, venture capital firms and intellectual property policy, etc.

All of these specific institutional arrangements are highly relevant to the generation, cumulative learning, productization and appropriation of economic rents of new technological innovations on the supply side. On the demand side, institutions facilitating word of mouth can be generalized as those facilitating the sharing of knowledge acquired during the learning-by-using process among users. Last but not least, institutions facilitating interactive learning among producers and users will enable the *ex post* improvement of innovations, thus further increasing the uptake.

Institutional co-evolution or innovation suggests that these and others are the strategic levers or mechanisms that innovation policy makers should turn to in order to facilitate the launch of new technological innovation cycles. In the context of innovation systems literature (Edquist, 1997), system failures due to missing links among important constituent elements in the system should also be tackled from the standpoint of institutional innovation to establish those missing links.

For the specific case of comparing PV deployment or productization in Japan and the US in terms of a physical technology and social technology framework, the efficiency of different combinations can also be explained in terms of a theoretical notion in institutional economics. Transaction cost is essentially the cost of using the market; it entails the search cost, the cost of contracting (ink cost) and other *ex post* monitoring costs. Wallis and North (1986) have suggested that the larger the transacting sector or the number of intermediary sectors in an economy, the higher the transaction cost. The case of the fragmented PV value chain in the US, then, would incur a higher transaction cost than that of Japan, in which a lot of the market contingencies are internalized within the boundary of a vertically integrated firm. This suggests that institutional co-evolution in the productization of PV in the US involves the continual *economization* of relevant transaction costs and the *re-allocation* of system integration labor. Institutional co-evolution also entails the emergence of institutions that facilitate interproject learning among the diversity of designs and independent system integrators and greater standardization in PV system engineering practices, thus shaping the PV industry in the US into a standards-based production organization (Langlois and Savage, 2001).

Indeed, according to the IEA (2003) and the Solar Electric Power Association[23] in the US, there is an increasing number of certification and training programs for PV system installers and integrators that are aimed at unifying or standardizing installation practices. Such standardization in training also facilitates cross-learning and knowledge reuse[24]

---

[23] See http://www.solarelectricpower.org/sepa.aspx/.

[24] Cross-learning (Shum, 2003) leads to shared routines and public interfaces among engineers or practitioners, giving rise to the "next bench design" which also enables knowledge reuse.

among different project designs, administrations, etc. In addition, in the realm of technical development or physical technology, there is now more standardization in the design, grid interconnection requirements and quality assurance of PV systems. The emergence of such programs, both social and physical, can be interpreted in terms of continual institutional co-evolution and physical technology evolution, respectively. This will lead to standards-based customization activities and hence greatly expedite and facilitate cross-learning among projects, leading to a dynamic economy of scope in the US' diversity-based PV deployment strategy that will compensate for the foregone mass production economy. The upshot is that there will be a better match between the social technology and the way PV is deployed in the US, which in turn will lead to a speedier diffusion.

10.5.2 *Conclusions and future work*

This chapter has used a novel approach to interpret different observed international solar PV installation and diffusion patterns in the specific category of utility grid-tied, small-scale PV systems. We adopted the theoretical notion of social technology and physical technology of Nelson and Sampat (2001) to hypothesize that such observed differences may be due to a disparity in how the general solar PV physical technology or principle is productized and in what kind of institution or social technology is used to bring these applications to the market of adopters. A fundamental motivation in our research was to argue that some combinations of the deployment or productization strategy of solar PV and the social technology may be more optimal than others in terms of the degree or extent of diffusion. The former can be said to achieve a better fit between deployment strategy and social technology than the latter group.

This notion of fit between technical change and institutions was first developed by Perez (1983) and Freeman (1992), but has yet to be empirically formulated for analysis. Our work here can be viewed as a first attempt to demonstrate such a theory of fit (Tidd, 2001) between institutions and technical change and their contingent interdependencies. The empirical findings reported in this chapter appear to confirm that Japan's mass deployment focus on a relatively standard application using a highly integrated value chain achieves a good fit, with minimal need for change in institutions or institutional complications. On the contrary, the US' solar PV deployment emphasizing diversity or customization using a fragmented industry structure does not confer institutional advantages, and calls for institutional co-evolution to improve learning among independent system integrators and the diversity of designs. In a sense, innovation management, especially its diffusion aspect, may have much to do with managing the interaction between how the new technology is deployed and the institutions bringing it to market. This combination will have a bearing upon the decision-making process of potential adopters, as is formulated in the probit model of diffusion, microscopically speaking. Without loss of generality, the framework of physical and social technologies and their joint effects on the innovation adoption decision-making environment of agents can serve as an analytical platform for characterizing the many aspects of institutions as a "technology for technical change", as first proposed by Paul David (see Arora *et al.*, 2006).

While this chapter has approached the deployment of renewable energy as a physical vs. social technology matching issue, this may be simplified since renewable energy deployment or the diffusion of environmental technology is contingent upon government subsidies and other policy instruments. Existing literature, however, tends to overemphasize financial policies such as buydowns and credits, and instead focuses upon aligning economic incentives or addressing economic externalities. Other policies, such as a renewables portfolio standard (RPS) and net metering, have been developed to boost production using the deployed renewable energy equipment.

Experts or policy makers, however, all agree that such financial-based policies should continually decrease and that the adoption of renewable energy must increasingly rely upon its own endogenous, self-propagating dynamics with minimal intervention. One way of approaching this is to formulate the possible synergies between financial policies and PV innovation dynamics and how the two can complement each other. We have suggested elsewhere (Shum and

Watanabe, 2009) that an innovation management framework can guide the targeted applications of such financial subsidies. This implies that government money should be applied to facilitate learning in the most disruptive element or subsystem in the implementation of a renewable energy technology or environmental innovation, in order to increase its likelihood and speed of diffusion. These difficulties tend to be locally based. More importantly, our proposal can be interpreted as extracting or discovering a new dimension to the energy policy space: the level of the *design hierarchy* at which subsidies are applied, rather than just blanket financial subsidies. Without loss of generality, such analysis can also be generalized to other generic renewable energy sources or environmental innovations in order for it to be leveraged in an interindustry study,[25] in addition to international comparisons.

References

Alderman, N. and Davies, S. (1990). Modelling regional patterns of innovation diffusion in the UK metalworking industries. *Regional Studies*, 24(6), 513–528.

Aoki, M. (2001). *Towards a Comparative Institutional Analysis.* Cambridge, MA: MIT Press.

Arora, A., Fosfuri, A. and Gambardella, A. (2006). Markets for technology: 'panda's thumbs', 'calypso policies' and other institutional considerations. In: C. Antonelli, D. Foray, B.H. Hall and W.E. Steinmueller (eds.), *New Frontiers in the Economics of Innovation and New Technology*, Cheltenham: Edward Elgar, pp. 323–361.

Bresnahan, T. and Greenstein, S. (1997). Technical progress and co-invention in computing and in the uses of computers. *Brookings Papers on Economic Activity: Microeconomics*, pp. 1–83.

Cabral, L. (2006). Equilibrium, epidemic and catastrophe: diffusion of innovations with network effects. In: C. Antonelli, D. Foray, B.H. Hall and W.E. Steinmueller (eds.), *New Frontiers in the Economics of Innovation and New Technology*, Cheltenham: Edward Elgar, pp. 427–437.

Davies, S. (1979). *The Diffusion of Process Innovations.* Cambridge: Cambridge University Press.

---

[25] We are grateful for Professor Nathan Rosenberg's suggestion to us on this issue when he was visiting the Tokyo Institute of Technology during the 2nd International SIMOT Symposium on February 27–28, 2006.

Dosi, G. (1988). The nature of the innovative process. In: G. Dosi, C. Freeman, R. Nelson, G. Silverberg and L. Soete (eds.), *Technical Change and Economic Theory*, London: Pinter, pp. 221–238.

Edquist, C. (1997). *Systems of Innovation: Technologies, Institutions, and Organizations*. London: Pinter.

Fleck, J. (2000). The artefact–activity couple. In: J. Ziman (ed.), *Technological Innovation as an Evolutionary Process*, Cambridge: Cambridge University Press, pp. 248–266.

Freeman, C. (1992). *The Economics of Hope: Essays on Technical Change, Economic Growth, and the Environment*. London: Pinter.

Geroski, P. (2000). Models of technology diffusion. *Research Policy*, 29, 603–625.

Geroski, P. (2003). *The Evolution of New Markets*. New York: Oxford University Press.

Ingersoll, E., Gallagher, D.C. and Vysatova, R.A. (2000). Industry development strategy for the PV sector. Available at http://www.crest.org/repp_pubs/articles/pv/2/2.html/.

International Energy Agency (IEA). (2003). *Co-operative Programme on Photovoltaic Power Systems — Task 1: Exchange and Dissemination of Information on PV Power Systems. National Survey Report of PV Power Applications in the United States of America*. IEA.

Jager-Waldau, A. (2004). *PV Status Report 2004 — Research, Solar Cell Production and Market Implementation of Photovoltaics*. Luxembourg: Office for Official Publications of the European Communities.

Kodama, F. (1995). *Emerging Patterns of Innovation: Sources of Japan's Technological Edge*. Boston: Harvard Business School Press.

Kodama, F. (2000). Innovation management in the emerging IT environments. In: *Proceedings of the First World Conference on Production and Operations Management — POM Facing the New Millennium: Evaluating the Past, Leading with the Present and Planning the Future of Operations, Sevilla, 2000*.

Langlois, R. and Savage, D. (2001). Standards, modularity, and innovation: the case of medical practice. In: R. Garud and P. Karnøe (eds.), *Path Dependence and Creation*, Mahwah, NJ: Lawrence Erlbaum Associates, pp. 149–168.

Lissoni, F. and Metcalfe, J. (1994). Diffusion of innovation ancient and modern: a review of the main themes. In: M. Dodgson and R. Rothwell (eds.), *The Handbook of Industrial Innovation*, Aldershot: Edward Elgar, pp. 106–141.

Lundvall, B. (1988). Innovation as an interactive process: from user-producer interaction to national systems of innovation. In: G. Dosi, C. Freeman, R. Nelson, G. Silverberg and L. Soete (eds.), *Technical Change and Economic Theory*, London: Pinter, pp. 349–369.

Maycock, P. (2005). Personal telephone interview.

Nelson, R. (2003). Physical and social technologies and their evolution. LEM Working Paper No. 2003/09, Laboratory of Economics and Management (LEM), Sant'Anna School of Advanced Studies, Pisa, Italy.

Nelson, R. and Sampat, N. (2001). Making sense of institutions as a factor shaping economic performance. *Journal of Economic Behavior and Organization*, 44, 31–54.

Ornetzeder, M. and Rohracher, H. (2006). User-led innovations and participation processes: lessons from sustainable energy technologies. *Energy Policy*, 34, 138–150.

Perez, C. (1983). Structural change and the assimilation of new technologies in the economic and social system. *Futures*, 15(4), 357–375.

Rogers, E. (2003). *Diffusion of Innovations*. New York: Free Press.

Schumpeter, J.A. (1939). *Business Cycles: A Theoretical, Historical and Statistical Analysis of the Capitalist Process*. New York: McGraw Hill.

Serchuk, A. and Singh, V. (1998). *Expanding Markets for PV: What to Do Next?* Washington, D.C.: Renewable Energy Policy Project (REPP).

Shum, K. (2003). The strategic implications of product platform. In: *Proceedings of the Mass Customization and Personalization Conference, Technical University of Munich, Munich, Germany.*

Shum, K. and Watanabe, C. (2004). Product diversification and its management. In: *Proceedings of the 13th International Conference on Management of Technology, IAMOT 2004, Washington, D.C., USA, April 3–7, 2004.*

Shum, K. and Watanabe, C. (2006a). Photovoltaic deployment strategies in Japan and the US — an institutional appraisal. *Energy Policy*, 35, 1186–1195.

Shum, K. and Watanabe, C. (2007). Towards an institutions-theoretic framework — comparing solar photovoltaic diffusion patterns in Japan and the US. *International Journal of Innovation Management*, 11(4), 565–592.

Shum, K. and Watanabe, C. (2009). An innovation management approach for renewable energy deployment — the case of solar photovoltaic (PV) technology. *Energy Policy*, 37(9), 3535–3544.

Stoneman, P. (2002). *The Economics of Technological Diffusion*. Oxford: Blackwell.

Stoneman, P. and Toivanen, O. (2006). Technological diffusion under uncertainty: a real options model applied to the comparative international diffusion of robot technology. In: C. Antonelli, D. Foray, B.H. Hall and W.E. Steinmueller (eds.), *New Frontiers in the Economics of Innovation and New Technology*, Cheltenham: Edward Elgar, pp. 438–470.

Tidd, J. (2001). Innovation management in context: environment, organization and performance. *International Journal of Management Reviews*, 3(3), 169–183.

Unruh, G. (2000). Understanding carbon lock-in. *Energy Policy*, 28, 817–830.

von Hippel, E. (2005). *Democratizing Innovation*. Cambridge, MA: MIT Press.

Wallis, J. and North, D. (1986). Measuring the transaction sector in the American economy, 1870–1970. In: S. Engerman and R. Gallman (eds.), *Long-Term Factors in American Economic Growth*, Chicago: University of Chicago Press, pp. 95–161.

Watanabe, C., Griffy-Brown, C., Zhu, B. and Nagamatsu, A. (2002). Inter-firm technology spillover and the "virtuous cycle" of photovoltaic development in Japan. In: A. Grubler, N. Nakicenovic and W.D. Nordhaus (eds.), *Technological Change and the Environment*, Washington, D.C.: Resources for the Future, pp. 127–159.

Watanabe, C. and Kondo, R. (2003). Institutional elasticity towards IT waves for Japan's survival — the significant role of an IT testbed. *Technovation*, 23(4), 307–320.

Watanabe, C., Kondo, R., Ouchi, N. and Wei, H. (2003). Formation of IT features through interaction with institutional systems — empirical evidence of unique epidemic behavior. *Technovation*, 23(3), 205–219.

Wene, C. (2000). *Experience Curves for Energy Technology Policy*. Paris: OECD/IEA.

Part III

Prediction of Future Patterns of Diffusion

Chapter 11

Forecasting Technology Diffusion

*Tugrul Daim, Nuri Basoglu, Nathasit Gerdsri
and Thien Tran*

11.1 Introduction

This chapter will describe a process for exploring the adoption of technological innovations. The process is extremely critical for those planning to introduce new products driven by emerging technological innovations. The process described has four steps which will be discussed (see Figure 11.1).

11.2 Technology Assessment

11.2.1 *Multi-criteria technology assessment*

There are several methodologies used for technology assessment (Daim and Kocaoglu, 2008a, 2008b, 2009; Tran and Daim, 2008). A large number of articles on technology assessment use decision analysis methods. The analytic hierarchy process (AHP) was found to be the most favored methodology. Merkhofer (1982) used a decision-focused technology assessment process including problem definition, alternative generation, deterministic analysis, probabilistic analysis, informational analysis and policy evaluation. Bard and Feinberg (1989) developed an assessment of electric and hybrid passenger vehicles in which they apply the deterministic multi-attribute utility theory and Monte Carlo simulation. Prasad and Somasekhara (1990)

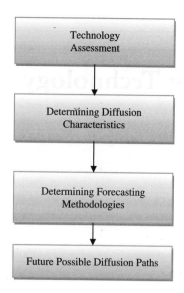

Figure 11.1.   The forecasting-for-diffusion process.

used an integration of the Delphi and AHP methods for choice of technologies in Indian telecommunications. Raju *et al.* (1995) evaluated five technology alternatives in toilet soap making that are ranked by the application of AHP. Prabhu and Vizayakumar (2001) developed the fuzzy hierarchical decision-making (FHDM) method, which synthesizes the concepts of multi-criteria decision-making methodology and fuzzy analysis. Meade and Presley (2002) used the analytic network process (ANP) as a model to evaluate the value of competing R&D project proposals. Winebrake and Creswick (2003) used AHP in conjunction with a scenario-building exercise (perspective-based scenario analysis or PBSA) to evaluate five fuel processor technology alternatives.

The characterization of technologies is key in order to be able to generate the correct evaluation variables and metrics. Koschatzky *et al.* (1996) introduced a graphical framework that shows the performance characteristics for selected key attributes of a product, process, technology or industry. Geisler (2002) provided a review of the technology evaluation metrics, including econometric methods, patents, process methods and bibliometrics. Smith and Byrd (1978) incorporated several technical criteria such as energy evaluation, economic evaluation and labor evaluation. Barbiroli (1990) introduced 16 parameters to evaluate the global advantage of a new technology, ranging from process reliability to change in the technological balance of the technology. Zhang *et al.* (2008) and Chen and Daim (2008) developed multi-criteria models for evaluating the diffusion of wireless technologies in China. Jordan and Daim (2007) developed a scoring model using multiple criteria for evaluating hybrid vehicle technologies. Hallum and Daim (2009) used AHP to evaluate different aerospace design alternatives. Daim *et al.* (2009) used AHP to evaluate alternative energy technologies.

11.2.2 Economic technology assessment

Economic methods are also used for assessing technologies. Gagnon and Haldar (1997) found that total savings, break-even point period, internal rate of return, accounting rate of return and total raw cost are the financial criteria most often mentioned by engineering managers. Tipping and Zeffren (1995) introduced a comprehensive "menu of metrics" that comprises 33 evaluation metrics, ranging from financial ratios to organizational measures, to determine the value of R&D investments in a corporation. McGrath and MacMillan (2000) introduced a process that incorporates various variables and the degree of uncertainty.

However, Chau and Parkan (1995) argued that choosing a manufacturing process based solely on cost analysis is not adequate since the process with best direct cost performance may not prove to be the best overall, and instead adopted a two-pronged approach which involves a regression analysis to determine the rankings in direct costs and a distance-based, multiple-attribute decision-making method. Hartmann (1999) introduced the technology balance sheet, which complements the trade balance sheet, to evaluate a company's technological potential; the technological and financial assessments are then consolidated into an overall evaluation to come up with the true value of the technology. Gagnon (1991) combined traditional financial discounting procedures for known cost data with expert opinions for estimating benefit values of the technologies; and incorporated engineering performance improvement, project volumes ranging from one to infinity, various time horizons and a comprehensive sensitivity analysis. Sohn and Ahn (2003) and Boer (1998) introduced further similar methods.

11.2.3 Technology assessment with modeling

Modeling is also used for evaluating variables that cannot be evaluated otherwise. Watson (1978) developed a computer-aided method for developing a graphical representation of system composition and structure in a technology assessment problem. Yap and Souder (1993) proposed a two-phase filter process for technology evaluation and selection with the application of a linear programming method. There is another group of researchers who have developed approaches to evaluate impacts that cannot be evaluated with other tools, including Keller and Ledergerber (1998), Wolstenholme (2003), Coates (1974), Ballard and Hall (1984), Jeong and Kim (1997), and Palm and Hansson (2006). Scenario analysis is also used by many researchers. Diffenbach (1981) used it to generate contextual scenarios representing variables that could influence the impact of the time-of-day (TOD) electricity rate. Chen et al. (1981) and Banuls and Salmeron (2007) also introduced scenario-based analyses.

11.2.4 Other emerging methods

In addition to multi-criteria analyses, economic analyses and modeling tools, there are several other methods covering areas among these major toolsets. Hellstrom (2003) proposed a framework for systemic innovation to reduce the risk associated with technology development. Wilhite and Lord (2006) developed online tools to assess the risk of a technology. Sharif and Sundararajan (1983) and Liang et al. (1999) provided comprehensive models incorporating multiple methods to evaluate technologies.

11.3 Technology Diffusion

There are several diffusion theories that could be used to understand the adoption of new technologies. The diffusion of innovations (DoI) is defined as "the process by which an innovation is communicated through certain channels over time among the members of a social system" (Rogers, 1962). Rogers (1995) defines an innovation as "an idea, practice, or object that is perceived as new by an individual or other unit of adoption". According to Rogers (1995), communication is "the process by which participants create and share information with one another in order to reach a mutual understanding", and communication channels are "the means by which messages get from one individual to another".

Bass (1969) developed an epidemiological model for the diffusion of consumer durables and other innovations. This model is useful in predicting technology introduction rates from a set of estimated values for the innovation and imitation factors. In the Bass model of diffusion, there is a market with m consumers who will ultimately adopt a technology. N_{t-1} is the number of people who have already adopted before time t. The model assumes that the probability that someone will adopt a technology given that he or she has not yet adopted it consists of two factors: a fixed factor p which reflects people's intrinsic tendency to adopt the new product; and a factor q which reflects word of mouth or social contagion, i.e. the larger the proportion of the market that has already adopted the technology, the more likely people are to adopt it. This model is represented by the following equation:

$$N_t = N_{t-1} + p(m - N_{t-1}) + q\frac{N_{t-1}}{m}(m - N_{t-1}),$$

where

m = market potential

p = coefficient of innovation

q = coefficient of imitation

N_t = total number of adopters of product up to time t.

According to the theory of reasoned action (TRA) developed by Fishbein and Ajzen (1975), the main determinant of an individual's behavior is the individual's intention, which in turn is influenced jointly by the individual's attitude and the subjective norm (see Figure 11.2). In TRA, attitude toward the behavior is defined as "the individual's positive or negative feelings about performing a behavior" (Fishbein and Ajzen, 1975). It is determined through an assessment of one's beliefs regarding the consequences arising from a behavior and an evaluation of the desirability of these consequences.

The technology acceptance model (TAM) developed by Davis (1986) can be considered as an adaptation of TRA. This model defines perceived ease of use and perceived usefulness as two determinants of attitude towards behavioral intention and usage (see Figure 11.3). In TAM, perceived ease of use is defined as "the degree

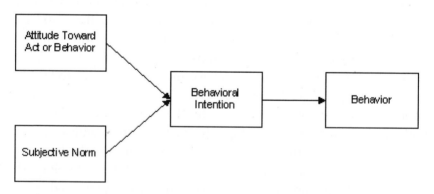

Figure 11.2.   Theory of reasoned action (Fishbein and Ajzen, 1975).

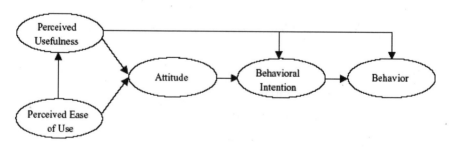

Figure 11.3.   Technology acceptance model (Davis, 1986).

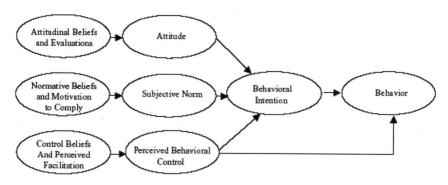

Figure 11.4.   Theory of planned behavior (Ajzen, 1991).

to which a person believes that using the system will be free of effort", whereas perceived usefulness is defined as "the degree to which a person believes that use of the system will enhance his or her performance" (Davis, 1986).

The theory of planned behavior (TPB) developed by Ajzen (1991) is another variant of TRA that takes into account the perceived behavioral control as a third determinant of an individual's behavioral intention to use a new system (see Figure 11.4). In TPB, perceived behavioral control is defined as "one's perception of the difficulty of performing a behavior" (Ajzen, 1991). TPB views the control that people have over their behavior as lying on a continuum from behaviors that are easily performed to those requiring considerable effort, resources, etc.

Diffusion models have been used extensively to explain different factors impacting technology adoption. Basoglu *et al.* (2007) and Kerimoglu *et al.* (2008) provide excellent background on the details of these models through the case of enterprise resource planning (ERP) software. Kargin *et al.* (2009a, 2009b) used these theories to explain the adoption factors of mobile services.

11.4 Determining Forecasting Methodology

According to Prehoda (1967), technology forecasting is the description or prediction of a foreseeable technological innovation, specific scientific refinement or scientific discovery that promises to serve some useful function. The outcomes of technology forecasting provide indications of the most probable time of occurrence. Bright (1967) defines technology forecasting as a systematic means to logically analyze technical attributes as well as economic attributes. Linstone (1999) argues that, since the end of the Cold War, the primary source of R&D funding has shifted from the military and government to private high-tech industry sectors, causing technology forecasting to become the driving force for the new era of R&D development. Various forecasting techniques are discussed by Bright and Schoeman (1973), Islam and Haque (1994), Martino (1983), Porter *et al.* (1991) and Twiss and Jones (1978). We will briefly review some of the tools used for technology forecasting below.

11.4.1 *Judgment-based methods*

Expert opinion provides mechanisms to gather and analyze information from a group of people who are considered to be experts in a particular field. The common approaches are interviews, meetings, surveys, the nominal group process and the Delphi technique. The Delphi technique is usually used in conjunction with other methods.

11.4.2 *Analytical methods*

Direct time series analysis assumes that time is a continuum extending from the past into the future. The only objective is to relate the past and the present to the future. If the past progress occurred in a recognizable pattern, there is a strong supposition that this trend will continue. Similarly, trend extrapolation allows forecasters to project future technical performance within the boundaries of a maximum limit which the technology cannot exceed. There are several approaches such as the substitution, Pearl, Gompertz and Fisher–Pry curves. These curves are used to forecast the substitution of one technology for another (Martino, 1983). Table 11.1 shows some of the most common transformations for technological growth curves as described by Porter *et al.* (1991).

The Gompertz model is often referred to as the "mortality model" in technology forecasting, as it produces an S-curve that rises more sharply but begins to taper off earlier than the Fisher–Pry model (Porter *et al.*, 1991). The Fisher–Pry model behaves very similarly to biological system growth models and thus is commonly referred to as the "substitution model", based on its application in forecasting whereby the rate of new technology will replace existent technology. Figure 11.5

Table 11.1. Typical growth models (Porter *et al.*, 1991).

Growth model	Transformation
Exponential	$Z = \log_{10} \Upsilon (\text{or} \ln \Upsilon)$
Pearl (Fisher–Pry, single variable)	$Z = \ln[(L - \Upsilon)/\Upsilon]$
Gompertz	$Z = \ln[\ln(L/\Upsilon)]$
Substitution	$Z = \ln[f(1 - f)]$

Note: L = upper growth limit; f = fraction of the market held by the new technology.

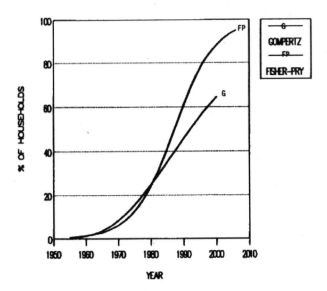

Figure 11.5. Fisher–Pry versus Gompertz models for cable television subscribers in the US (Porter *et al.*, 1991).

compares the Fisher–Pry and Gompertz models for cable television subscribers in the US.

Other analytical methods include regression analysis and data envelopment analysis. Both have been used for forecasting emerging wireless technologies (Anderson *et al.*, 2008; Kim *et al.*, 2009).

11.4.3 *Graphical methods*

Roadmapping, which is an emerging effective tool in the technology management field, has been widely utilized in the management of technology as a forecasting and planning management tool. Koen (1997) introduced the "enabling technology map" and the "source of technology map" as tools guiding technologists to focus on those technologies which provide competitive advantage to the company while outsourcing the more mature technologies. Holmes and Ferrill (2005) constructed a five-step process to help Singaporean small- and medium-sized enterprises (SMEs) create an operation and technology roadmap (OTR). Fleischer *et al.* (2005) developed a roadmapping tool to assess emerging technologies in the case of nanotechnologies. Phaal *et al.* (2004) developed a structured process that has started to be adopted by many in the field. Their approach, called the T-Plan, calls for multiple workshops to generate the key ingredients of the roadmaps. Daim and Oliver (2008) expanded this approach in the energy sector. They contended that a preliminary analysis of the organization is required for better results.

11.4.4 *Modeling methods*

Modeling, as in technology assessment, is a very useful tool for technology forecasting as well. Several different methods have been combined to create better models. Scenarios containing hypothetical sequences of events are constructed to focus attention on causal processes and decision points. Among the prior research, Winebrake and Creswick (2003) and Sager (2003) are good examples of using scenarios for technology forecasting. Both studies focused on future energy scenarios. Navam and Daim (2007) integrated scenarios with

AHP to develop a framework to forecast alternative fuels. Analogy is also used in conjuction with modeling. It involves a systematic comparison of the technology to be forecasted against some earlier technology that is believed to be similar in all or the most important aspects.

11.4.5 *Emerging technology indicators*

As we try to understand new technologies which we have not seen before, it becomes challenging to evaluate them due to the lack of past data. In these cases, publications and patents become very attractive to use. Daim *et al.* (2006) combined the use of publications and patents with scenarios and growth curves to develop forecasts for technologies such as fuel cell. Another study combined Bass curves with the use of patents and publications to forecast radio-frequency identification technologies (Daim and Suntharasaj, 2009). A recent study used publications and patents to forecast the competition between hard disk drives and flash memory (Daim *et al.*, 2008). Daim and Jordan (2008) developed a forecast for laptop battery technologies using this method. Martin and Daim (2008) incorporated the use of multiple indicators including research awards and demonstrated that, through understanding the time lags, one can use research awards to gain an insight into a much longer timeline in the future.

Rinne and Gerdsri (2003) classified forecasting techniques that are suitable for predicting the future development of emerging technologies by considering the type of technology and the time horizon of the forecast (Table 11.2). The type of technology can be addressed in three types: extensions of existing technologies, incremental emerging technologies and radical emerging technologies. Extensions of existing technologies use the same fundamental concepts and practices as existing technologies, with which they form a continuum. Both incremental and radical emerging technologies typically require new methods and processes. Incremental emerging technologies are borne from the adaptation, refinement and enhancement of existing technologies, while radical emerging technologies involve completely new concepts and delivery systems (Betz, 1998; Burgelman *et al.*, 1995).

Table 11.2. The classification of technology forecasting techniques categorized according to the type of technology and the time horizon of forecast (Rinne and Gerdsri, 2003).

Type of technology	Time horizon of forecast		
	Short range (<2 years)	Medium range (2–5 years)	Long range (>5 years)
Radical emerging technologies	Expert opinion (Delphi or NGD) Bibliometric analysis Scenario writing Causal model Judgment quantification (AHP)	Expert opinion (Delphi or NGD) Scenario writing Judgment quantification (AHP)	Expert opinion (Delphi or NGD) Scenario writing Judgment quantification (AHP)
Incremental emerging technologies	Expert opinion (SI, Delphi or NGD) Bibliometric analysis Patent analysis Analogy Scenario writing Lead-lag indicators Relevance tree Causal model Judgment quantification (AHP)	Expert opinion (Delphi or NGD) Scenario writing Causal model Judgment quantification (AHP)	Expert opinion (Delphi or NGD) Scenario writing Judgment quantification (AHP)

(Continued)

Table 11.2. (*Continued*)

Type of technology	Time horizon of forecast		
	Short range (<2 years)	Medium range (2–5 years)	Long range (>5 years)
Extensions of existing technologies	Expert opinion (brainstorming or SI)	Expert opinion (Delphi or NGD)	Expert opinion (Delphi or NGD)
	Patent analysis	Patent analysis	Scenario writing
	Direct time series analysis	Analogy	Causal model
	Trend extrapolation (Fisher–Pry substitution)	Scenario writing	Judgment quantification (AHP)
	Lead-lag indicators	Causal model	
	Regression	Simulation	
	Causal model	Morphological analysis	
		Relevance tree	
		Judgment quantification (AHP)	

Note: NGD = nominal group discussion; SI = structured interview.

The time horizon of forecasts is categorized as short range (less than 2 years), medium range (2–5 years) or long range (5–7 years). The predominant forecasting horizon for practitioners in the field is 2–5 years (Mignogna, 2002).

11.5 Case Study

This case study is provided to demonstrate the process of forecasting the diffusion of technological innovations. The case study is adopted from Daim *et al.* (2010), where diffusion of a technological innovation is analyzed in two different regions. A structured methodology roadmap was used to construct the forecast for the adoption of WiMAX technology. Figure 11.6 summarizes the steps taken in this analysis. This section will describe the assumptions and data utilized for each step.

This case study presents two distinct scenarios based on the selection of previous analogous products. By analyzing consumer behavior for previous products, one can begin to understand the market for new products. Each scenario represents a different analogous product characteristics set, technology and market structure. The scenarios were selected based on products that are comparable to WiMAX with respect to technology and impact to the consumer.

Many people today are new to the idea of mobile wireless networks. In fact, Clearwire first commercialized mobile WiMAX in September 2008 and it is currently the only service provider in the US, although other service providers are coming up to speed. However, given that most subscribers are likely to purchase bundled services and not WiMAX services exclusively, it was difficult to obtain real data for comparison against forecasted data in the US alone. Therefore, for the purposes of this project, real data were evaluated

Figure 11.6.   Methodology roadmap.

against the forecasted diffusion curves. For each of the scenarios presented, the Bass model was applied. The resulting curves provide estimates on how fast WiMAX will be adopted within the same period.

Knowledge of the market for this new product derives from knowledge on previous products of a similar category. This was the basic principle for choosing the parameters m, total market potential; p, innovators; and q, imitators. Since sales data are not yet available for WiMAX technology, the total market potential, m, was estimated from key statistics examined in past research of previously launched products. To determine m, scenarios 1 and 2 utilized 18.8 million people — the total population in the 375 cities where Clearwire provides its service — because we used real data from Clearwire for comparison with forecasted data. The coefficients of innovation, p, and imitation, q, have stronger mathematical fundamentals. Table 11.3 summarizes the parameter estimates for each scenario. Coefficient estimates were calculated based on a weighted average that took into account market structure, relative technology advantage and technology benefits. The weights given to each product score range from 1 to 10 and are subjective, based on the team's knowledge of the product.

To construct the forecast for the diffusion of WiMAX technology, the parameter estimates of m, p, and q were utilized as expressed by Ofek (2007):

$$S_t = p + (q/m)N_{t-1},$$

where S_t is the number of new adopters for the product during the time period t, and N_{t-1} is the cumulative number of adopters for the new product through the previous time period $(t-1)$.

Table 11.3. Parameter estimation per scenario.

	p	q	m
Senario 1	0.042	0.393	18.8
Senario 2	0.017	0.524	18.8

These parameters illustrate how fast or slow the adoption of WiMAX will occur. Market benchmarking of new technology introductions in the telecommunications industry was used to complement potential market forecasts for WiMAX. The model attempts to predict how many customers will eventually adopt the new product and when they will adopt it. If $q > p$, then imitation effects will dominate over the innovation effects; on the other hand, if $q < p$, then innovation effects will dominate and the highest sales will occur at introduction before sales decline in every period thereafter. Furthermore, the lower the value of p, the longer it takes to realize sales growth for the innovation. When both p and q are large, product sales will take off rapidly and fall off quickly after reaching a maximum (Lilien *et al.*, 2007).

Forecasting results are critical for management, as they provide data that help plan and implement strategies for the future. In this section of the chapter, the forecasting results will be explained. The penetration curves are steep and promise high product adaptability within the first decade of the life of the product. As the population of the US becomes more accustomed to getting things done "on the go", the introduction of WiMAX services will prove more successful. Figure 11.7 illustrates this trend: in the first 5 years, the product reaches ~40% penetration in scenario 1 and 20% penetration in scenario 2, but both scenarios reach 95% penetration by year 15.

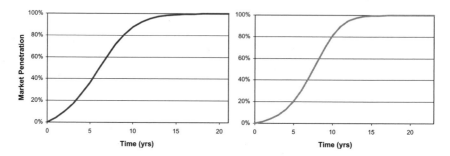

Figure 11.7.   Penetration curves for scenario 1 (left) and scenario 2 (right) (adapted from Daim *et al.*, 2010).

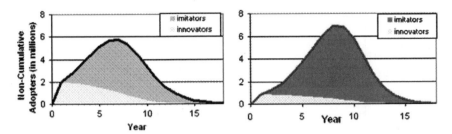

Figure 11.8. Imitator and innovator comparison for scenario 1 (left) and scenario 2 (right) (adapted from Daim *et al.*, 2010).

However, there is a distinct difference between the behaviors observed in the scenarios. Just like Wi-Fi before it, innovators have a major influence on the shape of the curve early in the adoption curve. Figure 11.8 compares innovator and imitator influence on the adoption curve. In both scenarios, as the number of imitators increases, the number of innovators decreases over time.

The influence of innovators is greater in scenario 1 than in scenario 2. Despite apparent similarities in the list of analogous products, the products chosen for scenario 1 offer high mobility and connectivity access, whereas in scenario 2 high speed is combined with the capability to process large sets of data. This observation shows that consumers are more interested in mobility rather than high speed. WiMAX intends to offer both of these functionalities, i.e. high mobility at broadband speed.

The actual number of Clearwire WiMAX subscribers (Fellah, 2008) was compared with the outcome of the forecast that resulted from the Bass model. Figure 11.9 summarizes the first two years of the life of the technology for Clearwire. Although Clearwire is not the only service provider in the US, it was chosen for this comparison because of its growing presence in the US. Since most subscribers do not subscribe exclusively to WiMAX services, it was difficult to distinguish the specific number of WiMAX subscriptions. The mean absolute error is 100,000 subscribers. Scenario 1 was chosen to compare against real data, as shown in Figure 11.9.

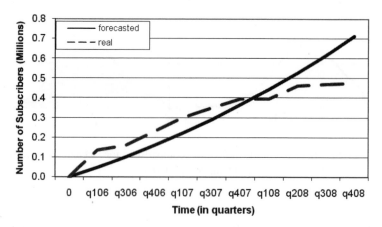

Figure 11.9.   Real data compared to the forecasted number of subscribers (adapted from Daim *et al.*, 2010).

11.6 Conclusions

We have presented a set of processes for developing diffusion forecasts for technologies. We started with technology assessment, and provided background knowledge on the types of methods and the application areas for each type. We then explained the technology diffusion theories and where they are applied. The final step was the classification of forecasting methods and where they are used. To demonstrate our discussion, we provided a case study that analyzes the diffusion of a new wireless technology, WiMAX, through the use of some of the methods discussed earlier in the chapter.

References

Ajzen, I. (1991). The theory of planned behavior. *Organizational Behavior and Human Decision Processes*, 50, 179–211.

Anderson, T., Daim, T. and Kim, J. (2008). Forecasting wireless technologies with DEA. *Technovation*, 28(9), 602–614.

Ballard, S.C. and Hall, T.A. (1984). Theory and practice of integrated impact assessment: the case of the Western Energy Study. *Technological Forecasting and Social Change*, 25(1), 37–48.

Banuls, V.A. and Salmeron, J.L. (2007). A scenario-based assessment model — SBAM. *Technological Forecasting and Social Change*, 74(6), 750–762.

Barbiroli, G. (1990). A new method to evaluate the specific and global advantage of a technology. *Technovation*, 10(2), 73–93.

Bard, J.F. and Feinberg, A. (1989). A two-phase methodology for technology selection and system design. *IEEE Transactions on Engineering Management*, 36(1), 28–36.

Basoglu, N., Daim, T. and Kerimoglu, O. (2007). Organizational adoption of enterprise resource planning systems: a conceptual framework. *Journal of High Technology Management Research*, 18(1), 73–97.

Bass, F. (1969). A new product growth model for consumer durables. *Management Science*, 15, 215–227.

Betz, F. (1998). *Managing Technological Innovation*. New York: John Wiley & Sons, Inc.

Boer, P. (1998). Traps, pitfalls, and snares in the valuation of technology. *Research-Technology Management*, 41(5), 45–54.

Bright, J.R. (1967). *Technological Forecasting for Industry and Government: Methods and Applications*. Englewood Cliffs, NJ: Prentice Hall.

Bright, J.R. and Schoeman, M.E.F. (1973). *A Guide to Practical Technological Forecasting*. Englewood Cliffs, NJ: Prentice Hall.

Burgelman, R.A., Maidique, M.A. and Wheelwright, S.C. (1995). *Strategic Management of Technology and Innovation*. Boston: McGraw-Hill.

Chau, O.L. and Parkan, C. (1995). Selection of a manufacturing process with multiple attributes: a case study. *Journal of Engineering and Technology Management*, 12, 219–237.

Chen, H. and Daim, T. (2008). Emerging technology assessment: modeling effective integration of the Internet and the mobile phones in China. *Journal of Technology Management in China*, 3(2), 194–210.

Chen, K., Jarboe, K. and Wolfe, J. (1981). Long-range scenario construction for technology assessment. *Technological Forecasting and Social Change*, 20(1), 27–40.

Coates, J.F. (1974). Some methods and techniques for comprehensive impact assessment. *Technological Forecasting and Social Change*, 6, 341–357.

Daim, T. and Jordan, S. (2008). A foresight based on scientific indicators. *Foresight*, 10(3), 43–54.

Daim, T., Kennedy, L., Choothian, W. and Ploykitikoon, P. (2008). Forecasting the future of data storage: case of hard disk drive and flash memory. *Foresight*, 10(5), 34–49.

Daim, T. and Kocaoglu, D. (2008a). How do engineering managers evaluate technologies for acquisition? A review of the electronics industry. *Engineering Management Journal*, 20(3), 19–30.

Daim, T. and Kocaoglu, D. (2008b). Exploring technology acquisition in Oregon, Turkey and in the U.S. electronics manufacturing companies. *Journal of High Technology Management Research*, 19(1), 45–58.

Daim, T. and Kocaoglu, D. (2009). Exploring the roles of technology assessment and acquisition in the competitiveness of US electronics manufacturing companies. *International Journal of Technology Management*, 48(1), 77–94.

Daim, T. and Oliver, T. (2008). Implementing technology roadmap process in the energy services sector: a case study of a government agency. *Technology Forecasting and Social Change*, 75(5), 687–720.

Daim, T., Patino, S.L., Jarpa, N. and Yoon, Y. (2010). WIMAX diffusion in USA and Korea: a comparative study integrating scenario planning and Bass model. *International Journal of Technology and Globalisation* (in press).

Daim, T., Rueda, G., Martin, H. and Gerdsri, P. (2006). Forecasting emerging technologies: use of bibliometrics and patent analysis. *Technological Forecasting and Social Change*, 73, 981–1012.

Daim, T. and Suntharasaj, P. (2009). Technology diffusion: forecasting with bibliometric analysis and Bass model. *Foresight*, 11(3), 45–55.

Daim, T., Yates, D., Peng, Y. and Jimenez, B. (2009). Technology assessment for clean energy technologies. *Technology in Society*, 31(3), 232–243.

Davis, F.D. (1986). A technology acceptance model for empirically testing new end-user information systems: theory and results. Doctoral dissertation, Massachusetts Institute of Technology, Cambridge, MA, USA.

Diffenbach, J. (1981). A compatibility approach to scenario evaluation. *Technological Forecasting and Social Change*, 19(2), 161–174.

Fellah, A. (2008). *Telecom Market Research and Analysis*. Montreal: Maravedis Inc.

Fishbein, M. and Ajzen, I. (1975). *Belief, Attitude, Intention, and Behavior: An Introduction to Theory and Research*. Reading, MA: Addison-Wesley.

Fleischer, T., Decker, M. and Fiedeler, U. (2005). Assessing emerging technologies — methodological challenges and the case of nanotechnologies. *Technological Forecasting and Social Change*, 72, 1112–1121.

Gagnon, R.J. (1991). Assessing strategies for obtaining advanced engineering technologies with highly uncertain benefits. *IEEE Transactions on Engineering Management*, 38(3), 210–222.

Gagnon, R.J. and Haldar, S. (1997). Assessing advanced engineering technologies. *International Journal of Technology Management*, 14(2/3/4), 439–469.

Geisler, E. (2002). The metrics of technology evaluation: where we stand and where we should go from here. *International Journal of Technology Management*, 24(4), 341–374.

Hallum, D. and Daim, T. (2009). A hierarchical decision model for optimum design alternative selection. *International Journal of Decision Sciences, Risk and Management*, 1(1–2), 2–22.

Hartmann, M.H. (1999). Theory and practice of technological corporate assessment. *Journal of Engineering and Technology Management*, 17(4), 504–521.

Hellstrom, T. (2003). Systemic innovation and risk: technology assessment and the challenge of responsible innovation. *Technology in Society*, 25, 369–384.

Holmes, C. and Ferrill, M. (2005). The application of operation and technology roadmapping to aid Singaporean SMEs identify and select emerging technologies. *Technological Forecasting and Social Change*, 72, 349–357.

Islam, M.N. and Haque, M.M. (1994). *Technology Planning and Control*. Dhaka, Bangladesh: World University Service Press.

Jeong, G.H. and Kim, S.H. (1997). A qualitative cross-impact approach to find the key technology. *Technological Forecasting and Social Change*, 55(3), 203–214.

Jordan, S. and Daim, T. (2007). Range based model for technology requirements: hybrid vehicle technology assessment case study. *International Journal of Automotive Technology Management*, 7(4), 314–326.

Kargin, B., Basoglu, N. and Daim, T. (2009a). Adoption factors of mobile services. *International Journal of Information Systems in the Service Sector*, 1(1), 15–34.

Kargin, B., Basoglu, N. and Daim, T. (2009b). Factors affecting the adoption of mobile services. *International Journal of Services Science*, 1(2), 29–52.

Keller, P. and Ledergerber, U. (1998). Bimodal system dynamic: a technology assessment and forecasting approach. *Technological Forecasting and Social Change*, 58, 47–52.

Kerimoglu, O., Basoglu, N. and Daim, T. (2008). Organizational adoption of information technologies: case of enterprise resource planning systems. *Journal of High Technology Management Research*, 19(1), 21–35.

Kim, J., Daim, T. and Anderson, T. (2009). A look at the future of wireless technologies. To appear in *Technology Analysis and Strategic Management*.

Koen, P.A. (1997). Technology maps: choosing the right path. *Engineering Management Journal*, 9(4), 7–11.

Koschatzky, K., Frenkel, A., Grupp, H. and Maital, S. (1996). A technometric assessment of sensor technology in Israel vs. Europe, the USA and Japan. *International Journal of Technology Management*, 11(5/6), 667–688.

Liang, S., Yuan, B. and Chow, L. (1999). A decision model linkage between technology forecasting, technology dominance and technology strategy. *International Journal of Technology Management*, 18(1/2), 46–55.

Lilien, G.L., Rangaswamy, A. and De Bruyn, A. (2007). The Bass model: marketing engineering technical note. Available at http://www.mktgeng.com/downloadfiles/technotes/TN08%20-%20Bass%20Model%20Technical%20Note.pdf/.

Linstone, H.A. (1999). TFSC: 1969–1999. *Technological Forecasting and Social Change*, 65, 1–8.

Martin, H. and Daim, T. (2008). Technology roadmapping through intelligence analysis: nanotechnology. *International Journal of Society Systems Science*, 1(1), 49–66.

Martino, J.P. (1983). *Technological Forecasting for Decision Making.* New York: North-Holland.

McGrath, R.G. and MacMillan, I.C. (2000). Assessing technology projects using real options reasoning. *Research-Technology Management,* 43(4), 35–49.

Meade, L.M. and Presley, A. (2002). R&D project selection using the analytic network process. *IEEE Transactions on Engineering Management,* 49(1), 59–66.

Merkhofer, M.W. (1982). A process for technology assessment based on decision analysis. *Technological Forecasting and Social Change,* 22(3–4), 237–265.

Mignogna, R.P. (2002). Popularity of technology forecasting methods. Available at Technology/Engineering Management, Inc. website (www.temi.com).

Navam, M. and Daim, T. (2007). Alternative motor fuels: a proposed forecasting framework using AHP and scenarios. *International Journal of Automotive Technology Management,* 7(4), 289–313.

Ofek, E. (2007). Forecasting the adoption of a new product. Harvard Business School Note 505-062, Boston, USA.

Palm, E. and Hansson, S.O. (2006). The case for ethical technology assessment. *Technological Forecasting and Social Change,* 73, 543–558.

Phaal, R., Farrukh, C.J.P. and Probert, D.R. (2004). Technology roadmapping — a planning framework for evolution and revolution. *Technological Forecasting and Social Change,* 71, 5–26.

Porter, A.L., Roper, A.T., Mason, T.W., Rossini, F.A. and Banks, J. (1991). *Forecasting and Management of Technology.* New York: Wiley.

Prabhu, R.T. and Vizayakumar, K. (2001). Technology choice using FHDM — a case of iron-making technology. *IEEE Transactions on Engineering Management,* 48(2), 209–222.

Prasad, A.V.S. and Somasekhara, N. (1990). The analytic hierarchy process for choice of technologies: an application. *Technological Forecasting and Social Change,* 38(2), 151–158.

Prehoda, R.W. (1967). *Designing the Future: The Role of Technological Forecasting.* London: Chilton Books.

Raju, U.S., Rangaraj, N. and Date, A.W. (1995). The influence of development perspectives on the choice of technology. *Technological Forecasting and Social Change,* 48, 27–43.

Rinne, M. and Gerdsri, N. (2003). Technology roadmaps: unlocking the potential of a field. Presented at the Portland International Conference on Management of Engineering and Technology (PICMET), Portland, OR, USA, 2003.

Rogers, E.M. (1962). *Diffusion of Innovations,* 1st ed. New York: The Free Press.

Rogers, E.M. (1995). *Diffusion of Innovations,* 4th ed. New York: The Free Press.

Sager, B. (2003). Scenarios on the future of biotechnology. *Technological Forecasting and Social Change,* 70, 109–129.

Sharif, M.N. and Sundararajan, V. (1983). A quantitative model for the evaluation of technological alternatives. *Technological Forecasting and Social Change*, 24(1), 15–29.

Smith, P.J. and Byrd, J. (1978). A preliminary technology assessment of a standardized container recycling system. *Technological Forecasting and Social Change*, 12(1), 31–39.

Sohn, S.Y. and Ahn, B.J. (2003). Multigeneration diffusion model for economic assessment of new technology. *Technological Forecasting and Social Change*, 70, 251–264.

Tipping, J.W. and Zeffren, E. (1995). Assessing the value of your technology. *Research-Technology Management*, 38(5), 22–39.

Tran, T. and Daim, T. (2008). A taxonomic review of methods and tools applied in technology assessment. *Technological Forecasting and Social Change*, 75(9), 1396–1405.

Twiss, B. and Jones, H. (1978). *Forecasting Technology for Planning Decisions*. New York: PBI-Petrocelli Books.

Watson, R.H. (1978). Interpretive structural modeling — a useful tool for technology assessment? *Technological Forecasting and Social Change*, 11(2), 165–185.

Wilhite, A. and Lord, R. (2006). Estimating the risk of technology development. *Engineering Management Journal*, 18(3), 3–10.

Winebrake, J.J. and Creswick, B.P. (2003). The future of hydrogen fueling systems for transportation: an application of perspective-based scenario analysis using the analytic hierarchy process. *Technological Forecasting and Social Change*, 70, 359–384.

Wolstenholme, E.F. (2003). The use of system dynamics as a tool for intermediate level technology evaluation: three case studies. *Journal of Engineering and Technology Management*, 20, 193–204.

Yap, C.M. and Souder, W.E. (1993). A filter system for technology evaluation and selection. *Technovation*, 13(7), 449–469.

Zhang, J., Daim, T., Choi, B. and Phan, K. (2008). A multiple-perspective model for technology assessment: case of mobile broadband technologies selection in China. *Journal of Technology Management in China*, 3(3), 264–278.

Chapter 12

Modeling and Forecasting Diffusion*

Nigel Meade and Towhidul Islam

12.1 Introduction

The modeling and forecasting of the diffusion of innovations has been a topic of practical and academic interest since the 1960s, when the pioneering works of Fourt and Woodlock (1960), Mansfield (1961), Floyd (1962), Rogers (1962), Chow (1967) and Bass (1969) appeared. The interest garnered by these papers can be judged by the numbers of citations for these papers on the ISI Web of Science, which were 148, 505, 13, 1,181, 74 and 895, respectively, in March 2009. Two papers, Fourt and Woodlock (1960) and Bass (1969), use "new product" rather than "technology" in their titles. Although the approach to modeling the diffusion of a technology or a new consumer durable is very similar, in recent years new product applications in marketing have tended to dominate in the overall diffusion literature.

The phenomenon of innovation diffusion is shown in a stylized form in Figure 12.1. Cumulative adoption and period-by-period adoptions are shown — which of these two representations is of

---

* This chapter is a modified and updated version of: Meade, N. and Islam, T. (2006). Modelling and forecasting the diffusion of innovation — a 25-year review. *International Journal of Forecasting*, 22, 519–545.

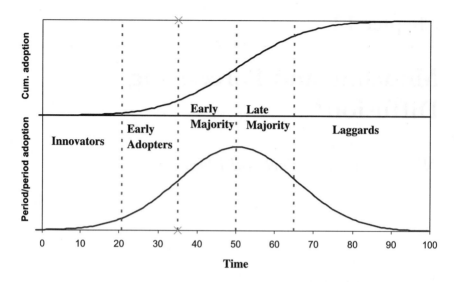

Figure 12.1.   Stylized diffusion curves.

greater importance depends on the application. For example, in the diffusion of mobile phones, a service provider is concerned about the demand on the infrastructure and is thus concerned with cumulative adoptions; a handset supplier is concerned with meeting demand and will thus want to model and forecast period-by-period adoptions. In this example, the service provider will want to know the level of adoption at a particular time and the eventual number of adopters; the handset provider will want to know the rate of adoption at a given time, the timing of peak demand and the magnitude of peak demand. As a counterpoint to the smooth curves of Figure 12.1, Figure 12.2 shows comparable information for the diffusion of residential telephones in the UK. The period-to-period adoptions in Figure 12.2 depart fairly drastically from the bell-shaped curve. The difficulties in forecasting are also demonstrated: in 1975, period-to-period demand appears to have peaked as decisions to expand production may have been canceled or postponed; however, in 1979, a 43% higher peak is reached.

The main models used for innovation diffusion were established by 1970. Of the eight different basic models listed in the Appendix

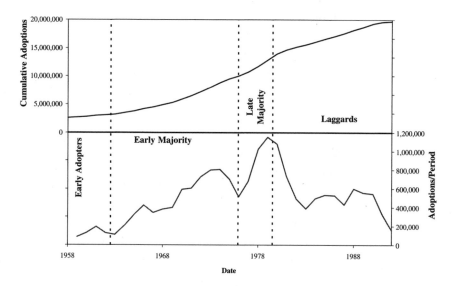

Figure 12.2. Diffusion of UK residential telephones.

at the end of this chapter (see Sections A12.1–A12.8), six had been applied in modeling the diffusion of innovations by this date. The main modeling developments from 1970 onwards have been in modifying the existing models by adding greater flexibility to the underlying models in various ways. The main categories of these modifications are listed below (in each case, a pioneering paper is cited as a proxy for research activity in this area):

- The introduction of marketing variables in the parameterization of the models (Robinson and Lakhani, 1975);
- Generalization of the models to consider innovations at different stages of diffusion in different countries (Gatignon *et al.*, 1989); and
- Generalization of the models to consider the diffusion of successive generations of a technology (Norton and Bass, 1987).

It is fair to say that, in most of these contributions, the emphasis has been on the explanation of past behavior rather than on

Table 12.1. Frequency of references by journal category.

Category	%
Marketing	31
Forecasting	27
Operations Research/ Management Science	13
Business/Economics	7
Other	22

forecasting future behavior. To quantify this comment and the previous comment about the preponderance of marketing studies, the references used in this paper are classified by their journals into the given categories (in decreasing order) in Table 12.1. There is little difference between the disciplines in terms of the freshness of their contributions: the average age of the marketing, forecasting and operations research/management science references is 15 years; and the average age of the business/economics references is 19 years.

During the last 25 years, there have been several reviews of diffusion models. These include Meade (1984), Mahajan and Peterson (1985), Mahajan *et al.* (1990, 1993a), Baptista (1999), Mahajan *et al.* (2000b) and Meade and Islam (2001). Meade (1984) emphasized several criteria for good practice in the use of growth curves for forecasting market development. These include:

- Model validity — the product should be adoptable rather than consumable (i.e. there should be an obvious upper bound to the saturation level);
- Statistical validity — the estimation of model parameters should be subject to significance tests; and
- Demonstrable forecasting ability and validity — the forecast should be contextually plausible and should be accompanied by some measure of uncertainty, ideally a prediction interval.

As we will see, it is still relatively easy to find applications where the model validity is dubious, the application of significance tests is widespread but not ubiquitous, and (when forecasting is included) the explicit discussion of uncertainty occurs in a minority of cases.

Baptista's (1999) review took an economic viewpoint. He focused on the diffusion of the innovation process between firms, and the roles that geography and interfirm networks play in knowledge transfer.

Mahajan *et al.* (1990, 1993a) offered a research agenda for the development of a sounder theory for diffusion in a marketing context and more effective practices (this agenda included several topics that were underway at the time). Their agenda includes:

- Increasing the understanding of the diffusion process at the level of the individual;
- Exploiting developments in hazard models as a means of incorporating marketing mix variables;
- Investigating the nature and effect of supply and distribution constraints;
- Modeling and predicting product take-off; and
- Making empirical comparisons with other sales forecasting models.

Of these items, the empirical comparisons have received the least attention. In this review, we shall look at modeling the diffusion of a single innovation in a single market, followed by the diffusion of an innovation in several (national) markets at the same time, and then the diffusion of successive generations of the same innovative technology. The length of each section obviously depends on the amount of work done on the topic discussed; thus, as the latter topics are newer and less researched, the relevant sections are shorter. Within each of these topics, we shall look at issues of modeling including the introduction of explanatory variables, estimation and forecasting accuracy. The most often encountered diffusion models are described in the Appendix; we will refer to these models where necessary and keep further equations within the text to a minimum.

12.2 The Diffusion of a Single Innovation in a Single Market

The path the cumulative adoption of an innovation takes between introduction and saturation is generally modeled by an S-curve. Examination of data sets suggests that this type of model is generally appropriate. A legitimate enquiry is, why is cumulative diffusion S-shaped? The two extreme hypotheses that explain this shape are those based on the dynamics of a (broadly homogeneous) population and those based on the heterogeneity of the population.

Taking the dynamics of the population first, Bass (1969) (see Section A12.1) suggested that individuals are influenced by a desire to innovate (coefficient of innovation, p) and by a need to imitate others in the population (coefficient of imitation, q). The probability that a potential adopter adopts at time t is driven by $p + qF(t)$, where $F(t)$ is the proportion of adopters at time t. Relating to the similarity of innovation diffusion with the spreading of an epidemic, imitation is often called a contagion effect. In a pure innovation scenario ($p > 0$, $q = 0$), diffusion follows a modified exponential curve (see Section A12.7); in a pure imitation scenario ($p = 0$, $q > 0$), diffusion follows a logistic curve (see Section A12.6). Other properties are that $p + q$ controls scale and q/p controls shape; note that the condition $(q/p) > 1$ is necessary for the curve to be S-shaped.

One of the first to use the heterogeneous population argument was Rogers (1962). He suggested that populations are heterogeneous in their propensity to innovate. Like a military attack, the innovators (2.5% of adopters) go "over the top" first, followed by the early adopters (13.5%), and then by the early majority (34%), the late majority (34%) and the laggards at the rear (16%). These percentages are based on the normal distribution (e.g. innovators are two standard deviations or more above the mean level of innovativeness). Put another way, individuals in a system have a threshold for adoption; innovators have a very low threshold. As the innovation becomes more widely adopted, the social pressure reaches more and more thresholds since, according to Rogers (1962), "Individual thresholds for adoption are normally distributed, thus creating the S-curve of diffusion". He also reported that early adopters are better educated, are more literate, have a higher social status, have a greater degree of upward social mobility and are richer than later adopters (Rogers, 1962).

This last property relates to income. An early mention of the income heterogeneity hypothesis was made by Duesenberry (1949). The heterogeneity of income distribution has been cited by several authors (e.g. Bonus, 1973) as a driver for the S-shape. The view is that the diffusion curve reflects the nature of income distribution: as the price of an innovation falls, more consumers can afford it. Provided the income distribution is bell-shaped and the price falls monotonically, an S-curve will result. In a critique of the Bass model, Russell (1980) did not like the terms "innovator" and "imitator" (a departure from the economist's world of rational agents who maximize utility under budget constraints). He preferred an individual-based model in which the individual has a threshold price: when the price of the innovation falls to this threshold, an innovation may be triggered. This argument leads via a log-normal distribution of income to an S-shaped curve. Russell referred to Bain (1963), who used a cumulative log-normal distribution to forecast the diffusion of televisions. However, Russell allowed for possible contagion within the income strata. Liebermann and Paroush (1982) provided an economic argument whereby income hetero-geneity, price and advertising are important drivers of the diffusion process.

Since the diffusion of an innovation is a complex process involving a large number of individual decisions, the diffusion of any one innovation will be due to elements of both extreme hypotheses. Van den Bulte and Stremersch (2004) performed a meta-analysis on the use of the Bass model applied to new product diffusion. The study involved 746 different Bass estimations spread over 75 consumer durables and 77 countries. The international comparison enabled them to test several sets of hypotheses, relat-ing the diffusion to both the national culture and the nature of the product. The contagion-based hypotheses for which they found support are that q/p ratios are:

- Negatively associated with individualism (individualism means more immunity to social contagion) or positively associated with collectivism;
- Positively associated with power distance (a measure of the hierarchical nature of the culture). The assumption here is that "classes" tend to adopt a new product at a similar time; and
- Positively associated with masculinity (cultures where there is a clear distinction between gender roles).

Contrary to their expectations, Van den Bulte and Stremersch (2004) found a negative association between q/p and uncertainty avoidance (a measure of how threatened people feel when faced with a novel opportunity). A positive association was found between q/p and the Gini coefficient of income inequality, supporting the income heterogeneity hypothesis. In cases where the products concerned had competing standards, e.g. VCRs (Betamax versus VHS) and PCs (DOS/Windows versus Apple), they found that this technological issue dominated the social or income effects.

Rogers (1995) linked other concepts to his framework (of heterogeneous innovativeness). The diffusion of an innovation will not proceed if the critical mass is not reached. This may occur if there is a discontinuity in the distribution of adoption thresholds. In this context, he makes a distinction between interactive and non-interactive innovations. The first adopter of a personal computer can start writing his own programs, but the first adopter of a telephone can do nothing until the second adopter acts. This argues for a critical mass of adopters to exist before diffusion really takes off. Adoption is slow before the critical mass exists (critical mass is the stage at which enough individuals have adopted the innovation so that further adoption is self-sustaining), and then diffusion accelerates and a contagion effect begins to take effect. Mahler and Rogers (1999) investigated the reasons given by German banks for the non-adoption of 12 telecommunications innovations. The reason given in 41% of cases was the low rate of diffusion of the innovations; this reason was very highly ranked regardless of the innovative history of the institution (whether it was classified as an innovator through to laggard). They pointed out that, in cases where there are competing standards for an innovation, each standard will need a critical mass before diffusion will accelerate.

In a study of the diffusion of imaging technology into US banks and insurance companies, Liberatore and Breem (1997) found that the logistic model best describes this process. They found no evidence of an innovation pressure (internal influence). Through a questionnaire analysis, they found that early adoption was related to the size of the organization, that is, larger organizations adopted the technology earlier.

Some technologies are dependent on each other. For example, Bayus (1987) studied the relationship between the compact disc and its hardware. Rogers (1995) distinguished between hardware and software: software is the understanding about what the technological hardware can achieve. Rogers contended that the software diffuses faster than the hardware. Geroski (2000) suggested the use of probit models to explain the decision of firms to adopt a technology; this appears to be a way of introducing the heterogeneity of firms into the adoption process.

In a study of the diffusion of 25 information technologies, Teng *et al.* (2002) used the Bass model to compare diffusion behavior. They found very low coefficients of innovation (internal influence); imitation (external influence) was the main driver for adoption in all cases. The technologies were clustered by saturation level and coefficient of imitation; five clusters were found. Email and fax were in one cluster with a low q and 100% saturation. Spreadsheet and PC were in a cluster with a high q and a 100% saturation level (interestingly, in contradiction to Rogers (1995), the parameter values for the hardware and software were almost identical). Imaging was in a cluster with a high q and a lower saturation level.

The time at which an innovative product is introduced may have an effect on the rate of its diffusion. At present, the evidence is slightly contradictory. Kohli *et al.* (1999) considered incubation time as a factor in innovation diffusion. Incubation time is the interval between the completion of product development and the beginning of "substantial" product sales. For example, patents on zips were taken out in 1893 and 1913, but sales did not take off until the 1930s. In a study of 32 products, they found a positive association between incubation time and time to peak sales, and a negative association between incubation time and the coefficient of innovation. They found no evidence that the incubation time was changing over time; this led them to comment that "innate innovativeness is not increasing". However, in a study specifically focused on this topic, Van den Bulte (2000) examined the change in the speed of diffusion of innovations over the period 1923–1996. Diffusion speed can be measured as the slope coefficient of the logistic curve, or the time taken to go from one level of penetration to another. He found a significant increase in speed over the period, attributing it to increased purchasing power, demographic changes and the types of products studied.

Some authors have used observed heterogeneity as a basis for qualitative forecasts of future diffusion patterns. Wareham *et al.* (2004) investigated socio-economic factors underlying the diffusion of the Internet and 2G mobile phones in the US. Mobile phone adoption was positively related to income, occupation and living in a metropolitan area. In addition, African-Americans adopted mobile phones significantly faster than other ethnic groups. As African-Americans and other ethnic groups are underrepresented in Internet use, they suggested that a likely possible route to Internet connectivity for these groups is via Internet-enabled mobile devices.

On a theoretical level, some authors have examined the behavior of populations, given specific forms of heterogeneity. Chatterjee and Eliashberg (1990) modeled adoption at the level of the individual, with heterogeneous perceptions of the innovation's performance. They showed that the Bass and other models can be considered special cases of their micro-modeling approach. Bemmaor (1994) and Bemmaor and Lee (2002) considered a population of individuals, where each individual's probability of adoption is given by a shifted Gompertz density function. The heterogeneity is driven by the "shift" parameter, which is distributed as a gamma random variable. Bemmaor and Lee showed that, under certain conditions, the observed diffusion is consistent with the Bass model. They further demonstrated that changing the parameters of the gamma distribution produces conditions under which the data are more or less skewed than the Bass curve. An asymmetric diffusion curve, such as the non-uniform responding logistic curve of Easingwood *et al.* (1981, 1983), can be reproduced under this framework. On forecasting accuracy, Bemmaor and Lee noted that the forecasting accuracy of their more flexible model is better than Bass' for one step ahead but deteriorates for longer horizons. In an interesting modeling development, Van den Bulte and Joshi (2007) segmented the market into two groups, "influentials" and "imitators". The adoption behavior of the influential segment affects the adoption behavior of the imitators, but not vice versa. Their analysis shows that the two-segment model tends to fit a range of data sets better than the gamma-shifted Gompertz model.

The geographical location of potential adopters is another form of heterogeneity that has received some attention. In a theoretical analysis, Goldenberg *et al.* (2000) examined innovation diffusion via percolation theory, which describes the heterogeneity of the population in a spatial context such that the "micro-structure" of the population is precisely defined. They used simulation to demonstrate that "social percolation" leads to a power law curve rather than exponential growth. The S-curve produced by this model has a very late point of inflection, very close to the saturation level. In an empirical study, Baptista (2000) examined the diffusion of numerically controlled machines and microprocessors in regions of the UK. He found that there were significant regional effects on the rate of diffusion.

12.2.1 *The use of explanatory variables in the diffusion model*

The diffusion of an innovation rarely takes place in a stable, unchanging environment. In recognition of this, there have been many attempts to include environmental variables within the diffusion model. An early example is Tanner (1974), who used GDP/capita and the cost of car usage as additional variables in the linearized logistic model [Equation (A12.17)] to forecast the growth of car ownership in the UK.

Typically, explanatory variables are incorporated into (1) market potential; (2) the probability of adoption or the hazard function; or (3) both, i.e. simultaneously into market potential and probability of adoption. Thus, in the first case, the environmental (or marketing mix) variables are hypothesized to determine the total number of eventual adoptions; whereas in the second case, the environmental variables are hypothesized to accelerate or retard adoption. Particularly in cases where the environmental variable is the product price, one could argue that this modeling approach supports the heterogeneity argument: a falling price brings the product within reach of more potential adopters. The question is whether to represent this likely increase in adoption by increasing the market potential or by increasing the probability of adoption. These approaches will be looked at in turn.

Some authors have made the saturation level (market potential) a function of price, advertising or some other measure of market activity. An early example of this was given by Mahajan and Peterson (1978), who used US housing starts to parameterize the market potential for washing machines. The impact of price on market potential has also been studied by Bass (1980), Bass and Bultez (1982), Kalish (1985) and Horsky (1990). One of the rationales used (see Mahajan and Peterson, 1978) is that a lower price would place the product within the budgetary limitations of a greater number of buyers, thus increasing the market potential. Approaching the incorporation of price into market potential from a different perspective, Horsky (1990) argued that the effective reservation price (e.g. price, the time the consumer spent to get the product, etc.) and wage rates are distributed across individuals according to an extreme value distribution. Thus, the market potential (the number of consumers who will buy the product) depends on the distribution of wage and price. The market potential will increase with either a reduction in the average price or an increase in income (or a reduction in the dispersion of the distribution of income).

Kalish (1985) characterized the diffusion of a new product in two stages, namely awareness and adoption. He suggested that consumers will buy a product if they are aware of it and if the risk-adjusted price falls below their reservation level. Thus, at a particular time, the market potential is the number of individuals who find the risk-adjusted price acceptable multiplied by the percentage of individuals who are aware of the product.

Karshenas and Stoneman (1992) introduced explanatory variables into market potential while modeling the diffusion of color televisions in the UK. Islam and Meade (1996) explored several formulations of the saturation level for UK business telephones using GDP-related variables. They found that the approach added insight into how the environment affected diffusion, but did not lead to an increase in forecasting accuracy.

Environmental variables are introduced into the probability, or hazard rate, of adoption by a variety of routes. These include parameterizing the coefficients of innovation or imitation (or their equivalents in non-Bass models), or introducing an extra multiplicative term. Robinson and Lakhani (1975) were the first to include price impact in the Bass model. They reformulated the Bass hazard function in this way:

$$h(t) = (\beta_0 + \beta_1 F(t)) \exp(-\beta_2 P(t)), \qquad (12.1)$$

where $P(t)$ is a price index (with $P(0) = 1$). They used this formulation as a tool to examine pricing strategies. Marginal pricing, which starts with a high price and then decreases with diffusion, was shown to be a poor strategy compared to either an optimal constant price or an optimal strategy (where the price starts low, rises to a peak and then falls). Variants of Equation (12.1) have been used by Dolan and Jeuland (1981) and Kalish (1983).

Horsky and Simon (1983) examined the effect of advertising on the probability of adoption. They modified the hazard function thus:

$$h(t) = \beta_0 + \beta_1 F(t) + \beta_2 \ln (A(t)), \qquad (12.2)$$

where $A(t)$ is the advertising expenditure at time t; and the coefficients β_0, β_1, β_2 are interpreted as measuring the effects of publicity, word of mouth and advertising, respectively. The model was shown to produce plausible estimates for the diffusion of a telephone banking service. Thomson and Teng (1984) proposed a model incorporating elements of Equations (12.1) and (12.2). Generalizing an approach by Thomson and Teng, Simon and Sebastian (1987) found that linking the imitation coefficient to advertising was the most effective way of using this information to model the diffusion of telephones in Western Germany. Their formulation is

$$h(t) = \beta_0 + \beta_1 F(t) + \beta_2 \alpha(A(t))F(t), \qquad (12.3)$$

where $\alpha(A(t))$ is a function of current and past advertising expenditure representing the advertising response.

Kamakura and Balasubramanian (1988) proposed a general model that allows price effects in the probability of adoption and in market potential. The model is a generalization of Equation (A12.1):

$$f(t) = (p + qF(t))P^{\alpha}(t)(H(t)P^{\beta}(t) - F(t)), \qquad (12.4)$$

where $H(t)$ is the proportion of households eligible to receive the innovation (for example, electrified households). This model nests simpler models, allowing for empirical testing of the nature of the price effect for particular data sets. They found that price affected adoption probability ($\alpha < 0$, $\beta = 0$) for relatively highly priced goods (refrigerators rather than blenders). Pursuing a similar theme to Kamakura and Balasubramanian and using a similar approach to Jain and Rao (1990), Parker (1992) incorporated a price elasticity term in a variety of models. For 11 out of 12 consumer durables, he found evidence of time-varying price elasticity.

In response to these modeling initiatives, Bass et al. (1994) developed a generalized Bass model (GBM) which allows the incorporation of marketing mix variables in the modeling of new product diffusion. They achieved this by introducing a "current marketing effort" factor, $x(t)$, into the hazard function of the Bass model:

$$h(t) = (p + qF(t))\, x(t), \qquad (12.5)$$

where

$$x(t) = 1 + \beta_1 \frac{\delta P(t)}{\delta t} + \beta_2 \max\left(0, \frac{\delta A(t)}{\delta t}\right). \qquad (12.6)$$

An attraction of this generalization is that if the marketing effort is more or less constant, then the model simplifies to the Bass model. They demonstrated that the GBM forecasts better than the Bass model for three consumer durables over various horizons (assuming crucially that the future behavior of the marketing variables is known). They further demonstrated empirically that their formulation is superior to making one or more of the parameters p, q or m a function of marketing variables.

Using the GBM in a proactive fashion in the spirit of Robinson and Lakhani (1975), Krishnan *et al.* (1999) derived optimal pricing strategies for product introduction. Using an objective function of cumulative net revenue over a planning horizon, they found that the optimal policy is to raise the price up until a specific time period and then monotonically reduce the price. The optimal timing of the peak price occurs well before peak sales. Earlier, Kalish and Lilien (1983) examined an optimal state price subsidy for accelerating the diffusion of beneficial technologies (such as alternative energy systems). In most cases, they found that the subsidy should decrease as diffusion accelerates.

In a study comparing models without and with explanatory variables, Putsis (1998) also compared different methods for estimation over several models. A central theme is the time-varying nature of the parameters of the diffusion model. These parameters may vary due to factors such as changes in the marketing mix, changes to the product or changes in consumer expectations. The approach offers an estimate of the current, rather than average, response to a marketing variable.

In a study using data for electrical products similar to Kamakura and Balasubramanian (1988) plus electronic products such as VCRs and CD players, Bottomley and Fildes (1998) used Kamakura and Balasubramanian's modeling framework to examine the effect of price information on forecasting accuracy. They found only one case, VCRs, where the full model shown in Equation (12.4) was needed (p, q, α, $\beta \neq 0$). Overall, they found little evidence of increased forecasting accuracy due to the inclusion of actual price information (let alone predicted price information).

12.2.2 *Estimation issues in single diffusion models*

Due to the nature of diffusion models, the estimation of parameters is generally a nonlinear problem. Estimation of the logistic model and some of its variants has been achieved by linear transformations followed by ordinary least squares (OLS) (for example, see Equation (A12.9)). A summary of these models is given by Young (1993). Lee and Lu (1987) further applied Box–Cox transformations to the linearly transformed data to forecast the diffusion of electronic switching systems in telecommunications. Meade and Islam (1995a) used nonlinear least squares (NLS) to fit a range of diffusion models to telecommunications data. Another approach is adaptive estimation, which recognizes the possibility that the parameters of the diffusion model may change over time. Meade (1985) applied the extended Kalman filter to estimate the logistic and Gompertz models for forecasting.

The most clearly documented story of the benefits of different fitting procedures is that of the Bass model. This story is described below. Although the Bass model is discussed here, the lessons learnt are likely to apply to non-Bass diffusion models as well.

12.2.2.1 *Estimation of the Bass model*

An attraction of the Bass model, when it was introduced in 1969, was that the coefficients of innovation, p, and imitation, q, and the market potential, m, could be estimated by OLS. This exploited the property of the discrete model that the binomial expectation of new adopters at time t was

$$\Upsilon_t - \Upsilon_{t-1} = \left(p + \frac{q}{m} \Upsilon_{t-1} \right)(m - \Upsilon_{t-1}), \qquad (12.7)$$

given that Υ_{t-1} adoptions had occurred by $t-1$. This is a discrete version of Equation (A12.1). Empirical experience shows that the OLS approach is prone to wrong signs, implying negative probabilities, and to unstable estimates. Schmittlein and Mahajan (1982) proposed a maximum likelihood estimation (MLE) approach, using a continuous model. The likelihood function is

$$L = (1 - G(t-1))^{M-\Upsilon_{t-1}} \prod_{i=1}^{t} (G(i) - G(i-1))^{\Upsilon_i - \Upsilon_{i-1}},$$

where $G(t)$ is defined in Equation (A12.3). This assumes that the adoptions are Bernoulli trials, with the probability of adoption changing between time periods. The benefits of this approach were demonstrated to be increased forecasting accuracy and more stable parameter estimates. Srinivasan and Mason (1986) argued that MLE tended to underestimate parameter standard errors and proposed an NLS approach. They suggested the minimization of the squared residuals $\sum u_t^2$ where

$$\Upsilon_t - \Upsilon_{t-1} = m(F(t) - F(t-1)) + u_t,$$

with $F(t)$ defined in Equation (A12.2). They found that the fitting and forecasting performance of NLS was very similar to MLE, but that both methods were superior to OLS.

These data have subsequently been used by several other authors. One of the data sets used describes the adoption of mammography by a group of 209 hospitals. This data set is used here to demonstrate and contrast the two objective functions of MLE and NLS. The data are shown in Figure 12.3. The adoptions peak in 1974 and forecasts

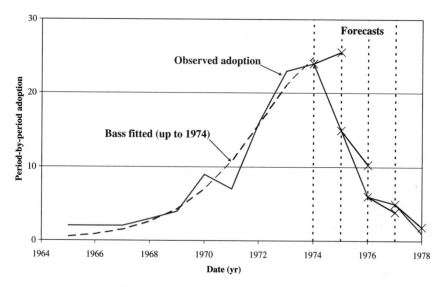

Figure 12.3. Diffusion of mammography in 209 US hospitals (with NLS fit and one-period-ahead forecasts).

are prepared one year ahead for the next four years. The relevant parameter estimates and objective functions are shown for MLE and NLS estimation in Table 12.2. Note that for both procedures the estimates of market potential (m) decrease with each new observation; the estimate of p (coefficient of innovation) tends to decrease and the estimate of q (coefficient of imitation) tends to increase with each observation. MLE favors higher estimates of market potential and the coefficient of innovation and a lower estimate of the coefficient of imitation than NLS. The mean absolute deviation (MAD) of one-step-ahead forecasts (shown in Figure 12.3) is lower for NLS. However, from 1976 onwards, the NLS estimate of market potential is less than the observed cumulative total of adoptions. In contrast, MLE estimates are plausible throughout this period.

In a different but related context, a comparison of new product trial forecasting models using consumer data sets, Hardie *et al.* (1998) found MLE to be noticeably better than NLS applied to period-to-period sales. However, over shorter series, they found NLS applied to cumulative sales comparable with MLE.

Table 12.2. Parameter estimates for the adoption of mammography by 209 US hospitals using NLS and MLE. (The relevant objective function values are shown in bold.)

Data used up to	Cumulative sales	*m*	*p*	*q*	MLE	MSE	1-step-ahead absolute error
NLS estimates							
1974	92	188.6	0.00206	0.5453	−323.3	**2.7**	10.6
1975	107	120.3	0.00073	0.7745	−374.8	**4.0**	4.3
1976	113	110.6	0.00038	0.8703	−402.6	**4.4**	1.1
1977	118	112.0	0.00044	0.8526	−421.5	**4.2**	0.8
1978	119	111.4	0.00041	0.8607	−427.6	**3.9**	
						MAD	4.2
MLE estimates							
1974	92	209.0	0.00328	0.4686	**−322.3**	3.3	9.7
1975	107	160.7	0.00395	0.4998	**−368.4**	7.0	10.4
1976	113	129.4	0.00324	0.5920	**−393.4**	8.9	1.8
1977	118	126.1	0.00299	0.6125	**−413.2**	8.2	2.6
1978	119	122.4	0.00254	0.6471	**−419.8**	7.8	
						MAD	6.1

Note: NLS, nonlinear least squares; MLE, maximum likelihood estimation; MSE, mean squared error; MAD, mean absolute deviation.

There are particular problems with the use of each of these objective functions. The use of MLE assumes the correct identification of the underlying random variable. Schmittlein and Mahajan (1982) assumed that individual adoption is a Bernoulli trial.

Bias in the NLS estimation of the Bass model was examined by Van den Bulte and Lilien (1997). The bias includes a tendency for the saturation level to be underestimated and close to the latest observed penetration, and a tendency for estimates of *q* to decrease as more data become available. In the mammography example, the former bias is very evident, but the latter is not apparent (see Table 12.2). They demonstrated through simulation that the biases exist, but that there is no simple solution: "expecting ... a handful of noisy data points to foretell the ultimate market size and the time path of market evolution is asking too much of too little data".

The use of NLS implicitly assumes that errors have the same variance throughout the time series. To overcome this constraint, Boswijk
and Franses (2005) borrowed from financial econometrics to propose
a new stochastic error process for the Bass model. Their approach is
designed to capture heteroscedastic errors and a tendency for the data
to revert to the long-term trend. They used CD diffusion data from
Bewley and Griffiths (2003) for a comparison of forecast accuracy of
their approach with Srinivasan and Mason's (1986) estimation procedure. They demonstrated that the latter parameter standard errors
were too low, giving overconfidence in parameter accuracy, while the
forecasts based on their formulation were more accurate for 9 out of
12 data sets. Fok and Franses (2007) developed this model further to
describe and compare the diffusion of academic papers in two econometric journals; here, diffusion was measured by the number of times
a paper was cited.

Srinivasan and Mason (1986) discovered the location of the minimum mean square error by a gradient-based search procedure. The
use of this type of search procedure implies that the objective function varies smoothly with the estimated parameters. There is a clear
consensus that using OLS to estimate the Bass model is non-optimal,
but the choice between NLS and MLE is less clear. The balance of
recent work has favored NLS, but it is too early to disregard MLE.
Innovative assumptions about the stochastic behavior of adoptions
can be more readily investigated by MLE. The use of heuristic, com-
putationally intensive search methods, such as genetic algorithms, for
NLS estimation (or MLE) deserves further research.

Other authors suggest that the estimation of the parameters p, q
and m as fixed values for a given data set is misguided because parameter values vary over time. Xie et al. (1997) applied the augmented
Kalman filter to estimate and forecast period-to-period adoption, $f(t)$.
They demonstrated their method on the Bass model applied to
Srinivasan and Mason's (1986) data sets, showing that it offers greater
accuracy in most cases (mammography is one of these cases; Xie et al.
quoted an MAD of 3.1, less than the values given in Table 12.2.) They
demonstrated how their framework can incorporate two or more
possible models with weightings that evolve in light of experience.

Goswami and Karmeshu (2004) used simulated annealing to fit a random coefficients version of the Bass model. Jiang *et al.* (2006) addressed the problem of left bias, which occurs when the data available do not go back to the actual introduction of the innovation. By using symmetry-based arguments, they suggested a method for correcting this bias. As they pointed out, their method produces equivalent results to the NLS method of Srinivasan and Mason (1986), where the time index is adjusted appropriately to recognize the delay between the first observation and introduction.

12.2.2.2 Use of diffusion models with little or no data

In many practical situations, predictions of new product sales are desirable before sufficient data are available for model estimation. A possible means of increasing available data is the use of higher-frequency data. Putsis (1996) found that the use of seasonally adjusted quarterly data leads to greater forecasting accuracy than the use of annual data, but found no further advantage with monthly data. In this situation of scarce data, forecasting by analogy is a possible approach. The Bayesian approach of Lenk and Rao (1990) is one possible approach in this context. These authors developed a hierarchical Bayes procedure to use information about prior innovations to forecast diffusion early on. The data are used in a cross-sectional manner, but the timing is based on a common time period of introduction rather than calendar time. The advantage of this approach over a single-series approach is that the experience of other innovation diffusions informs the parameter estimation for the series of interest. They found that their approach provides forecasts of slightly superior accuracy compared with MLE-based forecasts. In a study of the diffusion of home networking technology in Korea, Lee *et al.* (2008) used expert judgment to provide initial values of the Bass parameters. Bayesian estimation was used to update these estimates as fresh data became available.

The meta-analysis of Sultan *et al.* (1990) is a useful contribution to forecasting with little data. They found the coefficient of innovation to be fairly stable across the 213 applications they examined, with an average value of 0.03, while the coefficient of imitation was far more variable about its average of 0.38. They argued that this finding demonstrates the latter's sensitivity to marketing variables, in agreement with Kamakura and Balasubramanian's (1988) conclusions. Lee *et al.* (2003) described an application of the hierarchical Bayes procedure for forecasting sales of recorded music pre-launch. Their model is

$$f(t) = \lambda(t)m\,(1 - F(t)),\qquad\qquad (12.8)$$

where $\lambda(t)$ is a hazard function parameterized as a function of relevant exogenous variables describing the artist, the album and promotional activity. They showed that the incorporation of these variables reduced the pre-launch mean absolute percentage error (MAPE) from 69% to 52%; as sales data became available, the MAPE fell to around 30%.

Bass *et al.* (2001) prepared a pre-launch forecast of subscriptions to satellite television over a five-year horizon. The Bass model was used with parameter values chosen by a mixture of analogy and collection of intentions data from potential consumers. They described their forecast accuracy as "quite good".

12.2.3 *Modeling constrained diffusion*

In many of the historical examples used as diffusion data sets, such as telephones in the UK, US and elsewhere, supply constraints were present. In the case of fixed-line telephones, the reasons relate to the slow post-war recovery and the behavior of state monopolies. In the case of cellular telephones, supply restrictions can be a low capacity of installed base stations and the unavailability of services in some parts of the country. For example, cellular telephones in the US began operation in Chicago in 1983, in Los Angeles in 1984 and in the next phase in 30 other metropolitan areas (see Hausman, 2002). Sequential availability of interactive technology can be (and is) used as a business strategy because it allows the development of a critical mass in a particular area, before the service is launched in other parts of the country. Supply constraints continue to affect the satisfaction of demand of such desirable innovations as the iPod MP3 player. Jain *et al.* (1991) proposed an adaptation to the Bass model in which a third category of "waiting applicant" is introduced. This model was fitted to data describing the diffusion of fixed-line telephony in Israel. Islam and Fiebig (2001) extended this approach to carry out a multinational study estimating the saturation levels for fixed-line telephony in 46 supply-restricted countries. They used pooled cross-sectional estimates to forecast supply-restricted demand where little or no data was available.

Ho *et al.* (2002) looked at managing demand for new products in the presence of supply constraints. For example, this problem is faced by manufacturers of new products whose introduction is eagerly awaited by enthusiasts, such as PlayStation. They have to decide how much product to produce before launching the product. Optimal launch timing balances inventory costs against the possible loss of customers due to impatience. The main difficulty in implementation is that optimal timing and optimal capacity depend on the coefficient of imitation, q, whose estimation is most problematic. In this case, the estimate will have to be by analogy. Kumar and Swaminathan (2003) tackled the same problem almost simultaneously. The authors differed in their findings. The problem they addressed was this: if demand exceeds supply, should a monopolist damp down demand by building up inventory to satisfy later demand, or should the monopolist take the myopic view and satisfy demand as soon as possible? Ho *et al.* suggested that it is never optimal to delay filling demand; whereas Kumar and Swaminathan showed that, under a particular cost structure, the strategy of building up stock can be optimal.

12.2.4 *Modeling diffusion and replacement*

When modeling and/or forecasting sales of a new product, it is not possible in some situations to distinguish between first-time purchases of the product (adoptions) and replacement purchases. When the product is becoming mature, adoptions are a small proportion of total sales and the imperative is to model total sales rather than adoptions.

Olson and Choi (1985) proposed a decomposition of sales, S_t, into adoptions, y_t, and replacement sales, R_t. The Bass model is used for adoptions; and R_t depends on the density function, $\lambda(t)$, of the product lifetime (the Rayleigh distribution in the case of Olson and Choi) and past sales, as shown here:

$$R_t = \sum_{i=1}^{t} \left(\int_{i-1}^{i} \lambda(x)dx \right) S_{t-i}. \qquad (12.9)$$

Kamakura and Balasubramanian (1987) used a truncated normal distribution for $\lambda(t)$. Steffens (2001) has made Kamakura and Balasubramanian's approach dynamic by including a time-varying aggregate replacement distribution. The time to replacement is modeled as a function of price. In comparison with Kamakura and Balasubramanian's static model, Steffens found the dynamic model to be substantially more accurate than the static model over one- to five-year horizons. Islam and Meade (2000) compared seven different density functions for $\lambda(t)$ and a non-parametric version. They found that, over 42 data sets, there were many occasions where their MLE would not converge for combinations of data and density function. Overall, their non-parametric approach dominated the parametric models in terms of forecasting accuracy.

Some authors have used cross-sectional survey data to gain further insight into the replacement decision. Fernandez (2000) showed that the time to replacement for air conditioners can be modeled in terms of demographic, environmental and cost variables. Grewal *et al.* (2004) used attitude variables (derived from factor analysis) alongside variables describing the product and associated costs. Unfortunately, it is difficult to see how these studies can be harnessed to the time series forecasting approaches described above. Their value probably lies in a data-rich environment, where an owner, who is predicted to replace soon, can be persuaded to replace sooner.

A related problem is modeling the diffusion of a product with multiple purchases. For example, one household may have several televisions. This problem was addressed by Bayus *et al.* (1989) and Steffens (2003).

12.2.5 *Modeling the diffusion of multiple subcategories*

An innovative product may be available under separate subcategories. Many products such as mobile telephones are branded; thus, in this example, the subcategories are competing brands. Another example of subcategorization is where there are two or more competing standards, as with VCRs (see Section 12.2). One other categorization that has been studied is products acquired legally or illegally. Mahajan *et al.* (1993b) modeled the effect of a new entrant into an expanding market. Their approach is a development of the Bass model as represented by Equation (12.7):

$$Y_{i,t} - Y_{i,t-1} = p_i(m_i - Y_{i,t-1}) + \left(\frac{q_i}{m_i} Y_{i,t-1}\right)(M - Y_{t-1}), \quad (12.10)$$

where $Y_{i,t}$ represents the cumulative sales of subcategory i, m_i is the market potential of subcategory i, $Y_t = \sum_i Y_{i,t}$ and $M = \sum_i m_i$. They applied the model to competing brands of cameras offering "instant" photographs. Krishnan *et al.* (2000) criticized this model [Equation (12.10)] because sales of brand i are only affected by the cumulative buyers of brand i and no others (because of the term $\frac{q_i}{m_i} Y_{i,t-1}$). They proposed an alternative hazard function-based approach, where the hazard function for brand i is

$$h_i(t) = \frac{f_i(t)}{1 - F(t)} = p_i + q_i F(t). \quad (12.11)$$

Note that here the imitation process is driven by adopters of all brands rather than just brand i. An attraction of this formulation is that the subcategory models sum to a Bass model for the whole category. The model was fitted to three different markets for mobile telephones, showing that a late-arriving third brand could increase the speed of diffusion, increase the market potential or do both simultaneously.

Givon *et al.* (1995) used a model similar to Equation (12.11) for the diffusion of software where the sales of legal copies are known but the "sales" of pirated software are not. Given an estimate for the software market potential provided by a diffusion-based model of the number of extant personal computers, using UK data for spreadsheet and word processor sales, they demonstrated the interaction between these two subcategories. They found that users of pirated software were a dominant influence in the imitation component of diffusion; pirate users were estimated to outnumber legal users by six to one. Givon *et al.* (1997) extended their work to brands of the same software products, and found that piracy rates differed significantly between brands.

Kim *et al.* (2000) modeled competition between products that fulfill the same function, rather than different brands of the same product. Their work is discussed in more detail in Section 12.4. A range of other formulations for the interaction between the diffusions of related subcategories of products, such as prey-predator models, was discussed in Bayus *et al.* (2000). Lee *et al.* (2008) used conjoint analysis to describe the competition between technological alternatives in their study of the diffusion of home networking in Korea.

12.2.6 *Model selection and forecasting*

12.2.6.1 *Studies of comparative forecasting accuracy*

Armstrong *et al.* (1987) complained that little is known about the comparative performance of sales forecasting models in a given situation. In the situation of forecasting the diffusion of an innovation, one would expect a diffusion model to be more accurate than a time series model, such as the Holt–Winters model with a linear trend. Gottardi and Scarso (1994) compared the forecasting accuracy of ARIMA models with a selection of diffusion models. The non-symmetric responding logistic model of Easingwood *et al.* (1981) [Equation (A12.12)] was the most accurate, with the lowest MAPE. However, since many of the data sets are inappropriate as they describe consumption or production rather than diffusion, this empirical comparison is of little value.

Young (1993) used nine variations of growth curves to forecast 46 data sets. Forecast accuracy was compared over the last three data points. Harvey's model [Equation (A12.16)] was the most accurate model 13 times, while the Bass model (as implemented in Equation (12.7)) was the most accurate model 12 times.

Meade and Islam (1995a) used 14 variations of growth curve models to forecast the adoption of telephones in 15 different countries. For a kernel of nine series and nine growth curve models, relatively free of estimation problems, they used the Friedman test to compare forecasting accuracy. The most accurate models were the local logistic [Equation (A12.13)], Gompertz [Equation (A12.7)], logistic [Equation (A12.9)] and extended logistic (equivalent to the version of the Bass model in Equation (A12.2)) models. These were found to be significantly more accurate than the Bass (as implemented in Equation (12.7)), non-symmetric responding logistic [Equation (A12.12)] and flexible logistic [Equation (A12.11)] models. Hardie *et al.* (1998), using non-diffusion, consumer goods data, found that model fit was "largely unrelated" to forecasting performance.

Meade and Islam (1998) classified 29 diffusion models into three classes according to the timing of peak diffusion in relation to introduction and saturation. This was done in order to aid model selection. Using the criteria of model fit and short-term forecast stability in conjunction with members of each class, the prior probability that a data set belongs to each class was calculated. These prior probabilities allowed the calculation of a combined forecast. In 77% of the 47 data sets examined, the combined forecast was more accurate than the best-fitting model; the average improvement in root mean square error was 8%.

Bewley and Griffiths (2003) modeled the penetration of the compact disc (CD) in sound recording in 12 countries. They used the Bass model and versions of the flexible logistic model [Equation (A12.11)]. They found that, in ranking the relative accuracy of forecasts, the Box–Cox transformation variant of the flexible logistic model substantially outperformed the Bass model.

Bass *et al.* (2000) compared the one-step-ahead forecasting performance of four versions of the Bass model (the original version, the generalized version and two versions of a proportional hazard formulation of the Bass model) using three data sets. They found that one version of the proportional hazard model outperformed the other models in one-step-ahead forecasts. Bemmaor and Lee (2002) compared one- to three-step-ahead forecasting performance of the Bass model and the gamma-shifted Gompertz model using 12 products and services. The latter only outperformed the former for one-step-ahead forecasts. As the Bass model is a special case of the gamma-shifted Gompertz model, model parsimony becomes more important in long-range forecasting.

In summary, for homogeneous data sets, there is likely to be a preferred model, as shown by Meade and Islam (1995a) and Bewley and Griffiths (2003). However, for heterogeneous data sets, the evidence continues to point to the non-existence of a best forecasting diffusion model, as asserted by Meade and Islam (2001). In this case, the use of combined models as suggested by Meade and Islam (1998) is a low-risk approach.

12.2.6.2 *Use of prediction intervals*

A guide to the uncertainty associated with a forecast is desirable in any circumstance. Chatfield (1993) made the case for prediction intervals and cited reasons why they could be too narrow, such as taking parameter estimates as known values, assuming the normality of errors or assuming correct model identification. In the case of diffusion models, the case for being wary of these pitfalls is particularly strong. Several authors have suggested ways of generating prediction intervals.

Meade's (1985) use of the extended Kalman filter generated the information basis which, coupled with Monte Carlo simulation, allows the provision of a prediction interval for an arbitrary horizon. Migon and Gamerman (1993) used a Bayesian approach to forecasting diffusion via a generalized exponential growth model. This approach allows the computation of prediction intervals, and their model class included the logistic and Gompertz curves. Meade and Islam (1995b) compared three methods for computing prediction intervals. Each method takes into account both noise and the uncertainty of the parameter estimates. The methods compared were a Taylor series approximation of error variance, explicit modeling of the error density and the use of bootstrapping. They found the explicit density approach to be the most accurate.

Bewley and Griffiths (2003) used bootstrapping to generate prediction intervals for their CD penetration forecasts. Gutierrez *et al.* (2005) formulated a stochastic version of the Gompertz model that allowed them to provide confidence intervals for their out-of-sample forecasts.

12.2.7 *Applications*

Examples of Meade's (1984) concerns — where the saturation level has no bound (or meaning) — are given in applications by Suslick *et al.* (1995), who used the logistic model to forecast US crude oil production and world consumption of copper; and by Gutierrez *et al.* (2005), who forecasted the consumption of natural gas in Spain.

Mahajan *et al.* (1990) and Lilien *et al.* (2000) described generic uses of diffusion modeling in marketing. These uses include pre-launch forecasting (see Section 12.2.2.2), strategic decision analysis based on the product life cycle and the determination of the optimal timing of market entry.

Mahajan (1994) mentioned the importance of diffusion modeling in a variety of strategic applications. These include business valuation, where the business depends on products at various points in their life cycles; and relating capacity to demand, which is discussed in Section 12.2.3. Mahajan *et al.* (2000a, Table 1.1) documented eight published applications: two for pre-launch and launch strategic decisions, and six for post-launch strategic decisions.

In the realm of technologies studied, the area of telecommunications is particularly rich in published applications (nine of the references at the end of this chapter mention "telecommunications" or "telephones" in their titles) and unpublished conference papers by practitioners.

12.3 Modeling of Diffusion Across Several Countries

Modeling the diffusion of the same innovation in several countries offers a number of benefits. A practical forecasting advantage is that it helps overcome a perennial difficulty of using diffusion models for forecasting: their hunger for data. If an innovation is released in different countries at different times, it is desirable to be able to use the data from earlier adopting countries to predict the diffusion in later adopting countries. Modeling the effect of different national cultures on the diffusion process gives insight into the effect of national differences on the rate of adoption of the innovation. For example, the exercise may shed light on whether later adopting countries adopt more quickly than earlier adopters.

Addressing this last question, Takada and Jain (1991) used the Bass model for a cross-sectional analysis of the diffusion of durable goods in four Pacific Rim countries. They used the estimated coefficients to test hypotheses on country-specific effects and lead–lag time effects on the diffusion rates. They established significant differences in the coefficients of imitation between countries with different cultures, such as the US and Korea. They also found evidence that a lagged product introduction leads to accelerated diffusion.

The effect of lead–lag on the international diffusion of innovations has been addressed more recently by Ganesh and Kumar (1996), Ganesh et al. (1997), Kumar et al. (1998) and Kumar and Krishnan (2002). The premise is that the time lag grants additional time to potential adopters in the lagging markets to help them understand the relative advantage of the product, better assess the technology need and observe the experience of the lead country adopters' usage of the product. Kalish et al. (1995) argued that potential adopters in the lagging countries observe the introduction and diffusion of technology in the lead country. If the product is successful in the leading countries, then the risk associated with the innovation is reduced, thus contributing to an accelerated diffusion in the lagging countries.

Gatignon et al. (1989) proposed a methodology for modeling and forecasting the multinational diffusion of innovations based on the Bass model. For each country, the market potential is estimated; the coefficients of innovation and imitation are functions of national characteristics. For example, the coefficient of innovation for country i is

$$p_i = \beta_{p,i,0} + \sum_k \beta_{p,i,k} Z_{i,k} + e_{p,i}, \qquad (12.12)$$

where $Z_{i,k}$ represents a cultural variable; $\beta_{p,i,k}$, for $i = 0,1,\ldots$, are estimated coefficients; and $e_{p,i}$ is a disturbance term. The estimation of the model is achieved by generalized least squares. The cultural variables used to describe national cultural differences are cosmopolitanism (communication with foreign countries by post or by travel), mobility (car ownership) and the role of women in society (proportion of women in the workforce). The model was demonstrated on six innovations, ranging from lawn mowers to pocket calculators, in 14 European countries. The choice of national cultural variables, designed to capture a nation's propensity to innovate, has received much attention.

Talukdar *et al.* (2002) investigated the impact of a wide range of macroenvironmental variables on the parameters of the Bass model while modeling the diffusion of six products across 31 developed and developing countries. They found that, on average, the market potential in developing countries was a third of that in developed countries; and despite lagged introduction, the rate of adoption was slower in developing countries. They found that market potential was best explained by previous experience in the same country; in contrast, the probability of adoption was better explained by product experience in earlier adopting countries. Similar findings were reported by Desiraju *et al.* (2004), who modeled the diffusion of pharmaceutical drugs with the logistic model using data from 15 countries. In addition, they found that per capita expenditure on healthcare was positively related to the rate of adoption, while higher prices decreased adoption rates.

Innovativeness as a concept was discussed by Midgley and Dowling (1978), who suggested that there are two factors underlying the adoption of a new product/technology: the distribution of innate innovativeness in the population (echoing Rogers (1962)), and the communication between the population members (contagion). The realized behavior in the adoption of an innovation depends on the interplay between these factors. Lee (1990) investigated the innovativeness of nations empirically. A cross-sectional study of 70 nations was carried out in which innovativeness was represented by the proportion of the population owning a television. The significant predictor variables were GNP/capita, the proportion of the population that was literate, the proportion of scientists in the population and the proportion of GNP generated by the manufacturing sector. Lynn and Gelb (1996) compiled an index of national innovativeness based on a range of ownership of recently introduced products. They explained this index in terms of national traits developed by Hofstede (1984, 2001) — individualism and uncertainty avoidance — and purchasing power parity (PPP). These variables were significant in explaining the index, but not for all individual new products; for example, only PPP was necessary to explain the ownership of video cameras.

Steenkamp *et al.* (1999) further investigated national innovativeness alongside variables describing the individual. The dependent variable was the consumer's score on the "exploratory acquisition of products" scale developed by Baumgartner and Steenkamp (1996). On the individual level, measures of ethnocentrism, attitude towards the past (nostalgia) and education were used. On a national level, they used individualism, uncertainty avoidance and masculinity (greater emphasis on wealth and material goods in contrast to valuing people and helping others). They found that, on an individual level, both ethnocentrism and attitude towards the past were negatively related to innovativeness. On a national level, individualism and masculinity were positively related to innovativeness, while uncertainty avoidance was negatively related. In an exercise that provides a measure of national innovative capacity, Furman *et al.* (2002) modeled the innovativeness of different nations — measured by patent applications in the US — in terms of variables including income (GDP), research expenditure and the level of international trade.

Helsen *et al.* (1993) used a latent variable approach to simultaneously cluster nations into segments and estimate Bass coefficients, using 23 variables. Their factors (groupings of variables) were mobility, health, trade, life and cosmopolitanism. They found two or three segments (country groupings) that differed, depending on which innovation (color television, VCR or CD player) was considered.

12.3.1 *Estimation and model choice in multinational diffusion models*

Islam *et al.* (2002) compared several formulations of the parameters of the Bass and Gompertz models as functions of national variables for the diffusion of three telecommunications products. They pooled the estimation of the Gompertz growth parameter and the Bass coefficients, and made the market potential for each country a function of GDP/capita as a measure of wealth and various costs associated with product adoption. They found that the pooled Gompertz model offered plausible estimates of market potential and produced generally more accurate forecasts than single national models. Kumar and Krishnan (2002) developed a multinational Bass model that incorporates both simultaneous effects and lead–lag effects. Their framework allows the first country to introduce a technology to affect subsequent countries' rates of adoption, allows the later countries' adoption rates to affect those of earlier adopting countries, and allows adoption in different countries to have a simultaneous effect. Talukdar *et al.* (2002) and Desiraju *et al.* (2004) used a hierarchical Bayesian framework to estimate their pooled cross-sectional models.

12.3.2 *Applications*

Gruber and Verboven (2001) used a logistic model as the basis for modeling the diffusion of telecommunications within the European Union. They interpreted the introduction of digital mobile telephones as a relaxation of the capacity constraint imposed by analog technology. They further found that competition between suppliers increased the diffusion rate. They found a strong positive relationship between the timing of introduction (granting of licenses) and the subsequent rate of adoption. However, convergence in penetration levels between early and late countries is expected to occur relatively slowly. Frank (2004) used a similar approach to Gruber and Verboven to model the diffusion of mobile telephones in Finland. The equivalent of the imitation coefficient, q, was parameterized as a function of GDP/capita, a dummy variable identifying the introduction of GSM technology and a variable describing the proportion of fixed-line telephones. However, in contrast to Gruber and Verboven, only GDP/capita was found to be significant.

Kiiski and Pohjola (2002) examined the factors influencing the cross-country diffusion of the Internet. Using Internet hosts per capita as the diffusion variable, with a Gompertz-based model, they identified the main determinants of diffusion as GDP per capita and access cost. They also found that a greater proportion of post–15-year-olds in tertiary education led to faster diffusion.

Kalish *et al.* (1995) used a diffusion model normatively to examine under which conditions waterfall (sequential entry) and sprinkler (simultaneous entry) strategies should be selected when entering international markets.

12.4 Modeling of Diffusion Across Several Generations of Technology

Norton and Bass (1987) proposed an adaptation of the Bass model that considers different generations of a technology. Examples are the series of generations of mobile telephones and personal computers. In the Norton–Bass model, each generation of the technology attracts incremental population segments of potential adopters; in addition, later generations may attract potential adopters of earlier generations. This modeling approach has effectively succeeded the models on technological substitution, where one technology replaces its predecessor. Fisher and Pry (1971), Blackman (1972) and Sharif and Kabir (1976) used variants of the logistic model for technological substitution. Example substitutions were diesel for steam locomotives, and steel for wood in ship hulls. Meade (1989) contrasted the dynamics of the diffusion of color television, a retail product, with the diffusion of industrial products where the number of decision makers is small. A framework for a stochastic substitution model to model the properties of the different adopting populations was demonstrated. In a more recent example, the Gompertz model was used to forecast the substitution of electronic payments for cash in 10 European countries by Snellman *et al.* (2001).

The modeling innovations by Norton and Bass are that the new (generation of) technology attracts more potential adopters and that more than two generations of a technology can be considered simultaneously. Norton and Bass (1992) demonstrated their model on data from the electronics, pharmaceutical, consumer and industrial sectors. Speece and MacLachlan (1992) used the Norton–Bass model to model and forecast the adoption of successive generations of gallon milk containers. Mahajan and Muller (1996) extended the Norton–Bass model to allow adopters of early generations to skip generations; for example, an adopter of the first generation could replace it with third-generation technology. They demonstrated their model using generations of IBM mainframe computers. Islam and Meade (1997) demonstrated that the assumption of constant coefficients of innovation and imitation (p and q) over successive generations could be relaxed. In a study of multinational mobile telephone adoption, they demonstrated that the coefficient of imitation (q) tended to increase from generation to generation. Sohn and Ahn (2003) used the Norton–Bass model to demonstrate the cost/benefit analysis of introducing a new generation of information technology.

The case where demand data do not explicitly identify which generation of technology is purchased was discussed by Jun and Park (1999). They modeled consumer utility over time to allocate demand to the appropriate generation, and demonstrated their model on demand data for dynamic random access memory chips.

The Norton–Bass approach was extended by Kim *et al.* (2000), who considered the case where several devices compete to fulfill the same function, some of which are different generations of the same device. The example they considered was mobile telephony, where the competing devices were the pager, the analog mobile telephone, the digital mobile telephone, and a device for making but not receiving calls called the CT2. Applying their approach to the mobile telephony markets of Hong Kong and Korea, the Bass model was used to represent the numbers of subscribers to the pager and the CT2; the Norton–Bass model was used to represent the numbers of subscribers to the two generations of mobile telephones. The impact of competition between the devices was captured by making the market potential of each device a function of the subscriber base of its competitors. The out-of-sample accuracy of their approach was shown to be superior to the appropriate Bass or Norton–Bass alternative, and vastly superior to the naive alternatives of double exponential smoothing and linear regression.

An alternative modeling approach to that of Norton and Bass was demonstrated by Versluis (2002). He used a model developed by Marchetti (1977) that divides a technology's life cycle into growth, saturation and decline. The data were the diffusion of generations of dynamic random access memory chips. The comparison with other models showed a better fit than Norton–Bass; however, there was no out-of-sample comparison of forecasting accuracy.

12.4.1 *Use of explanatory variables in multi-generation models*

Speece and MacLachlan (1992) found that the inclusion of price as an explanatory variable in their milk container study improved forecasting accuracy (provided the future prices were known). Padmanabhan and Bass (1993) examined optimal pricing strategies for successive generations of technology. They found that the optimal strategy differs according to the nature of the producer (integrated monopolist or independent), the degree of cannibalization by the newer product of the old, and the degree of foresight of the producers.

Danaher *et al.* (2001) explored the use of price as a covariate in a variety of models of generations of mobile telephones. The models they compared for adoption time were the Bass model (no price effect), the generalized Bass model and a proportional hazards model which incorporates a Bass model of the baseline adoption (this is a multi-generation version of Jain (1992)). The proportional hazards approach provided a superior fit to the generalized Bass model, which failed to detect a price effect. They found evidence that a price skimming policy was used and was consistent with the Bass parameters (according to Kalish (1983), various combinations of values of p and q are consistent with a price skimming policy). They found that lowering the price of the earlier-generation mobile telephones increased the take-up of that generation and led to greater take-up of the succeeding generation (because of the greater number of subscribers). They further demonstrated that lowering the price of the succeeding generation led to a greater take-up of this generation while causing a proportionately smaller decrease in take-up of the earlier generation.

Pursuing a different variation of the Bass model, Jun and Park (1999) assumed that customers maximize their utility in deciding when to upgrade to (or adopt) a later generation of a technology. The probability of adoption is a function of the utility of the consumer, which in turn is a function of the product price. Jun *et al.* (2002) applied and developed this approach to forecast (1) the switch from analog to digital, and (2) the adoption of two competing digital services. Both analyses used Korean telecommunications data.

12.4.2 *Multi-technology models*

We have discussed the problem of forecasting the diffusion of a new product with little or no data. In this situation, using parameter estimates for a product analogous to the product of interest is a viable approach. Meade and Islam (2003) extended this idea by modeling the relation between the times to adoption of a technology by different countries. The dependence between the times to adoption by a country of two related innovations, the fax and the cellular telephone, was modeled in two stages. For the first stage, the choice of density function for the time to adoption — a Weibull density function — was used with its scale factor adapted to account for the economic and technological environments in different countries. In the second stage, describing the dependence relation, copulas were used. The Frank and Plackett copulas, coupled with the Weibull density function, using eight environmental variables, were shown to provide valuable insights into the effects of environmental variables on adoption times. Once a country has adopted one technology, the model of the dependence relation provides the conditional density of the time to adoption of the other technology.

12.5 Conclusions and Likely Further Research

The wealth of research into modeling and forecasting the diffusion of innovations is impressive and confirms its continuing importance as a research topic. In terms of practical impact, the main application areas are in the introduction of consumer durables and particularly in telecommunications. Telecommunications is an application that lends itself to modeling the effects of all the main themes identified here: the marketing mix, the multinational diffusion of services and the modeling of multi-generational diffusion.

In terms of research questions that are still open and those questions which have been resolved, the balance is strongly in favor of the former. For example, although there is some convergence of the most appropriate way to include marketing mix variables into the Bass model, there are several viable alternative models. This lack of closure is likely to continue simply because the processes underlying diffusion are far more complex than the models recognize and because lack of data allows only the de-selection of models which are obviously poor approximations of reality.

Future directions of research are likely to be in areas such as:

(1) Forecasting of new product diffusion with little or no data — There are two main reasons for this suggestion. One is that there is a demand for more accuracy; any reduction of the uncertainty will be valuable. The second is the increasing availability of

cross-sectional and time series data describing consumers. The availability of this type of data will allow better estimates of model parameters. The existence of these data is likely to encourage more normative modeling to refine pricing and marketing strategies; developments in real option valuation methods are likely to add to the value of these normative exercises. A priority among practitioners is to establish market potential as early as possible in the diffusion process, if possible before the process even begins. The identification of factors determining market potential is therefore a fruitful area of research. Possible approaches include a new meta-analysis, specifically focused on this agenda; or an analysis of existing meta-analyses such as those by Van den Bulte and Stremersch (2004) or Sultan *et al.* (1990). The development of a scale for imitation is also a profitable area of interest. This scale would complement the literature on an innovation scale (e.g. Steenkamp *et al.*, 1999) and would further facilitate forecasting the very early stages of diffusion.

(2) Forecasting with multinational models — This modeling area will continue to generate intense interest. One driver for this is the development of multinational telecommunications service providers. The launch of a new service across several companies is increasingly likely to be due to a multinational company's strategic plan, rather than the result of individual company decisions in the different countries. Again, there is scope for normative modeling for strategy evaluation.

(3) Forecasting with multi-generation models — Work in normative modeling in this area has already been published. The telecommunications application is likely to lead to multinational, multi-generational models for both forecasting and normative purposes.

We can be quite confident of one forecast: our list of suggestions has omitted some major future advances in diffusion modeling and forecasting. We look forward to discovering the nature of these omissions.

References

Armstrong, J.S., Brodie, R.J. and McIntyre, S.H. (1987). Forecasting methods for marketing — review of empirical research. *International Journal of Forecasting*, 3, 355–376.

Bain, A.D. (1963). Demand for new commodities. *Journal of the Royal Statistical Society, Series A*, 16, 285–299.

Baptista, R. (1999). Do innovations diffuse faster within geographical clusters? *International Journal of the Economics of Business*, 6, 107–129.

Baptista, R. (2000). The diffusion of process innovations: a selective review. *International Journal of Industrial Organization*, 18, 515–535.

Bass, F.M. (1969). A new product growth model for consumer durables. *Management Science*, 15, 215–227.

Bass, F.M. (1980). The relationship between diffusion rates, experience curves, and demand elasticities for consumer durable technological innovations. *Journal of Business*, 53, 51–67.

Bass, F.M. and Bultez, A.V. (1982). A note on optimal strategic pricing of technological innovations. *Marketing Science*, 1, 371–378.

Bass, F.M., Gordon, K., Ferguson, T.L. and Githens, M.L. (2001). DIRECTV: forecasting diffusion of a new technology prior to product launch. *Interfaces*, 31(May/Jun), S82–S93.

Bass, F.M., Jain, D. and Krishnan, T. (2000). Modeling the marketing-mix influence in new-product diffusion. In: V. Mahajan, E. Muller and Y. Wind (eds.), *New Product Diffusion Models*, London: Kluwer, pp. 99–122.

Bass, F.M., Krishnan, T. and Jain, D. (1994). Why the Bass model fits without decision variables. *Marketing Science*, 13(3), 203–223.

Baumgartner, H. and Steenkamp, J.-B.E.M. (1996). Exploratory consumer buying behavior: conceptualization and measurement. *International Journal of Research in Marketing*, 13(2), 121–137.

Bayus, B. (1987). Forecasting sales of new contingent products: an application to the compact disc markets. *Journal of Product Innovation Management*, 4(Dec), 243–255.

Bayus, B.L., Hong, S. and Labe, R.P. Jr. (1989). Developing and using forecasting models of consumer durables. *Journal of Product Innovation Management*, 6, 5–19.

Bayus, B.L., Kim, N. and Shocker, A. (2000). Growth models for multi-product interactions: current status and new directions. In: V. Mahajan, E. Muller and Y. Wind (eds.), *New Product Diffusion Models*, London: Kluwer, pp. 141–164.

Bemmaor, A.C. (1994). Modeling the diffusion of new durable goods: word-of-mouth effect versus consumer heterogeneity. In: G. Laurent, G.L. Lilien and B. Pras (eds.), *Research Traditions in Marketing*, Boston: Kluwer, pp. 201–213.

Bemmaor, A.C. and Lee, J. (2002). The impact of heterogeneity and ill-conditioning on diffusion model parameter estimates. *Marketing Science*, 21, 209–220.

Bewley, R. and Fiebig, D. (1988). Flexible logistic growth model with applications in telecommunications. *International Journal of Forecasting*, 4, 177–192.

Bewley, R. and Griffiths, W. (2003). The penetration of CDs in the sound recording market: issues in specification, model selection and forecasting. *International Journal of Forecasting*, 19(1), 111–121.

Blackman, W.A. (1972). A mathematical model for trend forecasts. *Technological Forecasting and Social Change*, 3, 441–452.

Bonus, H. (1973). Quasi-Engel curves, diffusion and the ownership of major consumer durables. *Journal of Political Economy*, 81, 655–677.

Boswijk, H.P. and Franses, P.H. (2005). On the econometrics of the Bass diffusion model. *Journal of Business and Economic Statistics*, 23(3), 255–268.

Bottomley, P.A. and Fildes, R. (1998). The role of prices in models of innovation diffusion. *Journal of Forecasting*, 17, 539–555.

Chatfield, C. (1993). Calculating interval forecasts. *Journal of Business and Economic Statistics*, 11, 121–135.

Chatterjee, R. and Eliashberg, J. (1990). The innovation diffusion process in a heterogeneous population: a micromodeling approach. *Management Science*, 36, 1057–1079.

Chow, G.C. (1967). Technological change and demand for consumers. *American Economic Review*, 57, 1117–1130.

Danaher, P.J., Hardie, B.G.S. and Putsis, W.P. (2001). Marketing-mix variables and the diffusion of successive generations of a technological innovation. *Journal of Marketing Research*, 38, 501–514.

Desiraju, R., Nair, H. and Chintagunta, P. (2004). Diffusion of new pharmaceutical drugs in developing and developed nations. *International Journal of Research in Marketing*, 21, 341–357.

Dolan, R.J. and Jeuland, A.P. (1981). Experience curves and dynamic demand models: implications for optimal pricing strategies. *Journal of Marketing*, 45(1), 52–62.

Duesenberry, J.S. (1949). *Income, Saving and the Theory of Consumer Behavior.* Cambridge, MA: Harvard University Press.

Easingwood, C., Mahajan, V. and Muller, E. (1981). A non-symmetric responding logistic model for forecasting technological substitution. *Technological Forecasting and Social Change*, 20, 199–213.

Easingwood, C., Mahajan, V. and Muller, E. (1983). A nonuniform influence innovation diffusion model of new product acceptance. *Marketing Science*, 2(Summer), 273–296.

Fernandez, V. (2000). Decisions to replace consumer durable goods: an econometric application of Wiener and renewal processes. *Review of Economics and Statistics*, 82(3), 452–461.

Fisher, J.C. and Pry, R.H. (1971). Simple substitution model of technological change. *Technological Forecasting and Social Change*, 3, 75–88.

Floyd, A. (1962). Trend forecasting: a methodology for figure of merit. In: J. Bright (ed.), *Technological Forecasting for Industry and Government*, Englewood Cliffs, NJ: Prentice Hall, pp. 95–105.

Fok, D. and Franses, P.H. (2007). Modeling the diffusion of scientific publications. *Journal of Econometrics*, 139, 376–390.

Fourt, L.A. and Woodlock, J.W. (1960). Early prediction of early success of new grocery products. *Journal of Marketing*, 25(Oct), 31–38.

Frank, L.D. (2004). An analysis of the effect of the economic situation on modeling and forecasting the diffusion of wireless communications in Finland. *Technological Forecasting and Social Change*, 71, 391–403.

Furman, J.L., Porter, M.E. and Stern, S. (2002). The determinants of national innovative capacity. *Research Policy*, 31, 899–933.

Ganesh, J. and Kumar, V. (1996). Capturing the cross-national learning effect: an analysis of an industrial technology diffusion. *Journal of the Academy of Marketing Science*, 24(4), 328–337.

Ganesh, J., Kumar, V. and Subramanian, V. (1997). Learning effects in multinational diffusion of consumer durables: an exploratory investigation. *Journal of the Academy of Marketing Science*, 25(3), 214–228.

Gatignon, H.A., Eliashberg, J. and Robertson, T.S. (1989). Modeling multinational diffusion patterns: an efficient methodology. *Marketing Science*, 8, 231–247.

Geroski, P.A. (2000). Models of technology diffusion. *Research Policy*, 29, 603–625.

Givon, M., Mahajan, V. and Muller, E. (1995). Software piracy: estimation of lost sales and the impact on software diffusion. *Journal of Marketing*, 59, 29–37.

Givon, M., Mahajan, V. and Muller, E. (1997). Assessing the relationship between user-based market share and unit sales-based market share for pirated software brands in competitive markets. *Technological Forecasting and Social Change*, 55, 131–144.

Goldenberg, J., Libai, B., Solomon, S., Jan, N. and Stauffer, D. (2000). Marketing percolation. *Physica A*, 284, 335–347.

Goswami, D. and Karmeshu. (2004). Study of population heterogeneity in innovation diffusion model: estimation based on simulated annealing. *Technological Forecasting and Social Change*, 71, 705–722.

Gottardi, G. and Scarso, E. (1994). Diffusion models in forecasting: a comparison with the Box–Jenkins approach. *European Journal of Operational Research*, 75, 600–616.

Gregg, J.V., Hassel, C.H. and Richardson, J.T. (1964). *Mathematical Trend Curves: An Aid to Forecasting*. Edinburgh: Oliver & Boyd.

Grewal, R., Mehta, R. and Kardes, F.R. (2004). The timing of repeat purchases of consumer durable goods: the role of functional bases of consumer attitudes. *Journal of Marketing Research*, 41(1), 101–115.

Gruber, H. and Verboven, F. (2001). The diffusion of mobile telecommunication services in the European Union. *European Economic Review*, 45, 577–588.

Gutierrez, R., Nafidi, A. and Gutierrez Sanchez, R. (2005). Forecasting total natural gas consumption in Spain by using the stochastic Gompertz innovation diffusion model. *Applied Energy*, 80, 115–124.

Hardie, B.G.S., Fader, P.S. and Wisniewski, M. (1998). An empirical comparison of new product trial forecasting models. *Journal of Forecasting*, 17, 209–229.

Harvey, A.C. (1984). Time series forecasting based on the logistic curve. *Journal of the Operational Research Society*, 35, 641–646.

Hausman, J. (2002). Mobile telephone. In: M.E. Cave, S.K. Majumdar and I. Vogelsang (eds.), *Handbook of Telecommunications Economics, Vol. 1: Structure, Regulation and Competition*, Amsterdam: Elsevier Science B.V., pp. 564–604.

Helsen, K., Jedidi, K. and DeSarbo, W.S. (1993). A new approach to country segmentation utilizing multinational diffusion patterns. *Journal of Marketing*, 57, 60–71.

Ho, T.-H., Savin, S. and Terwiesch, C. (2002). Managing demand and sales dynamics in new product diffusion under supply constraint. *Management Science*, 48, 187–206.

Hofstede, G. (1984). *Culture's Consequences: International Differences in Work-Related Values*. London: Sage.

Hofstede, G. (2001). *Culture's Consequences: Comparing Values, Behaviors, Institutions and Organizations Across Nations*, 2nd ed. Thousand Oaks, CA: Sage.

Horsky, D. (1990). A diffusion model incorporating product benefits, price, income and information. *Marketing Science*, 9, 342–365.

Horsky, D. and Simon, L.S. (1983). Advertising and the diffusion of new products. *Marketing Science*, 2(1), 1–17.

Islam, T. and Fiebig, D.G. (2001). Modelling the development of supply-restricted telecommunications markets. *Journal of Forecasting*, 20, 249–264.

Islam, T., Fiebig, D.G. and Meade, N. (2002). Modelling multinational telecommunications demand with limited data. *International Journal of Forecasting*, 18, 605–624.

Islam, T. and Meade, N. (1996). Forecasting the development of the market for business telephones in the UK. *Journal of the Operational Research Society*, 47, 906–918.

Islam, T. and Meade, N. (1997). The diffusion of successive generations of a technology: a more general model. *Technological Forecasting and Social Change*, 56, 49–60.

Islam, T. and Meade, N. (2000). Modelling diffusion and replacement. *European Journal of Operations Research*, 125, 551–570.

Jain, D.C. (1992). Marketing mix effects on the diffusion of innovations. Working paper, Kellogg Graduate School of Management, Northwestern University, Evanston, IL, USA.

Jain, D.C., Mahajan, V. and Muller, E. (1991). Innovation diffusion in the presence of supply restrictions. *Marketing Science*, 10, 83–90.

Jain, D.C. and Rao, R.C. (1990). Effect of price on the demand for durables: modeling, estimation, and findings. *Journal of Business and Economic Statistics*, 8(2), 163–170.

Jiang, Z., Bass, F.M. and Bass, P.I. (2006). Virtual Bass model and the left-hand data-truncation bias in diffusion of innovation studies. *International Journal of Research in Marketing*, 23, 93–106.

Jun, D.B., Kim, S.K., Park, Y.S., Park, M.H. and Wilson, A.R. (2002). Forecasting telecommunication service subscribers in substitutive and competitive environments. *International Journal of Forecasting*, 18, 561–581.

Jun, D.B. and Park, Y.S. (1999). A choice-based diffusion model for multiple generations of products. *Technological Forecasting and Social Change*, 61, 45–58.

Kalish, S. (1983). Monopolistic pricing with dynamic demand and production cost. *Marketing Science*, 2, 135–160.

Kalish, S. (1985). A new product adoption model with price, advertising and uncertainty. *Management Science*, 31, 1569–1585.

Kalish, S. and Lilien, G.L. (1983). Optimal price subsidy policy for accelerating the diffusion of innovation. *Marketing Science*, 2, 407–420.

Kalish, S., Mahajan, V. and Muller, E. (1995). Waterfall and sprinkler new-product strategies in competitive global markets. *International Journal of Research in Marketing*, 12, 105–119.

Kamakura, W.A. and Balasubramanian, S.K. (1987). Long-term forecasting with innovation diffusion models: the impact of replacement purchase. *Journal of Forecasting*, 6, 1–19.

Kamakura, W.A. and Balasubramanian, S.K. (1988). Long-term view of the diffusion of durables. *International Journal of Research in Marketing*, 5, 1–13.

Karshenas, M. and Stoneman, P. (1992). A flexible model of technological diffusion incorporating economic factors with an application to the spread of colour television ownership in the UK. *Journal of Forecasting*, 11, 577–601.

Kiiski, S. and Pohjola, M. (2002). Cross-country diffusion of the Internet. *International Economics and Policy*, 14, 297–310.

Kim, N., Chang, D.R. and Shocker, A.D. (2000). Modeling intercategory and generational dynamics for a growing information technology industry. *Management Science*, 46, 496–512.

Kohli, R., Lehmann, D.R. and Pae, J. (1999). Extent and impact of incubation time in new product diffusion. *Journal of Product Innovation Management*, 16, 134–144.

Krishnan, T.V., Bass, F.M. and Jain, D.C. (1999). Optimal pricing strategy for new products. *Management Science*, 45, 1650–1663.

Krishnan, T.V., Bass, F.M. and Kumar, V. (2000). Impact of a late entrant on the diffusion of a new product/service. *Journal of Marketing Research*, 37, 269–278.

Kumar, S. and Swaminathan, J.M. (2003). Diffusion of innovations under supply constraints. *Operations Research*, 51, 866–879.

Kumar, U. and Kumar, V. (1992). Technological innovation diffusion: the proliferation of substitution models and easing the user's dilemma. *IEEE Transactions on Engineering Management*, 39, 158–168.

Kumar, V., Ganesh, R. and Echambadi, R. (1998). Cross-national diffusion research: what do we know and how certain are we? *Journal of Product Innovation Management*, 15, 255–268.

Kumar, V. and Krishnan, T.V. (2002). Multinational diffusion models: an alternative framework. *Marketing Science*, 21, 318–330.

Lee, C. (1990). Determinants of national innovativeness and international market segmentation. *International Marketing Review*, 7(5), 39–49.

Lee, C.-Y., Lee, J.-D. and Kim, Y. (2008). Demand forecasting for new technology with a short history in a competitive environment: the case of the home networking market in South Korea. *Technological Forecasting and Social Change*, 75, 91–106.

Lee, J., Boatwright, P. and Kamakura, W. (2003). A Bayesian model for pre-launch sales forecasting of recorded music. *Management Science*, 49, 179–196.

Lee, J.C. and Lu, K.W. (1987). On a family of data-based transformed models useful in forecasting technological substitution. *Technological Forecasting and Social Change*, 31, 61–78.

Lenk, P.J. and Rao, A.G. (1990). New products from old: forecasting product adoption by hierarchical Bayes procedures. *Marketing Science*, 9, 42–53.

Liberatore, M.J. and Breem, D. (1997). Adoption and implementation of digital-imaging technology in the banking and insurance industries. *IEEE Transactions on Engineering Management*, 44, 367–377.

Liebermann, E. and Paroush, J. (1982). Economic aspects of diffusion models. *Journal of Economics and Business*, 34, 95–100.

Lilien, G.R., Rangaswamy, A. and Van den Bulte, C. (2000). Diffusion models: managerial applications and software. In: V. Mahajan, E. Muller and Y. Wind (eds.), *New Product Diffusion Models*, London: Kluwer, pp. 295–336.

Lynn, M. and Gelb, B.D. (1996). Identifying innovative national markets for technical consumer goods. *International Marketing Review*, 13, 43–57.

Mahajan, V. (1994). Commentary on Bemmaor, A.C., "Modeling the diffusion of new durable goods: word-of-mouth effect versus consumer heterogeneity". In: G. Laurent, G.L. Lilien and B. Pras (eds.), *Research Traditions in Marketing*, Boston: Kluwer, pp. 227–230.

Mahajan, V. and Muller, E. (1996). Timing, diffusion, and substitution of successive generations of technological innovations: the IBM mainframe case. *Technological Forecasting and Social Change*, 51(Feb), 109–132.

Mahajan, V., Muller, E. and Bass, F.M. (1990). New product diffusion models in marketing: a review and directions for research. *Journal of Marketing*, 54, 1–26.

Mahajan, V., Muller, E. and Bass, F.M. (1993a). New-product diffusion models. In: J. Eliashberg and G.L. Lilien (eds.), *Handbooks in Operations Research and Management Science, Vol. 5: Marketing*, Amsterdam: North-Holland, pp. 349–408.

Mahajan, V., Muller, E. and Wind, Y. (2000a). New product diffusion models: from theory to practice. In: V. Mahajan, E. Muller and Y. Wind (eds.), *New Product Diffusion Models*, London: Kluwer, pp. 3–24.

Mahajan, V., Muller, E. and Wind, Y. (eds.) (2000b). *New Product Diffusion Models*. London: Kluwer.

Mahajan, V. and Peterson, R.A. (1978). Innovation diffusion in a dynamic potential adopter population. *Management Science*, 24, 1589–1597.

Mahajan, V. and Peterson, R.A. (1985). *Models for Innovation Diffusion*. Newbury Park, CA: Sage.

Mahajan, V., Sharma, S. and Buzzell, R.B. (1993b). Assessing the impact of competitive entry on market expansion and incumbent sales. *Journal of Marketing*, 567, 39–52.

Mahler, A. and Rogers, E.M. (1999). The diffusion of interactive communication innovations and the critical mass: the adoption of telecommunications services by German banks. *Telecommunications Policy*, 23, 719–740.

Mansfield, E. (1961). Technical change and the rate of imitation. *Econometrica*, 29, 741–766.

Marchetti, C. (1977). Primary energy substitution models: on the interaction between energy and society. *Technological Forecasting and Social Change*, 10, 345–356.

McCarthy, C. and Ryan, J. (1976). An econometric model of television ownership. *Economic and Social Review*, 7, 256–277.

Meade, N. (1984). The use of growth curves in forecasting market development — a review and appraisal. *Journal of Forecasting*, 3, 429–451.

Meade, N. (1985). Forecasting using growth curves — an adaptive approach. *Journal of the Operational Research Society*, 36, 1103–1115.

Meade, N. (1989). Technological substitution: a framework of stochastic models. *Technological Forecasting and Social Change*, 36, 389–400.

Meade, N. and Islam, T. (1995a). Growth curve forecasting: an empirical comparison. *International Journal of Forecasting*, 11, 199–215.

Meade, N. and Islam, T. (1995b). Prediction intervals for growth curve forecasts. *Journal of Forecasting*, 14, 413–430.

Meade, N. and Islam, T. (1998). Technological forecasting — model selection, model stability and combining models. *Management Science*, 44, 1115–1130.

Meade, N. and Islam, T. (2001). Forecasting the diffusion of innovations. In: J.S. Armstrong (ed.), *Principles of Forecasting*, Boston: Kluwer, pp. 577–596.

Meade, N. and Islam, T. (2003). Modelling the dependence between the times to international adoption of two related technologies. *Technological Forecasting and Social Change*, 70, 759–778.

Midgley, D.F. and Dowling, G.R. (1978). Innovativeness: the concept and its measurement. *Journal of Consumer Research*, 4, 229–242.

Migon, H.S. and Gamerman, D. (1993). Generalized exponential growth models — a Bayesian approach. *Journal of Forecasting*, 12, 573–584.

Norton, J.A. and Bass, F.M. (1987). A diffusion theory model of adoption and substitution for successive generations of high-technology products. *Management Science*, 33, 1069–1086.

Norton, J.A. and Bass, F.M. (1992). Evolution of technological generations: the law of capture. *Sloan Management Review*, 33, 66–77.

Olson, J. and Choi, S. (1985). A product diffusion model incorporating repeat purchases. *Technological Forecasting and Social Change*, 27, 385–397.

Padmanabhan, V. and Bass, F.M. (1993). Optimal pricing of successive generations of product advances. *International Journal of Research in Marketing*, 10, 185–207.

Parker, P.M. (1992). Price elasticity dynamics over the adoption life cycle. *Journal of Marketing Research*, 29(3), 358–367.

Putsis, W.P. (1996). Temporal aggregation in diffusion models of first-time purchase: does choice of frequency matter? *Technological Forecasting and Social Change*, 51, 265–279.

Putsis, W.P. (1998). Parameter variation and new product diffusion. *Journal of Forecasting*, 17(3–4), 231–257.

Robinson, B. and Lakhani, C. (1975). Dynamic pricing models for new product planning. *Management Science*, 10, 1113–1122.

Rogers, E.M. (1962). *Diffusion of Innovations*. New York: The Free Press.

Rogers, E.M. (1995). *Diffusion of Innovations*, 4th ed. New York: The Free Press.

Russell, T. (1980). Comments on "The relationship between diffusion rates, experience curves and demand elasticities for consumer durable technological innovations". *Journal of Business*, 53(3), S69–S73.

Schmittlein, D.C. and Mahajan, V. (1982). Maximum likelihood estimation for an innovation diffusion model of new product acceptance. *Marketing Science*, 1(1), 57–78.

Sharif, M.N. and Islam, M.N. (1980). The Weibull distribution as a general model for forecasting technological change. *Technological Forecasting and Social Change*, 18, 247–256.

Sharif, M.N. and Kabir, C. (1976). System dynamics modeling for forecasting multi-level technological substitution. *Technological Forecasting and Social Change*, 9, 89–112.

Sharma, L.A., Basu, S.C. and Bhargava, S.C. (1993). A new model of innovation diffusion. *Journal of Scientific and Industrial Research*, 52, 151–158.

Simon, H. and Sebastian, K.-H. (1987). Diffusion and advertising: the German telephone campaign. *Management Science*, 33(4), 451–466.

Smith, F.E. (1963). Population dynamics in *Daphnia magna* and a new model for population growth. *Ecology*, 44, 651–663.

Snellman, J.S., Vesala, J.M. and Humphrey, D.B. (2001). Substitution of non-cash payment instruments for cash in Europe. *Journal of Financial Services Research*, 19(2/3), 131–145.

Sohn, S.Y. and Ahn, B.J. (2003). Multi-generation diffusion model for economic assessment of new technology. *Technological Forecasting and Social Change*, 70, 251–264.

Speece, M.W. and MacLachlan, D.L. (1992). Forecasting fluid milk package type with a multi-generation new product diffusion model. *IEEE Transactions on Engineering Management*, 39(2), 169–175.

Srinivasan, V. and Mason, C.H. (1986). Nonlinear least squares estimation of new product diffusion models. *Marketing Science*, 5(2), 169–178.

Steenkamp, J.-B.E.M., Hofstede, F.T. and Wedel, M. (1999). A cross-national investigation into the individual and national cultural antecedents of consumer innovativeness. *Journal of Marketing*, 63, 55–69.

Steffens, P.R. (2001). An aggregate sales model for consumer durables incorporating a time-varying mean replacement age. *Journal of Forecasting*, 20, 63–77.

Steffens, P.R. (2003). A model of multiple-unit ownership as a diffusion process. *Technological Forecasting and Social Change*, 70, 901–917.

Sultan, F., Farley, J.U. and Lehmann, D.R. (1990). A meta-analysis of applications of diffusion models. *Journal of Marketing Research*, 27, 70–77.

Suslick, S.B., Harris, D.P. and Allan, L.H.E. (1995). SERFIT: an algorithm to forecast mineral trends. *Computers and Geoscience*, 21, 703–713.

Takada, H. and Jain, D. (1991). Cross-national analysis of diffusion of consumer durable goods in Pacific Rim countries. *Journal of Marketing*, 55(Apr), 48–54.

Talukdar, D., Sudhir, K. and Ainslie, A. (2002). Investigating new product diffusion across products and countries. *Marketing Science*, 21(1), 97–114.

Tanner, J.C. (1974). Forecasts of vehicles and traffic in Great Britain. TRRL Report LR650, Transport and Road Research Laboratory, Department of Transport, Crowthorne, UK.

Tanner, J.C. (1978). Long-term forecasting of vehicle ownership and road traffic. *Journal of the Royal Statistical Society, Series A*, 141, 14–63.

Teng, T.C., Grover, V. and Guttler, W. (2002). Information technology innovations: general diffusion patterns and its relationships to innovation characteristics. *IEEE Transactions on Engineering Management*, 49, 13–27.

Thomson, G.L. and Teng, J.-T. (1984). Optimal pricing and advertising policies for new product oligopoly models. *Marketing Science*, 3, 148–168.

Van den Bulte, C. (2000). New product diffusion acceleration: measurement and analysis. *Marketing Science*, 19, 366–380.

Van den Bulte, C. and Joshi, Y.V. (2007). New product diffusion with influentials and imitators. *Marketing Science*, 26, 400–421.

Van den Bulte, C. and Lilien, G.L. (1997). Bias and systematic change in the parameter estimates of macro-level diffusion models. *Marketing Science*, 16, 338–353.

Van den Bulte, C. and Stremersch, S. (2004). Social contagion and income heterogeneity in new product diffusion: a meta-analytic test. *Marketing Science*, 23, 530–544.

Versluis, C. (2002). DRAMs, fiber and energy compared with three models of market penetration. *Technological Forecasting and Social Change*, 69, 263–286.

Wareham, J., Levy, A. and Shi, W. (2004). Wireless diffusion and mobile computing: implications for the digital divide. *Telecommunications Policy*, 28, 439–457.

Xie, J., Song, M., Sirbu, M. and Wang, Q. (1997). Kalman filter estimation of new product diffusion models. *Journal of Marketing Research*, 34, 378–393.

Young, P. (1993). Technological growth curves: a competition of forecasting models. *Technological Forecasting and Social Change*, 44, 375–389.

Appendix: An Annotated List of S-Shaped Diffusion Models

Notation: X_t is the cumulative number of adopters at time t. The saturation level is usually denoted by a (except in the case of the Bass model, where the conventional notation is used). Additional parameters are denoted by b and c. In some cases, where the diffusion curve is related to a density function, μ and σ are used.

Where possible, the models are presented as equations for cumulative adoption. Those that do not fit into this category appear as linearized trend models or nonlinear autoregressive models.

Models for Cumulative Adoption

A12.1 Bass model: Bass (1969) considered a population of m individuals made up of both innovators (those with a constant propensity to purchase, p) and imitators (those whose propensity to purchase is influenced by the amount of previous purchasing, $q(X_{t-1}/m)$). Here, we give the continuous time formulation used by Schmittlein and Mahajan (1982). The probability density function for a potential adopter to make an adoption at time t is

$$f(t) = (p + qF(t)) \, (1 - F(t)). \tag{A12.1}$$

The corresponding cumulative density function is

$$F(t) = \frac{1 - \exp(-(p+q)t)}{1 + \exp(q/p)\,(-(p+q)t)}. \tag{A12.2}$$

An alternative definition is

$$G(t) = cF(t), \tag{A12.3}$$

where c is the probability of eventual adoption. The expected number of adopters at time t is $cMG(t)$, where the size of the relevant population is M.

In some cases, it will be convenient to refer to the hazard function:

$$h(t) = \frac{f(t)}{1 - F(t)}. \tag{A12.4}$$

A12.2 Cumulative log-normal model:

$$X_t = a \int_0^t \frac{1}{y\sqrt{2\pi\sigma^2}} \exp\left(-\frac{(\ln(y)-\mu)^2}{2\sigma^2}\right) dy. \tag{A12.5}$$

This was used by Bain (1963). The model is asymmetric with a point of inflection before the 0.5 saturation level is reached.

A12.3 Cumulative normal model:

$$X_t = a \int_\infty^t \frac{1}{\sqrt{2\pi\sigma^2}} \exp\left(-\frac{(y-\mu)^2}{2\sigma^2}\right) dy. \tag{A12.6}$$

This was used by Rogers (1962). Its shape closely resembles the logistic model.

A12.4 Gompertz model:

$$X_t = a \exp(-c(\exp(-bt))). \tag{A12.7}$$

This was used by Gregg *et al.* (1964). The model is asymmetric about its point of inflection, which occurs before the diffusion has reached half the saturation level.

A12.5 Log-reciprocal model:

$$X_t = a \exp\left(\frac{1}{bt}\right). \tag{A12.8}$$

This was used by McCarthy and Ryan (1976).

A12.6 Logistic model:

$$X_t = \frac{a}{1 + c \exp(-bt)}. \tag{A12.9}$$

This was used by Gregg *et al.* (1964). The model is symmetric about its point of inflection (i.e. half of the potential adopters have the product at the point of inflection). The model was used in a linearized form by Mansfield (1961) (see Section A12.10).

There are many variations on the logistic theme, as shown below.

Log-logistic model:

$$X_t = \frac{a}{1 + c \exp(-b \ln(t))}. \tag{A12.10}$$

This was used by Tanner (1978). The replacement of *t* by *ln*(*t*) means that the curve is asymmetric about its point of inflection.

Flexible logistic (FLOG) model:

$$X_t = \frac{a}{1 + c\exp(-B(t))}. \qquad (A12.11)$$

This was used by Bewley and Fiebig (1988). A four-parameter generalization of the logistic growth curve, the FLOG model is sufficiently general to locate the point of inflection anywhere between its upper and lower bounds. By generalizing $B(t)$, the imitation effect, Bewley and Fiebig generated a range of models:

- Inverse power transformation (IPT) model, where

$$B(t) = b(1 + kt)^{1/k} - 1.$$

- Exponential logistic (ELOG) model, where

$$B(t) = b\frac{\exp(kt - 1)}{k}.$$

- Box–Cox model, where

$$B(t) = b\frac{(1 + t)^k - 1}{k}.$$

Non-symmetric responding logistic model:

$$X_t = \frac{a}{1 + c\exp(-bX_{t-1}^{\delta}t)}. \qquad (A12.12)$$

This was used by Easingwood *et al.* (1981). The underlying belief here is that the propensity to imitate, represented by b in the simple logistic model, changes in response to the number of adopters.

Local logistic model:

$$E(X(t + L \mid X_t = x_t)) = \frac{ax_t}{x_t + (a - x_t)\exp(-bL)}. \qquad (A12.13)$$

This was used by Meade (1985). The model forecasts logistic growth from the last known value of diffusion.

A12.7 Modified exponential model:

$$X_t = a - c \exp(-bt). \tag{A12.14}$$

This was used by Gregg *et al.* (1964). There is no point of inflection; the gradient decreases monotonically to the saturation level. Essentially, this is the model used by Fourt and Woodlock (1960).

A12.8 Weibull model:

$$X_t = a\left(1 - \exp\left(\left(\frac{t}{c}\right)^b\right)\right). \tag{A12.15}$$

This was suggested for use as a diffusion model by Sharif and Islam (1980).

Linearized Trend and Nonlinear Autoregressive Models

A12.9 Harvey model:

$$\ln(X_t - X_{t-1}) = b + c_1 t + c_2 \ln(X_{t-1}). \tag{A12.16}$$

This was proposed by Harvey (1984).

These remaining models assume a given saturation level, and X_t represents the proportion of adopters at time t.

A12.10 Floyd model:

$$\left[\frac{1}{1 - X_t}\right] + \ln\left(\frac{X_t}{1 - X_t}\right) = b + ct. \tag{A12.17}$$

This was proposed by Floyd (1962). Deleting the first term [in square brackets] in this equation gives the linearized form of the logistic model proposed by Mansfield (1961).

A12.11 Sharif–Kabir model:

$$\ln\left(\frac{X_t}{1-X_t}\right)+\sigma\left(\frac{1}{1-X_t}\right)=a+bt. \qquad (A12.18)$$

This is a linear combination of the Mansfield model and the Floyd model, as suggested by Sharif and Kabir (1976).

A12.12 KKKI model:

$$\left(\frac{q-pb}{q}\right)\ln(p+qX_t)-(b+1)\ln(1-X_t)=c+(q+p)t. \qquad (A12.19)$$

This was proposed by Kumar and Kumar (1992) as a technological substitution model derived from a population dynamics model by Smith (1963).

A12.13 SBB model:

$$X_t = X_{t-1}\exp(b\,(1-X_{t-1})). \qquad (A12.20)$$

This was proposed by Sharma *et al.* (1993).

Index